T0224164

Communications
in Computer and Information Science 712

Commenced Publication in 2007
Founding and Former Series Editors:
Alfredo Cuzzocrea, Orhun Kara, Dominik Ślęzak, and Xiaokang Yang

More information about this series at http://www.springer.com/series/7899

Dharm Singh · Balasubramanian Raman
Ashish Kumar Luhach · Pawan Lingras (Eds.)

Advanced Informatics for Computing Research

First International Conference, ICAICR 2017
Jalandhar, India, March 17–18, 2017
Revised Selected Papers

 Springer

Editors
Dharm Singh
Namibia University of Science and
  Technology
Windhoek
Namibia

Balasubramanian Raman
IIT Roorkee
Roorkee
India

Ashish Kumar Luhach
CTIEMT
Jalandhar, Punjab
India

Pawan Lingras
Department of Mathematics and Computing
  Science
Saint Mary's University
Halifax, NS
Canada

ISSN 1865-0929   ISSN 1865-0937 (electronic)
Communications in Computer and Information Science
ISBN 978-981-10-5779-3   ISBN 978-981-10-5780-9 (eBook)
DOI 10.1007/978-981-10-5780-9

Library of Congress Control Number: 2017947037

Printed on acid-free paper

This Springer imprint is published by Springer Nature
The registered company is Springer Nature Singapore Pte Ltd.
The registered company address is: 152 Beach Road, #21-01/04 Gateway East, Singapore 189721, Singapore

Preface

The International Conference on Advanced Informatics for Computing Research (ICAICR 2017) targeted state-of-the-art as well as emerging topics pertaining to advanced informatics for computing research and its implementation in engineering applications. The objective of this international conference is to provide opportunities for researchers, academicians, people from industry, and students to interact and exchange ideas, experience, and expertise on information and communication technologies. Besides this, participants were enlightened about current and emerging technological developments in the field of advanced informatics and its applications.

The International Conference on Advanced Informatics for Computing Research (ICAICR 2017) was hosted by Lyallpur Khalsa College of Engineering, Jalandhar, Punjab, India on March 17–18, 2017 in association with Namibia University of Science & Technology, Namibia, and technically sponsored by the CSI Chandigarh Chapter, India and the Southern Federal University, Russia.

We are highly thankful to our valuable authors for their contribution and our Technical Program Committee for their immense support and motivation towards making the first ICAICR 2017 a success. We are also grateful to our keynote speakers for sharing their precious work and enlightening the delegates of the conference. We express our sincere gratitude to our publication partner, Springer, for believing in us.

May 2017

Dharm Singh
Raman Balasubramanian
Ashish kr. Luhach
Pawan Lingras

Organization

Honorary Conference Chair

Dharm Singh   Namibia University of Science and Technology, Namibia

Conference General Chair

Raman Balasubramanian   IIT Roorkee, India

Conference Chair

Pao-Ann Hsiung   National Chung Cheng University, Chiayi, Taiwan

Conference Co-chairs

Upasana G. Singh   University of Kwazulu-Natal, South Africa
Chandra Kr. Jha   Banasthali University, Rajasthan, India
Ashish Kr. Luhach   CTIEMT, Jalandhar, Punjab, India
Abhijit Sen   Kwantlen Polytechnic University, Canada

Technical Program Committee

Chair

Pawan Lingras   Saint Mary's University, Canada

Co-chair

Poonam Dhaka   University of Namibia, Namibia

Members

K.T. Arasu   Wright State University Dayton, Ohio, USA
Mohammad Ayoub Khan   Taibah University, Saudi Arabia
Rumyantsev Konstantin   Southern Federal University, Russia
Wen-Juan Hou   National Taiwan Normal University, Taiwan
Syed Akhat Hossain   Daffofil University, Dhaka, Bangladesh
Zoran Bojkovic   University of Belgrade, Serbia
Sophia Rahaman   Manipal University, Dubai
Thippeswamy Mn   University of KwaZulu-Natal, Durban, South Africa
Lavneet Singh   University of Canberra, Canberra, Australia
Wei Wang   Xi'an Jiaotong-Liverpool University, China
Mohd. Helmey Abd Wahab   Universiti Tun Hussein Onn, Malaysia

Andrew Ware	University of South Wales, UK
Shireen Panchoo	University of Technology, Mauritius
Sumathy Ayyausamy	Manipal University, Dubai
Dharm Singh	Namibia University of Science and Technology, Namibia
Adel Elmaghraby	University of Louisville, USA
Almir Pereira Guimaraes	Federal University of Alagoas, Brazil
Fabrice Labeau	McGill University, Canada
Abbas Karimi	IAU, Arak, Iran
Kaiyu Wan	Xi'an Jiaotong-Liverpool University, China
Pao-Ann Hsiung	National Chung Cheng University, Chiayi, Taiwan
Paul Macharia	Kenya
Yong Zhao	University of Electronic Science & Technology of China, China
Upasana G. Singh	University of KwaZulu-Natal, South Africa
Basheer Al-Duwairi	Jordan University of Science and Technology, Jordan
M. Najam-ul-Islam	Bahria University, Pakistan
Ritesh Chugh	Central Queensland University, Rockhampton, Australia
Yao-Hua Ho	National Taiwan Normal University, Taiwan
Pawan Lingras	Saint Mary's University, Canada
Poonam Dhaka	University of Namibia (UNAM), Namibia
Amirrudin Kamsin	University of Malaya, Kuala Lumpur, Malaysia
Indra Seher	Central Queensland University, Sydney, Australia
Sung-Bae Cho	Yonsei University, Seoul, South Korea
Dong Fang	Southeast University, China
Huy Quan Vu	Victoria University, Melbourne, Australia
Sugam Sharma	Iowa State University, USA
Yong Wang	University of Electronic Science & Technology of China, China
T.G.K. Vasista	King Saud University, Riyadh, Saudi Arabia
Nalin Asanka Gamagedara Arachchilage	University of New South Wales, Australia
Durgesh Samadhiya	National Applied Research Laboratories, Hsinchu, Taiwan
Akhtar Kalam	Victoria University, Australia
Ajith Abraham	MIR Labs, USA
Runyao Duan	Tsinghua University, China
Miroslav Skoric	IEEE Section, Austria
Al-Sakib Khan Pathan	IIU, Malaysia
Arunita Jaekal	Windsor University, Canada
Pei Feng	Southeast University, China
Durga Toshniwal	IIT Roorkee, India
Satinder Kumar Sharma	IIT-Mandi, India

Ashish Anand	IIT-Guwahati, India
Somnath Dey	IIT-Indore, India
R.B. Mishra	IIT (BHU), India
Raman Balasubramanian	IIT Roorkee, India
Bhaskar Bisawas	IIT (BHU), India

Contents

Computing Methodologies

Information Systems

Security and Privacy

Network Services

Computing Methodologies

Fuzzy Based Efficient Mechanism for URL Assignment in Dynamic Web Crawler

Raghav Sharma[1], Rajesh Bhatia[1], Sahil Garg[2],
Gagangeet Singh Aujla[2], and Ravinder Singh Mann[3(✉)]

[1] PEC University of Technology, Chandigarh, India
rghvsharma4@gmail.com, rbhatia@gmail.com
[2] Thapar University, Patiala, Punjab, India
garg.sahill990@gmail.com, gagi_aujla82@yahoo.com
[3] Lyallpur Khalsa College of Engineering, Jalandhar, Punjab, India
mr.rsmann@gmail.com

Abstract. World wide web (WWW) is a huge collection of unorganized documents. To build the database from this unorganized network, web crawlers are often used. The crawler which interacts with millions of web pages needs to be efficient in order to make a search engine powerful. This utmost requirement necessitates the parallelization of web crawlers. In this work, a fuzzy-based technique for uniform resource locater (URL) assignment in dynamic web crawler is proposed that utilizes the task splitting property of the processor. In order to optimize the performance of the crawler, the proposed scheme addresses two important aspects, (i) creation of crawling framework with load balancing among parallel crawlers, and (ii) making of crawling process faster by using parallel crawlers with efficient network access. Several experiments are conducted to monitor the performance of the proposed scheme. The results prove the effectiveness of the proposed scheme.

Keywords: Web crawlers · Uniform resource locater · Static parallel crawler · Dynamic parallel crawler · Search engines · Fuzzy logic

1 Introduction

A crawler is a program that downloads and stores web pages for a web search engine. It plays a vital role in many fields of research, e.g. mining of twitter data for opinion mining [1] or finding the success ratio in project funding sites like Kickstart [2]. The crawlers are generally classified into two categories: unfocused and focused. The unfocused crawler creates an index of the entire web all around the globe. It develops and maintain a huge database of all domains including the network bandwidth and the processing speed. On the other hand, a focused crawler limits its processing up to semantic web zone by seeking out the pages which are relevant to the predefined taxonomy of topic. This avoids the irrelevant web regions to be crawled and reduces irrelevant items in the search result [3].

One of the most important strategy used to build database for specific communities is by collecting the domain-specific documents from the web. In this regard,

© Springer Nature Singapore Pte Ltd. 2017
D. Singh et al. (Eds.): ICAICR 2017, CCIS 712, pp. 3–17, 2017.
DOI: 10.1007/978-981-10-5780-9_1

focused crawlers try to initially "predict" that whether a target uniform resource locater (URL) is pointing towards a relevant and high-quality web page before actually fetching the page [4]. Generally, a web crawler starts its work from a single seed URL keeping it into a queue Q_0, where it keeps all the URLs to be extracted. From there, it extracts a URL based on some ordering and down- loads that page, extracts any URL in the downloaded page and put them in the same queue. It repeats this function until it is stopped. The major difficulty for a single process web crawler is that crawling the web may take months and in the mean time a number of web pages may have changed and thus, not useful for the end users. So, to minimize the download time, search engines execute multiple crawlers simultaneously known as parallel web crawlers. An effective architecture of a parallel crawler requires the no overlapping of the downloaded web pages using different parallel agents. Moreover, the coverage rate of the web should not be compromised within each parallel agents range. Next, the quality of web crawled should not be less than a single centralized crawler [5]. To achieve all these, com- munication overhead should be taken into account to achieve a trade-off among the objectives to build an optimized crawler. Besides these challenges, the major advan- tages of parallel crawler are scalability, network load dispersion, and network load reduction.

- Scalability: With millions of pages been added to the web daily, its almost impossible to crawl the web by a single process crawler.
- Network load dispersion: With parallel crawlers, we can disperse the load to multiple regions rather than overloading one local network.
- Network load reduction: Allowing parallel agents to crawl specific local data (of the same country or region of that of crawler), the pages will have to go through local network, thereby reducing the network load.

Now, to reduce the overlapping of the downloaded pages by parallel crawlers, the parallel agents need to coordinate. On that basis, the parallel crawler can be imple- mented in three ways; (1) Static parallel crawler, (2) Dynamic parallel crawler, and (3) Independent parallel crawler [6]. In independent parallel crawler, there is no coordination among the parallel agents. Each parallel agent continues crawling from its own seed URL. So, the overlap can be significant in this case unless the domain of crawl agents is limited and entirely different for each crawl agent. Rest of the two ways are elaborated as below.

- Static Parallel Crawler: In this, the web is partitioned by some logic and each crawler knows its own partition to crawl. So, there is no need of the central coordinator.
- Dynamic Parallel Crawler: In this, there is a central coordinator which assigns the URL to different parallel agents based on some logic i.e. the web is partitioned by the central coordinator at the run time.
- Independent Parallel Crawler: Here, there is no coordination among the parallel agents. Each parallel agent continues crawling from its own seed URL. So, the overlap can be significant in this case unless the domain of crawl agents is limited and entirely different for each crawl agent.

1.1   Static Parallel Crawler

For static parallel crawler, there is no need of the central coordinator. Instead, we need a good partitioning method to partition the web before the crawling. A number of partitioning scheme have been proposed such as, URL hash-based, site hash-based, and hierarchical schemes [7]. In URL hash-based, the page is sent to a parallel agent-based on the hash value of the URL. In site hash-based, the hash value is calculated only on the site name of the URL. In hierarchical, the partitioning is done on the basis of issues like country, language, and type of URL extension.

Major concern in the existing proposals of static parallel crawler is the mode of job division among the parallel agents. There are various modes of job division like firewall, crossover, and exchange. In the first mode, parallel agents crawl pages neglecting the inter-partition links. In the second mode, parallel agents crawls same partition links and when there are no more links left to crawl in the same partition, then it moves to inter-partition links to crawl them. In the third mode, parallel agents communicate using message exchanges whenever they encounter an inter-partition link in order to increase the coverage and decrease the overlap. The drawbacks of the static parallel crawler are as follow:

- Scalability: To reduce the overlap and increase the coverage, N! connections are required for URL transfer to appropriate parallel agent.
- Quality of web pages crawled: Each parallel agent is unaware of the web crawled by other agents. So, they don't have the global image of the web crawled and the decision of URL selection is based on its subset.

1.2   Dynamic Parallel Crawler

For dynamic parallel crawler, a central coordinator is required to assign URLs to different crawler agents. Figure 1 shows that each crawl agent behaves as a separate process crawler receiving the seed URL for its domain from the central coordinator. It then downloads the page from the web and extracts the URL links from the downloaded page and sends them to the central coordinator for assignment. The advantages of dynamic parallel crawler are explained as below.

- Crawling decision: Static parallel crawler suffers from poor crawling decision, i.e., which web page to crawl next. This is because no crawling agent has complete view of the web crawled. But in dynamic parallel crawler, the central coordinator has the global image of the web and the decision about the URL selection and assignment is taken by the central coordinator, not the crawl agents.
- Scalability: For dynamic parallel crawlers only N connections are needed by central coordinator for URL assignments, when the number of crawl agents are N. If a new crawl agent is added to the system, only one socket connection will be required between the crawl agent and the central coordinator.
- Minimizing web server load: To reduce the overload of a server, crawl agent sends the most important unvisited URL links to the crawl agents through the central coordinator. This decreases the load on a single web server.

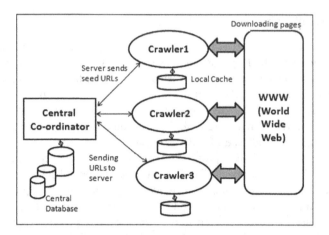

Fig. 1. Architecture of dynamic parallel crawler

Dynamic web crawler design poses a number of challenges as given below.

–   Which distribution algorithm should be used for URL assignment?
–   How to distribute jobs to different crawlers based on their health?
–   How to manage the already crawled pages to avoid replication of pages?

The main objective of this paper is the URL assignment strategies which is one of the important functionalities of the dynamic parallel crawler.

2   Related Work

In this section, the related work corresponding to web crawlers is divided into three subsections, i.e., hash-based approach, domain specific approach and virtualized URL assignment. Further, comparison is also provided in Table 1.

2.1   Hash Based Approach for URL Assignment

The hash based URL assignment scheme uses the key value of each URL to determine its crawl agent for parsing. Guerriero et al. [15] proposed the architecture for URL assignment by transforming the URL into a set of numerical information which represent coordinates of 3D space vector (x,y,z). Using this, a number of values can be generated from a single URL. Uniform Resource Identifier (URI) is a string of characters used to locate the host name. In [15], the URL strings have been defined in 3 ways i.e. scheme, domain and path, fragment, and query. Such elements are coordinate functions in the vector space. URI structure is transformed into 3D vector space over which a fuzzy clustering technique can be applied for the assignment of particular URL to a specified crawl agent. This scheme is easy to implement but the locality structure of the links is not reflected. Table 2 shows an example of URI parts.

Table 1. Summarization of related work

S. No.	Contributor	Title	Contributions
1	Cho and Garcia-Molina [8]	Parallel crawlers	• Listed three general architectures to avoid redundant crawling among parallel crawlers • Describes various crawling modes including the performance evaluation criteria for each crawling mode
2	Chau et al. [9]	Parallel crawling for online social networks	• Describes a framework on how to retrieve information from online social networks by crawling • Two tiers of parallelism are highlighted where multiple agents are controlled by master
3	Ahmadi-Abkenari and Selamat [7]	A clickstream-based focused trend parallel web crawler	• Demonstrates a web page importance metric based on the number of clicks per page over a period of time • Demonstrates an architecture of parallel crawler based on this ranking criteria
4	Batsakis et al. [10]	Improving the performance of focused web crawlers	• Classifies the crawlers as classified focused crawler, semantic crawler, learning crawler • Stress laid on crawlers capable of learning the content of relevant pages and paths leading to them
5	Yadav et al. [11]	An Approach to design incremental parallel web crawler	• Multi-threaded server-based architecture for incremental parallel web crawler has been designed • Helps to reduce overlapping, quality and network bandwidth problems
6	Arasu et al. [12]	Searching the web	• Discuss issues related to large data, indexing, updation and improving search engine working • Discuss case study of various ordering matrices
7	Bedi et al. [13]	A multi-threaded semantic focused crawler	• Semantic relevance between the web pages is computed dynamically depending upon distance between two concepts in ontology

(*continued*)

Table 1. (*continued*)

S. No.	Contributor	Title	Contributions
8	Zhao et al. [14]	SmartCrawler: 2-Stage crawler for harvesting deep-web interfaces	• Two-stage framework has been proposed for efficiently harvesting deep web interfaces • A link tree data structure eliminates the bias and retrieves web interfaces

Table 2. Coordinates of URI parts

URL parts	Substring	Coordinate
Scheme & domain	http://www.abc.com	X = 3487
Path	/index.php?	Y = 2241
Query & fragment	q = 1#session	Z = 744

2.2 Domain Specific Approach for URL Assignment

The approach for the dynamic partitioning of the web is based on the domain of the crawl agents that are influenced by the fact that web pages may link to pages having relevance to domain of the same page. So, after retrieving a web page, the crawl agent performs analysis for predicting the relevancy to one of the many domains of available crawl agents. Thus, breaking down a domain into subdomains can add up new crawl agents increasing the scalability of the system. The domain-oriented partitioning approach requires the initial seed URLs of various domains to be gathered which can be represented by some hub pages which consists of links to various highly relevant pages of different domains. Once the web page is downloaded, it is fed to parser, classifier and dispatcher module. Parser module extracts various HTML components of the specific page in order to get the list of new unvisited URLs from the specified page mentioned in the href attribute of the anchor tag. Later, the classifier module analyses the domain of the web page and adds it to the associated repository of its domain. Also, it tags the URL of the downloaded page with its domain in the same database that is used to store the unvisited URLs. Finally, the URL dispatcher sends the discovered URLs to the central coordinator performing three steps. In first step, it restores the relative address of hyper-links to absolute address which is important as a number of documents can refer to same URL. In second step, it aims to predict the domain of the discovered URLs using tagged URLs that can serve as the source of the newly discovered URLs reflecting the hyper-linked behavior of the web. Lastly, it can check for the duplication of the discovered pages with the pages of the same domain partition pool which have been visited.

2.3   Virtualized URL Assignment

In this approach, virtualization concept is used for the working of parallel crawlers. Here, multiple cores of processors are treated as virtual machines which interact with each other through a shared region or memory using virtual machine communication interface (VMCI). These virtual machines are treated as clusters and URLs belonging to same clusters are served by virtual machines of corresponding clusters [16]. Initially, there is a need of an injector module to provide the seed URLs which are used by clustering module for cluster formation. The clustering module calculates the hash value of the URLs and using the URI, the cluster belonging to URL is identified. Then, the URL is assigned to a virtual machine depending upon the threshold value of that machine which is decided as per the availability of the virtual machine.

2.4   Organization

The rest of the paper is organized as follows: Sect. 3 describes the proposed fuzzy technique for URL assignment. Section 4 discusses various results and Sect. 5 concludes the paper.

3   Proposed Fuzzy Based Mechanism for URL Assignment

In this work, a parallel architecture is proposed, where the systems can be geographically distributed. The flow of the proposed technique is shown in Fig. 2.

As shown in Fig. 3, the system has three main components: a fuzzy logic controller, a URL distributor, and some parallel agents.

- Fuzzy logic controller: The task of this component is load optimization among the parallel agents by monitoring the health of parallel agents in regular intervals. The parameters for fuzzy controller are discussed in Table 3.
- URL distributor: A set of URLs are selected by URL distributor and distributed to parallel agents using a fuzzy logic controller. Distributor receives, analyzes and store the aggregated results into central repository.
- Parallel agents: Each parallel agent works like a single centralized crawler starting from a single URL or a set of URLs and analyze every page specified by each URL. The link extractor analyses the page in order to identify the links and make a list of such links. The page downloader takes a new URL from this list and downloads the concerned page from the internet if it is not available in the local cache and sends it for analysis to link extractor. It sends the list of URLs with their health to the central coordinator as per crawl session. Finally, fuzzy logic controller distributes the load as per health.

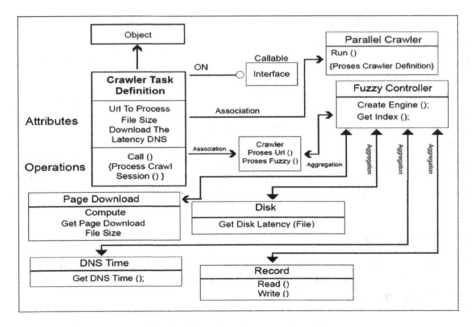

Fig. 2. Flowchart of proposed model

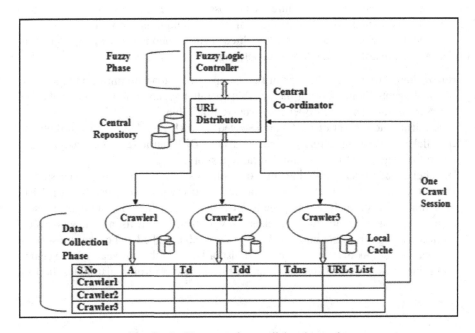

Fig. 3. Architecture of a parallel web crawler

Table 3. Parameters for fuzzy controller

S. No.	Factor(s)	Description	Possible fuzzy implications
1	Page size	An average 12 KB sized web page loads quickly. The more media on a page, the bigger the page size and the slower it will load	It has implications on factors including downloading time and utilization of bandwidth
2	Available cores/ machines	How many CPU core(s) and how many MIPS are available for processing new tasks	MIPS rating of a CPU is the number of low-level machine code instructions executed by a processor in a second
3	Storage/disk read/write latency	A host reads data from a logical unit number associated with the physical storage media. It slows down if large amount of data is written and stored while downloading. It is the average amount of time (ms) to complete read/write from the physical device	Larger the page size, larger is the disk requirement. If more cores are available the process will become parallel and faster. Latency is dependent on the underlying storage technology
4	Download time	It depends on the page size, processing power, and network bandwidth while it is transmitted from URL to crawler storage	Download time & bandwidth use increases with respect to page size
5	DNS resolution time	Time taken by authoritative DNS servers to respond to a request including domain, TLD, and root DNS server response times	If this is more, the discovery of URL response is slow, leading to build up of URL queue for processing

3.1 The Fuzzy Phase

The fuzzy logic is used to perform multiple tasks including (i) assignment of the URL to the priority queue for crawling sessions, and (ii) assignment of the URL to the machine or core used for invoking crawling sessions in the parallel crawlers. The proposed technique takes the assumptions as shown in Table 4.

Table 4. Assumptions for the proposed technique

- "A" be the last average page size in kb downloaded by a machine "m"
- "Td" be the last average time in seconds taken by a machine "m" to download "p" Pages
- "Tdd" is last average time (secs) taken by a machine "m" to save the "p" pages to the disk "d"
- "Tdns" be the Last Average Time in seconds taken by a machine "m" for DNS resolution
- "AL" = {normal, small, large} be the set of linguistic variable describing the "A" having discrete range of values
- "TdL" = {less, more} be the set of linguistic variable describing the "Td" having discrete range of values
- "TddL" = {less, more} be the set of linguistic variable describing the "Tdd" having discrete range of values
- "TdnsL" = {less, more} be the set of linguistic variable describing the "Tdns" having discrete range of values

The working of the proposed approach is shown in Algorithm 1.

Algorithm 1 The Proposed Algorithm

input: Variables from Table 4
output: URL Assignment
1: Initialize input variables
2: Set linguistic variables in accordance with the distribution of input variables
3: for each input variable do
4:    Set rules
5:    Initialize fuzzy inference engine
6:    Activate the fuzzy controller to assign the URLs to the queue "q" (Accumulation) of a particular machine "m"
7:    if AveragePageSize is "small" && TdL is "less" then
8:        Set Machine m ⟶Machine 1
9:    else if AveragePageSize is "large" && TdL is "more" then
10:       Set Machine m ⟶Machine 2
11:    end if
12: end for
13: Use $COG = \frac{\int_R \mu c(z).z dz}{\int_R \mu c(z).dz}$ to determine crisp output
14: Evaluate machine index from crisp values
15: Allocate url to machine m

4 Results and Discussion

The proposed scheme was evaluated in a simulated environment and the results obtained after regress crawling with different seed URLs are shown as below.

- Average DNS Time Statistics for Different Cores: Different cores checks the time taken by authoritative DNS servers to respond to a request for your domain or host. If this factor (DNS time) is more, the discovery of URL response will be slow, leading to build up of URL queue for processing. Figure 4 shows that the overlapping is significant for the DNS time statistics among the four different cores of the machine.

- Average Disk Latency Statistics for different cores: The Disk latency is the average time to complete read/write from the physical device. Figure 5 shows the time each

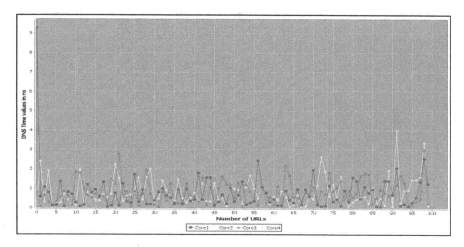

Fig. 4. Average DNS time statistics

core takes to complete the task of disk write after downloading the page. The result shows that there is a significant overlap in this case.

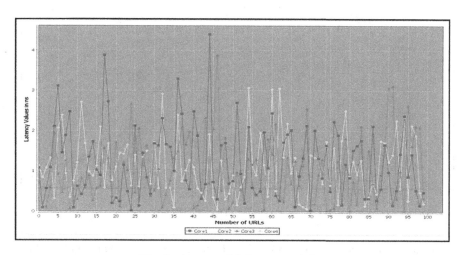

Fig. 5. Average disk latency statistics

- Average Downloading Statistics for different cores: The downloading time for the page depends on the page size while it is transmitted from URL to crawler storage. Figure 6 shows the downloading time (average) for different crawlers for a significant period of time.
- Average Page Size Statistics for different cores: This parameter affects the performance of crawlers in a great way as it directly affects the value of other parameters.

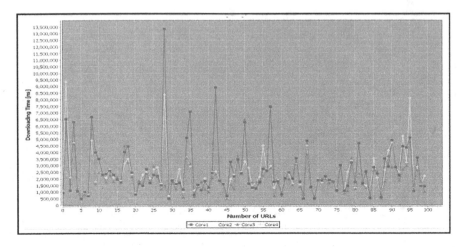

Fig. 6. Average downloading time statistics

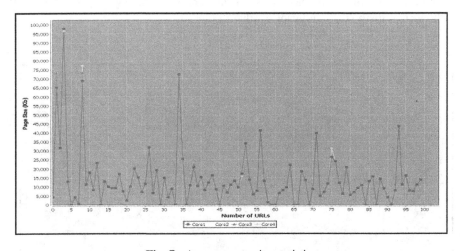

Fig. 7. Average page size statistics

The larger the page size, more is the downloading time and latency. Figure 7 shows the average page size crawled by each core.

- Average Time in Crawling First 10 URLs (in sec): We analyzed this performance on different seed URLs and then averaging the time for obtaining the performance parameter. It was found that for most of the seed URLs, the parallel approach proved to be the better one. The average time taken to crawl first 10 URLs was 95.5 s by simple crawler and 88.11 s by parallel crawler. This shows an approx 9% improvement in the performance of parallel crawler over the simple crawler. Figure 8 shows a pictorial representation of the same.

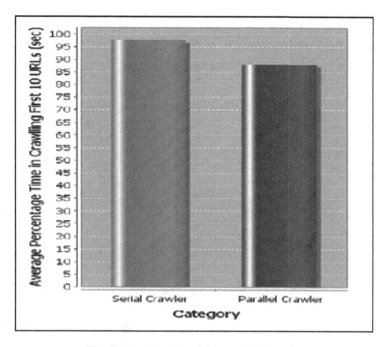

Fig. 8. Av. time of serial vs parallel crawler

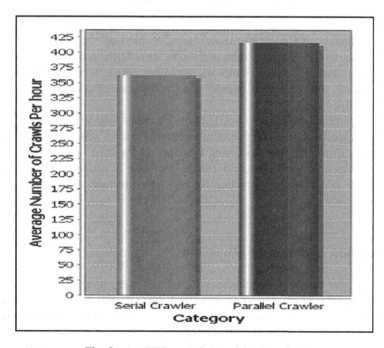

Fig. 9. Av. URLs crawled (serial vs parallel)

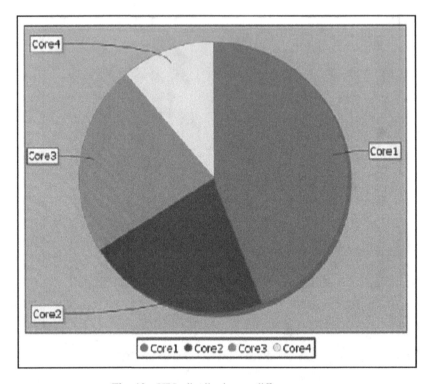

Fig. 10. URL distribution to different cores

- Average Number of Crawls per Hour: Here, we put both the simple and parallel crawler to crawl for an hour to analyze the number of URLs processed. From Fig. 9, it is evident that there is a significant difference between the number of URLs processed, i.e., 362 by simple crawler and 416 by parallel crawler (average taken out of the five cases).
- URL Assignment (Percentage Distribution): This factor shows the average number of URLs processed by different cores in a period of time. It was seen that about 40% URLs were distributed for processing by core1 on the basis of its health. Further, 25% of URLs were processed by core2, 25% by core 3, and 10% by core4. These results were obtained after crawling for one hour (average taken out of the five cases) (Fig. 10).

5 Conclusion and Future Directions

In this paper, the concepts of parallel web crawler were analyzed along with the implementation of parallel crawler in static and dynamic way. Due to drawbacks of static parallel crawlers, a new approach for URL assignment to crawl agents based on their health monitoring is proposed using fuzzy logic. Various parameters such as DNS time, page download time, disk time, and page size are used as input to fuzzy controller. The behavior of simple crawler and the proposed parallel crawler has been evaluated using extensive simulations. The results depict that parallel crawler is better than the serial crawler. The proposed scheme helps in optimal utilization of CPU power and bandwidth. This is due to the assignment being done as per health of the resources and network conditions. Further, the dynamic assignment strategy overcomes the limitations of static parallel crawler which needed N! connections to increase the size of the crawler.

References

1. Grover, S., Aujla, G.S.: Twitter data based prediction model for influenza epidemic. In: 2nd IEEE International Conference on Computing for Sustainable Global Development (INDIACom), pp. 873–879, March 2015
2. Etter, V., Grossglauser, M., Thiran, P.: Launch hard or go home!: predicting the success of kickstarter campaigns. In: 1st ACM Conference on Online Social Networks, pp. 177–182 (2013)
3. Seyfi, A., Patel, A.: A focused crawler combinatory link and content model based on t-graph principles. Comput. Standards Interfaces **43**, 1–11 (2016)
4. Lu, H., Zhan, D., Zhou, L., He, D.: An improved focused crawler: using web page classification and link priority evaluation. Math. Probl. Eng. (2016)
5. Merlet, J.-P., Gosselin, C., Huang, T.: Parallel mechanisms. In: Springer Hand-book of Robotics, pp. 443–462. Springer, Heidelberg (2016)
6. Marin, M., Paredes, R., Bonacic, C.: High-performance priority queues for parallel crawlers. In: 10th ACM Workshop on Web Information and Data Management, pp. 47–54 (2008)
7. Ahmadi-Abkenari, F., Selamat, A.: An architecture for a focused trend parallel web crawler with the application of clickstream analysis. Inf. Sci. **184**(1), 266–281 (2012)
8. Cho, J., Garcia-Molina, H.: Parallel crawlers. In: 11th ACM International Conference on World Wide Web, pp. 124–135 (2002)
9. Chau, D.H., Pandit, S., Wang, S., Faloutsos, C.: Parallel crawling for online social networks. In: 16th ACM International Conference on World Wide Web, pp. 1283–1284 (2007)
10. Batsakis, S.E., Petrakis, G., Milios, E.: Improving the performance of focused web crawlers. Data Knowl. Eng. **68**(10), 1001–1013 (2009)
11. Yadav, D., Sharma, A., Sanchez-Cuadrado, S., Morato, J.: An approach to design incremental parallel webcrawler. J. Theoret. Appl. Inf. Technol. **43**(1), 08–29 (2012)
12. Arasu, A., Cho, J., Garcia-Molina, H., Paepcke, A., Raghavan, S.: Searching the web. ACM Trans. Internet Technol. **1**(1), 2–43 (2001)
13. Bedi, P., Thukral, A., Banati, H., Behl, A., Mendiratta, V.: A multi-threaded semantic focused crawler. J. Comput. Sci. Technol. **27**(6), 1233–1242 (2012)
14. Zhao, F., Zhou, J., Nie, C., Huang, H., Jin, H.: Smartcrawler: a two-stage crawler for efficiently harvesting deep-web interfaces. IEEE Trans. Serv. Comput. **9**(4), 608–620 (2016)
15. Guerriero, A., Ragni, F., Martines, C.: A dynamic URL assignment method for parallel web crawler. In: IEEE International Conference on Computational Intelligence for Measurement Systems and Applications, pp. 119–123, September 2010
16. Bhaginath, W.R., Shingade, S., Shirole, M.: Virtualized dynamic URL assignment web crawling model. In: International Conference on Advances in Engineering Technology Research, pp. 1–7, August 2014

Towards Filtering of SMS Spam Messages Using Machine Learning Based Technique

Neelam Choudhary[(✉)] and Ankit Kumar Jain

Computer Engineering Department, National Institute of Technology,
Kurukshetra, Haryana, India
neelamchoudhary197@gmail.com, ankitjain@nitkkr.ac.in

Abstract. The popularity of mobile devices is increasing day by day as they provide a large variety of services by reducing the cost of services. Short Message Service (SMS) is considered one of the widely used communication service. However, this has led to an increase in mobile devices attacks like SMS Spam. In this paper, we present a novel approach that can detect and filter the spam messages using machine learning classification algorithms. We study the characteristics of spam messages in depth and then found ten features, which can efficiently filter SMS spam messages from ham messages. Our proposed approach achieved 96.5% true positive rate and 1.02% false positive rate for Random Forest classification algorithm.

Keywords: SMS spam · Mobile devices · Machine learning · Feature selection

1 Introduction

Short Message Service (SMS) is one of the popular communication services in which a message is sent electronically. The reduction in the cost of SMS services by telecom companies has led to the increased use of SMS. This rise attracted attackers which have resulted in SMS Spam problem. A spam message is generally any unwanted message that is sent to user's mobile phone. Spam messages include advertisements, free services, promotions, awards, etc. People are using SMS messages to communicate rather than emails because while sending SMS message there is no need of internet connection and it is simple and efficient [1].

The SMS Spam problem is increasing day by day with the increase in the use of text messaging. There are various security measures available to control SMS Spam problem but they are not so mature. Many android apps [2–4] are also on play store to block spam messages but people are not aware of these apps due to lack of knowledge. Other than apps the filtering techniques available mainly focuses on email spam as email spam is one of the oldest problem [5] but with the popularity of mobile devices, SMS spam is the one of the major issue these days.

SMS is one of the cheapest ways to communicate and can be considered as the simplest way to perform phishing attacks as mobile devices contain sensitive and personal information like card details, username, password, etc. [6–8]. Attackers are finding different ways to steal this information from mobile devices and SMS is one of the easiest ways. Smishing i.e. SMS based Phishing is more popular these days in which

© Springer Nature Singapore Pte Ltd. 2017
D. Singh et al. (Eds.): ICAICR 2017, CCIS 712, pp. 18–30, 2017.
DOI: 10.1007/978-981-10-5780-9_2

user sends malicious link via SMS and asks user to visit that link and steals sensitive information from user's mobile device. There are various detection approaches available for detecting mobile phishing like QR code, machine learning based, biometric based, matrix code reader based, knowledge based and authentication based [9].

SMS spammers can purchase any mobile number with any area code to send spam messages so that it becomes difficult to identify the attacker. US tatango learning center provided the list of top 25 SMS Spam area codes used by spammers [10]. Moreover, top 5 SMS Spam messages [11] are shown in Fig. 1.

Payment Protection Insurance	Quick Loans	Accident Compensation
IMPORTANT - You could be enititled upto $3,160 in compensation from mis-sold PPI on a credit card or loan. Please reply PPI for info or STOP to opt out.	A Loan for $950 is approved for you if you receive this SMS. 1 min. verification & cash in 1 hr at www.co.uk to opt out reply STOP	You have still not claimed the compensation you are due for the accident you had. To start the process please reply YES. To opt out text STOP.

Debt Forgiveness	Pension Reviews
Due to a new legislation, those struggling with debt can now apply to have it written off. For more information text the word INFO or to opt out text STOP	Our record indicate your pension is under Performing to see higher growth and up to 20% cash release reply PENSION for a free review. To opt out reply STOP.

Fig. 1. Top 5 popular SMS spam messages

In 2014, a report was released by Cloud mark in which they stated that how spammers used Twilio to send 385,000 spam messages [12]. National Fraud Intelligence Bureau (NFIB) published a media report about the latest scams which was analyzed by action fraud in 2016 [13]. Spammers are targeting bank customers these days by sending spam messages for asking their bank account details, ATM pin number, password, etc. and the customer thinks that the message is coming from the bank and he/she may give all the details to the spammer. A report was published by ACMA that how bank customers are becoming the victim of SMS Spam attacks [14].

In our proposed approach main aim is to filter the spam and ham SMS using machine learning algorithms. We have used a feature set of 10 features for classification. These features can differentiate a spam SMS from ham SMS. Machine learning techniques were effective in email spam filtering as it helps in preventing zero-day attacks and provides the high level of security. The Same approach is being used for mobile devices in order to prevent from SMS Spam problem but in the case of SMS Spam features will be different from email spam as the size of the text message is small and the user uses less formal language for text messages. And text message is simple without any graphic content and attachments.

The rest of the paper is organized as follows: First of all, Sect. 2 discusses the related work, Sect. 3 presents our proposed model including features that we have selected for our experiment. Section 4 presents the experimental detail including the dataset collection, results of our experiment. Finally, Sect. 5 presents conclusion and future work.

2 Related Work

A number of SMS Spam messages detection techniques are available these days like android apps to block spam messages, filtering spam messages using classification algorithms, etc. In this section, we will review the SMS Spam detection techniques by filtering spam messages based on feature selection using machine learning techniques.

El-Alfy and AlHasan [15] have proposed a model for filtering text messages for both email and SMS. They have analyzed different methods in order to finalize a feature set such that complexity can be reduced. They have used two classification algorithms i.e. Support Vector Machine (SVM) and Naïve Bayes and 11 features i.e. URLs, likely spam words, emotion symbols, special characters, gappy words, message metadata, JavaScript code, function words, recipient address, subject field and spam domain. They have evaluated their proposed model on five email and SMS datasets.

Jialin et al. [16] have proposed a message topic model (MTM) for filtering Spam messages. Messages Topic Model (MTM) considers symbol terms, background terms and topic terms to represent spam messages and it is based on the probability guess of latent semantic analysis. They have used k-means algorithm to remove the sparse problem by training SMS spam messages into random irregular classes and then aggregating all SMS spam messages as a single file such that to capture word co-occurrence patterns.

Chan et al. [17] have presented two methods for SMS Spam filtering i.e. feature reweighting method and good word attack. Both methods focus on the length of the message along with considering the weight of message. Good word attack focuses on deceiving the output of classifier by using least number of characters while for feature reweighting method they have introduced a new rescaling function for rescaling the weights. They have evaluated the experiment on two datasets i.e. SMS and comment.

Delany et al. [18] discuss different approaches available for SMS Spam filtering and the problems associated with the dataset collection. They have analyzed a large dataset of SMS spam and used ten clusters i.e. ringtones, competitions, dating, prizes, services, finance, claims chat, voicemail and others.

Xu et al. [19] have detected SMS Spam messages using content-less features. They have used 2 classification algorithms i.e. SVM and k-nearest neighbor (KNN) and feature set consisting of 3 features i.e. static, temporal and network for their experiment. They found that by combining temporal and network features SMS Spam messages can be detected more accurately and with good performance. Moreover, they also found the ways filter SMS Spam messages by using features that contain graph-topology and temporal information thus excluding the content of the message.

Nuruzzaman et al. [20] used Text Classification techniques on independent mobile phones to evaluate their performance of filtering SMS spam. The training, filtering, and updating processes were performed on an independent mobile phone. Their proposed model was able to filter SMS spam with some good accuracy, less storage consumption, and good enough processing time without using a large amount of dataset or any support from computer.

Uysal et al. [21] have proposed a method for SMS Spam filtering by using two feature selection based approaches i.e. chi-square metrics and information gain in order to select discriminative features. They have also developed a real time mobile application for SMS Spam filtering based on android application. They have used two different Bayesian based classification algorithms i.e. probabilistic and binary. According to the authors, their proposed system is highly accurate in detecting both spam and legitimate messages.

Yadav et al. [22] developed a model SMSAssassin for SMS Spam filtering. They have used a feature set of 20 lightweight features and two machine learning algorithms i.e. Support Vector Machine (SVM) and Bayesian learning. They have collected a dataset of 2000 messages from users within the time span of two months. In their proposed model whenever the user gets some message over his phone, then SMSAssassin initially captures that message without user's knowledge, fetches feature values, and sends theses values to the server for classification. If the messages are reported as spam, then the user will not be able to see that message and it will be redirected to spam folder.

Hidalgo et al. [23] have analyzed that how Bayesian filtering technique can be used to detect SMS Spam. They have built two datasets one in English and another in Spanish. Their analysis shows that Bayesian filtering techniques that were earlier used in detecting email spam can also be used to block SMS Spam.

3   Proposed Methodology

The main objective of our approach is to classify the spam SMS messages as soon as it received on the mobile phone, regardless of newly created spam message (zero-hour attack). In this, we firstly collected dataset and finalized the features for our experiment. After finalizing features, we extracted the features from the messages (ham and spam) to create a feature vector. These feature vectors are used for training and testing purposes. Our proposed system takes the decision based on ten features. Figure 2 shows the system architecture of our proposed approach. In the training phase, a binary classifier is generated by applying the feature vectors of spam and ham messages. In the testing phase, the classifier determines whether a new message is a spam or not. At the end we get classification results for different machine learning algorithms and performance is evaluated for each machine learning algorithm such that we can get the best algorithm for our proposed approach.

3.1   Feature Selection

Feature selection is a very important task for the SMS Spam filtering. Selected features should be correlated to the message type such that accuracy for detection of spam message can be increased. There is a length limit for SMS message and it contains only text (i.e. no file attachments, graphics, etc.) while in the email, there is no text limit and

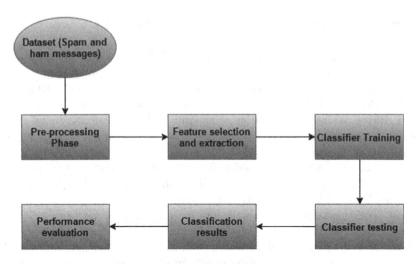

Fig. 2. System architecture

it contains attachments, graphics, etc. SMS message is usually of two types i.e. ham (legitimate) message and spam message. Spam and ham messages can be differentiated using various features. Identification of good feature that can efficiently filter spam SMS messages is a challenging task. Moreover, we study the characteristics of spam messages in depth and find some features, which are useful in the efficient detection of spam SMS. The features that we have extracted and evaluated for our proposed approach are summarized as follows:-

- *Presence of Mathematical Symbols* - Spammers usually uses mathematical symbols for creating spam messages. For example, symbol + can be used for free services messages. Mathematical symbols that we have considered in our experiment are +, −, < , > , / and ^. The first feature is defined as S_1 which could be 1 if any mathematical symbol is present in the message.

$$S_1 = \begin{cases} 1 & Mathematical\,symbol \\ 0 & No\,mathematical\,symbol \end{cases} \tag{1}$$

- *Presence of URLs* - We consider the presence of URLs as a feature since harmful spam SMS contains URLs and asks the user to visit those URLs to provide their personal details, debit/credit card information, password or to download some file (file containing the virus). The second feature S_2 which could be 1 if any URL (http or www) is present in the message.

$$S_2 = \begin{cases} 1 & URL\,is\,present \\ 0 & No\,URL \end{cases} \tag{2}$$

- *Presence of Dots* - The presence of dots seems to be good indicator for legitimate messages because people use dots while chatting. Moreover, People often use dots to separate the sentence, or words so that it becomes easy for the receiver to read the message. We define the presence of dots as feature S_3, which will be 1 if the message contains dots.

$$S_3 = \begin{cases} 1 & Dot\,is\,present \\ 0 & No\,Dot \end{cases} \qquad (3)$$

- *Presence of special symbols* - The presence of special symbols usually refers to spam messages because spammers use special symbols for various reasons. E.g. special symbol "$" is being used to represent money in the dollar in fake award messages, similarly symbol "!" is used to the special attention of user like CON-GRATULATIONS! WINNER!, etc. Special symbols that we have used in our approach are !, *, &, # and $\sim$. The fourth feature is defined as S_4 which would be 1 if any special symbol is present.

$$S_4 = \begin{cases} 1 & Special\,symbol \\ 0 & No\,Special\,symbol \end{cases} \qquad (4)$$

- *Presence of emotions* - The presence of emotion symbols seems to be a good indicator for legitimate messages because a person usually uses emotions while chatting. For example emotion :) is used for happy face, emotion :(is used for sad face, emotion -_- is used for angry face, etc. Emotion symbols that we have considered for our experiment are :), :(, -_-, :p, :v, :*, :o, B-) and :'(. We define the presence of emotions as feature S_5.

$$S_5 = \begin{cases} 1 & Emotions \\ 0 & No\,Emotions \end{cases} \qquad (5)$$

- *Lowercased words* - Checks if the message contains lowercased words or not as all lowercased words in a message can be used to seek user's attention. The presence of lowercased words is given by feature S_6 as:-

$$S_6 = \begin{cases} 1 & Lowercased\,words \\ 0 & No\,Lowercased\,words \end{cases} \qquad (6)$$

- *Uppercased words* - We consider the presence of uppercased words as a feature as spammers usually use uppercased words to seek user's attention. For example, WON, PRIZE, FREE, RINGTONE, ATTENTION, etc. The seventh feature is S_7 given by rule:-

$$S_7 = \begin{cases} 1 & Uppercased\,words \\ 0 & No\,Uppercased\,words \end{cases} \qquad (7)$$

- *Presences of Mobile Number* - We consider the presence of mobile number as a feature in order to identify spam messages because spammers usually give mobile number in a message. They ask the users to dial on the given number and when user dials on the given number, attacker on the other side ask for user's personal details, bank details, etc. For example, "you have won a $2,000 price! To claim, call 09050000301". We define the presence of mobile number as feature S_8.

$$S_8 = \begin{cases} 1 & \textit{Mobile Number} \\ 0 & \textit{No Mobile Number} \end{cases} \tag{8}$$

- *Keyword specific* - The presence of suspicious keywords like send, ringtone, free, accident, awards, dating, won, service, lottery, mins, video, visit, delivery, cash, Congrats, Please, claim, Prize, delivery, etc. are considered as spam keywords because these keywords are generally used to attract users in spam messages. We define ninth feature as S_9 which will be 1 if message contains spam keywords otherwise it will be 0.

$$S_9 = \begin{cases} 1 & \textit{Presence of spam keywords} \\ 0 & \textit{No spam keywords} \end{cases} \tag{9}$$

- *Message Length* - It includes the total length of the message including space, symbols, special characters, smileys, etc. The text limit of SMS messages is 160 characters only. We define tenth feature as S_{10} which counts the total length of each message.

Table 1 shows that how each feature value is extracted from ham and spam messages.

Table 1. SMS message feature value for ham and spam messages

Feature type	Have you finished work yet?) (Ham message)	CONGRATULATIONS! Nokia 3650 video camera phone is your Call 09066382422 Calls cost 150 ppm Ave call 3 min vary from mobiles 16 + Close 300603 post BCM4284 Ldn WC1N3XX (Spam message)
Presence of mathematical symbols	0	1
Presence of URLs	0	0
Presence of dots	0	0
Presence of special symbols	0	0
Presence of emotions	1	0
Lowercased words	1	1
Uppercased words	0	1
Presence of mobile number	0	1
Keyword specific	0	1
Message length	30	157

4 System Design, Implementation and Results

Our aim is to construct a new classification model which can filter spam SMS efficiently. This section presents implementation details, dataset, the brief summary of machine learning algorithms and performance evaluation measures to judge the performance of our proposed approach. The detection of spam SMS is a binary classification problem where various features are used to train the classifier.

4.1 Dataset Collection

The SMS dataset that we have used for our experiment contains 2608 messages out of which 2408 collected from SMS Spam Corpus publically available [24] and 200 collected manually which consists of 25 spam messages and 175 ham messages. The SMS Spam Corpus v.0.1 consists of following two sets of messages:

- SMS Spam Corpus v.0.1 Small - It consists of 1002 ham messages and 82 spam messages. This corpus is useful and has been used in the research [23, 25].
- SMS Spam Corpus v.0.1 Big - It consists of 1002 ham messages and 322 spam messages. This corpus is useful and has been used by the researchers in their research work [26].

4.2 Machine Learning Algorithms

After extracting features, classification accuracy is being tested on WEKA tool using five machine learning algorithms: Naïve Bayes, Logistic Regression, J48, Decision Table, and Random Forest. These algorithms [27] are described in brief as:-

- *Naïve Bayes* - Naïve Bayes classification algorithm is based on Bayes theorem [28]. In Naïve Bayes assumptions between predictors is independent. It is simple and easy to use so it can be used for large datasets.
- *Logistic Regression* - In this machine learning algorithm the dependent variable is categorical and measures the relationship between the independent variable and categorical dependent variable using the logistic function.
- *J48* - J48 uses a training data o already classified samples and it is a java implementation of the C4.5 classification algorithm. This algorithm basically constructs a decision tree where is each feature is represented by the node.
- *Decision Table* - Decision table is a machine learning algorithm that represents a set of rules and in this result is good only for some continuous features.
- *Random Forest* - Random Forest algorithm is best machine algorithm for a large number of datasets. It basically constructs a set of decision trees at training phase and then each tree operates on randomly chosen attributes.

4.3   Evaluation Metrics

In order to evaluate the effectiveness of our proposed approach, we will consider eight possible outcomes i.e. true positive rate, false positive rate, true negative rate, false negative rate, f1 score, accuracy, precision, and recall. These are the standard metrics to judge any spam detection system. These evaluation metrics are described in brief as follows:-

- True Positive Rate (TP) - It denotes the percentage of spam messages that were accurately classified by the machine learning algorithm. If we denote spam messages as S and spam messages that were accurately categorized as P, then

$$TP = \frac{P}{S} \tag{10}$$

- True Negative Rate (TN) - It denotes the percentage of ham messages that were accurately categorized as ham messages by the machine learning algorithm. If we denote ham message as H and ham messages that were accurately categorized as ham by Q, then

$$TN = \frac{Q}{H} \tag{11}$$

- False Positive Rate (FP) - It denotes the percentage of ham messages that were wrongly categorized as spam by the machine learning algorithm. If we denote ham messages as H and ham messages that were wrongly classified as spam by R, then

$$FP = \frac{R}{H} \tag{12}$$

- False Negative Rate (FN) - It denotes the percentage of spam messages that were incorrectly classified as ham message by the machine learning algorithm. If we denote spam messages as S and number of SMS spam messages that were incorrectly classified as ham by T, then

$$FN = \frac{T}{S} \tag{13}$$

- Precision - It denotes the percentage of messages that were spam and actually classified as spam by the classification algorithm. It shows the exact correctness. It is given as:-

$$Precision = \frac{TP}{TP + FP} \tag{14}$$

- Recall - It denotes the percentage of messages that were spam and classified as spam. It shows the completeness. It is given as:-

$$Recall = \frac{TP}{TP + FN} \qquad (15)$$

- F-measure - It is defined as the harmonic mean of Precision and Recall. It is given as:-

$$\text{F-measure} = \frac{2 * Precision * Recall}{Precision + Recall} \qquad (16)$$

- Receiver Operating Characteristics (ROC) area - In this an area is plotted between True Positive Rate and False Positive Rate for different threshold values.

4.4   Results and Discussions

Various experiments are performed to evaluate the performance of our proposed SMS Spam detection system. Initially we have selected features on the basis of behavior of spam and ham messages and then extracted these features from the dataset to get the feature vector. After extracting features from the dataset, various classification algorithms like Naïve Bayes, Logistic Regression, J48, Decision Table and Support Vector Machine (SVM) is being applied to get the performance metrics. We have used WEKA tool for classification and have used cross validation of 10-fold in which 90% of data is used for training purpose and remaining 10% data for testing purpose. Table 2 presents the results of our proposed approach on various classification algorithms i.e. Naïve Bayes, Logistic Regression, J48, Decision Table and Support Vector Machine (SVM) algorithm. Receiver Operating Characteristics (ROC) curve for our proposed approach is shown in Fig. 3.

Table 2. Results of proposed approach on various machine learning algorithms

Algorithm	TP rate	FP rate	Precision	ROC area	F-measure	Recall
Naïve Bayes	0.941	0.077	0.948	0.985	0.943	0.941
Logistic regression	0.959	0.135	0.958	0.989	0.958	0.959
J48	0.961	0.143	0.960	0.953	0.960	0.961
Decision table	0.960	0.133	0.959	0.984	0.960	0.960
Random forest	0.965	0.102	0.965	0.983	0.965	0.965

After comparing the performance metrics for various machine learning algorithms we have analyzed that best results were achieved by Random Forest Classification Algorithm. The Random Forest machine learning algorithm achieved the best classification results with the high accuracy. Moreover, we achieved 96.5% true positive rate and 1.02% false positive rate with Random Forest machine learning algorithm. Random Forest classification algorithm basically constructs a set of decision trees at training phase and then each tree operates on randomly chosen attributes.

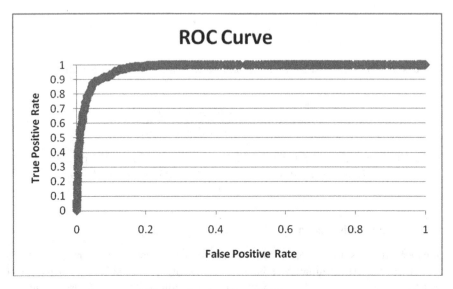

Fig. 3. Random forest ROC area

After getting the results a comparative study is done such that to compare our results with the previous results. Table 3 shows the comparative study of our proposed approach with the previous approach available in the literature.

Table 3. Comparative study of our approach with previous approach

Paper	Machine learning algorithm	TP rate
Content based spam detection [15]	SVM	95.5
Proposed approach	Random forest	96.5

5   Conclusion and Future Work

The SMS Spam problem is increasing nowadays with the increase in the use of text messaging. SMS Spam filtering is the big challenge these days. In this paper, we propose a technique for SMS Spam filtering based on 10 feature using five machine learning algorithms namely Naïve Bayes, Logistic Regression, J48, Decision Table and Random Forest. The dataset that we have used in our work consists of 2608 messages out of which 2408 messages were collected from the SMS Spam Corpus v.0.1 publically available and 200 messages collected manually. Out of all classification algorithms, Random Forest Classification Algorithm gives best results with 96.1% true positive rate.

In our future work, we will try to add more features as best spam features help in detecting spam messages more accurately. We will also try to collect more and more datasets from the real world.

References

1. Mobile Commons Blog. https://www.mobilecommons.com/blog/2016/01/how-text-messaging-will-change-for-the-better-in-2016/
2. SMS Blocker Award. https://play.google.com/store/apps/details?id=com.smsBlocker&hl=en
3. TextBlocker. https://play.google.com/store/apps/details?id=com.thesimpleandroidguy.app.messageclient&hl=en
4. Androidapp. https://play.google.com/store/apps/details?id=com.mrnumber.blocker&hl=en
5. Puniškis, D., Laurutis, R., Dirmeikis, R.: An artificial neural nets for spam e-mail recognition. Elektronika ir Elektrotechnika **69**, 73–76 (2006)
6. Jain, A.K., Gupta, B.B.: Phishing detection: analysis of visual similarity based approaches. Secur. Commun. Netw. **2017** (2017). Article ID 5421046. doi:10.1155/2017/5421046
7. Gupta, B.B., Tewari, A., Jain, A.K., Agrawal, D.P.: Fighting against phishing attacks: state of the art and future challenges. Neural Comput. Appl. 1–26 (2016). doi:10.1007/s00521-016-2275-y
8. Jain, A.K., Gupta, B.B.: A novel approach to protect against phishing attacks at client side using auto-updated white-list. EURASIP J. Inf. Secur. 1–11 (2016). doi:10.1186/s13635-016-0034-3
9. Choudhary, N., Jain, A.K.: Comparative Analysis of Mobile Phishing Detection and Prevention Approaches (Accepted)
10. Tatango Learning Center. https://www.tatango.com/blog/top-25-sms-spam-area-codes/
11. Adaptive Mobile Press Releases. https://www.adaptivemobile.com/press-centre/press-releases/five-top-spam-texts-for-2012-revealed-in-adaptivemobiles-ongoing-threat-ana
12. Cloudmark Report. https://www.tatango.com/blog/sms-spammers-exploit-twilio-send-385000-spam-text-messages/
13. Action Fraud News. http://www.actionfraud.police.uk/news/latest-scams-to-watch-out-for-apr16
14. ACMA Cybersecurity Blog. http://www.acma.gov.au/theACMA/engage-blogs/engage-blogs/Cybersecurity/Banks-targetted-by-SMS-phishing-scam
15. El-Alfy, E.S.M., AlHasan, A.A.: Spam filtering framework for multimodal mobile communication based on dendritic cell algorithm. Future Gen. Comput. Syst. **64**, 98–107 (2016). doi:10.1016/j.future.2016.02.018
16. Jialin, M., Zhang, Y., Liu, J., Yu, K., Wang, X.: Intelligent SMS spam filtering using topic model. In: International Conference on Intelligent Networking and Collaborative Systems (INCoS), pp. 380–383. IEEE (2016). doi:10.1109/INCoS.2016.47
17. Chan, P.P.K., Yang, C., Yeung, D.S., Ng, W.W.Y.: Spam filtering for short messages in adversarial environment. Neurocomputing **155**, 167–176 (2015). doi:10.1016/j.neucom.2014.12.034
18. Delany, S.J., Buckley, M., Greene, D.: SMS spam filtering: methods and data. Expert Syst. Appl. **39**, 9899–9908 (2012). doi:10.1016/j.eswa.2012.02.053
19. Xu, Q., Xiang, E.W., Yang, Q., Du, J., Zhong, J.: SMS spam detection using non-content features. IEEE Intell. Syst. **27**(6), 44–51 (2012)
20. Nuruzzaman, M.T., Lee, C., Abdullah, M., Choi, D.: Simple SMS spam filtering on independent mobile phone. Secur. Commun. Netw. 1209–1220 (2012). doi:10.1002/sec.577
21. Uysal, A.K., Gunal, S., Ergin, S., Gunal, E.S.: A novel framework for SMS spam filtering. In: International Symposium on Innovations in Intelligent Systems and Applications (INISTA), pp. 1–4. IEEE (2012). doi:10.1109/INISTA.2012.6246947

22. Yadav, K., Kumaraguru, P., Goyal, A., Gupta, A., Naik, V.: SMSAssassin: crowdsourcing driven mobile-based system for SMS spam filtering. In: 12th Workshop on Mobile Computing Systems and Applications, pp. 1–6. ACM (2011). doi:10.1145/2184489. 2184491

23. Hidalgo, J.M.G., Bringas, G.C., Sánz, E.P., García, F.C.: Content based SMS spam filtering. In: ACM Symposium on Document Engineering, pp. 107–114. ACM (2006). doi:10.1145/ 1166160.1166191

24. SMS Spam Corpus. http://www.esp.uem.es/jmgomez/smsspamcorpus

25. Cormack, G.V., Hidalgo, J.M.G., Sánz, E.P.: Feature engineering for mobile (SMS) spam filtering. In: 30th Annual International ACM SIGIR Conference on Research and Development in Information Retrieval, pp. 871–872. ACM (2007). doi:10.1145/1277741. 1277951

26. Cormack, G.V., Hidalgo, J.M.G., Sánz, E.P.: Spam filtering for short messages. In: 16th ACM Conference on Conference on Information and Knowledge Management, pp. 313–320. ACM (2007). doi:10.1145/1321440.1321486

27. Ayodele, T.O.: Types of machine learning algorithms. In: New Advances in Machine Learning. INTECH Publisher (2010)

28. Machine Algorithm Algorithms. http://machinelearningmastery.com/naive-bayes-for-machine-learning

Intelligent Computing Methods in Language Processing by Brain

Ashish Ranjan[1(✉)], R.B. Mishra[2], and A.K. Singh[2]

[1] Department of Humanistic Studies, IIT BHU, Varanasi, India
ashishr.rs.hss15@itbhu.ac.in
[2] Department of Computer Science & Engineering, IIT BHU, Varanasi, India
ravibm@bhu.ac.in, aksingh.cse@iitbhu.ac.in

Abstract. Language processing by brain focuses on experimental, theoretical and psychological study of the brain functioning while processing language. Techniques of dynamic brain imaging and behavioral study require mathematical modeling and methods to explore the scenario. Intelligent computing methods model the observed behavior and process images to obtain clear picture of the brain. This paper illustrates the various models and methodology of neurolinguistic with special emphasis on intelligent computing methods in the field. Finally a comparative study of research going on aphasia and dyslexia has been done.

Keywords: Neurolinguistic model · fMRI · EEG · MEG · PET-scan · ERP · SOM

1 Brain Anatomy of Language Processing

Human brain is divided into two hemisphere-left hemisphere and right hemisphere. In human left hemisphere is prominent part for language processing in brain. About 97% of right handed people and about 19% of left handed people have language processing area in right hemisphere [1]. Language specific areas of the brain were first discovered by Broca and Wernicke by autopsies of patients suffering from various language related problems before their death. They found damaged area in their brain was consistently located in the left hemisphere, and these areas are named as Broca area and Wernicke area named after them as shown in Fig. 1. Later, these discoveries were confirmed by Wilder Penfield and Herbert Jasper by brain surgery of patients giving local anesthesia while keeping them conscious and recording their experience [1]. Present day research takes advantage of different brain imaging techniques like FMRI, PET-scan and response recording techniques like EEG, MEG. Also the target community, which was previously only patients suffering from languages difficulties has been replaced by normal person, women and children. It has been found that women uses both the hemisphere while Children are found to be adaptive to brain injury that is if left hemisphere of child is injured the child may develop language capability in its right hemisphere. Studies have been done on character level, word level, and syntax level to find out broader view of language processing regions [1]. Recording the image of brain area while communication, reading, learning and listening has also explored the picture

© Springer Nature Singapore Pte Ltd. 2017
D. Singh et al. (Eds.): ICAICR 2017, CCIS 712, pp. 31–41, 2017.
DOI: 10.1007/978-981-10-5780-9_3

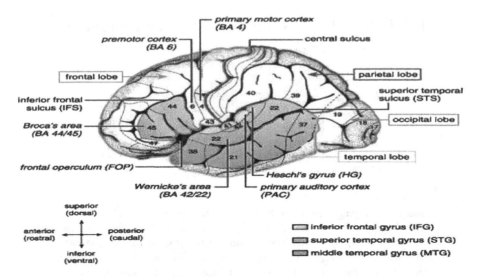

Fig. 1. Brain anatomy for language processing [2]

a lot. However this is not the whole about regions involved in language processing it is just a beginning. Based on above discussion the methodological trend and their findings in language processing by brain research can be summarized into following Table 1.

Broca's [1, 3, 4] - This was the first language area in the human brain which was discovered by Paul Broca a French neurologist by autopsy of patient and named as Broca's area after him. This is located in frontal lobe of the brain is mainly responsible for speech production. Inability to speak is termed as aphasia and hence inability to produce speech was termed as Broca's aphasia. Broca's is also responsible for understanding complex aspect of grammar in communication.

Wernicke's [1, 3] - This language region of the brain was discovered by Carl Wernicke a German neurologist and named after him. This region was discovered by

Table 1. Trends in neuro-linguistic research

Period	Target group for research	Procedure	Result
19th century	People having language related disorder after their death	Autopsy	Language processing area is located in left hemisphere
20th century	People with brain injury	Brain surgery	Functioning module explored distributed
Late 20th century to upto	Healthy people including women and children	Neuroimaging techniques- FMRI, PET SCAN, Neuropsychologica -1 techniques	processing area and distributed nature of processing for same condition

autopsy of a patient who can speak well but unable to understand the speech of others. This is located at upper portion of the temporal lobe just behind the auditory cortex. This area is related to speech comprehension and naming things i.e. mental dictionary. The problem of not understanding speech is known as Wernicke's aphasia or receptive aphasia.

Arcuate fascilicus [1] - Broca's and Wernicke's are connected by tracts of nerves called arcuate fascilicus. Damage to arcuate fascilicus results an aphasia called conduction aphasia. People suffering from conduction aphasia can understand speech and can produce speech but they are unable to repeat words or sentence they hear.

Angular Gyrus [5] - It is located near parietal lobe and occipital lobe. It enables us to associate multiple types of language related information whether visual, auditory or sensory. Perceived words are associated with different images, sensations and ideas only due to this part. Inactive angular gyrus can result in problems like alexia (inability to read), dyslexia (difficulty with reading), and agraphia (inability to write). However dyslexia can involve other region of the brain.

Visual cortex [5] - it is the area of cerebral cortex involved in processing of visual information.

2   Experimental Methods for Language Processing in Brain [6]

2.1   Historical Methods

a. **Autopsy** [1] – The classical investigation of brain lesion analysis of Broca, Wernicke and other in 19th century was based on post-mortem autopsies of patients of language disorder particularly aphasia.
b. **Wada Test** [1] (interacarotid sodium amytal test) – This method was used to study inter and intra hemispheric differences in handling language function. In this method using an aesthesia carotid arteries were made non-functioning and hemispheric functions were recorded before surgery. This method was used mainly in the case of epilepsy.
c. **Cerebral angiography** [7] – It is radiological technique to explore vascular structure by injecting a contrast substance into the carotid artery to make blood vessel visible in angiogram. This was mainly used to find out the blockage in blood vessels. This method was risky as it involves the chances of stroke.

2.2   Present Day Methods

Static Recording

a. **Computed tomography (CT)** [8] - This is a radiographic method in which brain is examined by a narrow beam of X-ray in very thin slices. The X-ray beam is rotated round the head and passed into it. On the other side the quality and quantity of beam is recorded from which the image of black, white and grey shade is obtained.

b. **Magnetic resonance imaging (MRI)** [9] - This measures the magnetic activity of hydrogen atom nuclei. An external magnetic field is applied around the brain which makes the hydrogen nuclei to align themselves in a single plane. With external radio frequency transmitter signals are transmitted to make them align on different pattern and soon after the signal they return to their original pattern releasing electromagnetic signal. These signals are recorded by computer which converts them into images of gray, black and white shade.

Dynamic Recording: Imaging

a. **FMRI** [10] - Functional magnetic resonance imaging is one the most commonly used technique for the study of language processing in the brain. In this method functional MR image of blood oxygenation level is analyzed to account the local neuronal activity. With the increased local neuronal activity blood flow also increases which results increase in oxygenated blood that is disproportionate to the increased need of oxygen for neuronal activity. Due to this, paramagnetic deoxygenated hemoglobin generated susceptibility effect is reduced. This leads to an increased signal intensity on $T2^*$-weighted MR images in active brain areas. FMRI technique is used in patient care suffering from different neurological disease and in research both. This is due to the fact that classical model of language processing is oversimplified. Recent studies based on FMRI imaging techniques and PET-scans have revealed that no unequivocal association was found in types of aphasia and lesion location [11]. The problems related to lesion in specific part are not constant and also vary patient to patient

b. **PET** [11] - Positron emission tomography is an isotopic technique which records the physiological changes in the brain by inserting glucose tagged with radioactive sodium positron in the body. The positron collides with electron and both get annihilated releasing two photons (gamma rays) which move in opposite directions. The detector circling the brain detects the photon and image is produced. The active area of the brain uses more energy i.e. more glucose so more photons are released and computer translate these as warmer colour as green or blue. This methodology produce a three dimensional map of the brain with relative activities in different regions.

c. **MEG** - [12] Magnetoencephalography is a functional neuroimaging technique which record small changes in the magnetic field produced by electric current naturally occurring in the brain in response to a particular activity. Arrays of SQUIDs (superconducting quantum interference devices) are currently the most common magnetometer, while the SERF (spin exchange relaxation-free) magnetometer is being investigated for future machines. This measures the neural transmission more directly than blood flow or metabolism data.

Dynamic Recording: Electrical activity

a. **EEG** - [13] Electroencephlogram track and record brain wave pattern of electrical activity. In this method small electrodes of thin wire are placed on scalp and these send signal to computer to record. Normal electrical activity make recognizable pattern while abnormal pattern indicates seizures or other problems. Altered levels of consciousness can easily be detected and EEG is very useful diagnostic tool for this case. It is specialized mechanism to record second language processing. The time resolution of EEG technique capture the rapidly changing electrical response to individual words, morpheme, or speech sounds. Generally it used to measure how second language has been understood based on average response.

b. **ERP** [14] - Evoked or event related potential is electrical activity which is result of the reaction of central nervous system to sensory stimulation. They are recorded by electrodes in same manner as EEG. It adopts an averaging technique to remove disturbances and reveals the acute response. The ERP is a typical series of positive and negative peaks, representing earlier and later stages of information processing. The advantage of using ERP is that, it is very inexpensive and allows fine temporal measurement of cognitive processing.

3   Neurolinguistic Computational Models [15]

Current neurolinguistic computational models are built upon the core idea of artificial intelligence which believes that brain is like digital computer. However the processing in brain is massively parallel and there is no specific memory module to access information. But assumption of modularity in brain functioning is key element of all these models. In spite of many constraints in modeling the brain processing there are two views brain modeling one relies on structured modeling and other on unstructured modeling or emergent modeling.

3.1   Structured Models

a. **Module level structured models** - This model attempts to localize the processing area in the brain. A familiar example of this type of model is Geschwind [16] model which suggest that language comprehension begin with receipt of signal by auditory cortex in temporal lobe and passed to Wernicke's area for lexical processing and then over arcuate fasciculum to Broca's area where reply is planned and output is sent to motor cortex for articulation. Although this model is problematic as there is little evidence that Wernicke's area functions as association cortex with any specific linkage to lexical or linguistic processing. Broca area has problems also although it is well defined anatomically. But it is not possible to locate the specific area for specific aphasia. However recent FMRI technique supports the cluster based functionality module in specific area which support the module level structured models. Also studies on children and development disorder in which specific language disorder is explained as the particular link to specific area is damaged.

b. **Neuron-level structured model** - Morton's logogen model [17] was most successful model of this type. In this model there was a master neuron devoted to a particular word. When this central unit was activated it further triggers the further units in phonology, orthography, meaning, and syntax. McClelland and Rumelhart [18] developed IA model. IA model account context effect in letter perception. This model was very successful in explaining speech production, reading, lexical semantic and second language learning. The problem with this model is that it is far from reality. It is not possible to associate a particular neuron with particular word in practice.

3.2 Emergent Models

a. **Self-organizing map** - To overcome the limitations of IA model PDP (Parallel Distributed Processing) model was proposed by Rumelhart which which relies on backprogation and successful in dealing with the distributed nature of memory in the brain. MacWhinny shown that PDP model was unable to represent localist representation of word leading to difficult morphological and syntactical processing. Kohonen [19] proposed Self Organizing Feature Map (SOFM) to handle all these problems. SOFM is difficult for language processing but its extension and further research are very impressive. It has been used by Mikkulainen et al. [20] for visual system. DevLex-II word learning model of Li et al. [21] illustrate the operation of this model. This model has three local maps-auditory map, concept map and articulatory map to represent the learning in children. There is possibility to extend the map based on addition of neuron or overlaying new feature.

b. **Syntactic Emergence** - Elman [22] proposed a simple recurrent back-propagation connection to predict the next word. This model assumes the comprehension is highly constructive and goal is to find the next word. MacDonald [23] has presented a model to ambiguity resolution. This model has excellently modeled the temporal properties of sentence processing. Macwhinny [24] proposed construction grammar. This framework emphasizes the role of individual lexical item in early grammatical learning.

c. **Lesioning Emergent** Model: After the syntactic model has been built lesioning model are built to study the aphasic symptoms of the brain. In this model lesioning is done by removing the hidden units, removing connection, rescaling weight, removing input or adding noise to the system. It has been shown that various method of lisioning network produce similar effects [25]. Plaut and Shallice [26] developed a model of deep dyslexia using lesioning technique.

4 Mathematical Methods

4.1 ANN

Artificial neural network is basic electronic model which mimic the structure and function of the brain. Neural network consists of processing neuron as node and information flow from one to another with proper channel. Each node can have one or more input associated with some weight. Each neuron does some computation on it input. The output may be input to some other neuron or can be output of the system. Basic source of learning of brain is by experience and neural network work in same fashion. The language acquisition in children and second language learning paradigm can be explained by neural network based models. Self-organizing map model of Kohenen [19] and SRN model of Elman [27] are neural network based model to explain language acquisition.

4.2 SVM

The use of support vector machine in brain image analysis is increasing day by day due to its capability in capturing multivariate relationship in the data. Brain image analysis based on univariate voxel-wise analysis fails in the cases where statistical test upon registered stereotaxic space result into spatially complex difference and involves a combination of different voxel or brain structure [28]. The support vector methods have solved these problems at great level, [29, 30]. These approaches allow capturing complex multivariate relationship in data and successfully applied to variety of neurological condition in classification [31, 32]. A lot of application in image segmentation and classification problems is done now a day.

4.3 Bayesian Approach to Brain Function

In field of behavioral science and neuroscience cognitive ability based on statistical principle is explained by Bayesian approach. It assumes that internal probabilistic model nervous system is maintained by processing sensory information using Bayesian probability. It explains and investigates the capacity of nervous system in uncertain situation. Human perceptual and motor behavior is modeled with Bayesian statistics. Landy et al. [33], Jacobs [34], Goldreich [35] had worked using Bayesian decision theory. Georghe and Hawkins [36] work on cortical information processing which is also called hierarchical temporal memory is based on Bayesian network of Markov chain.

5 Comparative Study of Recent Research Work Focused on Aphasia and Dyslexia

We have compared the recent trend of research focused on aphasia and dyslexia as in Table 2 and found that the behavioural studies and neuro-imaging techniques both are equally important in research community.

Table 2. Comparative study of recent research work on aphasia and dyslexia

Author name	Work	Disease	Methodology
Warren et al. [37]	Structural prediction	Aphasia	Behavioral
Hanne et al. [38]	Sentence comprehension and morphological study	Aphasia	Behavioral
Cruice et al. [39]	Verb use study by different group	Aphasia	Behavioral
Della Rosa et al. [40]	Functional recovery in aphasia	Aphasia	fMRI
Toumiranta et al. [41]	Vocabulary acquisition	Aphasia	Behavioral
Wang et al. [42]	Functional deficit in clause and nominal phrases	Aphasia	Behavioral
Bart den Ouden et al. [43]	Argument effect in action verb naming	Aphasia	fMRI
Sebastian et al. [44]	Semantic processing in English-Spanish bilingual	Aphasia	Behavioral
Karni et al. [45]	Differential effect of word presentation rate	Dyslexia	fMRI
Oren and Breznitz [46]	Bilingual reading comparison	Dyslexia	ERP
Shiran and Breznitz [47]	Recall range and information processing speed	Dyslexia	ERP
Richard et al. [48]	Morphological spelling treatment in children	Dyslexia	fMRI
Leeuwan et al. [49]	Brain mapping study of two month infant	Dyslexia	fMRI
Dandache, S. et al. [50]	Reading and phonological skill of children	Dyslexia	Behavioral

6 Conclusion

This paper illustrates the historical perspective in language processing by brain along with technique and tradition. Various data acquisition techniques for brain research have been briefly explained in the field. Various neuro-linguistic computational models have been discussed. Research in the field requires mathematical knowledge to model the observed behaviour to computational model. A brief account of the mathematical methods employed has been discussed, though the list is not perfect and requires including many more. Finally a comparative study of research going on diseases aphasia and dyslexia has been given. From this research it is clear that importance of classical models and methods are still valid and it is not always require having costly machine for research work. Other views of research other than imaging are also equally important.

References

1. George, C.: Boeree: Speech and the Brain (2004). http://webspace.ship.edu/cgboer/speechbrain.html
2. Friederici, A.D.: The brain basis of language processing: from structure to function. Physiol. Rev. Publ. **91**(4), 1357–1392 (2011)
3. Broca area: The Editors of Encyclopædia Britannica. https://www.britannica.com/science/Broca-area
4. Grodzinsky, Y., Santi, A.: The battle of Broca region. Trends Cogn. Sci. **12**(12), 474–480 (2008)
5. Anatomy of Speech & Language. http://memory.ucsf.edu/brain/language/anatomy
6. Methods of Investigating Brain and Language. http://bbi3215psycholinguistics.wikifoundry.com
7. Cerebral Angiography. http://www.radiologyinfo.org/en/info.cfm?pg=angiocerebral
8. C.T Scan Wikipedia. https://en.wikipedia.org/wiki/CT_scan
9. Despotović, I., Goossens, B., Philips, W.: MRI segmentation of the human brain: challenges, methods, and applications. Comput. Math. Methods Med. **2015** (2015). Article ID 450341
10. Dogil, G., Ackermann, H., Grodd, W., Haider, H., Kamp, H., Mayer, J., Riecker, A., Wildgruber, D.: The speaking brain: a tutorial introduction to fMRI experiments in the production of speech, prosody and syntax. J. Neurolinguistics **15**, 59–90 (2002)
11. Cathy, J.: Price: a review and synthesis of the first 20 years of PET and fMRI studies of heard speech, spoken language and reading. Neuroimage **62**(2), 816–847 (2012)
12. Magnetoencephalography: Wikipedia. https://en.wikipedia.org/wiki/Magnetoencephalography
13. Gouvea, A.C.: (FIU): current advances in neurolinguistics: the use of electroencephalography (EEG) to study language. Neurociência da Linguagem **7**(2) (2011)
14. Yu, Y., Lu, S., Zhu, W., Li, C., Lin, Z., Wu, J.: Application of ERP in neurolinguistics: a review of recent studies. Neurosci. Biomed. Eng. **4**(3), 195–201
15. Macwhinney, B., Li, P.: Neurolinguistic computational models. In: Handbook of the Neuroscience of Language
16. Geschwind, N.: Specializations of the human brain. Sci. Am. **241**, 180–199 (1979)
17. Morton, J.: A functional model for memory. In: Norman, D.A. (ed.) Models of Human Memory, pp. 203–248. Academic Press, New York (1970)
18. McClelland, J.L., Rumelhart, D.E.: An interactive activation model of context effects in letter perception: part 1. An account of the basic findings. Psychol. Rev. **88**, 375–402 (1981)
19. Kohonen, T.: Self-organizing Maps, 3rd edn. Springer, Berlin (2001)
20. Miikkulainen, R., Bednar, J.A., Choe, Y., Sirosh, J.: Computational Maps in the Visual Cortex. Springer, New York (2005)
21. Li, P., Zhao, X., MacWhinney, B.: Dynamic self-organization and early lexical development in children. Cogn. Sci. **31**, 581–612 (2007)

22. Elman, J.L., Bates, E., Johnson, M., Karmiloff-Smith, A., Parisi, D., Plunkett, K.: Rethinking Innateness. MIT Press, Cambridge (1996)
23. MacDonald, M.C., Pearlmutter, N.J., Seidenberg, M.S.: Lexical nature of syntactic ambiguity resolution. Psychol. Rev. **101**(4), 676–703 (1994)
24. MacWhinney, B., Hillsdale, N.J.: Lawrence Erlbaum. The competition model. In: MacWhinney, B. (ed.) Mechanisms of Language Acquisition, pp. 249–308 (1987)
25. Bullinaria, J.A., Chater, N.: Connectionist modelling: implications for cognitive neuropsychology. Lang. Cogn. Process. **10**, 227–264 (1995)
26. Plaut, D., Shallice, T.: Deep dyslexia: a case study of connectionist neuropsychology. Cogn. Neuropsychol. **10**, 377–500 (1993)
27. Elman, J.l.: Distributed representations, simple recurrent networks, and grammatical structure. Mach. Learn. **7**, 195–225 (1991)
28. Davatzikos, C.: Why voxel-based morphometric analysis should be used with great caution when characterizing group differences. NeuroImage **23**(1), 17–20 (2004)
29. Vapnik, V.N.: The Nature of Statistical Learning Theory. Springer, Heidelberg (1995)
30. Scholkopf, B., Smola, A.J.: Learning with Kernels. MIT Press, Cambridge (2001)
31. Lao, Z., et al.: Morphological classification of brains via high-dimensional shape transformations and machine learning methods. NeuroImage **21**(1), 46–57 (2004)
32. Fan, Y., et al.: COMPARE: classification of morphological patterns using adaptive regional elements. IEEE TMI **26**(1), 93–105 (2007)
33. Hudson, T.E., Maloney, L.T., Landy, M.S.: Optimal compensation for temporal uncertainty in movement planning. PLoS Comput. Biol. **4**(7) (2008)
34. Jacobs, R.A.: Optimal integration of texture and motion cues to depth. Vis. Res. **39**(21), 3621–3629 (1999)
35. Goldreich, D.: A Bayesian perceptual model replicates the cutaneous rabbit and other tactile spatiotemporal illusions. PLoS ONE **2**(3), e333 (2007)
36. George, D., Hawkins, J.: Towards a mathematical theory of cortical micro-circuits. PLoS Comput. Biol. **5**(10), e1000532 (2009). doi:10.1371/journal.pcbi.1000532
37. Warren, T., Dickey, M.W., Lei, C.M.: Structural prediction in aphasia: evidence from either. J. Neurolinguistics **39**, 38–48 (2016)
38. Hanne, S., Burchert, F., De Bleser, R., Vasishth, S.: Sentence comprehension and morphological cues in aphasia: what eye-tracking reveals about integration and prediction. J. Neurolinguistics **34**, 83–111 (2015)
39. Cruice, M., Pritchard, M., Dipper, L.: Verb use in aphasic and non-aphasic personal discourse: what is normal? J. Neurolinguistics **28**, 31–47 (2014)
40. Della Rosa, P.A., Canini, M., Borsa, V.M., Marien, P., Cappa, S.F., Abutalebi, J.: Functional recovery in subcortical crossed and standard aphasia. J. Neurolinguistics **27**(1), 103–118 (2014). doi:10.1016/j.jneuroling.2013.09.004
41. Tuomiranta, L., Gronroos, A.M., Martin, N., Laine, M.: Vocabulary acquisition in aphasia: modality can matter. J. Neurolinguistics **32**, 42–58 (2014)
42. Wang, H., Yoshida, M., Thompson, C.K.: Parallel functional category deficits in clauses and nominal phrases: the case of English agrammatism. J. Neurolinguistics **27**(1), 75–102 (2014)
43. Bart den Ouden, D., Fix, S., Parrish, T.B., Thompson, C.K.: Argument structure effects in action verb naming in static and dynamic conditions. J. Neurolinguistics **22**(2), 195–215 (2009)
44. Sebastian, R., Kiran, S., Sandberg, C.: Semantic processing in Spanish-English bilinguals with aphasia. J. Neurolinguistics **25**(4), 240–262 (2012)
45. Karni, A., Morocz, I.A., Bitan, T., Shaul, S., Kushnir, T., Breznitz, Z.: An fMRI study of the differential effects of word presentation rates (reading acceleration) on dyslexic readers' brain activity patterns. J. Neurolinguistics **18**(2), 197–219 (2005)

46. Oren, R., Breznitz, Z.: Reading processes in L1 and L2 among dyslexic as compared to regular bilingual readers: behavioral and electrophysiological evidence. J. Neurolinguistics **18**(2), 127–151 (2005)
47. Shiran, A., Breznitz, Z.: The effect of cognitive training on recall range and speed of information processing in the working memory of dyslexic and skilled readers. J. Neurolinguistics **24**(5), 524–537 (2011)
48. Richards, T.L., Aylward, E.H., Berninger, V.W., Field, K.M., Grimme, A.C., Richards, A. L., Nagy, W.: Individual fMRI activation in orthographic mapping and morpheme mapping after orthographic or morphological spelling treatment in child dyslexics. J. Neurolinguistics **19**(1), 56–86 (2006)
49. Leeuwen, T.V., Been, P., Herten, M.V., Zwarts, F., Maassen, B., der Leij, A.V.: Two-month-old infants at risk for dyslexia do not discriminate /bAk/ from /dAk/: a brain-mapping study. J. Neurolinguistics **21**(4), 333–348 (2008)
50. Dandache, S., Wouters, J., Ghesquière, P.: Development of reading and phonological skills of children at family risk for dyslexia: a longitudinal analysis from kindergarten to sixth grade. Dyslexia **20**(4), 305–329 (2014). doi:10.1002/dys.1482

Classification Algorithms for Prediction of Lumbar Spine Pathologies

Rajni Bedi[1(✉)] and Ajay Shiv Sharma[2]

[1] Computer Science and Engineering Department,
Lyallpur Khalsa College of Engineering, Jalandhar, Punjab, India
avirajni@gmail.com
[2] Information Technology Department, Guru Nanak Dev Engineering College,
Ludhiana, Punjab, India
2ajayshiv@gmail.com

Abstract. Classes can be predicted correctly in the dataset using Classification. For the present study, weka data mining tool is used to predict the lumbar spine pathologies. In this work dataset is firstly classified using different algorithms and then it is determined that which classification algorithm performs better for predicting lumbar spine pathologies. Lumbar spine diseases are predicted with identification of symptoms in patients. We have evaluated and compared six classification algorithms using different evaluation criteria. For the present work, the multilayer perceptron algorithm gives best results to predict the lumbar spine pathologies. This model can be used by the radiologists for lumbar spine pathologies prediction.

Keywords: Lumbar disc disease · Lumbar spinal stenosis · Spondylolisthesis · Intervertebral disc

1 Introduction

Statistics from the World Health Organization shows that 80% of people have back pain in lumbar spine in their lifetime [1]. It is the most common cause of interference with work and routine daily activities. The National Institute of Neurological disorders and stroke estimates that American spends at least $50 billion annually on health care and treatment for Low Back Pain (LBP) [1]. The common causes of Lower Spine Pain are Lumbar Disc Disease (LDD), Lumbar Spinal Stenosis (LSS) and Spondylolisthesis. Main cause of LDD is the desiccation and degeneration of the soft nucleus of the intervertebral disc in the lumbar spine. This is also termed as herniated lumbar disc [2] as shown in Fig. 1. With aging, the intervertebral disc dries up and because of dehydration the disc decreases in height. Due to this outer ring (annulus) of the disc gets deteriorated and nucleus of the disc gets herniated out. This herniated nucleus then compresses the adjacent nerve roots and causes pain, numbness and weakness on that side of the leg. LSS is a frequently encountered painful and potentially disability condition. LSS is a condition that occurs when the passageway within the vertebral column become narrowed due to bulging disc, ligamentum flavum and facet joint hypertrophy [3] and constrict the nerve roots contained within them.

© Springer Nature Singapore Pte Ltd. 2017
D. Singh et al. (Eds.): ICAICR 2017, CCIS 712, pp. 42–50, 2017.
DOI: 10.1007/978-981-10-5780-9_4

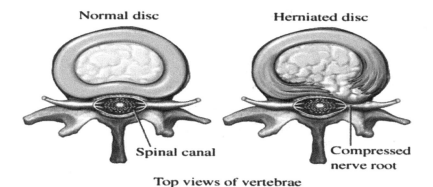

Fig. 1. A spine segment illustrating herniated disc

Figure 2 illustrates Lumbar Spinal Stenosis. Lumbar spinal stenosis causes pain in the lower back and back of the legs which increases on prolonged standing and walking [3].

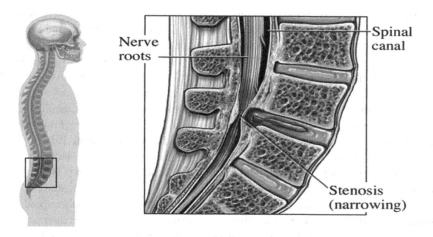

Fig. 2. Image illustrating Lumbar Spinal Stenosis

Spondylolisthesis is a forward shift of one vertebrae body on another (Fig. 3). This vertebral slip occurs due to degenerative disease of facet joints or to a developmental break or elongation of L5 Lamina causing an L5/S1 spondylolisthesis.

Data Mining Techniques may be used in various fields like reporting and treatment in medical field, stock trading, marketing and finance. We have used classification techniques for the diagnosis of lumbar spine pathologies. The present predictive model can act as a tool to assist the doctors and radiologist to provide the information regarding type of lumbar spine problem a patient is having.

Spondylolisthesis

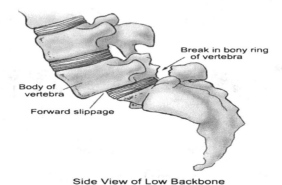

Fig. 3. Image of spine illustrating Spondylolisthesis

2   Literature Review

Ramana and Babu studied different classification algorithms to classify liver patient's dataset. They used different criteria like Sensitivity, Specificity, Accuracy and Precision to evaluate their algorithms [4]. Nookala et al. compared different classification algorithms on cancer data base to predict occurrence of cancer in patients [5]. Exarchos et al. used partial decision trees and association rules to predict symptoms of Parkinson's disease (PD [6]. Koziol et al. employed decision trees for diagnosis of prostate cancer [7]. In the year 2010, Shin et al. used the association rules for medical image classification in hypertensive patients [8]. Aljumah et al. studied a regression-based data mining technique for predictive analysis of diabetic treatment [9]. In 2012, Osmanbegovic along with his co-author used different data mining techniques for making student performance predicting model [10]. Williams et al. used Naïve Bayes and Decision Tree algorithms to predict risk of breast cancer [11]. Dangare et al. used Decision Trees, Naive Bayes, and Neural Networks algorithms to analyze prediction systems for heart disease. These classifiers were also compared based on their accuracy [12]. In his research work Dhamodharan used distinct patients' symptoms to predict major liver diseases by using Bayes and Tree algorithms and compared them based on their accuracy measure. They inferred that Naïve Bayes algorithm can predict the diseases with higher classification accuracy than the FT tree algorithm [13].

3   Problem Formulation

Due to large number of patients in developing countries, resources are scarce that results in large number of undiagnosed and misdiagnosed cases. Also the treatment is merely based on virtual perception of radiologists. So justification is required to satisfy the patients. We can overcome the human errors and can use machine learning to build the predictive model using the past history and clinical examinations of patients to aid the clinical findings of lumbar disc disease, stenosis and spondylolisthesis. Various classification algorithms have been analyzed comparatively in the present study.

4 Methodology

In the current study, the emphasis is on classifying the patients on the basis of type of Lumbar Spine Pathology. With an aim to achieve this, different classification algorithms are trained with the patients' dataset. After the training of the classification algorithm, we get a prediction model that predicts the lumbar spine problems that a patient is having depending upon the patient examinations and clinical characteristics. Different classification algorithms are also compared on the basis of different criteria. For classifying the dataset, Weka data mining tool (Waikato Environment for Knowledge Analysis) was used.

4.1 Classification Algorithms

In Weka, we have different categories of classifiers such as Tree based classifiers, Bayes, Functions, Rules etc. In the present study, we have selected mix of these classification algorithms like Naive Bayes, Multilayer Perceptron, SVM, J48, Random forest and Decision Table to study Lumbar Spine dataset. Their classification accuracy and performance are also studied.

Brief background on these algorithms is given in the following section.

Naive Bayes Algorithm
The Naive Bayes algorithm represents supervised learning method for classification. It uses Bayes Theorem with strong independence assumptions. Its main advantage is that every attribute of data set being classified is independent of value of any another attribute. It needs few records of training data for evaluating the attributes required for classification.

J48
A J48 decision tree is a type of supervised learning methods for classification. For selecting an attribute to split the data, the information gain of various attributes is calculated. The attribute with highest normalized information gain is selected to split the population into two or more subpopulations.

Random Forest
It is an ensemble learning method for classification. In this, at training time a large number of decision trees are constructed and then the mode of classes of individual trees is calculated and used as the output class. It generally enhances the performance of the final model.

Decision Table
In weka, it is a good tool for performing classification. This algorithm is divided into two parts- an inducer and a visualizer. In this algorithm, data is divided hierarchically depending upon most suitable splitter in the given dataset. The inducer selects the most

important attributes for splitting the data, and the associated visualizer displays the resulting model graphically.

SMO

This algorithm is mainly used for solving the optimization problems. It divides the problem into a number of sub-problems, which are then solved analytically. It is used for training support vector machines.

In Support Vector Machine (SVM), we construct hyperplanes that divides the data into separate classes. Then the hyperplane that is having the largest distance to the nearest training data point is selected as the best hyperplane.

Multilayer Perceptron (MLP)

Multilayer perceptron has been used in wide variety of tasks such as prediction and classification. It consists of a system of simple interconnected neurons or nodes. The neuron output is calculated as the weighted sum of its inputs to which a nonlinear sigmoid function is applied. Back-propagation algorithm is used to find out weights in the learning phase.

This classification algorithm is known for its decision speed and good generalization capacity.

4.2 Evaluation Criteria for Classification

The main objective of this research proposal is to classify and predict various Lumbar Spine diseases using dataset of various patients with symptoms of spinal disease. This also involves comparing the classification algorithms for Lumbar Spine Data based on the various input parameters like Accuracy, Kappa Statistics, and Area under ROC, F-Measure, Mean Absolute Error and RMSE (Root Mean Square Error). For the performance evaluation the WEKA data mining tool is used. In this model, the training and testing data are selected randomly from the data set to measure accuracy and other different parameters.

4.3 Data Set

This is a prospective study to be conducted in the outpatient department of Joshi Neuro Trauma Centre, Jalandhar and Johal Multispecialty Hospital, Jalandhar for a duration of seven months from 1/1/2016 to 31/7/2016. Patients visiting the OPD with chief complaint of back pain, male or female, in the age group of 30 to 65 years are evaluated. The data acquired by each patient are shown in Table 1. The present study predicts the type of following Lumbar Spine pathologies: Lumbar Disc Disease, Stenosis or Spondylolisthesis.

Table 1. Attributes used in the dataset

Attributes	Values	Comments
Age	Age in years	Age of Patient
Gender	M, F	M-Male, F-Female
Backache	Mild, Moderate or Severe	History of Backache
Radicular Pain-Side	L, R, B or No	Pain in Left Leg (L), Right Leg (R), Both Legs (B) or No pain in legs (No)
Radicular Pain-Site	L1-L2, L2-L3, L4-L5, L5-S1	Nerve roots from L1 to S1 supply different areas of the leg that can be clinically judged
Radicular Pain	Continue, Walking, Working or No	Pain while walking, working, continuous or no pain
Bowel and Bladder Involvement	Yes, No	Involvement of Bowel and Bladder
Numbness/Tingling	Yes, No	Any Numbness or Tingling in Legs or Feet
Motor Weakness	Yes, No	Any weakness in Legs or Feet
Back Deformity	Sideways, Forward	Any Deformity in back
SLR	Positive, Negative	Straight Leg Raising is positive or negative

5 Results and Discussion

In this section the results of different classifiers are discussed. To classify the cause of Lumbar Spine Problem correctly, the different measures are calculated for different classifiers. The various performance measures are shown in Table 2.

Table 2. Various performance measures

Algorithm	Accuracy (%)	F-Measure	Kappa Statistics	ROC	MAE	RMSE
Naive Bayes	95.71	0.957	0.942	0.999	0.0402	0.1189
SMO	90	0.899	0.8645	0.962	0.2583	0.3237
Multilayer Perceptron	98.57	0.986	0.9807	1	0.0256	0.0817
J48	88.57	0.881	0.8458	0.932	0.0651	0.2379
Random Forest	97.14	0.971	0.9613	1	0.0816	0.1451
Decision Table	84.29	0.833	0.7871	0.968	0.1966	0.2625

5.1 Analysis of Parameters

Kappa Statistics
We can observe from Table 2 that Multilayer perceptron classifier has largest value of K (0.9807) as compared to other classifiers of Lumbar Spine dataset. This leads us to the fact that there is a perfect aggrement between the classifier and ground truth.

Mean Absolute Error (MAE)
According to Table 2 data, SMO classifier achieves maximum MAE values i.e. 0.2583 and multilayer perceptron classifier has minimum MAE values (0.0256). So Multilayer Perceptron predicts result that is almost equivalent to the true value of the Lumber Spine parameters.

Root Mean Squared Error (RMSE)
The result shows that Multilayer perceptron has the lowest error rate i.e. 0.0817.

Depending on above three parameters performance of the algorithms are compared and shown in Fig. 4. It is observed from the figure that multilayer perceptron gives near accurate results and SMO gives poor results for the same parameters.

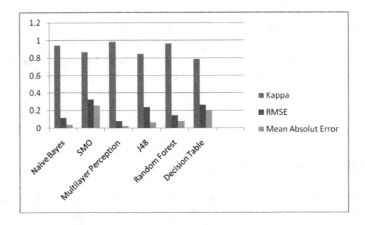

Fig. 4. Kappa statistics and error rates

Classification Accuracy
Figure 5 shows that multilayer perception algorithm gives highest classification accuracy i.e. 98.57% and Decision Table algorithm gives least classification accuracy i.e. 84.29%. From the above facts it can be concluded that Multilayer Perceptron performs best in case of Lumbar Spine dataset.

Area Under ROC
From Table 2 it is observed that both the Multilayer Perceptron and Random Forest has same ROC value i.e. 1. Even the Naive Bayes algorithm performs well according to ROC value i.e. 0.999.

F-Measure
F-Measure of Multilayer Perceptron is highest i.e. 0.9807 and Decision Table is having least value i.e. 0.833.

ROC values and F-Measures of different classifiers are represented graphically in Fig. 6.

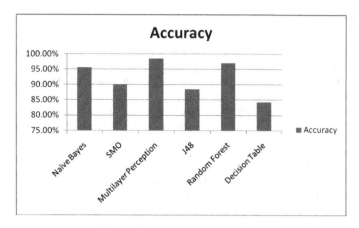

Fig. 5. Accuracy

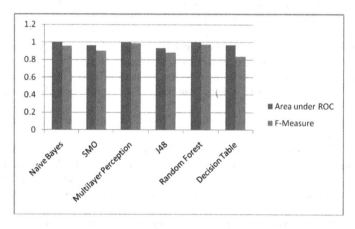

Fig. 6. Area under ROC and F-Measure

6 Conclusion

Disc anomalies such as Lumbar Disc Disease, Lumbar Spinal Stenosis and Spondy-lolisthesis are the main causes of lumbar spine pain. The present study can be used to assist the radiologist and doctors to predict the disc problem depending upon patients' clinical symptoms. In the present model, different classification algorithms were used for predicting lumbar spine diseases and it was found that Multilayer Perceptron outperforms as compared to other algorithms.

References

1. NINDS: National institute of neurological disorders and stroke (ninds): low back pain fact sheet, NIND brochure (2008)
2. Arthur, F.D., Agur, A.M.R.: Atlas of Anatomy, 11th edn. Lippincott Williams and Wilkins, Philadelphia (2004)
3. Markman, J.D., Gaud, K.G.: Lumbar spinal stenosis in older adults: current understanding and future directions. Clin. Geriatr. Med. **24**, 369–388 (2008). doi:10.1016/j.cger.2007.12.007
4. Ramana, B.V., Babu, M.S.P.: Liver classification using modified rotation forest. Int. J. Eng. Res. Dev. **1**, 17–24 (2012)
5. Nookala, G.K.M., Pottumuthu, B.K., Orsu, N., Mudunuri, S.B.: Performance analysis and evaluation of different data mining algorithms used for cancer classification. Int. J. Adv. Res. Artif. Intell. **2**, 49–55 (2013). doi:10.14569/IJARAI.2013.020508
6. Exarchos, T.P., Tzallas, A.T., Baga, D., Chaloglou, D., Fotiadis, D.I., Tsouli, S., Diakou, M., Konitsiotis, S.: Using partial decision trees to predict Parkinson's symptoms: a new approach for diagnosis and therapy in patients suffering from Parkinson's disease. Comput. Biol. Med. **42**, 195–204 (2012). doi:10.1016/j.compbiomed.2011.11.008
7. Koziol, J.A., Feng, A.C., Jia, Z., Wang, Y., Goodison, S., McClelland, M., Mercola, D.: The wisdom of the commons: ensemble tree classifiers for prostate cancer diagnosis. Bioinformatics **25**, 54–60 (2009). doi:10.1093/bioinformatics/btn354
8. Shin, A.M., Lee, I.H., Lee, G.H., Park, H.J., Park, H.S., Yoon, K.I., Lee, J.J., Kim, Y.N.: Diagnostic analysis of patients with essential hypertension using association rule mining. Healthc. Inf. Res. **16**, 77–81 (2010). doi:10.4258/hir.2010.16.2.77
9. Aljumah, A.A., Ahamad, M.G., Siddiqui, M.K.: Application of data mining: diabetes health care in young and old patients. J. King Saud Univ.-Comput. Inf. Sci. **25**, 127–136 (2013). doi:10.1016/j.jksuci.2012.10.003
10. Osmanbegovi, E., Suljic, M.: Data mining approach for predicting student performance. Econ. Rev. **10**, 3–12 (2012)
11. Williams, K., Idowu, P.A., Balogun, J.A., Oluwaranti, A.: Breast cancer risk prediction using data mining classification techniques. Trans. Netw. Commun. **3**, 1–11 (2015)
12. Dangare, C.S., Apte, S.S.: Improved study of heart disease prediction system using data mining classification techniques. Int. J. Comput. Appl. **47**, 44–48 (2012). doi:10.5120/7228-0076
13. Dhamodharan, S.: Liver disease prediction using bayesian classification. In: 4th National Conference on Advanced Computing, Applications & Technologies, pp. 1–3 (2014)

Keyword Based Identification of Thrust Area Using MapReduce for Knowledge Discovery

Nirmal Kaur$^{(\boxtimes)}$ⓘ and Manmohan Sharmaⓘ

School of Computer Application,
Lovely Professional University, Jalandhar, India
nirmal019@gmail.com, manmohan.19673@lpu.co.in

Abstract. Keyword based identification generally used in many applications like Web pages, Query processing, Searching interfaces with dealing the power of data mining algorithms which contributes effective and efficient work in large datasets. Keywords are most important terms in documents or text fields to get some interesting knowledge for fulfill the discovery goal. The goal of this paper is to specify the Thrust Area for particular searched keyword in computer science field by this interface. This paper use MapReduce framework with some modification and search the keyword from database to identify the Thrust Area. The proposed interface is mapped on the processed query resulting in the relevant information extracted from the given datasets. MapReduce can work with keywords in large datasets such as sorting, counting frequency etc. with high efficiency. Experimental work has also been carried out to analyses the performance on various parameters such as the time taken by each input source to make clusters and identify Thrust Areas.

Keywords: Knowledge discovery · Keyword matching · Keyword-based identification · MapReduce · Information retrieval

1   Introduction

Knowledge discovery is used to find motivating and essential useful designs patterns or procedures in data and briefly produce the complete information extraction method, as well as however data are stored and retrieved, it produce cost-effective and efficient algorithms to explore huge information, it shows how to visualize and interpret the results, and also to build and support the communication between machine and human. It generally considers support for knowledge and analyzing the application domain [1]. Knowledge Discovery approaches lead to discovering the knowledge about inductive learning, semantic query optimization, Bayesian statistics, and knowledge extraction for expert systems. KDD processes include the characteristics of data integration, data exploration, and a frequency distribution by matching some keywords and find relevant information in the relevancy of data. Data mining is the essential process of Knowledge discovery. The investigation in databases and data origination has presented ascend to an approach to compact with store and control this useful information for further decision making [2]. With the help of Data Mining the knowledge is extracted from two datasets by predicting the factors and comparison between the classes of the information or data

© Springer Nature Singapore Pte Ltd. 2017
D. Singh et al. (Eds.): ICAICR 2017, CCIS 712, pp. 51–62, 2017.
DOI: 10.1007/978-981-10-5780-9_5

classified using the classification technique. Knowledge discovery plays an important role in information retrieval system for information extraction using searching algorithms and to optimize the searching process, the used algorithm should be efficient. In order to measure the efficiency of an algorithm, the complexity should be polynomial with respect to time and space [3]. Text categorization used in textual databases for divide the text into different classes, such as text classification. Data mining is a region of strong activity for developing new algorithms and techniques as a research topic but additionally an application area wherever realistic advantage are to be created [4]. This paper presents the Keyword based identification process which also used in term-weighting, counting and sorting. Keyword based identification process includes the query search form interface and give the appropriate results suitable for that query. Further sections explain the important types of knowledge which contributes in the process.

1.1 Keyword-Based Identification Process

Keyword based identification generally used in many applications like Web pages, Query processing, Searching interfaces with dealing the power of data mining algorithms which contributes effective and efficient work in large datasets. In databases, various keywords matching and pattern matching algorithm developed by these techniques such as Frequent item set, Sequential pattern searching, probability based keyword searching, n-gram etc. keywords are most important terms in document or text fields. In every class containing keywords in C1 (k_1, k_2, k_3 ,......., k_n). The occurrence frequency of any keyword in database can be calculated as Term Frequency (TF) and Inverted Document Frequency (IDF). Keyword based identification is a very useful operation in the previous applications, like data integration, data repositing, distributed query processing and so on [5]. Keyword search concluded in structured data format such as relational databases [6–8] taking benefits of an arrangement of database and information retrieval techniques. One of the most significant problems for facilitating such as query facility is to be choosing the most convenient data sources related to the keyword query. Mostly Information retrieval systems used keyword-frequency statistics for textual databases [9]. Data mining techniques have previously been utilized for text exploration by extracting co-occurring relationships as descriptive phrases from document collection [10]. A keyword based approach used in any database for the purpose of retrieval of data from the database based on keyword search using different technologies such as CGI (Common Gateway Interface), JavaScript and Servlet, Java Swing etc., these programs accept query from user and processed query with keyword matching mechanism and give appropriate result to the user [11]. Knowledge representation in documents by term vectors lead to high dimensionality problem in index terms in textual data so clustering methods can be used to overcome these problems [12].

1.2 MapReduce Framework

MapReduce works as a programming model to produce huge data sets and an interface for processing and generating clusters from data sets. In this model the written programs are parallelized and executes naturally on wide clusters [13]. The main concept behind map reduce is "mapping" your data set into a collection of (key, value) pairs, and then it reducing overall datasets by grouping the datasets with the same key.

The proposed technique utilizes functionality of the recognized MapReduce algorithm for counting word frequencies in a large text files. MapReduce work flow starts with the framework that split the data inputs into segments. The script takes input data and maps the data into <key, value> pairs according to our requirements [14]. Mapper are used to Map the key in different input sources and then reducer creates the blocks of keyword by apply sorting and then blocks are divided into single block by counting key value as per their frequency. To deal with a specific problem it is preferable to use world class solution like MapReduce.

The paper is organized as follows. Section 2, some related work are discussed. Section 3, presented the objectives of study. Section 4, presented the methodology of work. Section 5, discussed the experimental results. Conclusions and the future work are presented in Sect. 6.

2 Related Work

In related work the existing Keyword based identification techniques for knowledge discovery and existing work of MapReduce framework for searching and mapping has been described.

A system for keyword based searching in databases was proposed in [11] and describes a prototype for searching in a database named Mragyati. This system implemented as data retrieval system on the web using common gateway interface and java script. The results were shown by ranking of query in database and also provide the answer of foreign key concept in database. A survey of keyword querying in database presented in [15] described about the BANKS which is an integrated database for keyword querying and interactive browsing. Implemented an approach based on Dijkstra shortest path algorithm. The system used for keyword based searching in relational databases name DBExplore which has implemented in [16] by using web server and commercial databases. It provides interaction to user by a browser interface and provides efficient keyword searching utility. A system DISCOVER in [17] which is useful for finding relevant candidate networks without redundancy in data. It provides a simple interface for querying keyword on a search engine that associated with relationships and attached via more than one tuple. Also provides a candidate network generation algorithm with efficiency and define greedy algorithm for creating a near optimal execution plan.

A technique for automatic query which retrieves the information and build relationship between user and text databases developed in [18]. It used different domains, target relations and databases with low effort and also improves the efficiency of extraction techniques. Qxtract improved the extracting relation and design the system by using Bootstrapping algorithm. An architecture named ESKO in [19] supports highly efficient keyword based search framework which creates virtual documents from database by joining tuples and for indexing and keyword search processing used DB2 net search extender. Experiment results shows keyword queries response time is collaborative for representative queries. A method proposed in [9] for solves the selection problem that effectively encapsulates the relations between keywords in a relational database over the sources found and developed effective ranking based methods that defines the keyword relationship for a given keyword query. The overview of keyword querying and ranking of those keywords in database and also shows the mapping process of keywords in SQL queries, automated ranking etc. provides in [20] discussed evaluation technique for keyword queries based on inverted list in IR System.

The precision of search queries specified weight of keywords for success and also verified efficiency and effectiveness of the queries improved in [21]. The interface was designed which contain five modules such as data collection, extraction of data, processing their indexing and search queries executions and last interface interaction. The search engine named SWEE for searching queries with effectively and efficiently. Two problems in relational databases to improve the effectiveness and efficiency for keyword searching were overcome in [22] and an efficient ranking algorithm with a ranking model was proposed that performed the experiments on real data sets. Introduced a new index which provide efficiency in time and size factors. The ranking algorithm takes less time from existing algorithms. The semantic matching work for keyword matching in Information Retrieval systems was described in [23] and proposed a hybrid fuzzy ontology for querying and hybrid method for keyword matching. Used keyword matching algorithm for measured the space in keywords and apply fuzzy arrangements for match keywords from all database in IR System and also describe the algorithm for matching relevant paths. They improved keyword based IR systems by providing better search mechanism.

Hierarchical clustering method for large datasets with MapReduce Framework was provided in [24]. The method provides efficiency including two techniques such as Batch Updating and Communication cost and Co-occurrence based similar dataset and feature selection to reduce the memory requirements for huge datasets or feature vectors. A model based on Hadoop MapReduce which can be mapped the processed query and extract the relevant information from datasets was designed in [25]. K-means clustering for partition the terms into related concepts and classes was used in it and performed text preprocessing and clustering by using term frequency and inverted document frequency. Experimental results show the precision and recall versus no of documents F-measure and error rate. A new approach to examine the keyword queries with MapReduce algorithm was proposed in [26] results in efficient and effective on graph data sets. Proposed baseline method for keyword queries by using MapReduce. This framework partitions the large graphs into small graphs than Reduce the SIterationand compared the execution time of two approaches SOverlapping and SIteration by emulates the top k-keywords values running on different queries with different number of keywords. A framework by using domain ontology in [27] for finding articles and hot topics by using MapReduce algorithm. It sorts keywords automatically and titles from particular hot topics in XML bibliography datasets. They created the dataset and extract the keywords from main topic and sub topic then mapping articles by MapReduce mapping process from keywords, titles and abstract of publications. MapReduce algorithm works for calculate the title then count the each topic year wise then sort the highest topic called hot topic.

3 Objectives

1. To develop an interface for keyword searching and find out the thrust area on the basis of that keyword from database.
2. To calculate time consumed by each input source with respect to size of data.

4 Methodology

To get the knowledge about all keyword based querying process and develop an interface as an application to find out the Thrust Area in Computer Science Field. In this paper created a GUI for building the interface used Java Swing language and implement the modified MapReduce algorithm. This paper proposes work for store the keywords data in various input streams in the form of text files which can make number of files according to our requirement. After that apply MapReduce counting approach that extracts the keyword data from files and sort the keywords according to high counting. At this point performed sorting based on counting of keywords instead of keyword frequency then compute the time taken by each input source with respect the size of data and then connect Database for find searched keyword from there and specify the Thrust Area for that particular keyword.

4.1 Overview of Framework

In this paper, performed a mechanism for keyword-based identification to get the Thrust Area for that keyword by using MapReduce Framework (Fig. 1).

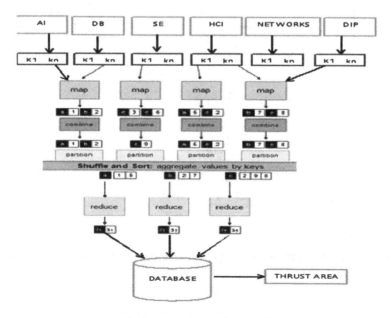

Fig. 1. Overview of framework

In first step created a pool of Dump files which contain the keywords data of various disciplines in computer science and make different clusters according to their disciplines. Build a framework using Java Swing for searching keywords for their respective disciplines. Apply MapReduce algorithms with some modifications which counts the keywords frequency appeared in different files and sort the keyword by its high counting then match that searched keyword which has high counting from the database. When Keyword matches from the database then specify the thrust area based on that keyword. Calculate the time taken by each input source and define the number of clusters made by that keyword. In modified algorithm sorting is not w.e.f keywords as available in MapReduce algorithm instead do sort using count value so that frequency of keywords can be found for further Thrust Area.

4.2 Flow Chart

(See Fig. 2).

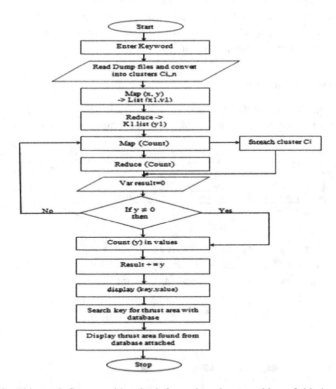

Fig. 2. This work flow provides the information about working of this interface.

4.3   Pseudo Code

Map(Key, value=Datasets in clusters Ci):
mapping(x,y) -> list(x1,y1)
reducing(x1, newlist(y1)) -> y2

Input: A set of key/value pairs
Mapper (Keyword Count)
1.   foreach cluster Ci (i=1 : N)
2.   map(Key X, Value Y):
3.   for each word w in value:
4.   display(w, 1)
5.   end
6.   end
7.   **Reduce (key=keyword, value= count):**
8.   Reducer (Keyword Count)
9.   reduce(key, values):
10. result = 0
Output
11. for count y in values:
12. result += y
13. display (key, result)
14. end

In this work performed the sorting value in counting y from different cluster which results produced and display the highest count keyword found from file. Then identify the thrust area for highest count keyword found and display the thrust area found for that particular keyword searched.

This paper shows the results of implementation according to querying keywords and also time taken by each input sources. Results show that when entered the keyword for searching Thrust Area number of cluster made by that keyword and show all keywords by counting in output. Then match the high counted keyword from the database and specify the Thrust area. Also Show the Frequency of keyword in each discipline area. For example if entered the keyword "cryptography" then it will show the thrust area for this keyword is "Networks and Security".

5   Experimental Results

The experimental results identify the Thrust Area for any searched keyword in Computer Science Field and also show the frequency of that keyword in all disciplines. Based on high counting of particular keyword specify the Thrust Area from Database. Results included these factors:

1. Time taken for such data source and cumulative time to process all input data sources.

2. Cluster formulations n + m.
   where n = No of Data sources and m = no of sub data sources.
3. Thrust Area Identification.

This table shows the time consumption in seconds on various trials from input resources taken by us (Table 1).

Table 1. Time consumption in seconds on various trials (input resources taken 7)

Trial No.	Time taken (sec)
First	28.9
Second	34.1
Third	17.9
Fourth	24.5
Fifth	30.1

Calculations for each input unit show the graph of time calculations per unit or dataset of input files (Fig. 3).

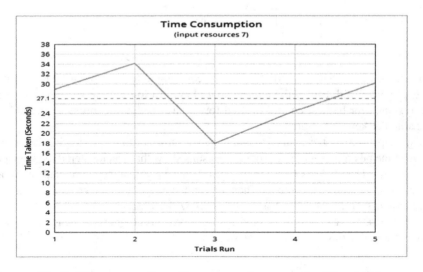

Fig. 3. Time consumption with same no. of resources for different trials

After calculating the time consumption by trials then calculate the time taken by each input resources and also describe clusters for each input resources (Table 2).

This graphs shows the work of cluster formulations for each discipline area and calculating the time taken by each input source (Fig. 4).

This graph shows results on the basis of searched keyword and shows the frequency of that keyword according to all disciplines and specifies the Thrust Area for

Table 2. Clusters formation and time consumption for increasing input resources

S.No.	Input resources (Disciplines)	Clusters	Time taken (sec)
1.	AI	5	0.06
2.	DATABASE	23	0.72
3.	SE	30	2.53
4.	HCI	47	4.57
5.	DIP	65	7.69
6.	Information system	80	12.65
7.	NETWORKS	99	17.42

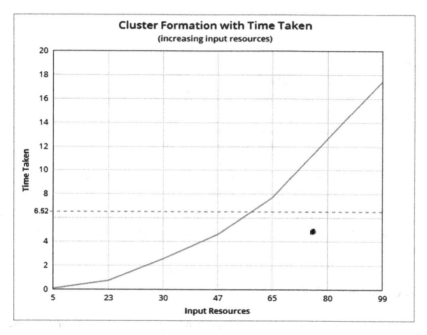

Fig. 4. Cluster formulation with increasing input resources time consumption

that keyword. In this take various disciplines files as input 1, input 2.........input n. For Example if entered the keyword "cryptography" then it will show the thrust area for this keyword is "Networks and Security" (Fig. 5).

This work defines knowledge about particular searched keyword and shows the relationship of that keyword to the particular area according to keyword frequency.

For building this interface used MapReduce algorithm with some modification and after apply counting approach from this algorithm. After performed counting on keywords then match the keyword from our database and specify the Thrust Area in computer science disciplines based on keyword identification. This work fulfills the goal of keyword based identification of thrust area. There are various techniques available in keyword based searching from database and we used the MapReduce

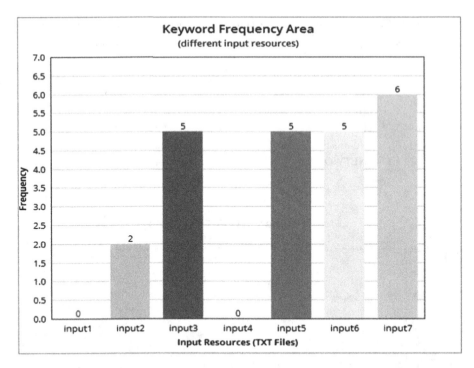

Fig. 5. Keyword frequency measurement in different areas

algorithm which used in Google ranking and also used in Hadoop for big data. This technique is used for ranking, sorting and counting word frequencies for textual databases.

6 Conclusions and Future Work

In this paper build an interface for keyword searching and counting their frequencies according to input datasets and make clusters based on particular keyword and if keyword found in database then specify the thrust area for that particular keyword and check the frequency of keywords in respective areas. Results show that when entered the keyword for searching Thrust Area number of cluster made by that keyword and show all keywords by counting in output. Then match the high counted keyword from the database and specify the Thrust area. This is an architecture based research to enhance and carried out the earlier solution in an efficient way. Although for this research there is no technical invention but there is a contribution of a new architecture implementation. In which clubbed MapReduce with knowledge discovery.

In future work we can improve the efficiency of this work and add more keywords in database of different areas such as Medical, Chemical, and Electronics etc. Also add an interface for submitting a research paper from author and store the keywords automatically in database. Then we can get more efficient and effective results.

References

1. Cios, K.J., Pedrycz, W., Swiniarski, R.W., Kurgan, L.: Data Mining: A Knowledge Discovery Approach. Springer, Heidelberg (2007)
2. Ramagari, B.M.: Data mining techniques and application. Indian J. Comput. Sci. Eng. (2011)
3. Feldman, R., Dagan, I.: Knowledge discovery in textual databases (KDT). In: Proceedings of KDD, vol. 95 (1995)
4. Mcgarry, K.: A survey of interestingness measures for knowledge discovery. Knowl. Eng. Rev. (2005). Cambridge University Press
5. Shvaiko, P., Euzenat, J.: A survey of schema-based matching approaches. In: Spaccapietra, S. (ed.) Journal on Data Semantics IV. LNCS, vol. 3730, pp. 146–171. Springer, Heidelberg (2005). doi:10.1007/11603412_5
6. Agrawal, S., Chaudhari, S., Das, G.: DBXplorer: a system for keyword-based search over relational databases. In: ICDE IEEE (2002)
7. Balmin, A., Hristidis, V., Papakonstantinou, Y.: ObjectRank: authority-based keyword search in databases. In: VLDB (2004)
8. Bhalotia, G., Hulgeri, A., Nakhe, C., Chakrabarti, S., Sudarshan, S.: Keyword searching and browsing in databases using BANKS. In: ICDE (2002)
9. Yu, B., Li, G., Sollins, K.: Effective keyword based selection of relational database. In: SIGMOD (2007)
10. Kalesha, P., Rao, M., Kavitha, C.: Efficient preprocessing and patterns identification approach for text mining. Int. J. Comput. Trends Technol. (2011)
11. Sarda, N.L., Jain, A.: A system of keyword based and searching in databases. Arxiv.org (2001)
12. Beil, F., Ester, M., Xu, X.: Frequent term-based text clustering. In: SIGKDD (2002)
13. Dean, J., Ghemawat, S.: MapReduce: Simplified Data Processing on Large Clusters. Google Inc. (2004)
14. Maclean, D.: A very brief introduction to MapReduce, for CS448G (2011)
15. Hulgeri, A., Bhalotia, G., Nakhrey, C., Chakrabarti, S.: Keyword search in databases. In: Bulletin of the IEEE Computer Society Technical Committee on Data Engineering (2001)
16. Agarwal, S., Chaudhari, S., Das, G.: DBExplorer: a system for keyword-based search over relational databases. In: Proceedings of the 18th International Conference with Hashing and Other Known Compression Techniques (2002)
17. Hristidis, V., Papakonstantinou, Y.: DISCOVER: keyword search in relational databases. In: Proceedings of the 28th VLDB Conference (2002)
18. Agichtein, E., Gravano, L.: Querying text databases for efficient information extraction. In: Proceedings of the IEEE ICDE (2003)
19. Su, Q., Widom, J.: Indexing relational database content offline for efficient keyword based search. In: International Database Engineering & Application Symposium (2005)
20. Chaudhari, S., Das, G.: Keyword querying and ranking in databases. In: Proceedings of the VLDB Endowment (2009)
21. Qin, Z., Li, P.: SWEE: approximately searching web service with keywords effectively and efficiently. © IEEE (2010)
22. Li, L., Petschulat, S.: Efficient and effective aggregate keyword search on rational databases. Int. J. Data Warehous. Min. (2012)
23. Uthayan, K.R., Anandha, V.: Hybrid ontology for semantic information retrieval model using keyword matching indexing system. Res. Artic.@ Sci. World J. (2015)

24. Sun, T., Shu, C.: An efficient hierarchical clustering method for large datasets with Map-Reduce. In: International Conference on Parallel and Distributed Computing, Application and Technologies (2009)

25. Rao, P.S., Prasad, M.H.M.K., Reddy, K.T.: An efficient semantic ranked keyword search of big data using Map Reduce. Int. J. Database Theory Appl. (2015)

26. Hao, Y., Cao, H.: Efficient keyword search on graphs using MapReduce. In: IEEE International Conference on Big Data (2015)

27. Swaraj, K.P., Manjula, D.: A fast approach to identify articles in hot topics from XML based big bibliographic datasets. Cluster Comput. **19**, 837–848 (2016). doi:10.1007/s10586-016-0561-1

An Efficient Genetic Algorithm for Fuzzy Community Detection in Social Network

Harish Kumar Shakya[✉], Kuldeep Singh, and Bhaskar Biswas

Department of Computer Science and Engineering,
Indian Institute of Technology (BHU), Varanasi, India
{hkshakya.rs.cse,kuldeep.rs.cse13,
bhaskar.cse}@iitbhu.ac.in

Abstract. A new fuzzy genetic algorithm proposed for community identification in social networks. In this paper, we have used matrix encoding that enables traditional crossover between individuals and mutation takes place in some of the individuals. Matrix encoding determines which node belongs to which community. Using these concepts enhance the overall performance of any evolutionary algorithms. In this experiment, we used the genetic algorithm with the fuzzy concept and compared to other existing methods like as crisp genetic algorithm and vertex similarity based genetic algorithm. We employed the three real world dataset strike, Karate Club, Dolphin in this work. The usefulness and efficiency of proposed algorithm are verified through the accuracy and quality metrics and provide a rank of proposed algorithm using multiple criteria decision-making method.

Keywords: Community detection · Fuzzy modularity · Genetic algorithm · Metrics · Social network

1 Introduction

Social Network has become an important part of the daily lives of almost everybody. So studying the evolution of communities in such social network has become necessary for the study of the studies of urban development, criminology, social marketing, and several other areas. One of the main Application of Social Network is in marketing. With a large percentage of population over Social network sites, targeting ads at specific population has become an important part. Now to do so, we need to identify specific communities to whom we would like to target particular ads, and so community detection in these social network sites has become a subject of research. Billions of people online, so billions of nodes Accuracy has become an important issue.

We have targeted social networks because of their huge popularity and over billions of people on these sites. They can be connected via several things. These things can be specific interests in various fields such as sports, music, fashion, gadgets, etc. this interest helps us form communities to which we can target the specific products. In this Proposed work, we can make a particular individual belong to more than one community, so nothing in this will be binary but a percentage, which determines how much

© Springer Nature Singapore Pte Ltd. 2017
D. Singh et al. (Eds.): ICAICR 2017, CCIS 712, pp. 63–72, 2017.
DOI: 10.1007/978-981-10-5780-9_6

of the person's time or interest is in that particular community. Community Structure possesses different meanings when it comes to Application fields.

If we take an example of WebPages, then a community structure can be a group of WebPages having similar themes such as WebPages about movies. Here our main focus is social networks. So a community frame in a social network can be identified by similar characteristics that different nodes possess. Social networks possess complex structure.

Community formations are quite common in real (complex) networks. Social networks include community groups based on shared location, interests, occupation, etc. Community structure in a network usually is a display of some important hidden prototype and thus can make deeper our understandings of some phenomenon and also enable useful applications.

The main feature of graph representation in a real world is clustering. In this technique, we can analyze the set of vertexes in the same group and the other one. It is also called the community detection. If the various nodes lie in the different community, it means he contains a variety of property. Clusters are formed by applying a particular algorithm. Obviously, every Algorithm forms different clusters.

The results of such Algorithm can be compared by fitness function called Modularity as we will see further in the report. Before that, we will discuss the Algorithm used by us for detecting community structures.

We use an evolutionary technique for detecting communities. After my long review [4–6, 9, 10] about the traditional algorithm and evolutionary algorithms, we will find much expectation for the genetic algorithm in further experiments. One of most precious and the widely used algorithm is the Genetic algorithm. This algorithm based on Darwin's theory of evolution, Just as the chromosomes of different individuals are diverse and evolve with each generation with the theory of survival of the strongest. Here the individuals are operated upon using specific techniques, and then a solution set is created, in which the best of them is taken and again operated. An iteration of this takes place until we have a good enough solution set.

Till now much of the focus has been on the disjoint detection of communities. That is Individual communities having no relation with each other were being detected. The assumption made is that a network has dense connections around certain nodes and more connections there rather than any other nodes in the network. However, in real life, this is not the case. A person who has a family group can belong to other groups as well. These groups can be friends, workgroup, sports group, etc.

So basically real life network is not a simple collection of individual communities connected to each other, but a social network has nodes that belong to different communities. So an overlap is an important property that needs to be incorporate in our network detection. Hence in this paper, we talk about overlapping community detection algorithms that detect a set of groups that are not necessarily disjoint. There could be vertexes that belong to more than one community.

2   Valuation Functions

2.1   Modularity

Objective Function Modularity [2, 3] is employed to calculate however separated the various vertex sorts from one another, and it will be calculated as follows.

$$Q = \frac{1}{2m} \sum_{i,j} A_{ij} - \frac{k_i k_j}{2m} \qquad (1)$$

Here, Q represents quality function modularity, m represents some edges, A_{ij} represents an entry of contiguousness matrix, k_i, k_j represents the degrees of vertex i, j severally, c_i, c_j represents the part of vertex i, j and (x, y) = 1 if x = y, zero otherwise.

2.2   Normalized Mutual Information

It has extensively utilized measures to analysis the network community detection algorithms [1]. It equals to one if the detected communities and their ground truth square measure identical whereas the worth is zero if the communities' square measure strictly distinct with the ground truth. It will be defined as

$$I_{nom}\left(X, \breve{Y}\right) = \frac{2I(X,Y)}{H(X) + H(Y)} \qquad (2)$$

$$H(X) = -\sum_x P(x) \log P(x) \qquad (3)$$

$$H(X|Y) = -\sum_{x,y} P(x,y) \log P(x|y) \qquad (4)$$

2.3   Omega-Index

It is employed to calculate overlapped communities and utilized to estimate the quantity of clusters during which the vertex involve [14].

$$\frac{1}{|v|^2} \sum_{u,v \ V} \{|C_d| = |C_g|\} \qquad (5)$$

Where C_d, C_g, represent the set of ground truth communities, identified communities correspondingly, that the pair of vertices u and v shares.

2.4   Simple Modularity and Fuzzy Modularity

Two concepts of modularity are different in the aspect that in simple GA, the vertex either belongs to a particular community or not. However, in Fuzzy GA we a node can belong to a certain community as a percentage. Simple GA cannot be applied to Fuzzy Algorithm as it simple GA treats the relation between nodes and community as binary and not as a fraction. Hence we devised a different qualitative measure for fuzzy [7, 8].

2.4.1   Zhang Fuzzy Modularity

In this objective function [16] the community detection procedure in begins by partitioning V with spectral bunch applied to G using FCM, once the eigenvector illustration of G is chosen. When a fuzzy c-partition $U \in Mf\ c_n$ is found this manner, the partition is reborn to a possibilistic c-partition $U\lambda \in Mf\ c_n$ of V as follows:

A threshold λ is chosen (presumably $0 < \lambda < 1$), so accustomed extract from the kth row of $U \in MF\ c_n$ the vertex set $V_k = \{i|u_k\ i > \lambda, 1 \leq i \leq n\}$. for every vertex i in V_k, the corresponding entry of $(U\lambda)$ k (the kth row of $U\lambda$) is set to one. when a omit all k rows of U is completed, the remaining $(non - 1)$ entries in $U\lambda$ are set to zero.

2.4.2   Liu Fuzzy Modularity

In this [17] objective function initiates with a partition and then categorizes the nodes in pursuance of the most membership regulation (which is commonly called calcifying the partition).

$$Q_l = \frac{1}{\|W\|} \sum_{k=1}^{c} \sum_{i,j \in V_k} \left[\left(\frac{u_{ki} + u_{ki}}{2} \right) w_{ij} - p_e(i,j) \right] \tag{6}$$

$$d_f(i) = \sum_{j \in V_k} \left(\frac{u_{ki} + u_{kj}}{2} \right) w_{ij}$$
$$+ \sum_{r \notin V_k} \left(\frac{u_{ki} + (1 - u_{kr})}{2} \right) w_{ir} \tag{7}$$

3   Experimental Work

In Proposed work, we have used the individual encoding of the chromosomes of the Genetic Algorithm. Chromosomes are encoded into binary matrix [1].

$$M = \begin{pmatrix} m_{11} & m_{12} & \cdots & m_{1t} \\ m_{21} & m_{22} & \cdots & m_2 \\ \vdots & \vdots & \ddots & \vdots \\ m_{n1} & m_2 & \cdots & m_{nt} \end{pmatrix} \tag{8}$$

The Binary Matrix where M is an $n \times t$ matrix, $t\ (1 < t < n)$ is the number of communities after partitioning G. n is the number of nodes. Each m_i, j indicates how much of the node belongs to a particular community. Without Overlapping these values are binary. However, when overlapping Communities are taken into account, then these values are between 1 and 0. Now this will follow two rules.

$$\sum_{j-1}^{t} m_{ij} = 1$$

$$\sum_{i-1}^{n} m_{ij} > 0 \tag{9}$$

Population initialization takes place in which we have used node similarity matrix. It was done because similar nodes that have a high probability of being in the same node are initialized in one community. Then Crossover and Mutation operation are done.

In crossover operation, crossover the 80% of the top solution from the total solution. Modulation operator is applied to the least 20% of the solution. Then with initial population and the resultant population, the best half is chosen. The Quality of the chromosomes is measured through a suitable operator Now to measure the quality of the solution we have used the Modularity operator as it gave better and more consistent result than it's alternative. Then many iterations of the above are run until the modularity does not increase.

4   Experimental Analysis

In this experiment, we employed three different datasets to analyze accuracy and quality of proposed algorithm. We compared proposed algorithm to various version of genetic algorithms. One is simple genetic algorithm [15], and another is a genetic algorithm with node similarity [1]. The results are given below (Table 1).

Table 1. Value description of parameters

Parameter	Value	Description
Pn	100	Number of individuals
Pc	0.8	Crossover individuals
Pm	0.2	Mutation individuals
Nmax	100	Number of iterations
alpha	1/(2*no of communities)	Threshold values

4.1   Strike Dataset [11]

In a wood-processing facility, workers started strike; the communication structure among the employees in the form of a graph is given below. In Fig. 1, represent the graphical view of strike dataset in a single color but after applied the SGA we have to find the communities denoted the different colors. Similarly applied the VGA resultant is available in (III) graph. In last graph (IV), we have defined the three colors, but the red color defines the fuzzy communities and overlapping communities. This process is followed to the other datasets also in given below Figs. 2 and 3.

(i)   (ii)   (iii)   (iv)

Fig. 1. Community-based graphical representation for Strike dataset

(i)   (ii)   (iii)   (iv)

Fig. 2. Community-based graphical representation for Karate club dataset

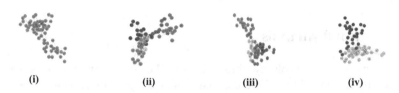

(i)   (ii)   (iii)   (iv)

Fig. 3. Community-based graphical representation for Dolphin dataset

4.2   Karate Club Dataset [12]

Zachary's Karate Club [12] is a renowned social network of a university karate club explained in "An Information Flow Model for Collision and Fission in small set" paper by Zachary.

4.3   Dolphin Dataset [13]

The description of the data set is as follows - A directionless social network of frequent relations among 62 dolphins in a society living off Doubtful Sound, New Zealand, as compiled by Lusseau et al. [13].

In this experiment, we have found the results in different format means graphical and tabular for used datasets. In Table 2, represent the whole result with accuracy and quality functions for all datasets. We have used NMI, entropy, and omega as accuracy parameters while using modularity, conductance, and coverage as quality parameters.

First of all, we talk about the Dolphin dataset; FGA has got the higher values for NMI = 0.7864, Omega = 0.9264, and Coverage = 0.94968. Similarly, Entropy = 0.2135 and Conductance = 0.36653 have got the lower value compare to the other algorithm. Entropy and conductance have contained the inverse property mean lower

Table 2. Accuracy and quality metric values for various datasets

Datasets	Algorithms	NMI	Entropy	Modularity	Omega	Conductance	Coverage
Dolphin	SGA	0.470468	0.529532	0.5122226	0.707033	0.935054	0.7924528
	VGA	0.370501	0.629499	0.4816265	0.636171	1.741664	0.7169811
	FGA	0.786448	0.213552	0.1462689	0.926494	0.3665375	0.9496855
Karate club	SGA	0.56209	0.437911	0.4003123	0.84492	1.416041	0.7692308
	VGA	0.491055	0.508945	0.4151052	0.802139	1.15	0.7564103
	FGA	0.661445	0.338555	0.2948628	0.855615	0.301607	0.9871795
Strike	SGA	0.68407	0.315933	0.5557479	0.85507	0.5996503	0.86842
	VGA	0.78437	0.21563	0.5619806	0.91304	0.59033639	0.8684f2
	FGA	0.59047	0.40953	0.3771963	0.82971	0.1311688	0.97368

value get the good community structure and vice versa. So it means Fuzzy based Genetic Algorithm good performance for this dataset.

In karate club dataset, similarly FGA have got the higher values NMI = 0.66144, Omega = 0.85561 and Coverage = 0.987179 compare to SGA and VGA algorithm. FGA have also had good performance for this dataset because it has contained the lower Entropy = 0.33855 and Conductance = 0.301607. Modularity only has gained the lower value 0.29486 compare to other available algorithms.

In Strike dataset, VGA has got the higher NMI = 0.78437, Omega = 0.91304, Modularity = 0.56198 and Entropy = 0.21563 have contained the lower value. Only Conductance = 0.1311 and Coverage = 0.97368 have supported the FGA algorithm.

Finally, we analyzed that FGA have performed good for large datasets but average performance for the small datasets. It means fuzzify genetic algorithm find the overlapping communities and maintain the accuracy and quality also. Another fact is that VGA is good for the small datasets. FGA have good performance for the whole datasets (Strike, Karate, and Dolphin) but main focus on the accuracy of the proposed algorithm. In Table 3, we will show the final results with proposed algorithm compare to other algorithms called MCDM rank table. It contains the MCDM (Multiple criteria decision making) ranks [14]. In this rank system, we will summarize the both quality

Table 3. MCDM ranking score obtained for different datasets

Datasets	Algorithms	MCDM Rank
Dolphin	SGA	0.398
	VGA	0.165
	FGA	**0.945**
Karate club	SGA	0.255
	VGA	0.246
	FGA	**0.821**
Strike	SGA	0.444
	VGA	**0.656**
	FGA	0.425

and accuracy metrics as a single score value. Figures 4, 5, 6 represents the MCDM graphs for individual datasets for all the algorithms. According to the graphs, we will easily show that which algorithm is better to score comparing to other. FGA have got the highest MCDM score For Dolphin and Karate club datasets. It means we have

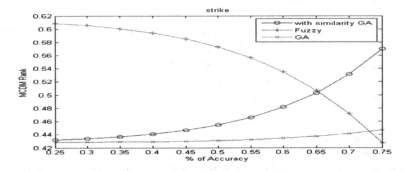

Fig. 4. MCDM ranking graphs for Strike datasets with variation of accuracy and quality.

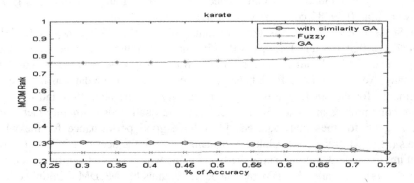

Fig. 5. MCDM ranking graphs for Karate club datasets with variation of accuracy and quality.

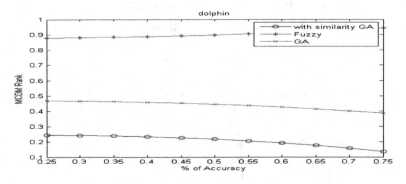

Fig. 6. MCDM ranking graphs for Dolphin datasets with variation of accuracy and quality.

proved that proposed FGA have better performed compare to existing Genetic algorithms. The new fuzzy algorithm (FGA) is also hopeful for further work with new ideas.

5 Conclusion and Future Work

In this experiment genetic algorithm for community detection in social networks, matrix encoding empowers traditional individual crossover and no additional requirement of decoding. Initial individuals generated by measuring distance are diverse yet retain an acceptable level of accuracy. As evident from MCDM graphs, the fuzzy based algorithm gives a better result than other crisp community algorithms. In, the future complexity of the algorithm could also be minimized by using a better quality function. Accuracy could also be increased. In further we will use the fuzzy concept with new version of Genetic algorithm means vertex similarity based genetic algorithm and other evolutionary algorithm like as differential evolution and co-operative co-evolutionary differential evolution algorithm.

References

1. Li, Y., Liu, G., Lao, S.Y.: A genetic algorithm for community detection in complex networks. Journal of Central South University **20**(5), 1269–1276 (2013). doi:10.1007/s11771-013-1611-y
2. Newman, M.E., Girvan, M.: Finding and evaluating community structure in networks. Phys. Rev. E **69**(2), 026113 (2004). doi:10.1103/PhysRevE.69.026113
3. Newman, M.E.: Fast algorithm for detecting community structure in networks. Phys. Rev. E **69**(6), 066133 (2004). doi:10.1103/PhysRevE.69.066133
4. Chikhi, N.F., Rothenburger, B., Aussenac-Gilles, N.: Community structure identification: a probabilistic approach. In: 2009 International Conference on Machine Learning and Applications, ICMLA 2009, pp. 125–130. IEEE, December 2009. doi:10.1109/ICMLA.2009.66
5. Chang, C.S., Hsu, C.Y., Cheng, J., Lee, D.S.: A general probabilistic framework for detecting community structure in networks. In: 2011 Proceedings IEEE INFOCOM, pp. 730–738. IEEE, April 2011. doi:10.1109/INFCOM.2011.5935256
6. Hartigan, J.A., Wong, M.A.: Algorithm AS 136: A k-means clustering algorithm. J. R. Stat. Soc. Series C (Appl. Stat.) **28**(1), 100–108 (1979). 10.2307/2346830
7. Bezdek, J.C., Ehrlich, R., Full, W.: FCM: the fuzzy c-means clustering algorithm. Comput. Geosci. **10**(2–3), 191–203 (1984). doi:10.1016/0098-3004(84)90020-7
8. Lancichinetti, A., Fortunato, S., Kertész, J.: Detecting the overlapping and hierarchical community structure in complex networks. New J. Phys. **11**(3), 033015 (2009). doi:10.1088/1367-2630/11/3/033015
9. Riedy, J., Bader, D.A., Jiang, K., Pande, P., Sharma, R.: Detecting communities from given seeds in social networks. Georgia Institute of Technology (2011)

10. Hafez, A.I., ella Hassanien, A., Fahmy, A.A., Tolba, M.F.: Community detection in social networks by using Bayesian network and expectation maximization technique. In: 2013 13th International Conference on Hybrid Intelligent Systems (HIS), pp. 209–214. IEEE, December 2013. doi:10.1109/HIS.2013.6920484
11. Michael, J.H.: Labor dispute reconciliation in a forest products manufacturing facility. For. Prod. J. **47**, 41–45 (1997)
12. Zachary, W.: An information flow model for conflict and fission in small groups. J. Anthropol. Res. **33**, 452–473 (1977)
13. Lusseau, D., Schneider, K., Boisseau, O.J., Haase, P., Slooten, E., Dawson, S.M.: The bottlenose dolphin community of doubtful sound features a large proportion of long-lasting associations. Behav. Ecol. Sociobiol. **54**(4), 396–405 (2003). doi:10.1007/s00265-003-0651-y
14. Kou, G., Peng, Y., Wang, G.: Evaluation of clustering algorithms for financial risk analysis using MCDM methods. Inf. Sci. **275**, 1–12 (2014). http://dx.doi.org/10.1016/j.ins.2014.02.137
15. Tasgin, M., Herdagdelen, A., Bingol, H.: Community detection in complex networks using genetic algorithms. arXiv preprint arXiv:0711.0491 (2007)
16. Zhang, S., Wang, R.S., Zhang, X.S.: Identification of overlapping community structure in complex networks using fuzzy c-means clustering. Phys. A **374**(1), 483–490 (2007). doi:10.1016/j.physa.2006.07.023
17. Liu, J.: Fuzzy modularity and fuzzy community structure in networks. Eur. Phys. J. B-Condens. Matter Complex Syst. **77**(4), 547–557 (2010). https://doi.org/10.1140/epjb/e2010-00290-3

Predicting the Outcome of Spanish General Elections 2016 Using Twitter as a Tool

Prabhsimran Singh[1,3(✉)], Ravinder Singh Sawhney[2,3],
and Karanjeet Singh Kahlon[1,3]

[1] Department of Computer Science, Guru Nanak Dev University,
Amritsar, India
prabh_singh32@yahoo.com, karanvkahlon@yahoo.com
[2] Department of Electronics Technology, Guru Nanak Dev University,
Amritsar, India
sawhney.ece@gndu.ac.in
[3] Guru Nanak Dev University, Amritsar, India

Abstract. In recent years, twitter has become a popular micro blogging tool among the people world over. These persons post small messages depicting their likes and dislike towards a certain entity e.g. election results. These messages can be used to predict their opinion towards a political party in general or an individual candidate in particular. This paper takes into consideration numerous tweets related data towards the context of 2016 Spanish General Elections. Next, we have tried to establish a relationship between the tweets gathered during the campaigning period and actual vote share that various political parties received in 2016 Spanish General Elections. We have developed a tool in ASP.Net and collected 90154 tweets from 6th June to 26th June 2016 and computed our results based on these tweets. Finally, we compared our computations to establish a close co-relation with the actual results. The factors those may have caused small variance, are minutely investigated upon to give us better insight so as elucidate even closer predictions for future events.

Keywords: Twitter · Tweet · Opinion mining · Sentiment analysis · Election prediction

1 Introduction

Twitter was launched in 2006 and since then it is gaining popularity among the youth elite and educated class all around the world, to express their anguish as well as pleasure related to social, political as well as economic events. According to recent figures, approximately 58 million tweets are being tweeted every day or 2.5 million tweets in an hour [1]. This large amount of data has provided newer visions and ideas about research in this area for the researchers. This data also includes tweets that may relate to a political party in general or a candidate in particular. During election times these tweets if processed properly can be used to predict the winner of the upcoming election using sentiment analysis. Sentiment analysis is a hybrid field consists of

© Springer Nature Singapore Pte Ltd. 2017
D. Singh et al. (Eds.): ICAICR 2017, CCIS 712, pp. 73–83, 2017.
DOI: 10.1007/978-981-10-5780-9_7

human psychology and computer science that deals with the analysis of one's opinion or sentiment towards an entity [2].

Our aim in this paper is to share the captured information from tweets after processing it using our mathematical & computational approach and predict the winner of the 2016 Spanish General Elections. We have tried an earnest effort to establish a relationship between the number of positive tweets that a party is receiving to actual vote share that a party got in the election. In our research, we have considered the top four parties contesting the 2016 Spanish General Elections. This was the second time in last 6 months that Spain was having the public opinion as the last elections held on 20th December 2015 produced a hung house i.e. not a single party got the absolute majority [3].

The main reasons for choosing Spanish General Elections for our research topic is that Spain is a developed country [4], secondly literacy rate of the country is 98% [5], thirdly 84% population has access to the internet in one form or the other [6]. So this gives a strong foundation to our research that the data being collected consist of like and dislikes of the major section of the society belonging to the entire population of the country.

2   Related Work

Using Twitter for election prediction along with sentiment analysis is a relatively newer yet growing field. In this section we focus on the previous work in which the researchers have used number of tweets for the election prediction.

Tumasjan et al. [7], applied their research on German Federal Elections. They used a very simple technique i.e. counting the number of tweets that contains the name of the party or its leaders. They collected 104,300 tweets involving 6 German political parties over a period of 27 days. Despite being a simple technique, it was able to predict correct results.

Choy et al. [8], carried their research work to predict the winner of 2011 Singapore Presidential Elections. In addition to counting the number of positive tweets they also classified tweets in different age groups. Since the time period of tweet collection was only 8 days, the predicted results were incorrect.

Nooralahzadeh et al. [9], did their research in order to predict the winner of 2012 Presidential elections held in two developed countries i.e. France and USA. Their work had an addition feature of a scoring function which along with number of positive tweets gave accurate predictions for both the countries.

Prasetyo and Hauff [10], emphasized on the use Twitter for election prediction in developed countries stating that it is more accurate and precise technique. They carried their work to predict the outcome of 2014 Indonesia's Presidential Elections and further compared the results with 20 offline poll predictions where Twitter outperformed all these predictions.

Khatua et al. [11], correctly predicted the outcome of 2014 Indian General Elections. They mainly focused on two main alliances NDA lead by BJP and the UPA lead by Congress. They calculated the vote share based on the tweets that each party or each candidate was receiving. Further, they said only tweets mentioning one name should be considered as tweets having 2 or more names create a lot of problems.

Burnap et al. [12], used a baseline model for prediction of 2015 UK general elections. They stressed that previous works were not true predictions as they were performed after the actual results were announced. They predicted the results based on tweet analysis before the actual results were announced. However the results predicted by them were incorrect, but the concept of true prediction made their work stand out from others.

Srivastava et al. [13], gave a mapping function that was able to convert tweet share into seat share. They collected positive tweets for three main parties AAP, BJP and Congress contesting 2015 Delhi Assembly Elections. The positive tweets showed that AAP will be the victorious party as it got more than 54% tweet share. Further using their proposed function they accurately predicted the seat share of each party.

3 Proposed Methodology

The proposed technique initiates with the collection of tweets from the Twitter. Tweet collection is based on the hashtags (#) of the party and its Presidential candidate. Once tweets are collected, the process of data cleaning is done in which unwanted web links, hashtags (#) are removed. After cleaning the data, the process of sentiment analysis is performed on each tweet in order to extract the sentiment from the tweet and finally based on this sentiment analysis positive tweet score is calculated for each party. The graphical flow of the process is explained in Fig. 1.

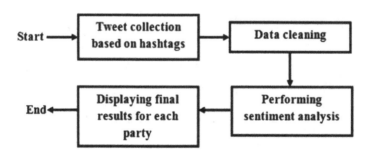

Fig. 1. Flowchart of proposed methodology

4 Implementation and Results

For carrying out our research work we build a computational tool in ASP.Net using visual studio 2012 express edition [14]. In addition to this, we used Tweetinvi API [15] for tweet collection. The tweets were collected based on the hashtags (#) of the political party and Presidential candidate. Table 1 show details of hashtags (#) used for tweet collection. Figure 2 shows the screenshot of the tool while performing the tweet collection operation.

Table 1. Hashtags used

Party name	Hashtags (#) used	
	Party	Presidential candidate
People party	#pp	#rajoy
PSOE	#psoe	#pedrosanchez
Unidos podemos	#unidospodemos	#igleasias
Citizen party	#csteam	#albertrivera

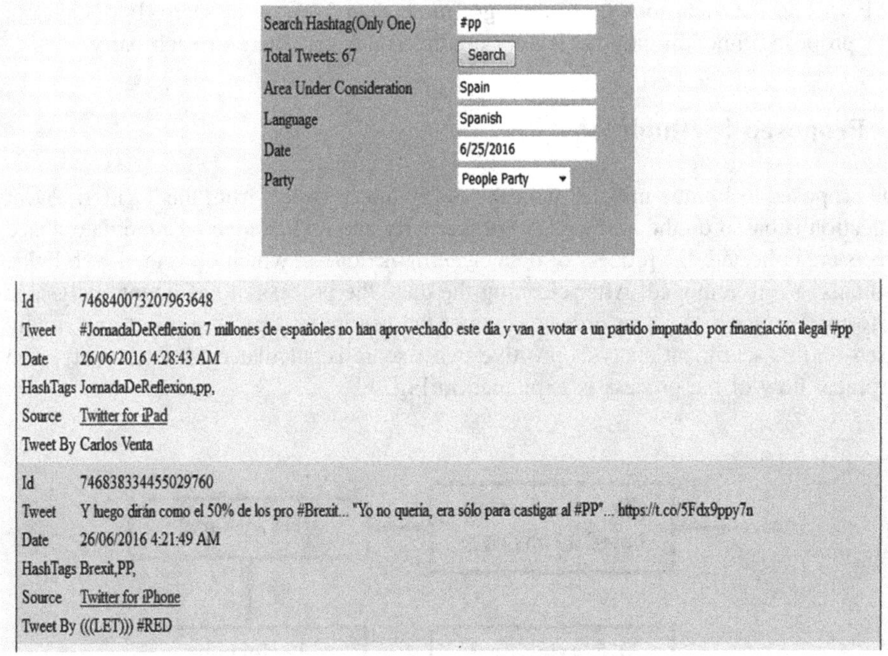

Search Hashtag(Only One)	#pp
Total Tweets: 67	Search
Area Under Consideration	Spain
Language	Spanish
Date	6/25/2016
Party	People Party

Id	746840073207963648
Tweet	#JornadaDeReflexion 7 millones de españoles no han aprovechado este día y van a votar a un partido imputado por financiación ilegal #pp
Date	26/06/2016 4:28:43 AM
HashTags	JornadaDeReflexion,pp,
Source	Twitter for iPad
Tweet By	Carlos Venta

Id	746838334455029760
Tweet	Y luego dirán como el 50% de los pro #Brexit... "Yo no quería, era sólo para castigar al #PP"... https://t.co/5Fdx9ppy7n
Date	26/06/2016 4:21:49 AM
HashTags	Brexit,PP,
Source	Twitter for iPhone
Tweet By	(((LET))) #RED

Fig. 2. Screenshot of the computational tool

The main aim of our research was to find the relationship between the tweet share and the actual vote share the party is receiving in 2016 Spanish General Elections. For this we focused on top 4 parties i.e. People Party, PSOE, Unidos Podemos and Citizen Party. Now we will discuss each stage of the process.

(a) Tweet Collection: Using the developed tool we collected 90154 tweets from 6th June 2016 to 26th June 2016, which actually was the voting day. The daily breakup of tweets that each party got is shown in the Table 2, while pictorial representation of daily tweet collection is given by Fig. 3.

Table 2 clearly shows that people party and unidos podemos got major share of daily tweets, while citizen party received the least number of daily tweets. In total people party got 35988 (39.9%) tweets, PSOE got 20379 (22.6%) tweets, unidos podemos got

Table 2. Daily tweet collection for each party

	People party	PSOE	Unidos podemos	Citizen party
06-06-16	907	504	1201	148
07-06-16	1404	623	1060	59
08-06-16	1091	484	831	44
09-06-16	1052	576	1073	32
10-06-16	1314	1188	1544	68
11-06-16	1321	649	1276	26
12-06-16	1390	1119	1171	1670
13-06-16	904	653	914	440
14-06-16	3875	1918	2553	596
15-06-16	2302	770	1096	216
16-06-16	2283	825	1829	241
17-06-16	1686	895	1301	206
18-06-16	1506	715	1577	237
19-06-16	1857	540	1074	277
20-06-16	1132	725	2277	166
21-06-16	2283	1019	902	180
22-06-16	2248	876	1630	163
23-06-16	3037	836	1490	145
24-06-16	1714	1810	1705	186
25-06-16	1891	2899	1058	94
26-06-16	791	755	754	243
Total	*35988*	*20379*	*28316*	*5437*
Mean	*1799.40*	*1018.95*	*1415.80*	*271.85*
% age	*39.9*	*22.6*	*31.4*	*6.0*

28316 (31.4%) tweets and citizen party got 5437 (6.0%) tweets. Certain events like debate on 13th June, 2016 lead to high data collection on the proceeding day as people were posting their thoughts about the debate.

The tweets collected were either in English language or Spanish language. Spanish language was selected as it the national language of Spain. In fact out of the total 90154 tweets, 77595 tweets were in Spanish language that means 86% of total tweets were in Spanish language. Figure 4, shows graphical representation of tweet collected in different languages.

(b) Tweet Cleaning: In this phase unwanted web links and hashtags (#) are removed. Data cleaning is very important step before performing sentiment analysis because these unwanted web links and hashtags (#) can alter the results of sentiment analysis. The tweet cleaning operation is performed in automated fashion using the same tool used for tweet collection. Figure 5 shows screenshot of the tweet cleaning operation performed by the tool. Tweet cleaning is performed for both Spanish and English language, an example of this is shown in Table 3. The basic idea behind this phase is to remove that part of tweet that is not required for sentiment detection.

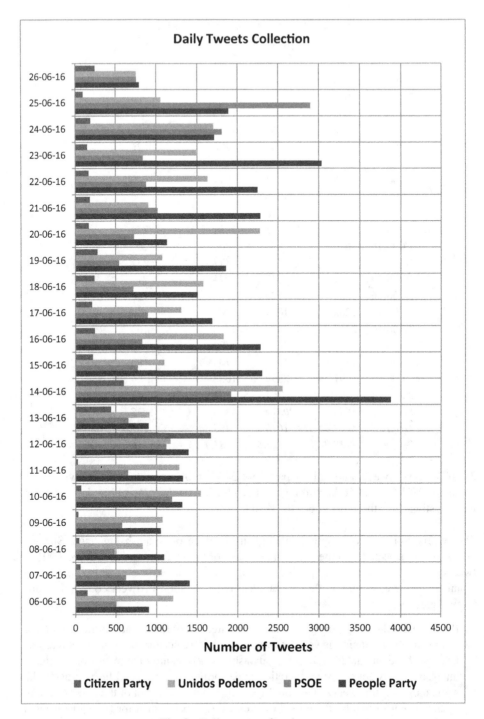

Fig. 3. Daily tweets of each party

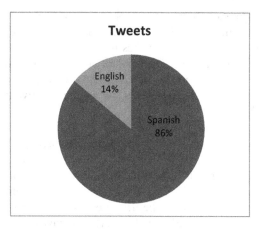

Fig. 4. Daily tweets of each party

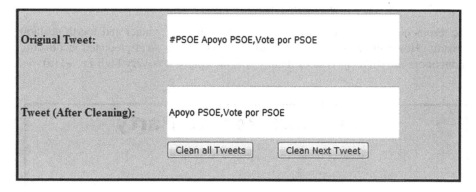

Fig. 5. Screenshot of tweet cleaning process

Table 3. Showing the tweet cleaning phase

Language	Original tweet	Tweet after data cleaning
English	I support PP #PP, #Rajoy, #Debate https://www.youtube.com/watch?v=FraiuCkzmu8	I support PP
Spanish	Apoyo PSOE, Vote por PSOE #PSOE	Apoyo PSOE, Vote por PSOE

(c) Checking Positive Sentiments: For this phase, we have created a database of words and phrases in English as well as in Spanish language, which shows positive sentiment in one form or the other. The reason for developing our own sentiment analysis technique was that most of the standard sentiment analysis techniques work only for English language. Though this was a time consuming task, yet every effort was made to add all the possible words and phrases in the database.

A total of four different data lists are created, one each for tweets of all Spanish parties under consideration. All the tweets from each data list are scanned one by one and if they contain any word or phrase that matches in the database, then the polarity of the tweet is set to positive otherwise null. Once polarity of all tweets in data list is checked, we compute the positive tweet count as per Eq. 1. An important point to be noted here is that we are only considering positive tweets and not the negative tweets. An example of this is shown in Fig. 6.

$$PositiveTweetCount = \sum (PositivetweetsinDataListA) \qquad (1)$$

(d) Final Results: The result of sentiment analysis showed that people party is likely to get maximum vote share, as they were getting maximum positive tweet count according to our technique. The detail results are shown in Table 4.

(e) Comparison to Actual Results: In this phase, we have compared our calculated results to the actual election results [16]. Further we calculated the Mean Absolute Error (MAE). Table 5 shows the comparison results, while Fig. 7 shows the graphical representation of the comparison.

The results clearly show that we were able to predict the winner and fourth position correctly. However results of second and third place party were predicted incorrectly. Furthermore the MAE in case of unidos podemos party was very high i.e. +11.03%.

Fig. 6. Example of sentiment analysis

Table 4. Final results

Party name	Positive tweets	Positive tweet%	Calculated position
People party	5655	33.77%	I
PSOE	4086	24.40%	III
Unidos podemos	5379	32.13%	II
Citizen party	1641	9.80%	IV

Table 5. Comparison of results [16]

Party name	Calculated results	Actual results	MAE	Calculated position	Actual position
People party	33.77%	33.03%	+0.74%	I	I
PSOE	24.40%	22.66%	+1.74%	III	II
Unidos podemos	32.13%	21.10%	+11.03%	II	III
Citizen party	9.80%	13.05%	−3.25%	IV	IV

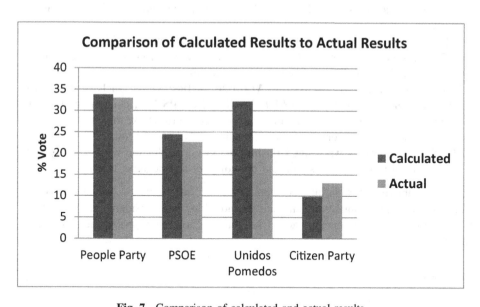

Fig. 7. Comparison of calculated and actual results

5   Conclusions and Future Work

This paper explored the newest field of performing sentiment analysis based on the tweets and then predicting the election outcome of the event using tweets. The aim of the paper was to find the relationship between the tweet share and actual vote share that a party receives during an election. We implemented our research taking the case study of 2016 Spanish General Elections held on 26th June, 2016. We collected 90154 tweets over the span of 20 days for the top 4 Spanish political parties. At end, we calculated the positive sentiment score of each party.

The results predicted by us were deserved to be in line with the actual accurate results. We were correctly able to detect the position of party finishing first and fourth i.e. people party and citizen party. However the technique used by us is still not perfect as it produced wrong prediction for the party finishing second and third. Moreover the mean absolute error in case of unidos podemos party was quite significant. We considered that the following factors could have been responsible for our predictions differing from the actual results.

(a) **Spanish Language:** Since 85% of the tweets collected were from Spanish language, it became extremely difficult for us to understand and apply operation to check these tweets for positive sentiments.

(b) **Re-Tweets were not removed:** In our technique we did not apply any mechanism to remove the re-tweets, so getting same tweet again and again for checking positive sentiment gave wrong results.

(c) **Phrase and words used for checking positive sentiments:** As explained earlier, Spanish being an alien language to us, we might have missed local phrases and words that are used by local people to show their positive sentiment towards a party.

(d) **Concept of Twitter Bomb was not Checked:** As explained by Gaurav et al. [17], the concept of Twitter bomb i.e. multiple tweets from same person should have been checked. This highly influenced our results.

(e) **Tweets Containing Mention of Multiple Parties:** Tweets such as **"PEOPLE PARTY IS WINNING, BEWARE PSOE. #PP #PSOE"**, contains multi party mention so it becomes extremely difficult to process a tweet like this as it is showing positive sentiment for one party while negative sentiment for other.

(f) **Negative Tweets were not Considered:** In our evaluation we have only concentrated on positive tweets, and did not consider any negative tweets.

All the above factors influenced the accuracy of our prediction in one way or the other. By moderating our computational tool and taking into consideration these factors for future work we can develop a technique that can accurately predict the outcome of any elections.

References

1. Statisticbrain Twitter Facts. http://www.statisticbrain.com/Twitter-statistics/
2. Liu, B.: Sentiment analysis and opinion mining. Synth. Lect. Hum. Lang. Technol. **5**(1), 1–167 (2012). doi:10.2200/S00416ED1V01Y201204HLT016
3. Spanish General Elections Results December (2015). http://www.infoelectoral.mir.es/min/busquedaAvanzadaAction.html
4. IMF Report. http://www.imf.org/external/pubs/ft/weo/2015/01/weodata/groups.htm
5. CIA literacy Rate Report. https://www.cia.gov/library/publications/resources/the-world-factbook/fields/2103.html

6. CIA Internet User Report. https://www.cia.gov/library/publications/resources/the-world-factbook/rankorder/2153rank.html

7. Tumasjan, A., Sprenger, T.O., Sandner, P.G., Welpe, I.M.: Predicting elections with twitter: what 140 characters reveal about political sentiment. In: ICWSM 10, pp. 178–185 (2010)

8. Choy, M., Cheong, M.L.F., Laik, M.N., Shung, K.P.: A sentiment analysis of Singapore Presidential Election 2011 using Twitter data with census correction. arXiv preprint arXiv: 1108.5520 (2011)

9. Nooralahzadeh, F., Arunachalam, V., Chiru, C.: 2012 presidential elections on Twitter–an analysis of how the US and French Election were reflected in tweets. In: 2013 19th International Conference on Control Systems and Computer Science (CSCS), pp. 240–246. IEEE (2013). doi:10.1109/CSCS.2013.72

10. Prasetyo, N.D., Hauff, C.: Twitter-based Election Prediction in the developing world. In: Proceedings of the 26th ACM Conference on Hypertext & Social Media, pp. 149–158. ACM (2015)

11. Khatua, A., Khatua, A., Ghosh, K., Chaki, N.: Can# Twitter_Trends predict election results? Evidence from 2014 Indian General Election. In: 2015 48th Hawaii International Conference on System Sciences (HICSS), pp. 1676–1685. IEEE (2015) doi:10.1109/HICSS.2015.202

12. Burnap, P., Gibson, R., Sloan, L., Southern, R., Williams, M.: 140 characters to victory?: using Twitter to predict the UK 2015 General Election. Electoral Stud. (2015). doi:10.1016/j.electstud.2015.11.017

13. Srivastava, R., Kumar, H., Bhatia, M.P. Jain, S.: Analyzing Delhi Assembly Election 2015 using textual content of social network. In: Proceedings of the Sixth International Conference on Computer and Communication Technology 2015, pp. 78–85. ACM (2015). doi:10.1145/2818567.2818582

14. Visual Studio 2012. https://www.visualstudio.com/en-us/downloads/download-visual-studio-vs.aspx

15. Tweetinvi API. https://www.nuget.org/packages/TweetinviAPI/

16. Spanish General Election Results, June 2016. http://www.infoelectoral.mir.es/min/busquedaAvanzadaAction.html

17. Gaurav, M., Srivastava, A., Kumar, A., Miller, S.: Leveraging candidate popularity on Twitter to predict election outcome. In: Proceedings of the 7th Workshop on Social Network Mining and Analysis, p. 7. ACM (2013). doi:10.1145/2501025.2501038

Priority Based Service Broker Policy for Fog Computing Environment

Deeksha Arya[(✉)] and Mayank Dave

National Institute of Technology, Kurukshetra, Haryana, India
deekshasheokand@gmail.com, mdave@nitkkr.ac.in

Abstract. With an increase in number of services being provided over the Internet, the number of users using these services and the number of servers/Datacentres providing the services have also increased. The use of Fog Computing enhances reliability and availability of these services due to enhanced heterogeneity and increased number of computing servers. However, the users of Cloud/Fog devices have different priority of device type based on the application they are using. Allocating the best Datacentre to process a particular user's request and then balancing the load among available Datacentres is a widely researched issue. This paper presents a new service broker policy for Fog computing environment to allocate the optimal Datacentre based on users' priority. Comparative analysis of simulation results shows that the proposed policy performs significantly better than the existing approaches in minimizing the cost, response time and Datacentre processing time according to constraints specified by users.

Keywords: Service broker · Cloud computing · Fog computing · Load balancing

1 Introduction

The term "Fog computing," first proposed by Cisco in 2011, is defined as a distributed computing paradigm that extends the services provided by the cloud to the edge of the network [1, 2]. Fog servers are deployed in the proximity of users to ensure higher availability of computing resources. Different users of Fog/Cloud have different priorities based on the application they are using or the data they want to store on the internet. Further, various service providers have different characteristics such as initialization time, the cost of storing the data, the speed of processing of data and fault rate [3]. Allocating the best Datacentre (DC) to process a particular user's request depends on the definition of "best Datacentre" which further depends on the priority of user submitting the request. For some applications, the user might prefer minimum response time irrespective of the cost whereas sometimes the priority may be to keep the budget low without applying any hard constraint on response time. Due to these reasons, there is a need to make an optimal allocation of the best possible Datacentre on users' request based on the current priorities. Another issue of importance is overloading of the Cloud/Fog Datacentres [4–7]. In case several users have the same order of priorities, the best Datacentre satisfying the given criteria would soon get overloaded resulting in decreased performance and increased waiting time. Thus, there must be a mechanism to redirect the users' requests to another Datacentre having sufficient

© Springer Nature Singapore Pte Ltd. 2017
D. Singh et al. (Eds.): ICAICR 2017, CCIS 712, pp. 84–93, 2017.
DOI: 10.1007/978-981-10-5780-9_8

resources, also termed as load balancing across the available Datacentres. Service Broker (see Fig. 1) is a computing service which acts as an interface between user and Datacentres and performs the task of load balancing as well as the optimal allocation of users' requests to appropriate Datacentres. This paper presents a new service broker policy for Fog computing environment which takes the decision based on users' priority. Our comparative analysis of performance in terms of cost, response time and Datacentre processing time shows that the proposed priority based policy performs significantly better than the existing approaches according to constraints specified by users and is thus recommended for a user-oriented system. The remaining paper is structured as follows. Section 2 presents a brief survey of existing schemes for optimal allocation of DCs. Section 3 provides detailed design and working of the scheme we are proposing followed by Sect. 4 which describes the possible scenarios and simulation set-up for evaluating the performance of our scheme. Section 5 compares the proposed approach with existing approaches for the scenarios described in Sect. 4. Section 6 concludes the paper and provides direction for future work.

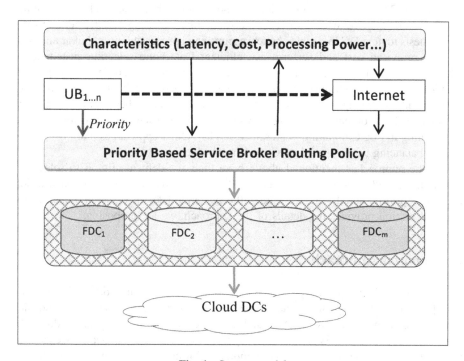

Fig. 1. System model

2 Related Work

Various approaches, also termed as "Service Broker Policies," have been proposed to deal with the allocation of the optimal Datacentre to serve the users' request. However, the definition of "optimality" is different for different approaches. Some of the approaches consider proximity as the decision factor [8]; some consider response time [7, 8] and some focus on the cost of execution [4, 9]. Cloud Analyst [8, 10] is an open source Toolkit built directly on top of CloudSim Toolkit [11] and was proposed by Wickremasinghe et al. in 2009. Cloud Analyst provides various tools and methods for simulating the Cloud and for evaluating its service performance. By making some modifications, it can be extended to simulate the algorithms designed for Fog computing environment as well. For the purpose of directing the users' requests to the best DC, the three Service Broker policies included in Cloud Analyst are: (i) Closest Datacentre policy, (ii) Dynamically Reconfigurable Service Broker policy and (iii) Optimized Response time Service Broker policy. Closest Datacentre policy is based on network latency; Dynamic Reconfigurable Service Broker policy relies on dynamic load at DCs, and the third one is based on response time of DCs. Naha and Mohamed [4] proposed cost-aware service brokering and performance sentient load balancing algorithms in the cloud. Rekha and Dakshayini [9] proposed a cost-based DC selection policy for large scale networks. Manasrah et al. [12] present a variable service broker routing policy (VSBRP). VSBRP is a heuristic-based technique that aims to minimize response time by selecting a DC based on communication channel bandwidth, latency and the size of the job. To reduce the overloading of DCs, the service broker using VSBRP redirects the user requests to next DC that yields better response and processing time. Jaikar and Noh [13, 14] proposed cost and performance efficient Datacentre selection system for a federated cloud. The policies mentioned above were originally proposed for Datacentre selection in Cloud computing environment, but can be made suitable for Fog computing environment by making some changes. There are a few approaches for Service Broker intended for Fog computing environment [5–7, 15]. One such algorithm for resource provisioning in Fog Computing is presented in [14]. Other approaches like [5–7] focus on load balancing across the Fog DCs at Virtual Machine level.

All the approaches mentioned above have their pre-defined criteria to select the optimal DC for allocation of users' requests. This paper presents a new approach which uses users' priority and the current state of the system to take the decision dynamically. The next section provides the details of the approach, we are proposing.

3 Proposed Approach

Figure 1 shows the proposed system model. Users clustered in the form of User-bases (UB) [8], access the Fog/Cloud Datacentres via the internet. For instance, we consider m number of Fog Datacentres (FDCs) and n number of UBs in the system. Although, the number of DCs and UBs present in the system may change dynamically, we assume that the service broker always has the complete information of the number of DCs or UBs present in the system at any time. Our approach works by assigning a value γ to each DC, which acts as optimality index for the DCs. The value γ is calculated based on users' priority and DC characteristics, using Eq. (3) presented in the next subsection. Service broker acts as an interface between the internet and Fog/Cloud DCs and selects the DC to serve users' request based on the value of γ. For optimal allocation, the DC with the highest value of γ is selected. Moreover, for load balancing, the broker decreases the value of γ corresponding to selected DC so as to reduce the probability of selecting this DC again. Further, to incorporate the dynamic nature of Fog computing environment, dynamic reconfiguration is included. Considering that the response time of a DC is directly proportional to its current latency, which is also a measure of network congestion and Datacentre overloading, γ is updated dynamically using Eq. (4) based on the current latency of a DC.

We divide the working of our approach in 3 main steps: (i) Initialization, (ii) Selection of best DC and (iii) Dynamic reconfiguration, which are elaborated below. In this paper, we provide only the significant details of proposed approach. We have used Cloud Analyst to implement the proposed policy and the essential functionalities like handling Virtual Machines (VMs), controlling the communication across different regions of the world, handling of simultaneous requests by the application servers, etc., have been kept same. The following subsections present the step-by-step procedure of our approach.

3.1 Initialization

The initialization part of the scheme covers the procedure of assigning the optimality index to DCs and is implemented by the following four sub-steps:

(a) Read users' priority for minimizing the cost and response time in terms of high (3), medium (2), low (1) and very low (0).

(b) Assign values to Time coefficient (C_{Time}) and Cost coefficient (C_{Cost}) on the basis of users' priority in the range 0 to 3. If both the coefficients C_{Time} and C_{Cost} are assigned the value zero, it represents the case when users don't have any specific priority for minimizing cost or response time. For such a case, we modify the coefficients and assign the values $(C_{Time}) = C_{Time}) = 3$, so as to provide the best possible service to the users.

(c) Calculate normalized processing power ($Power_{norm}$) and normalized cost ($Cost_{norm}$) corresponding to each Datacentre present in the system as follows:

$$Power = 0;$$
$$\text{for } (i = 1 \, to \, Number_{units})$$
$$\{$$
$$\text{for } (j = 1 \, to \, \# \, Processors_i)$$
$$Power = Power + power_{ij};$$
$$\}$$

$$Power_{norm} = \frac{Power}{100}; \tag{1}$$

$$Cost_{norm} = \left(\left(Cost_{DataTransfer} + Cost_{VM} \right) * 100 \right); \tag{2}$$

where $Number_{units}$ represents the number of physical hardware units associated with the DC, $\# Processors_i$ represents the number of processors in i^{th} hardware unit, $power_{ij}$

represents the processing power of jth processor of ith hardware unit. $Cost_{DataTransfer}$ represents the data transfer cost for the DC (\$/Gb), $Cost_{VM}$ represents the cost per VM for the DC (\$/hour).

(d) Calculate the initial value of γ corresponding to each Datacentre present in the system as follows:

$$\gamma = (C_{Time} * Power_{norm}) - (C_{Cost} * Cost_{norm}); \tag{3}$$

The following subsection describes the procedure for optimal allocation of DCs to serve the users' requests.

3.2 Selection of Best Datacentre

For the purpose of optimal allocation, the service broker selects the closest Datacentre with highest value of γ. The user's request is then assigned to this DC and after the assignment, for preventing the DC from getting overloaded, the γ value associated with this DC is decreased by a fixed value C thereby decreasing the chances of its selection for the next time. The following subsection provide details about dynamic upgradation/degradation of optimality index on the basis of current performance of the DCs.

3.3 Dynamic Reconfiguration

To incorporate the dynamic nature of Fog computing environment, we provide a mechanism to alter optimality index of DCs dynamically. For dynamic reconfiguration, the service broker monitors the performance of DCs and if the current latency of a DC (*CurrLatency*) say DCi is found to be lesser as compared to the best response time of this DC (*Best_{i})* so far, the broker increases the optimality index of this DC using Eq. 4, thereby increasing the chances of its allocation for the next request. The following lines describe the process of dynamic reconfiguration.

$$
\begin{aligned}
&\text{for } (i = 1 \; to \; m) \; \{ \\
&\quad \text{if } (CurrLatency_i \; != \text{null}) \{ \\
&\quad \text{if } (Best_i \; != \text{null}) \{ \\
&\qquad \text{if } (\; CurrLatency_i \; of \; DC_i < \; Best_i \;) \; \{ \\
&\qquad \quad \gamma_i = \gamma_i + \frac{Best_i - CurrLatency_i}{Best_i} * 10; \qquad (4) \\
&\qquad \quad Best_i = CurrLatency_i \; ; \\
&\qquad \} \; \text{else} \quad \gamma_i = \gamma_i - 1 ; \\
&\quad \} \; \text{else} \quad Best_i = CurrLatency_i \; ; \\
&\}\}
\end{aligned}
$$

4   Simulation Setup

The simulation tool Cloud Analyst has been used for implementing and analyzing the performance of the proposed scheme. For current simulation, we focus on User-Fog interaction. Fog-Cloud interaction can be implemented in the same way as User-Fog interaction by considering the Fog DCs as users and Cloud DCs as service providers. The simulation was run for sufficient period (1 day) so as to cover both peak as well as off-peak hours to analyze the efficiency of proposed approach. The configurations used for DCs, UBs and load balancing, are described in Tables 1, 2, and 3 respectively. To demonstrate the Fog computing environment, heterogeneous Datacentres are considered. The Fog datacentre FDC1 contains two physical hardware units with three processors each. However, the units differ in the processing speed of processors. For unit-1, the speed of processors is 500 MIPS, and for unit-2, the processing speed is 1000 MIPS. FDC2 contains one hardware unit with four processors each having processing speed 1000 MIPS. FDC3 includes three hardware units each having four processors with processing speed 10000 MIPS. FDC4 and FDC5 both contain one hardware unit with three processors. The processors of FDC4 have processing speed 100 MIPS each. For processors of FDC5, the speed is 200 MIPS.

Table 1. Datacentre configuration

Name	Cost per VM $/Hr	Data transfer cost $/Gb	Physical HW units
FDC1	1.6	0.2	2
FDC2	2.4	0.7	1
FDC3	5	3	3
FDC4	0.1	0.1	1
FDC5	0.24	0.14	1

Table 2. User base configuration

Name	Requests per user per Hr	Peak hours start (GMT)	Peak hours end (GMT)	Avg. peak users	Avg. Off-peak users
UB1	120	3	9	5000	500
UB2	60	3	9	1000	100
UB3	60	3	5	1500	150

Table 3. Load balancing and grouping factor configuration

User grouping factor in UBs (Represents number of users simultaneously active from a single user base)	1000
Request grouping factor in Datacentres (Represents number of simultaneous requests a single application server instance can support)	50
Executable instruction length per request (bytes)	100
Load balancing policy across Virtual Machines in a single Data centre	Throttled

For evaluation purpose, we compare our approach with two existing approaches and simulate the six cases mentioned in Table 4. In case (i), we applied the existing approach "Load Based Dynamic Reconfigurable DC selection [8]" which selects the Datacentres based on current load on DCs, irrespective of users' current priority. In case (ii), (iii) and (iv), we have used the proposed approach which considers users' priority and current load on the DCs to select optimal Datacentre and thus allocates different Datacentres in different cases, despite having the same configuration of DCs and UBs in all the cases. Case (v) uses "Service Proximity" based approach [8] which selects the closest DC to serve the users' request irrespective of users' priority and current load on the DCs. If multiple DCs are present in the proximity of the user, the approach selects one of the available DCs randomly. In case (vi), we have used proposed approach without using dynamic reconfiguration. The next section compares the performance of our priority-based approach with the existing schemes.

Table 4. Description of different cases for simulation

Case	Approach used	Users' priority	Whether load on DCs considered?
(i)	Load based dynamic reconfigurable policy [8]	*Not considered*	Yes
(ii)	Proposed approach	Minimize cost, Keeping the time less	Yes
(iii)	Proposed approach	Minimize time, No restriction on cost	Yes
(iv)	Proposed approach	Minimize cost, No restriction on time	Yes
(v)	Service Proximity based approach [8]	*Not considered*	No
(vi)	Proposed approach	Minimize time, Keeping the cost low	No

5   Results

For the evaluation of performance of our approach, we consider the following three parameters:

(a) Cost (the total cost of running the application for a day)
(b) Average Response time (the average time taken by the system in responding to users after the submission of their requests)
(c) Average DC processing time (the average time taken by the DCs to process the users' requests).

Figures 2, 3 and 4 respectively shows the comparison of average cost, response time and processing time for the 6 cases mentioned in Sect. 4. Evidently, the proposed priority based approach performs better than the existing approaches according to constraints specified by users. For case (ii), where the users' priority is to "minimize cost, keeping the time less $(C_{Time} = 1, C_{cost} = 3)$", the proposed approach works accordingly and outperforms the approach used in case (i) regarding both cost as well as time (response time and Datacentre processing time). For case (iii), where the users' priority is to "minimize time, no restriction on cost $(C_{Time} = 3, C_{cost} = 0)$", the proposed priority based approach although results in a higher cost than case (ii), handles the constraint on minimizing the time very well. Similarly, in case (iv), the proposed approach minimizes the cost as per users' priority $(C_{Time} = 0, C_{cost} = 3)$ along with preventing the DCs from getting overloaded by using dynamic reconfiguration. The approaches used in case (v) and case (vi) although give better results than those used in case (i), (ii), (iii) and (iv) but are not recommended for Fog computing environment since these approaches do not use/allow load based dynamic reconfiguration and thus can result in overloading of DCs. Also, for Fog computing environment, the main characteristic is its dynamic nature and load on DCs needs to be considered for taking decision dynamically. Further, the current simulation was run only for 24 h, but in the long term, the performance of DCs degrades due to overloading and so does the result of approaches used in case (v) and (vi). Thus the comparative analysis of the results proves the effectiveness of our approach in incorporating the users' requirements without any degradation in the performance.

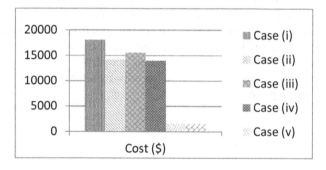

Fig. 2. Comparison of average cost for the cases described in Table 4.

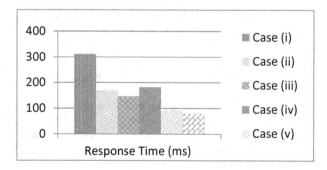

Fig. 3. Comparison of average response time for the cases described in Table 4.

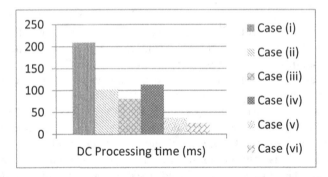

Fig. 4. Comparison of average DC processing time for the cases described in Table 4.

6   Conclusion and Future Work

This paper presents a new service broker policy for Fog computing environment to select the optimal Datacentre to be allocated to users' request on the basis of users' priority and current load on the DCs. Simulation results show that this approach performs better than the existing approaches in minimizing the cost as well as response time and Datacentre processing time according to constraints specified by users. By analyzing the results, the proposed approach is recommended for a customized environment where users have different priorities based on the application they are using. However, even if the users don't have any specific priority, our approach sets the parameters by itself to provide the optimized performance. Future work will be based on extending the proposed policy by associating it with the concept of secure data processing at the nodes. Again, the level of security required will be decided on the basis of users' current priority.

References

1. Bonomi, F.: Connected vehicles, the internet of things, and fog computing. In: 8th ACM International Workshop on Vehicular Inter-Networking (VANET), pp. 13–15. ACM, Las Vegas (2011)
2. Bonomi, F., Milito, R., Zhu, J., Addepalli, S.: Fog computing and its role in the Internet of Things. In: Proceedings of the first edition of the MCC workshop on Mobile cloud computing, pp. 13–16. ACM (2012). doi:10.1145/2342509.2342513
3. Dastjerdi, A.V., Gupta, H., Calheiros, R.N., Ghosh, S.K., Buyya, R.: Fog computing: principals, architectures, and applications. In: Internet of things: principles and paradigms, 1st edn., Chap. 4, pp. 1–26. Elsevier (2016)
4. Naha, R.K., Mohamed, O.: Cost-aware service brokering and performance sentient load balancing algorithms in the cloud. J. Netw. Comput. Appl. **75**, 47–57 (2016). Elsevier
5. Ningning, S., Chao, G., Xingshuo, A., Qiang, Z.: Fog computing dynamic load balancing mechanism based on graph repartitioning. IEEE China Commun. **13**(3), 156–164 (2016). doi:10.1109/CC.2016.7445510. IEEE

6. Verma, S., Yadav, A.K., Motwani, D., Raw, R.S., Singh, H.K.: An efficient data replication and load balancing technique for fog computing environment. In: 3rd International Conference on Computing for Sustainable Global Development, pp. 5092–5099. IEEE (2016)

7. Verma, M., Bhardwaj, N., Yadav, A.K.: Real-time efficient scheduling algorithm for load balancing in fog computing environment. Int. J. Inf. Technol. Comput. Sci. **4**, 1–10 (2016). doi:10.5815/ijitcs.2016.04.01. MECS Press

8. Wickremasinghe, B.: CloudAnalyst: a CloudSim-based tool for modeling and analysis of large scale cloud computing environment, MEDC Project Report, University of Melbourne (2009)

9. Rekha, P.M., Dakshayini, M.: Cost-based Datacentre selection policy for large-scale networks. In: International Conference on Computation of Power, Energy, Information and Communication (ICCPEIC). IEEE, pp. 18–23 (2014). doi:10.1109/ICCPEIC.2014.6915333

10. Wickremasinghe, B., Calheiros, R.N., Buyya, R.: Cloud analyst: a CloudSim-based visual modeler for analyzing cloud computing environments and applications. In: Proceedings of the 24th IEEE International Conference on Advanced Information Networking and Applications (AINA), pp. 446–452. IEEE (2010). doi:10.1109/AINA.2010.32

11. Calheiros, R.N., Ranjan, R., Beloglazov, A., Rose, C.A.F., Buyya, R.: CloudSim: a toolkit for modeling and simulation of cloud computing environments and evaluation of resource provisioning algorithms. Softw.: Pract. Exp. **41**, 23–50 (2011). doi:10.1002/spe.995. Wiley

12. Manasrah, A.M., Smadi, T., Almomani, A.: A variable service broker routing policy for data center selection in cloud analyst. J. King Saud Univ. - Comput. Inf. Sci. **29**(3), 365–377 (2017)

13. Jaikar, A., Kim, G.R., Noh, S.Y.: Effective Datacentre selection algorithm for a federated cloud. Adv. Sci. Technol. Lett. (Cloud Super Comput.) **35**, 66–69 (2013). doi:10.14257/astl.2013.35.16. SERSC

14. Jaikar, A., Noh, S.Y.: Cost and performance effective Datacentre selection system for scientific federated cloud. Peer-to-Peer Netw. Appl. **8**, 896–902 (2015). doi:10.1007/s12083-014-0261-7

15. Agarwal, S., Yadav, S., Yadav, A.K.: An efficient architecture and algorithm for resource provisioning in fog computing. Int. J. Inf. Eng. Electron. Bus. (IJIEEB) **8**, 48–61 (2016). doi:10.5815/ijieeb. MECS Press

Software Remodularization by Estimating Structural and Conceptual Relations Among Classes and Using Hierarchical Clustering

Amit Rathee[(⊠)] and Jitender Kumar Chhabra

Department of Computer Engineering, National Institute of Technology,
Kurukshetra 136119, India
amit1983_rathee@rediffmail.com,
jitenderchhabra@gmail.com

Abstract. In this paper, we have presented a technique of software remodularization by estimating conceptual similarity among software elements (Classes). The proposed technique makes use of both structural and semantic coupling measurements together to get much more accurate coupling measures. In particular, the proposed approach makes use of lexical information extracted from six main parts of the source code of a class, namely comments, class names, attribute names, method signatures, parameter names and method source code statements zone. Simultaneously, it also makes use of counting of other class's member functions used by a given class as a structural coupling measure among classes. Structural coupling among software elements (classes) are measured using information-flow based coupling metric (ICP) and conceptual coupling is measured by tokenizing source code and calculating Cosine Similarity. Clustering is performed by performing Hierarchical Agglomerate Clustering (HAC). The proposed technique is tested on three standard open source Java software's. The obtained results encourage remodularization by showing higher accuracy against the corresponding software gold standard.

1 Introduction

In object-oriented systems, classes act as a primary composing element, which group the associated data and the functionality together. Also, when a software is developed, these classes are grouped together into various modules called packages. These modules are expected to possess higher cohesion and low coupling properties. But this structure starts deteriorating with time because of continuous maintenance activities performed on it for changing requirements. During maintenance new classes are added and older ones may be modified or deleted. Hence, resulting in architectural erosion. This may also happen due to not following the object-oriented guidelines properly because of the pressure to deliver the software early in the market. All these activities degrades class cohesion and coupling. So, to reduce maintenance activity, a new and efficient approach is needed, which can detect this degradation and ultimately, restructure the software system to minimize the maintenance.

In this paper, dependency among classes are measured and highly dependent/coupled classes are identified. Such classes need remodularization to maintain

D. Singh et al. (Eds.): ICAICR 2017, CCIS 712, pp. 94–106, 2017.
DOI: 10.1007/978-981-10-5780-9_9

structural quality. In this paper, we propose a new approach to measure coupling among classes that is used further for restructuring of the software architecture by performing hierarchical agglomerate clustering (HAC). The proposed approach focuses on reducing coupling among classes by doing restructuring. In proposed approach, coupling among classes is based on both structural and conceptual coupling analysis. The conceptual coupling is analysed based on semantic relations among classes. Two classes possess higher structural coupling if they are using each other's functionality by calling each other's member functions and accessing member variables. So, the structural coupling is measured by counting the in-flow and out-flow of information, called Information-Flow-based Coupling (ICP), among classes of the given software. To measure semantic coupling and hence conceptual dependency, we first extract tokens from six main zones of a class namely: comments, class names, attribute names, method signatures, parameter names and method source code statements zone and then performed Latent Semantic Indexing (LSI) to reduce dimensionality. The extracted tokens from these zones are further normalized using Porter Stemmer's algorithm [31] and TF-IDF value of each token is measured. Then, cosine similarity among classes of the software is computed as semantic dependency. Finally, we combine both measurements to get the final coupling among classes. Since, the extracted tokens strongly represent the corresponding domain of the software, so, they reflect the conceptual coupling among classes.

The rest of this paper is organized as follows: Sect. 2 gives the literature survey, Sect. 3 gives the details of the proposed work, Sect. 4 shows the experiment and results obtained and finally Sect. 5 gives conclusions and future work remarks.

2 Literature Survey

Lots of ideas have already been proposed in literature aiming at supporting software system restructuring and remodularization in the world of software engineering. Since the 80's, many authors have researched and proposed techniques in term of metrics, frameworks, etc. to increase overall quality of systems.

Many graph based techniques had been proposed by Cimitile and Visaggio [1], Shaw et al. [15], and Antoniol et al. [3] which aims at identifying strongly connected subgraphs in the Call Graph representation of the system under study. van Deursen and Kuipers [5] and Tonella [4] also proposed the re-modularization of software system by using concept analysis technique, which extracts the group of objects that share some common attributes among them. Mancoridis et al. [16] proposed algorithms to automatically recover the underlying software architecture from source code. They have used a search-based clustering approach to recover the software modular structure. Mitchell and Mancoridis [6] used the same approach and developed Bunch tool for automatic system decomposition into a more cohesive modular structure. Harman et al. [7] and Seng et al. [8] have also proposed system decomposition techniques which makes use of search-based approaches and various soft computing techniques. Abdeen et al. [9] have proposed and implemented a heuristic search-based technique for optimizing inter-package coupling. Abdellatief et al. [17] provided various component-based system dependency metrics which are based on graph methods. Qiu et al. [18]

also proposed methods to measure software similarity based on the structural properties derived from UML diagrams. Savic et al. [19] proposed a SNEIPL tool for the automatic extraction of dependencies using software network and enriched Concrete Syntax Tree (eCST) representation of the source code.

Component classification and similarity measurement is also done based only on lexical information. Srinivas et al. [20] gives a similarity metric based on the lexical properties and representation of the component in vector form. Another set of conceptual coupling matrices is proposed by Poshyvank based on the semantic information present in identifiers and comments from the source code. Kagdi et al. [30] proposed another set of metrics for measuring the conceptual similarity between the method-method, method-class and class-class.

The combined use of both conceptual and structural measures have also been studied in the literature by many researchers [2, 10–13, 21–23, 27–29]. Bavota et al. [13, 14] used graph theory to identify various extract package refactoring opportunities. These refactoring operations tries to remove promiscuous package problem in software system, i.e. a package is assigned more responsibilities that should have been divided in separate packages. Maletic and Marcus [10] have proposed an approach which makes use of both semantic and structural data to propose refactoring decisions that are helpful in reducing maintenance efforts and other reengineering activities of software systems. Kuhn et al. [11] extended the work by Maletic and Marcus by giving a visualization support for the clusters and their semantic relationships. Adritsos and Tzerpos [24] presented LIMBO, a hierarchical algorithm for software clustering. The clustering algorithm proposed counts both structural and non-structural attributes to reduce the maintenance activity of a software system by decomposing it into clusters. Corazza et al. [21–23] presented a clustering based approach to divide OO system into subsystems, by considering only lexical information extracted from the source code and then using a partitioning algorithm to build more cohesive subsystems. Belle et al. [25] proposed an approach based on both linguistic and structural data to recover the underlying architecture of OO Systems. Measuring structural and conceptual coupling based on the structural and conceptual information and using it to remodularize software system using HAC clustering is the main characteristics of our approach. The combined approach to estimate similarity measurement and remodularization using structural and semantic coupling in literature have also been proposed similar to our approach, but, no one in literature have proposed a combined approach which aims at dividing the source code in different zones to measure semantic coupling and simultaneously used in-flow and out-flow information counting to measure structural coupling together. The approach of dividing the source code into various zones and extracting tokens for similarity measurement is more accurate because most of the conceptual information's introduced by programmer are covered by these zones. The in-flow & out-flow measurement of information also gives a direct measurement of actual structural coupling present in source code.

3 Proposed Approach

The proposed approach focus on the measurement of conceptual coupling between different Java classes belonging to a software system and then use that information in performing remodularization. The proposed approach is depicted in Fig. 1. It is based on measuring both Structural and Semantic Coupling among classes. As today's software are built by following proper standards and guidelines by programmers. So, lots of valuable semantic information is already present in the source code in the form of member-variable names, class-names, function-names, parameter-names etc. and they are strongly related with the concept of the class i.e. the idea implemented by the class. This idea motivates us to extract those words from source code in the form of tokens and use them for dependency calculation. Similarly, classes are also structurally coupled due to the usage of each other's member function. This motivates us to measure Structural Coupling among classes also. Further, these two dependencies information, Semantic & Structural Coupling, are combined together after normalizing Structural Coupling and used for clustering using a hierarchical agglomerative clustering algorithm.

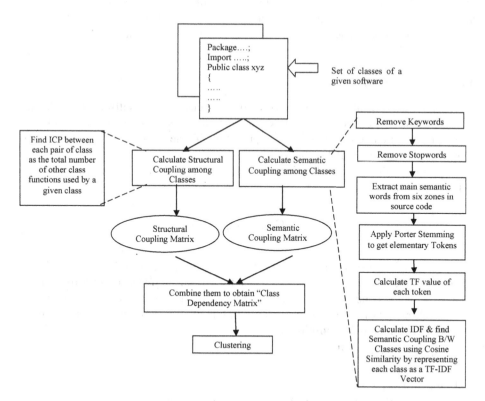

Fig. 1. Proposed methodology to measure conceptual coupling among classes

The source code can be considered as a systematic collection of lexical information, which are present in various parts. We have found that most of these information's are mostly present in following six parts/zones of source code:

1. Comments Zone.
2. Class Name Zone.
3. Attribute Names Zone.
4. Method Signatures Zone.
5. Parameter Names Zone.
6. Method Source Code Statements Zone.

The Comments Zone includes two sections: Javadoc & Comments provided by the programmers. This zone provides documentation related to class and used mainly for maintenance activities. The Class Name Zone includes class definition section present in source code. The Attribute Name Zone includes all member variables defined in a class definition. The Method Signature Zone includes all class member function's prototype statements. It also includes user defined data types used as parameters. The Parameter Names Zone section includes all the variables used in a class member function's definition as parameter names. And finally the Method Source Code Statements Zone consists of all the statements present inside the class member function's definition body. The proposed work is divided into following subsections:

3.1 Semantic Similarity

In the first step, we find the similarity among all classes of a software by utilizing lexical information extracted from different zones of classes and the cosine similarity technique in which each class Ci is represented in the form of lexical vector Vi consisting of token's TF-IDF value and then similarity among two classes Ci and Cj is calculated through corresponding lexical vectors Vi and Vj respectively by using the following formula:

$$\text{CoSim} (C_i, C_j) = \frac{V_i \cdot V_j}{\|V_i\| * \|V_j\|} \tag{1}$$

Finally, we get a square matrix called **Semantic Coupling Matrix (SeCM)** of size n where n is the total number of classes in a software. The SeCM is a symmetric matrix because semantic coupling among any two class C_i and C_j is unidirectional in nature. The overall process is represented as an algorithm consisting of the following steps:
   // Finding Semantic Coupling Matrix

1. Remove all keywords.
2. Remove Stopwords.
3. Extract tokens.
4. Normalize tokens by applying Porter Stemmer Algorithm.
5. Divide tokens into various zones.
6. Calculate the frequency of each token.

7. Represent each class as a vector in TF-IDF form.
8. Calculate Cosine Similarity between each pair of class to obtain **Semantic Coupling Matrix (SeCM).**

The working of the above algorithm is explained with the help of two java classes as shown in Fig. 2. The keyword removal step consists of filtering out all standard words of java like int, public, class and predefined class names such as serializable, hashtable etc. As the Javadoc and comments consist of English language sentences, so it is necessary to remove all common words called stopwords to get an accurate similarity measure. In our example, the stopwords are a, to, of and in. After this step, the next step is to extract all major words as lexical information and apply java's Camel NameCase Style division to get more rooted elements. E.g. schoolYear is divided into two tokens: school and year respectively. In the next step, the porter stemming algorithm is applied to normalize ambiguity due to plurals, verbs etc. e.g. handle, handling and handler will represent the same token rather than three separate tokens. This gives better control over semantic similarity measurement.

```
/* A public class to handle SemesterWise details of a student
*/
    public class Semester implements Serializable {
        // a list of member variables
        private int schoolYear;
        private int semNum;
        private String semCode;
        private Hashtable studEnrolled = new
        Hashtable();
        private Hashtable subjOpen = new Hashtable();
        // a list of public member functions
        public Semester() { .....}
        public Semester(int sy, int sem) {.......}
        public void enrollStudent (Student thisStudent) {.....}
        public int getSchoolYear() {.....}
        public String getSemCode() {.....}
        public int getSem() {.....}
        public void openSubject(Subject thisSubject) {.....}
        public void setSem(int newSem) {.....}
    }
                    Semester.java
```

```
/* A class to handle Students personal details in a university */
    public class PersonRecord implements Serializable {
        // a list of member variables
        private String firstName;
        private String lastName;
        private String middleName;
        private String middleInitial;
        private static int count;
        // a list of member functions
        public Person(){int a;......}
        public Person(String fn, String ln, String mn){.....}
        public String getFirstName(){......}
        public String getLastName(){......}
        public static int getCount(){....}
        public void setFirstName(String str){......}
        public void setLastName(String str){.....}
        public static void setCount(){.....}
    }
                    Person.java
```

Fig. 2. Sample java files

Finally, all tokens are extracted and their frequency count is recorded separately for each class. A complete list of these tokens is as shown below in Table 1. Finally, this information is represented as vector and similarity is calculated using Eq. (1).

3.2 Structural Similarity

In the second step, we find the similarity among the classes by utilizing the structural properties. We consider Information-Flow-based Coupling (ICP) as a structural similarity measure. In this we measure total number of member functions of other classes called/ used by the given class as the structural coupling, i.e. ICP measures the total

Table 1. Token list extracted from four zones of two sample files

Zone	Semester.java		Person.java	
	Token name	Frequency	Token name	Frequency
Comments	handle	1	handle	1
	semester	1	student	1
	wise	1	person	1
	detail	1	detail	1
	student	1	university	1
	list	2	list	2
	member	2	member	2
	variable	1	variable	1
	function	1	function	1
Class name	semester	1	person	1
	serialize	1	record	1
	–	–	serialize	1
Attribute name	school	1	first	1
	year	1	name	3
	sem	2	last	1
	num	1	middle	2
	code	1	initial	1
	stud	1	count	1
	enrol	1	–	–
	subj	1	–	–
	open	1	–	–
Method signature	semester	2	person	2
	sem	3	first	2
	enrol	1	name	4
	student	2	last	2
	school	1	count	2
	year	1	–	–
	code	1	–	–
	open	1	–	–
	Subject	2	–	–
	–	–	str	2
Parameter	Sy	1	fn	1
	sem	1	ln	1
	–	–	mn	1
Source code statement	–	–	a	1

amount of inflow and outflow of information from a class. The overall process is represented in the form of an algorithm consisting of the following steps:

// Finding Structural Coupling Matrix

1. Find ICP coupling matrix between each pair of class, which measures the total no. of method invocations.
2. Represents the result in **Structural Coupling Matrix (StCM)** and normalize the entries to the range [0…1].

The ICP is calculated for each pair of classes and results in the generation of Structural Coupling Matrix of order nxn, where n is the total number of classes under study. The ICP between two classes C_i and C_j is calculated using following formula:

$$ICP(C_i, C_j) = \sum_{k=1}^{k=|call(C_i,C_j)|} calls(C_i, C_j) \tag{2}$$

Here, calls (C_i, C_j) denote the total number of functions $\left(m_1, m_2 \ldots \ldots, m_j \right) \varepsilon C_j$ called by class Ci. Similarly, because, StCM is not symmetric due to the directional nature of structural coupling among classes. So, it is necessary to make it symmetric. To do this, ICP (C_j, C_i) is calculated as mentioned below just to possess symmetry relation:

$$ICP(C_j, C_i) = max\left(ICP(C_i, C_j), ICP(C_j, C_i) \right) \tag{3}$$

3.3   Combining Structural and Semantic Coupling Matrix

In this step, we combine the two similarity matrix SeCM & StCM together. Here, first of all, before addition of entries, the entries of the StCM must be normalized because it contains 0 as minimum and its maximum value is unbounded. Whereas, our semantic coupling matrix's entries are in the range [0…1]. To combine the two metrics in a single similarity measure we will first normalize the structural matrix values in the range [0…1]. To do this, the below mentioned formula as used by Bavota et al. [13] is used to normalize each entry $C_{i, j}$ of the structural coupling matrix (StCM):

$$C_{i,j} = \frac{\left(C_{i,j} - min(StCM) \right)}{max(StCM) - min(StCM)} \tag{4}$$

Here, min (StCM) & max (StCM) are the minimum and maximum values in Structural Coupling Matrix (StCM) respectively.

After normalization, matrices StCM & SeCM are added together, resulting in final coupling matrix for the system as Class Dependency Matrix (CDM). It is a symmetric nxn matrix, where n is the total no. of classes in the system, and it represents the overall coupling (structural + semantic) among classes of a given software.

3.4   Clustering Using Hierarchical Agglomerate Clustering

The last step in software remodularization is the clustering process. It aims to recover the underlying software architecture by regrouping classes based on dependency relations. Here, the clustering is performed using an HAC. Agglomerate hierarchical algorithms starts with each entity (class) assigned to individual cluster, which are in turn combined together until we get a single large cluster containing all the entities. Various types of hierarchical clustering algorithms have been discussed in [26]. We have used Complete Linkage Hierarchical Algorithm. In computing distance d of newly formed cluster from existing clusters with distance d1 & d2 as d = max (d1, d2). The Complete Linkage is chosen because it gives more cohesive and uniform clusters [26]. It results in a tree with each node representing a cluster and the height of the tree represents the dissimilarity among clusters. For performing software remodularization, this tree needs to be cut at appropriate height to have a group of clusters rather than one. This process is depicted in Fig. 3 below. Here, the system is divided into two clusters by cutting the tree at cut point 1. The first cluster contains E1–E3 and the second E4, E5 entities. Similarly, we can divide the system into four clusters by cutting at cut point 2.

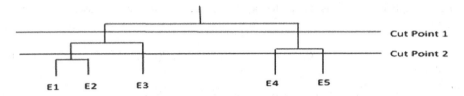

Fig. 3. A hierarchical tree divided into two clusters by cutting tree at cut point

Given a set of N entities (classes) which needs to be regrouped together, and an N*N distance (or similarity) matrix, the HAC is done by following algorithmic steps:

1. Assign each entity Ei having feature vector Ef1, Ef2,......, EfN to single cluster, so that initially there are total N clusters, each having just one item.
2. Find the minimum distinct (most similar) pair of clusters and merge them into a single cluster, so that now there are total N-1 clusters.
3. Again Calculate distances (similarities) between the newly created cluster and each of the old ones using Complete Linkage method.
4. Repeat steps 2 and 3 until all entities have been joined into a single cluster of size N.

4   Experimentation and Results

To validate the proposed methodology, we conduct our experiment on three freely available open source java software's whose details is given in Table 2. The table defines the software name, its version, total number of classes, thousand lines of code (KLOC) count and total number of packages in software. The semantic information extraction and dependency calculation is done using a tool specially designed by the authors. Whereas, the structural dependencies are calculated using Stan4J Tool.

Table 2. Description of software system under study

System	Version	#Classes	KLOC	#Packages
Junit	4.5	27	2.74	4
Easy mock	2.4	63	3.06	3
Servlet-API	2.3	40	2.84	4

The proposed approach has been evaluated using expert criteria approach. The collected clustering results P_C is compared against clustering obtained from expert opinions P_G as gold standards. The comparison has been performed by finding out Precision & Recall Metrics and ultimately calculating the f-measure for each software. Table 3 shows the f-measure values of each software under study. The results indicates positive measurement of cohesion based on structural and conceptual relations among entities of a software system. As two entities can be in the same cluster called Intra pair or they may be in different cluster called Inter pair. So, precision and recall can be defined as:

Table 3. Precision, recall & F-measure values

System	Precision	Recall	F-Measure
Junit	0.62	0.35	0.52
Easy mock	0.91	0.40	0.62
Servlet-API	0.67	0.64	0.66

Precision: Precision is defined as the percentage of intra pairs given by the clustering method which are also intra in the expert partition. The value of precision of the constructed package P_C and original package P_G is calculated using following formula:

$$\text{Precision } P_i = \frac{|C(P_{Ci}) \cap C(P_{Gi})|}{|C(P_{Ci})|}$$

Recall: Recall is defined as the percentage of intra pairs in the expert partition which are identified by the clustering method. The value of recall from the constructed package PC and original package PG is calculated using following formula:

$$\text{Recall } P_i = \frac{|C(P_{Ci}) \cap C(P_{Gi})|}{|C(P_{Gi})|}$$

Here, $C(P_{Ci})$ & $C(P_{Gi})$ is the total number of classes in the ith constructed package P_{Ci} and original package P_{Gi}. Since the above two metrics measure two different aspects regarding a software partition, so, we further evaluated F-measure metric to make balance between two results. The F-measure value of ith package is obtained from the corresponding precision and recall using following formula:

$$\text{F - measure}\,P_i \;=\; 2 * \frac{PrecisionP_i * Recall\,P_i}{PrecisionP_i + Recall\,P_i}$$

5   Conclusion and Future Work

In this paper, we proposed a technique to measure the conceptual similarity among classes of an OO Software which is ultimately used for performing software remodularization using hierarchical agglomerate clustering to obtain better architecture. Based on the above experiment and results, it can be concluded that using a combination of both structural & conceptual coupling measure, gives better dependency indication rather than using them as individuals. The present work is mainly based on measuring the Cosine Similarity & ICP among classes and in future many other techniques and metrics for finding similarity can be tested and a comparison can be further done. Also, in future inter module/package dependency can be tested using the same proposed technique. The methodology can be modified and tested to suite other OO languages such as C++ etc. Furthermore, other clustering technique can be used & tested to provide appropriate grouping.

References

1. Cimitile, A., Visaggio, G.: Software salvaging and the call dominance tree. J. Syst. Softw. **28** (2), 117–127 (1995)
2. Marcus, A., Poshyvanyk, D., Ferenc, R.: Using the conceptual cohesion of classes for fault prediction in object-oriented systems. IEEE Trans. Softw. Eng. **34**(2), 287–300 (2008)
3. Antoniol, G., Di Penta, M., Casazza, G., Merlo, E.: A method to re-organize legacy systems via concept analysis. In: Proceedings of 9th International Workshop on Program Comprehension, Toronto, Canada, pp. 281–292 (2001)
4. Tonella, P.: Concept analysis for module restructuring. IEEE Trans. Softw. Eng. **27**(4), 351–363 (2001)
5. van Deursen, A., Kuipers, T.: Identifying objects using cluster and concept analysis. In: Proceedings of 21st International Conference on Software Engineering, Los Angeles, California, USA, pp. 246–255 (1999)
6. Mitchell, B.S., Mancoridis, S.: On the automatic modularization of software systems using the bunch tool. IEEE Trans. Softw. Eng. **32**(3), 193–208 (2006)
7. Harman, M., Hierons, R.M., Proctor, M.: A new representation and crossover operator for search-based optimization of software modularization. In: Proceedings of the Genetic and Evolutionary Computation Conference, New York, USA (2002)
8. Seng, O., Bauer, M., Biehl, M., Pache, G.: Search-based improvement of subsystem decompositions. In: Proceedings of the Genetic and Evolutionary Computation Conference, Washington, Columbia, USA, pp. 1045–1051 (2005)
9. Abdeen, H., Ducasse, S., Sahraoui, H.A., Alloui, I.: Automatic package coupling and cycle minimization. In: Proceedings of the 16th Working Conference on Reverse Engineering, Lille, France, pp. 103–112 (2009)

10. Maletic, J., Marcus, A.: Supporting program comprehension using semantic and structural information. In: Proceedings of 23rd International Conference on Software Engineering. Toronto, Ontario, Canada, pp. 103–112 (2001)
11. Kuhn, A., Ducasse, S., Gîrba, T.: Semantic clustering: identifying topics in source code. Inf. Soft. Technol. **49**(3), 230–243 (2007)
12. Scanniello, G., Risi, M., Tortora, G.: Architecture recovery using latent semantic indexing and k-means: an empirical evaluation. In: Proceedings of International Conference on Software Engineering and Formal Methods, pp. 103–112 (2010)
13. Bavota, G., De Lucia, A., Marcus, A., Oliveto, R.: Software re-modularization based on structural and semantic metrics. In: Proceedings of International Working Conference on Reverse Engineering, pp. 195–204. IEEE Computer Society (2010)
14. Bavota, G., Oliveto, R., Gethers, M., Poshyvanyk, D., De Lucia, A.: Methodbook: recommending move method refactorings via relational topic models. IEEE Trans. Softw. Eng. **40**(7), 671–694 (2014)
15. Shaw, S.C., Goldstein, M., Munro, M., Burd, E.: Moral dominance relations for program comprehension. IEEE Trans. Softw. Eng. **29**(9), 851–863 (2003)
16. Mancoridis, S., Mitchell, B.S., Rorres, C., Chen, Y.-F., Gansner, E.R.: Using automatic clustering to produce high-level system organizations of source code. In: Proceedings of 6th International Workshop on Program Comprehension, Ischia, Italy. IEEE CS Press (1998)
17. Abdellatief, M., Sultan, A.B.M., Ghani, A., Jabar, M.A.: Component-based software system dependency metrics based on component information flow measurements. In: Sixth International Conference on Software Engineering Advances, IARIA (2011)
18. Qiu, D.H., Li, H., Sun, J.L.: Measuring software similarity based on structure and property of class diagram. In: 6th International Conference on Advanced Computational Intelligence (ICACI). IEEE (2013)
19. Savic, M., Rakic, G., Budimac, Z., Ivanovic, M.: A language-independent approach to the extraction of dependencies between source code entities. IST **56**, 1268–1288 (2014). Elsevier
20. Srinivas, C., Radhakrishna, V., Rao, C.V.G.: Software component clustering and classification using noval similarity measure. In: 8th International Conference Interdisciplinarity in Engineering (INTER-ENG), Romania (2014)
21. Corazza, A., Di Martino, S., Scanniello, G.: A probabilistic based approach towards software system clustering. In: Proceedings of European Conference on Software Maintenance and Reengineering, pp. 89–98. IEEE Computer Society (2010)
22. Corazza, A., Di Martino, S., Maggio, V., Scanniello, G.: Investigating the use of lexical information for software system clustering. In: Proceedings of European Conference on Software Maintenance and Reengineering, pp. 35–44. IEEE Computer Society (2011)
23. Corazza, A., Martino, S., Maggio, V., Scanniello, G.: Weighing lexical information for software clustering in the context of architecture recovery. Empir. Softw. Eng. **21**, 72–103 (2016)
24. Andritsos, P., Tzerpos, V.: Information-theoretic software clustering. IEEE Trans. Softw. Eng. **31**(2), 150–165 (2005)
25. Belle, A.B., Boussaidi, G.E., Kpodjedo, S.: Combining lexical and structural information to reconstruct software layers. Inf. Softw. Technol. **74**, 1–16 (2016)
26. Maqbool, O., Babri, A.H.: Hierarchical clustering for software architecture recovery. IEEE Trans. Softw. Eng. **33**(11), 759–780 (2007)
27. Prajapati, A., Chhabra, J.K.: Improving modular structure of software system using structural and lexical dependency. Inf. Softw. Technol. **82**, 96–120 (2017). (Elsevier, SCI)
28. Parashar, A., Chhabra, J.K.: An approach for clustering class coupling metrics to mine object oriented software components. Int. Arab J. Inf. Technol. **13**(3), 239–248 (2016). (SCI)

29. Prajapati, A., Chhabra, J.K.: Preserving core components of object-oriented packages while maintaining structural quality. Procedia Comput. Sci. **46**, 833–840 (2015). (Elsevier)
30. Kagdi, H., Gethers, M., Poshyvanyk, D.: Integrating conceptual and logical couplings for change impact analysis in software. Empir. Softw. Eng. **18**, 933–969 (2013)
31. Porter, M.F.: An algorithm for suffix stripping. Program **14**(3), 130–137 (1980)

Requirements Traceability Through Information Retrieval Using Dynamic Integration of Structural and Co-change Coupling

Jyoti$^{(\boxtimes)}$ and Jitender Kumar Chhabra

National Institute of Technology, Kurukshetra, India
jjangra2@gmail.com, jitenderchhabra@gmail.com

Abstract. Requirement Traceability (RT) links correlate requirements to their corresponding source code and helps in better requirement understanding, reusability and other software maintenance activities. Since a major portion of software artifacts is in the form of text, for finding these links Information Retrieval (IR) techniques based on textual similarity are widely adopted for Requirement Traceability. But it is hard to find RT links when artifacts have less textual description. So, for finding these links indirectly non-textual techniques like structural information based, co-change history based, ownership based are used with IR. However, if the results of IR contain false positives, the combined approach may increase them further. So, instead of directly combining, this paper proposes an automatic technique for RT by first improving the IR approach and then combining it with the non-textual based techniques. Also, we present a new non-textual based technique based on weighted integration of structural coupling and change history based coupling of classes for retrieving indirect links. The results show that our proposed approach performs better than the existing methods which use coupling information complementary to IR.

Keywords: Requirement Traceability · Dynamic integration · Co-change coupling · Structural coupling

1 Introduction

During development of a system, software artifacts, e.g. requirement documents, use-cases, design artifacts, and other UML diagrams are maintained along with source code. Correlation among these artifacts helps in various domains like program comprehension, software maintenance, impact analysis and reusability [1]. Requirement Traceability (RT) links correlate requirements to their corresponding source code [2]. Moreover, it assists in better understanding of requirements, verifying implementation of all claimed requirements, and at the same time, it also ensures that no unspecified functionality has been implemented [2]. But, with the evolution of software, RT links are not updated to the extent of changes made to the system [3]. To address this issue, researchers proposed various Information Retrieval (IR) techniques [4–7] for maintenance (updation) of RT links. These IR techniques are based on textual similarity as

© Springer Nature Singapore Pte Ltd. 2017
D. Singh et al. (Eds.): ICAICR 2017, CCIS 712, pp. 107–118, 2017.
DOI: 10.1007/978-981-10-5780-9_10

most of the content in software artifacts is in the form of text. The documents having high textual similarity, have a high probability of being correlated/linked [3]. IR relies on the application domain terms used by programmers while writing source code items, e.g. functions, identifiers, comments, variables and other artifacts [3]. Before applying the IR approach, a preprocessing (stemming) on artifacts is done to split identifiers of source code (wherever applicable) and to remove the irrelevant information (e.g. stop words) from documents [3]. After preprocessing step, a term-by-document matrix is formed. An entry w_{ij} in the matrix represents the weightage of the ith term in the jth artifact [4, 5]. This matrix is passed as an input to IR-based approaches [4]. Vector Space Model (VSM) [4, 5] is the most basic IR model. In VSM, cosine similarity among columns (vectors) of the matrix is used to form a ranked list. Links in the ranked list having similarity higher than a particular threshold (t), are treated as candidate links [3, 4]. But since, meaning of the word may change with context (Polysemy) and different words may have the same meaning (Synonymy) [6, 7], direct matching of documents on the basis of text is not enough. Also, certain artifacts inherently have less textual information (e.g. Abstract classes, Interfaces) [7]. Due to all of these possibilities, many times it becomes hard to distinguish between actual links and false positives, especially in the lower part of the ranked list. Due to these limitations many researchers observed that obtained ranked list from IR may result into large number of false positives and actual correlation among them may remain undetected [2, 3, 5, 6, 8]. So, to find RT links, non-textual similarity based techniques are used in combination with IR to retrieve these links indirectly. Among non-textual based methods, coupling among classes is the most commonly used for retrieving indirect links between use-cases and source code [8–11]. But, if the obtained ranked list from IR has many false positives, then its combination with other approaches may increase the number of false positives [12]. To address these issues, the main contributions of this paper are:

1. An approach for retrieving RT links is proposed, which combines improved version of IR with coupling based schemes.
2. The impact of maintenance related changes on structural coupling and co-change coupling has been investigated to find out their relative weights.
3. A scheme is proposed for finding indirect links by using dynamic integration of structural and co-change coupling.
4. Comparative analysis of the proposed approach with two different alternate approaches has been carried out.

The rest of the paper is organized as follows. Existing methodologies for RT along with their limitations are described in Sect. 2. Section 3 elaborates the proposed RT technique. Section 4 presents comparative study and Sect. 5 finally concludes the paper.

2 Related Work

IR techniques based on textual similarity, e.g. VSM [4, 5], Probabilistic-based [4] and LSI-based [6, 7] gives almost similar performance [13]. Since it is not necessary that the relevant documents always use similar terms and certain artifacts inherently have less textual information (e.g. Abstract classes, Interfaces) [7]. Due to which it becomes hard to distinguish between actual links and false positives, especially in the lower part of the list [2, 3, 5, 6, 8]. So, the approaches require manual efforts to filter out the correct links from the ranked list [7, 14–16]. To reduce the efforts needed by the software engineer, approaches like incremental approach [16], link count based approach [17], smoothening-filter based method [18], and transitive-relations based approach [19] are used. Although, these approaches improve the IR technique but these approaches are mostly dependent on textual similarity of documents. Instead of relying on the textual similarity, certain complementary approaches that are non-textual are often used with IR [10–12]. Two commonly used methods are structural coupling based [8, 9] and co-change coupling based [10, 11].

Structural coupling based IR techniques find the indirect links by determining coupling based on inheritance relationship, method calls, variables used of other classes, etc. IR schemes using structural information are extremely desirable [8, 20, 21]. But they are found to be less useful because if IR techniques results already contain some false positives, the combined approach may increase them further [9, 12]. To overcome this, [9] proposed an approach, but the problem is that it is still semi-automatic approach and it requires a lot of manual effort for filtering out candidate links. For bigger software, this kind of manual processing is neither possible nor desirable because of cost and time [12]. Another problem is that the structural design degrades with the changes made to the system [10, 22–24]. To address this problem, change history based approaches in combination with IR are used [10, 11]. It is based on the idea that classes co-changed together in the commits are correlated [10, 11, 22, 25]. But during initial phases of development, change history is less prominent than structural information due to less number of commit reports logged. So, instead of using them individually as in [8–11], their weighted combination can give better results. This paper presents a weighted scheme which assigns weights to structural coupling and change history based techniques dynamically. The next section describes the proposed RT scheme in detail.

3 Working Methodology

This paper proposes an approach for finding RT links. Scheme comprises of two steps as shown in Fig. 1. In first step direct links are found. First of all, the direct links within requirements (Horizontal traceability Links) and between use cases and source code (Vertical Traceability Links) are recovered using IR-based approaches. The non-textual based approaches are used for finding correlation among the classes. In the second step, the weighted matrix is formed representing the similarity among the artifacts. Next, this matrix is taken as an input and indirect links are found using matrix multiplication method [26]. After applying appropriate threshold resulting links are obtained. The working of the proposed approach is described in detail in following sub-sections.

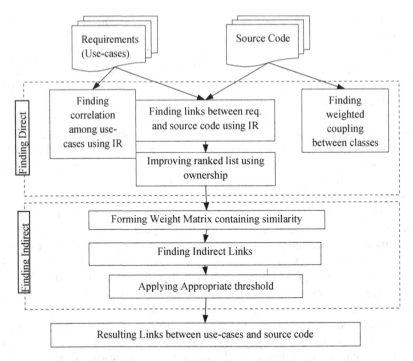

Fig. 1. Proposed approach for RT links recovery

3.1 Identifying Direct Links

In the first step, we find out the direct links present in all possible combinations of artifacts (usecases-usecases, usecases-source code and source code-source code).

Finding Direct RT Links Using Improved IR Approach. In this step we find the RT links using IR model as in [5]. Proposed approach improves simple IR approach using developer's context by adding a bonus as done by Diaz et al. [12]. Author's context is found by combining the documents written by the same author into a single document. A requirement r_i's IR similarity with every author's context is found, whosoever results in maximum similarity, say author A_k, bonus is added to the similarity value between r_i and classes written by author A_k. The bonus is added to an average of maximum and minimum similarity values [12]. Bonus helps in improving the textual similarity value of correct links and it becomes easy to discard false positives. Improved similarity between r_i and c_k is denoted by ImIRSim(r_i, c_k), and is calculated as follows (normalized between 0 and 1):

$$\text{ImIRSim}(r_i, c_k) = \frac{\text{IRSim}(r_i, c_k) + \text{avg}_{r_i}}{1 + \text{avg}_{r_i}} \tag{1}$$

Here, $\text{IRSim}(r_i, c_k)$ is the IR similarity between r_i and c_k and avg_{r_i} is the average of the maximum and minimum similarity value of r_i with source code classes. Thus, direct links between requirement and classes are found.

Finding Links Among Requirements Using IR Approach. Most of the time, requirements are well documented and contain more textual information. While finding RT links using IR there is a huge conceptual gap between terms used in these types of artifacts, which is not the case when we find traceability links within requirements. Our approach uses VSM based model [4, 5] as it is among the best two IR approaches [27]. As in [5], we obtain IR similarity among requirements. IR similarity between r_i and r_k is denoted by $\text{IRSim}(r_i, r_k)$.

Finding Links Between Classes Using Weighted Non-textual Based Approach. In this step, we find coupling between classes using a weighted combination of change history based and structural based. During initial phases of development, the structural information provides better coupling information between classes in comparison to change history based techniques due to less number of commit reports logged [23]. However, as the software evolves and multiple versions come into the picture, the structural design degrades and change history becomes more prevalent in determining the correlation between classes [10, 11, 22]. The paper suggests the dynamic integration of structural and co-change coupling schemes. Weightage of structural approach is high initially, but as the software evolves weight of change history increases. Weightage varies with the software evolution and increase in the number of commits. Three sub-steps involved in this process are described below.

Structural Coupling. In this step, we find the structural similarity between the classes same as in [26]. Structural similarity (StrSim) given by Eq. (2)

$$\text{StrSim}(c_i, c_j) = \frac{|x_{i,j}|}{|x_i| + |M_i|} \tag{2}$$

Here, $|x_{i,j}|$ is the number of methods invoked by class c_i of class c_j, $|x_i|$ is the total number of functions called by class c_i and $|M_i|$ is the total number of methods in c_i.

Co-change Coupling. In this step, we find the coupling between the classes as in [26] using change history. Authors have used proximity to find the association between classes as given by Eq. (3).

$$\text{CHSim}(c_i, c_j) = \frac{|c_i \cap c_j|}{|c_j|} \tag{3}$$

Here, $|c_i \cap c_j|$ represents the number of commits in which both classes co-change together and $|c_i|$, denotes the number of commits having only class c_i.

Dynamic Integration of Structural and Co-change Coupling. As the structural design degrades with the changes made to the system [10, 22, 23] but change history gives better coupling information. But, during initial phases of development, change history is less prominent than structural information due to less number of commit reports logged. So, instead of using them individually as in [8–11], a new technique for finding coupling information dynamic integration is presented in this paper. Based on the percentage of classes changed weightage of structural and co-change coupling dynamically changes. The weight varies with the percentage of classes changed up to this version as shown below in Eq. (4).

$$NonTxSim(c_i, c_j) = (\mu)CHSim(c_i, c_j) + (1-\mu)StrSim(c_i, c_j) \tag{4}$$

$$\lambda = \frac{\text{number of classes changed}}{\text{total classes}} \tag{5}$$

$$\mu = \begin{cases} 0.2 \text{ if } \lambda \leq 0.2 \\ \lambda \text{ if } 0.2 < \lambda < 0.8 \\ 0.8 \text{ if } \lambda \geq 0.8 \end{cases} \tag{6}$$

Here, λ denotes the percentage of classes changed. As the classes change, structural design degrades [10, 11, 23] and change history weightage increases. Although with modifications, design degrades, still the structural coupling has its importance. Similarly in case of change history, when there are less number of commits, it does not give much information, but still, has little relevance. So, we have formulated μ such that when λ is lesser than 0.2 we take $\mu = 0.2$, If λ is greater than 0.8, we take $\mu = 0.8$ and when it is in range 0.2 to 0.8 we take $\mu = \lambda$. Thus, in every case, minimum weightage of both co-change and structural coupling is at least 0.2. For example, in project iTrust [28] the number of classes changed up to a particular version is summarized in Table 1. Up to version 11.0, 93 distinct classes are modified out of 243 total classes. For this dataset $\lambda = 0.38$ and $\mu = 0.38$. Weightage of change history based approach will be 0.38 and for structural based will be 0.62. By using these step described in subsect. 3.1 direct links are found. Next subsection describes steps used for finding indirect links in detail.

Table 1. Dataset of iTrust from version 6.0 to 11.0

Version	Commit	Files changed	Classes changed	Classes
6.0	8	24	2	208
7.0	26	136	8	198
8.0	24	203	24	193
9.0	70	951	68	211
10.0	7	961	90	218
11.0	13	989	93	243

3.2   Identifying Indirect Links

In this step indirect links are found. First matrix is formed showing direct similarity among artifacts. Next by using matrix multiplication resulting links are obtained.

Formation of Weight Matrix. In this step, we combine the correlation found from Subsect. 3.1 into a single weight matrix. If the total number of artifacts (requirement and source code classes) are N, then a weight matrix (WM) is of the order of N by N is formed.

Matrix Multiplication to Find Indirect Links. Matrix obtained in previous sub-step is taken as an input. In this sub-step, we recover the indirect links using matrix multiplication as in [26] because it considers all possible indirect links with a variation that instead of multiplying N times, we only multiply 5–6 times to reduce the complexity. We multiply WM^0 to itself which gives WM^1, to find indirect links of level 1 (means indirect coupling through one level). Similarly, WM^k is obtained, here k is taken based on the accuracy required. By adding the WM^0, WM^1, WM^2, WM^3.....WM^k, Resultant matrix (M) gives both direct and indirect links between requirements and source code. By choosing appropriate threshold, artifacts having similarity higher than threshold are chosen as correct links. Hence, RT links are obtained between use-cases and source code.

4   Results

As the proposed approach uses a weighted combination of change history and structural information based approaches for finding coupling among classes, a project having freely available source code, change history, well-documented use-cases, and traceability matrix is needed for validating results. Java project iTrust [28] used in [11], fits in above requirements. So, this paper uses it for validating the proposed methodology. Table 2 describes further details about the project. The original traceability matrix maintained by developers maps from use-cases to methods implementing them. So, we form a mapping between use-cases to classes (Oracle$_{iTrust}$) using available original traces, as our approach works for the class level granularity. Oracle$_{iTrust}$ matrix is used for validating the results.

Table 2. Details of project iTrust

Project name	Version number	Number of classes	Number of use-cases	Number of traces	KLOC
iTrust	11.0	243	34	603	25

4.1   Results Evaluation

For comparison of our proposed approach with structural and co-change coupling schemes, three well-known metrics Precision, Recall and F-measure are used, as done by most of the researchers [5–7, 10, 12, 22] as shown in by Eqs. (7), (8) and (9) respectively.

$$Precision = \frac{|Retrv \cap Corct|}{|Retrv|} \tag{7}$$

$$Recall = \frac{|Retrv \cap Corct|}{|Corct|} \tag{8}$$

$$F - measure = \frac{2 * Precision * Recall}{Precision + Recall} \tag{9}$$

Here, Retrv is set of retrieved links and Corct is set of correct links. As described in Sect. 3.1. for evaluating correlation among artifacts for finding RT links IR approaches are used. For this purpose, we use VSM based TraceMe [29] tool as VSM is among the best two IR approaches [27]. Comparison of TraceMe tool [29] with other available tools ADAMS Re-Trace [30], ReqAnalyst [31], etc. for RT link recovery has been done in [29], showing TraceMe as the best tool for RT link recovery. Our approach dynamically integrates structural and co-change coupling scheme as described in Sect. 3.

In project iTrust the number of classes changed up to a particular version is summarized in Table 2. Up to version 11.0, 93 distinct classes are modified out of 243 total classes. For this dataset $\lambda = 0.38$ and $\mu = 0.38$ are evaluated using Eqs. (3), (4) and (5). Weightage of change history based approach will be 0.38 and for structural based will be 0.62. So, by taking weightage 38% for co-change coupling and 62% for structural coupling ranked list is obtained using the approach described in Sect. 3. Resulting links are compared with Oracle$_{iTrust}$ and Precision, Recall and F-measure are evaluated. We have compared our approach with structural coupling and co-change coupling schemes in combination with IR, using Precision (%), Recall (%) and F-measure by varying threshold in range 0.0 to 1.0 with step-size 0.10 as shown in Figs. 2, 3 and 4 respectively. Step size 0.1 is taken to get a perfect tradeoff between accuracy of results and efforts required for calculations. If we take the step size greater that 0.1 (e.g. 0.2, 0.3) then we may miss important changes and if we will take less than 0.1 required calculations will be high. As shown in Fig. 4 F-measure for structural based approach and change history is not more than 0.35 whereas in case of proposed approach even 0.56 is achieved for range 0.4 to 0.6. Also, Fig. 2 shows that better precision can be achieved at lower threshold values for the proposed approach, which results into reduction of intensive efforts needed for filtering the false positives. So, threshold in range 0.4 to 0.6 is suggested for iTrust version 11.0.

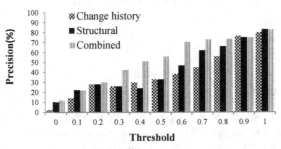

Fig. 2. Comparison based on Precision

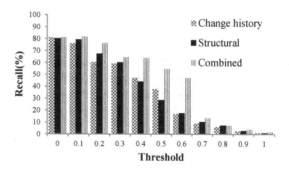

Fig. 3. Comparison based on Recall

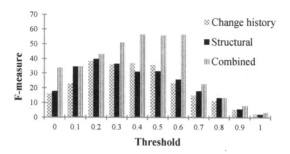

Fig. 4. Comparison based on F-measure

Based on above discussions and results, it is clear that the proposed approach can be used for finding more number of correct links with better precision in comparison to co-change coupling and structural coupling schemes. The proposed approach reduces the efforts required by software developers in finding actual correlation among artifacts. The proposed approach has been found to perform significantly better than others for every threshold value, although the best range of threshold value is software dependent and can be decided only after detailed experimentation.

5   Conclusion and Future Work

To improve IR, non-textual techniques like structural and co-change coupling among classes are frequently used in combination with IR. Unfortunately, if resulting output from IR approach contains some false positives, the combined approach may increase them further. To overcome this problem, we propose an automatic approach, in which we first improve IR using code ownership information and then use non-textual information for recovering indirect co-relation among artifacts. When commits are less, structural information is much more useful than change history approach for finding coupling. On contrary, as code evolves, the design degrades resulting in poor performance of structural information based technique in comparison to change history approach. Due to which, dynamic integration of structural and co-change coupling as complementary to IR is suggested. We have compared our approach with existing approaches by taking Precision, Recall, and F-measure metrics into consideration by varying threshold with step size 0.1. The results show that our combined approach outperforms the existing IR techniques for all threshold values and threshold in range 0.4 to 0.6 is suggested. Hence, proposed approach can assist software developers in better program understanding and software maintenance by finding actual correlation among artifacts.

The suggested threshold value is limited to this software only. In future, a detailed experimentation will be done to suggest threshold for other types of software applications. Also, indirect link recovery scheme can be improved in future to reduce the calculation efforts. For acceptability of our results, detailed study on softwares will be done having detailed documentation and change history.

References

1. Palmer, D.: Traceability in software requirements engineering. In: Thayer, R.H., Dorfman, M. (eds.), Los Alamitos, CA, pp. 412–422. IEEE Computer Society Press (2000)
2. Wright, S.: Requirements Traceability - What?, Why? and How?. In: Proceedings of the Colloquium by the Institution of Electrical Engineers Professional Group C1 (Software Engineering), London (1991)
3. Antoniol, G., Canfora, G., Casazza, G., Lucia, A.D., Merlo, E.: Recovering traceability links between code and documentation. IEEE Trans. Softw. Eng. **28**(10), 970–983 (2002). doi:10. 1109/TSE.2002.1041053
4. Harman, D.: Ranking algorithms. In: Information Retrieval: Data Structures and Algorithms. Prentice-Hall, Englewood Cliffs, NJ. pp. 363–392 (1992)
5. Baezayates, R., Ibeironeto, B.: Modern Information Retrieval, pp. 363–392. Prentice-Hall, Addison Wesley (1999)
6. Deerwester, S., Dumais, S.T., Harshman, R.: Indexing by latent semantic analysis. J. Am. Soc. Inf. Sci. **41**(6), 391–407 (1990)
7. Lucia, A.D., Fasano, F., Oliveto, R., Tortora, G.: Recovering traceability links in software artifact management systems using information retrieval methods. ACM Trans. Softw. Eng. Methodol. **16**(4), 13–63 (2007). doi:10.1145/1276933.1276934. Article no. 13
8. McMillan, C., Poshyvanyk, D., Revelle, M.: Combining textual and structural analysis of software artifacts for traceability link recovery. In: Proceedings of TEFSE, pp. 41–48 (2009). doi:10.1109/TEFSE.2009.5069582
9. Panichella, A., McMillan, C., Moritz, E., Palmieri, D., Oliveto, R., Poshyvanyk, D., Lucia, A.D.: When and how using structural information to improve IR-based traceability recovery. In: Proceedings of the 17th European Conference on Software Maintenance and Reengineering, Genova, Italy, pp. 199–208. IEEE CS Press (2013). doi:10.1109/CSMR. 2013.29
10. Kagdi, H., Maletic, J.I., Sharif, B.: Mining software repositories for traceability links. In: ICPC, pp. 145–154. IEEE Computer Society (2007). doi:10.1109/ICPC.2007.28
11. Ali, N., Jaafar, F., Hassan, A.E.: Leveraging historical co-change information for requirements traceability. In: 20th Working Conference on Reverse Engineering (WCRE), pp. 361–370 (2013). doi:10.1109/WCRE.2013.6671311

12. Diaz, D., Bavota, G., Marcus, A., Oliveto, R., Takahashi, S., Lucia, A.D.: Using code ownership to improve IR-based traceability link recovery. In: ICPC, San Francisco, CA, USA, IEEE, pp. 123–132 (2013). doi:10.1109/ICPC.2013.6613840

13. Marcus, A., Maletic, J.I.: Recovering documentation-to-source-code traceability links using latent semantic indexing. In: Proceedings of 25th International Conference on Software Engineering, Portland, OR, pp. 125–135 (2003)

14. Lucia, A.D., Fasano, F., Oliveto, R., Tortora, G.: Enhancing an artefact management system with traceability recovery feature. In: Proceedings of the 20th IEEE International Conference on Software Maintenance (ICSM), pp. 306–315 (2004). doi:10.1109/ICSM.2004.1357816

15. Lucia, A.D., Oliveto, R., Sgueglia, P.: Incremental approach and user feedbacks: a silver bullet for traceability recovery? In: 22nd IEEE International Conference on Software Maintenance (ICSM), pp. 299–309 (2006). doi:10.1109/ICSM.2006.32

16. Lucia, A.D., Fasano, F., Oliveto, R., Tortora, G.: Can information retrieval techniques effectively support traceability link recovery? In: Proceedings of the 14th IEEE International Conference on Program Comprehension (ICPC), pp. 307–316 (2006). doi:10.1109/ICPC.2006.15

17. Bavota, G., Lucia, A.D., Oliveto, R., Tortora, G.: Enhancing software artifact traceability recovery processes with link count information. Inf. Softw. Technol. J. Elsevier, pp. 163–182 (2014). doi:10.1016/j.infsof.2013.08.004

18. Lucia, A.D., Penta, M.D., Oliveto, R., Panichella, A., Panichella, S.: Improving IR-based traceability recovery using smoothing filters. In: Proceedings of the 19th International Conference on Program Comprehension, pp. 21–30. IEEE (2014). doi:10.1109/ICPC.2011.34

19. Nishikawa, K., Oshima, K., Washizaki, H., Mibe, R., Fukazawa, Y.: Recovering transitive traceability links among software artifacts. In: ICSME, Bremen, Germany, pp. 576–580. IEEE (2015). doi:10.1109/ICSM.2015.7332517

20. Parashar, A., Chhabra, J.K.: Improving modular structure of software system using structural and lexical dependency. Inf. Softw. Technol. 82, 96–120 (2017). doi:10.1016/j.infsof.2016.09.011

21. Parashar, A., Chhabra, J.K.: Harmony search based remodularization for object-oriented software systems. Comput. Lang. Syst. Struct. **47**(2), 153–169 (2017). doi:10.1016/j.cl.2016.09.003

22. Parashar, A., Chhabra, J.K.: Package restructuring based on software change history. Natl. Acad. Sci. Lett. **40**, 1–7 (2016). doi:10.1007/s40009-016-0472-y

23. Parashar, A., Chhabra, J.K.: Mining software change data stream to predict changeability of classes of object-oriented software system. Evolv. Syst.- Interdiscip. J. Adv. Sci. Technol. **7**(2), 117–128 (2016). doi:10.1007/s12530-016-9151-y

24. Parashar, A., Chhabra, J.K.: Measurement of package-changeability by mining change-history. In: Procedia Comput. Sci. 46 443–448 (201). doi:10.1016/j.procs.2015.02.042

25. Parasha, A., Chhabra, J.K.: An approach for clustering class coupling metrics to mine object oriented software components. Int. Arab J. Inf. Technol. **13**(3), 239–248 (2016)

26. Parashar, A., Chhabra, J.K.: Assessing impact of class change by mining change associations. In: Int. Arab J. Inf. Technol. (IAJIT) (2016, accepted paper)

27. Abadi, A., Nisenson, M., Simionovici, Y.: A traceability technique for specifications. In: Proceedings of the 16th IEEE International Conference on Program Comprehension, pp. 103–112 (2008). doi:10.1109/ICPC.2008.30

28. iTrust: Role-Based Healthcare Project. http://agile.csc.ncsu.edu/iTrust/

29. Bavota, G., Colangelo, L., Lucia, A.D., Fusco, S., Oliveto, R., Panichella, A.: TraceME: traceability management in eclipse. In: 28th IEEE (ICSM) (2012). doi:10.1109/ICSM.2012. 6405343
30. Lucia, A.D., Oliveto, R., Tortora, G.: ADAMS Re-Trace: traceability link recovery via latent semantic indexing. In: ICSE, pp. 839–842 (2008). doi:10.1109/CSMR.2005.7
31. Lormans, M., Deursen, A.V.: Can LSI help reconstructing requirements traceability in design and test? In: CSMR, pp. 45–54 (2006). doi:10.1109/CSMR.2006.13

Information Systems

Bilingual Code-Mixing in Indian Social Media Texts for Hindi and English

Rajesh Kumar$^{(\boxtimes)}$ and Pardeep Singh

Department of Computer Science and Engineering,
National Institute of Technology Hamirpur, Hamirpur 177-005, India
rajesh11335@gmail.com, AVAGAMAN@gmail.com

Abstract. Code Mixing (CM) is an important in the area of Natural Language Processing (NLP) but it is more challenging technique. There are many techniques available for code-mixing but till now less work has been done for code mixing. In this paper we discussed the various approaches used for code mixing and classifying existing code mixing algorithm according to their techniques. Most of people do not always use the Unicode that means only one language during chatting on Facebook, Gmail, Twitter, etc. If some people do not understand the Hindi language, then it is very difficult task for these people to understanding the meaning of code-mixedsentences. For correct Hindi words we used the converter form Hindi words to English words. But most of the words are not correct words according to dictionary and also the code-mixed sentences contained the short form, abbreviation words, phonetic typing, etc. So we have used the character N-gram pruning which is one of the most popular and successful technique of Natural Language Processing (NLP) with dictionary based approaches for language identification of social media text. This paper proposed a scheme which improve the translation by removing the phonetic typing, abbreviation words, shortcut, Hindi word and emotions.

Keywords: Code mixing (CM) · Natural language processing (NLP) · Creative typing (CT) · Abbreviation (A) · Contracted (C) · Code switching (CS) · Language identification (LID)

1 Introduction

Code-Mixing refer to mixing the two or more languages written in roman script, like Hindi and English, English and Bengali and so on, along with short form, abbreviation words, phonetic typing and emotions. Code-mixing occur when someone who don't express their words in common language like English (which know both) but they express these words in own language (another local language but not in English). Detecting the language of social media texts such as twitter data or Facebook data is a challenging task because the social media texts do not contain the appropriate as dictionary that is, the words contained shortcuts, contracted words, phonetic typing, etc. This is the main reason that in social media texts, there are highly percentage of spelling error due to creative spellings ("ni8" for "night"), wordplay ("freeee" for "free"), abbreviations ("LOL" for "laugh out loud" and so on [1]. There is many

© Springer Nature Singapore Pte Ltd. 2017
D. Singh et al. (Eds.): ICAICR 2017, CCIS 712, pp. 121–129, 2017.
DOI: 10.1007/978-981-10-5780-9_11

research on detect the language of social media texts but more of them are for only English words, whereas the words of social media texts are mixture of languages along with creative typing, shortcuts. In social media, non–English speakers do not always use common language (one language) to write their own language, one can say that the maximum possibility of social media texts is code mixed type. The automatic language detector fails for social media texts and also it is very challenging task to detect the language at word level [1]. We know that social media text is in code-mixed form so understanding the meaning of words is very difficult to users. One has say that, due to anomaly the language of words represents to another and for correcting these types of words there is no any algorithm is available. So it is found that, a word can be written in more than one different words (spelling are different). For example, the word bajar is found written as: bazar, bazaar, bajaar, bajjar, bazzar [2].

These are Few Types of Words in Code Mix Text in Indian Social Media:

Abbreviations: This types of words are made by adding the first character of all words. we can say that this is a short form of words. e.g. the abbreviation of "laugh out loud" is 'LOL'.

Wordplay: This type of words contains repeated single character in a words. The user used this type of words to express their emotions. In this anomaly the spelling of a word is extended by repeating one of the character multiple times. e.g. "Gooddddddd" for 'good' [2].

Slang words: The internet and mobile user has its own way to write the text for expressing someemotions. Sometimes it is different from a general term which used more frequently, the user used this type of word for reducing the number of character in words by giving phonetic effect to the words. e.g. "gud ni8" for 'good night', "f9" for 'fine', "4ever" for 'forever', "10q" for 'thank you'.

Phonetic Variation: Pronunciation of a word may depend on the dialects of a language. These variations result in a single word having multiple spellings when written in Roman script. e.g. the word "bhi" could be written as: v, bhe, be, vi.

2   Background and Related Works

As English is a universal language and it is found very often in code-mixed words with some other language. This is especially true because most of the people used English language for studied or spoken in the community as the second language. In such cases, the user is most probably used English with his/her local language like (Hindi, Bengali, Marathi or any other local languages) to form code-mixing [3]. Most of the people use two languages at the same time in same conversation, this is the natural tendency of human due to this bilingual (e.g. mixing of Hindi and English, English and Bengali) is exist. The phenomenon of code-mixing has been occurring since last 30 years. Gold [4] investigate the problem of language identification and also tackle the problem of code switching and he describe some feature of its.

It has recently drawn wider attention. Several linguists, we can say that if the speaker use two or more languages to speak or write the utterance in same conversation at the same time may be utterance change or not is known as linguistic code switching [5]. Nguyen and Dogruöz [6] they firstly use dictionary lookup approach for defining the language of word, if words are not found in dictionaries, then they used language model, this is called dictionary with language model. In language model they build a character n-gram language model for each language where maximum n-gram length is 5.

Using automatic language identification, one can focus on identifying both spoken language as well as written texts. One has been studied the language identification of speech where, the Markov chain model is a function which defined the probabilistic function of language [7]. Dutta et al. [8] investigate the problem for ambiguous word they follow the post-processing method (that is compare the language of previous and next word for detecting the language of current word). But there is problem because this is not a legal to predict the language of ambiguous word as compare to previous and next word language [1].

One hasinvestigated the problem for language identification of words they given theapproach using SVM with n-gram count and they produced better result as compared to language model. Canvar and Trenkle [9] has used n-gram language models for text categorization which is very popular for language identification. They proposed an approach for language identification using n-gram profiling and pruning. In this they create the language profile of each language and calculate the weight between word profile and each language profile and then select the language of words which has smallest distance as compared to each language profile. They used the feature of n-gram pruning and dictionary model in SVM classification for language identification. Since 1980s it is defined that code switching has a part of bilingual and multilingual language use [1]. Code switching is the term which is defined as those sentence which has alternation in language in same conversation. One has said that in code mixing the most used language is known as matrix language and the another local language is known as embedded language. The detection of language of alternation code switching is very difficult task because in alternation code switching the sentences contains the words which belong to alternate languages. Like first word of sentence is in English then other word is different from English it may be Hindi, Bengali or any other [10].

There are Following Types of Code Switching Such as:

Intra sentential switching: The sentence which contains two or more than two languages are known as intra sentential switching. e.g. kitni cute baby hai.

Inter sentential switching: In inter sentential switching the first sentence in one language and another sentence is in totally different language (in bilingual Hindi and English) if one sentence is in English then next sentence will be on Hindi language.

Tag switching: If the user used either the tag line, or word, or both form language English to Hindi is called tag switching.

One has distinguished between "mixing" and "switching" is that, in mixing the topic of matter is constant and all have knowledge about both languages. While in switching the matter of conversation may be changed [1].

3 Methodology

In this paper, we identify the language of words, remove the phonetic typing, abbreviation words, shortcut, Hindi words and emotions. First of all, we break the data set (input) into sentences and then we break the sentences into words (one by one). After breaking the sentence into words we stored the words of sentence in a list. And from list, we take a word for identifying the language of words of a sentence until the sentence not end (means word is null). First we check the word in English dictionary if the word is found then we store the word in the output list (we make a list for storing the output) and go for next word.

   If the word is not found in English dictionary the we go for Hindi dictionary (according to flow chart from Fig. 1), if it found in Hindi dictionary then we convert the Hindi word into corresponding English word and stored into output list and go for next word. And if the word is also not found in any dictionary (neither English nor Hindi dictionary) then we check for Abbreviation (A), Shortcuts (S), Contracted words (C) and Creative Typing (CT). For these types of words, we keep a list which contained these types of words with their respective original word. If the word is found in any one from these types of words, then we replaced the word by their respective original word and stored into output list and go for next word. Else the word is not found in any dictionaries (Hindi and English) and also not found in any type of words from A, S, C and CT. Then we go for spell checker, in spell checker there are two sections, first is detection of wordplay and another is correct the misspell words. Then we check for wordplay, the wordplay word is like "ohhhhhhhhh", this type of words is an incorrect English word, because the detector fails to detect the language of this type of words. This is incorrect due to users to express their feeling. For detection of wordplay one has used regular expression and removed the repeating character that presents three times consecutively by a single character that character is same character in words (same as repeating character), and after correcting the word we stored it into output list and go for next word. Else if it is not the wordplay word then we go for correction for misspell word, for correcting the misspell words, we use the most popular technique of Natural language processing (NLP) is character N-gram pruning along with dictionary based, after correcting the misspell word stored the correct word in output list and go for next word. Similarly, for each word of each sentences.

3.1 Language Identification (LID)

We tackle two major challenges when we identifying the language of words in code-mixing social media text. Firstly, people often used the words which is not appropriate from dictionary means the words has not correct spell for both either Hindi or English words. Secondly, some Hindi words are similar to English words and also having the same spelling. Here, the sub-objective is that we have to identify the language of words of code-mixed social media text which contained English words and Hindi words. one has said that, Social media text contains a named entities (NEs) which first character is capital and this type of words are from any languages like Hindi or English. So, we consider the NEs as normal words. Thus, language of words is English (E), Hindi (H) [8].

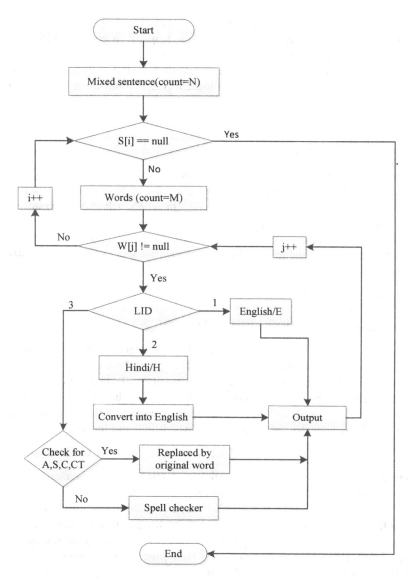

Fig. 1. Flow chart of methodology

3.2 Dictionary Based Detection

We can use the dictionary for language identification and also check for spelling error or not, for example if the word is belonging to English language but it not found in dictionary then the maximum probability for error in spelling of words. One has one this technique for the identification of language, but he faced with a many problems due to the social media text is full of noise like user used the words which is not based on dictionary or they used anomaly which dictionary never detect the language of words. In dictionary based method for language identification, first of all check the words from dictionary, the most probably that the language is either English or Hindi. First of all, find the words in English dictionary, if it found then check for next words, otherwise find the words in Hindi dictionary (Hindi WorldNet). If the words have not found in any dictionary then go for spelling checker, Abbreviation words, phonetic errors, contracted words, shortcuts, etc.

3.3   Character N-Gram Pruning

Character N-gram pruning is a technique which is used to extract the group of characters from a word. One can use this technique to correct those types of words which has misspell in either prefix in words or suffix in words. Character n-gram is most popular and successful technique of NLP. we can take the value of n for n-gram is different length at the same time. One has said that we can append blanks to prefix and suffix of the string when the length of n is more than the letter of extracted words. For example, we apply character n-gram on the word "GOOD" then we get,

Bi-grams: _G, GO, OO, OD, D_
Tri-grams: _GO, GOO, OOD, OD_, D_ _
Quad-grams: _GOO, GOOD, OOD_, OD_ _, D_ _ _

In general, we can say that, the number of bigram, trigram, quad grams and so on, has N + 1 extracted words where N is the length of original word. The benefit of using n-gram is that every string is decomposed into small words, and the other benefit of n-gram is that after apply the n-gram on word the words are broken into different many words which size is small as compare to original words so we can easily remove misspell words by consider only those words which is found in dictionary [9].

If the Words are not Found in any Dictionaries, then Check for Followings:

Detection of shortcuts: In conversations, maximum text which containedshort forms of words like "engg" for "engineering", "fav" for "favorite". For correcting shortcuts words, we keep a list and their corresponding original words.

Detection of Abbreviation words: identifyingthe language of ambiguous words which occur in both the languages (Hindi and English) is by default marked as English [5]. e.g. the abbreviation word "Gun", meaning in English is "weapon" whereas in Hindi the meaning is "characteristics", "advantage" etc. For detecting the abbreviation words, we keep a list and match the ambiguous words from list and replaced by corresponding original words.

Detection of contracted words: For contracted words we also keep the list, if the words are found in the list then we replaced the contracted words by their corresponding original words. e.g. the contracted words "I've", this word will replace by the original word "I have" form the list which contains contracted words.

Detection of Wordplay: There are some words in social media text that are created by users, e.g., "ohhhhhhhhh". From example the word "ohhhhhhhhh" is misspelled English word. We can say that this types of words are misspelled by users. For detecting these types of words one has used regular expression and removed the repeating character that presents three times consecutively by a single character (single character is the repeated character) [8]. If the words are not the wordplay, then there is a need of algorithm for detecting and correcting the misspell words. which is character n-gram pruning with dictionary based technique. In this technique, first of all pruned the words using character n-gram (Assume the maximum value of n is 5) and after pruning make a list which contain the pruned words by their frequencies (maximum to minimum), for finding the language of words we match the pruned words in dictionary [9].

Ex: - homea
If N = 3 → hom, ome, mea
If N = 4 → **home(/E)**, omea
If N = 5 → homea

4 Analysis of Methodology

In this section, we are going to discuss the experiments we carried out and the results obtained. From the above Fig. 1, first of all we define the boundary of sentences and then break the sentences into words. After that we apply techniques for language identification. We have used one of the most popular techniques for language identification of word which is character n-grams with dictionary-based technique.

First we have checked the words in English dictionary if found then mark "\E" for English else we go for Hindi dictionary if found in Hindi dictionary then mark "\H" for Hindi and convert the words into appropriate English words which gives the same meaning. If the word has not found in any dictionary means the word is misspelling, then we check for Shortcuts (S), Abbreviation (A), Creative typing (CT) and Contracted words (C). We keep a list which contained these types of words and their corresponding original words. If the words are found in one of from these words in the list, then we replaced that word by corresponding original words. Otherwise we go for spell checker. In spell checker we have used the character n-gram pruning with dictionary based. We consider the language of ambiguous word is English(/E) and also we first find the words in English dictionary so, in this methodology by default the language of ambiguous words will be English(/E). First of all, we pruned the misspell word and store them into local memory by their frequencies (from maximum to minimum) and then we compared from dictionary and then mark the language of the misspell words. Matching the pruned word from maximum to minimum frequencies in dictionary.

We are Going to Discuss some Sentences of Code Mixed Types:

Sentence 1: Mujhe phy me 65 aud math me 88 marks hai
Google Trans: I have 88 in Math and 65 in physics marks.
Algo + Google Trans: I have88 in mathematics and 65 in physics marks.

Sentence 2: But mai physics padhana chahta hu DU me
Google Trans: But I want to study Physics in DU.
Algo + Google Trans: But I want to study physics in Delhi University

In this sentence 2, here the word "DU" is abbreviation word for 'Delhi University' and "phy" is the short form of 'physics'. We can say that if the sentence is belonging to only one language (like Hindi) without any anomaly or there is not code mixing in sentence then the Google translation give the betterperformance but if there is code mixing in sentences (mixing of any two languages like Hindi and English) and also anomaly is present then the google translation give wrong output or less performance as compared to performance of translating the sentences which contain only one language without anomaly.

Sentence3: Bt I am nt eligbl 2 dt course due 2 my 12th marks
Google Trans: Bt I am nt eligbl 2 dt course due 2 my 12thmarks
Algo + Google Trans: But I am not eligible to that course due to my 12th marks

In sentence 3, the "nt" is creative typing for 'not', "4" is also creative typing for 'for', "dt" is creative typing for 'that', and "bcoz" is short form of 'because'. These types of shortcuts, creative typing, abbreviation word has been removed by the methodology which we have discussed in Sect. 1.3 and after applying the methodology machine translation will give the better performance as compared to simple Google translation. The Google translator give better performance when the sentence is belonging to only one language either English or Hindi, but if there is mixing of languages in a single sentence then the translator gives the wrong output which does not make any sense and also when there are some shortcuts, creative typing, abbreviation words are present in sentence then the translator definitely give the wrong answer.

5   Conclusion

This paper has presented the study of detecting the code mixing context like social media texts. In social medial texts, the identification of language is very difficult task, at word level or taken level. In each sentence of social media can contain the words which belong to several languages. This paper considered only two languages (English and Hindi). First identify the language of words and convert the Hindi word into English word. This paper removed the problem due to shortcuts, abbreviation words, contracted words, creative typing, wordplay and also remove the misspell word. Used character n-gram with dictionary based which is most popular and successful technique for language identification of words.

References

1. Das, A., Gambäck, B.: Code-mixed in social media text. In: Proceedings of the 11th International Conference on Natural Language Processing, Goa, India, December 2014
2. Sharma, S., Srinivas, P., Balabantaray, R.: Text normalization of code mix and sentiment analysis. In: International Conference on Advances in Computing, Communications and Informatics (ICACCI) (2015)

3. Shrestha, P.: Incremental n-gram approach for language identification in code switched text. In: Proceedings of the First Workshop on Computational Approaches to Code Switching, Doha, Qatar, 25 October 2014, pp. 133–138. Association for Computational Linguistics (2014)
4. Gold, E.M.: Language identification in the limit. Inf. Control **10**(5), 447–474 (1967)
5. Sharma, S., Srinivas, P., Balabantaray, R.: Sentiment analysis of code- mix script. In: International Conference on Computing and Network Communications (CoCoNet) (2015)
6. Nguyen, D., Dogruöz, A.S.: Word level language identification in online multilingual communication. In: Proceedings of the Conference on Empirical Methods in Natural Language Processing, ACL, Seattle, Washington, pp. 857–862, October 2013
7. House, A.S., Neuburg, E.P.: Toward automatic identification of the language of an utterance. Preliminary methodological considerations. J. Acoust. Soc. Am. **62**, 708–713 (1977)
8. Dutta, S., Saha, T., Banerjee, S., Naskar, S.: Text normalization in code-mixed social media text. In: IEEE 2nd International Conference on Recent Trends in Information Systems (ReTIS) (2015)
9. Cavnar, W.B., Trenkle, J.M.: N-gram based text categorization. In: Proceedings of the Third Annual Symposium on Document Analysis and Information Retrieval, pp. 161–175 (1994)
10. Das, A., Gambäck, B.: Identifying languages at the word level in code-mixed indian social media text. In: Proceedings of the 11th International Conference on Natural Language Processing, Goa, India, pp. 169–178, December 2014

Performance Evaluation and Comparative Study of Color Image Segmentation Algorithm

Rajiv Kumar[1]([⊠]) [iD] and S. Manjunath[2]

[1] Botho University, Gaborone, Botswana
rajiv.kumar@bothouniversity.ac.bw
[2] BNM Institute of Technology, Bangalore, India
smanjunath@bnmit.in

Abstract. In this research paper, authors have been proposed the color image segmentation algorithm by using HSI (hue, saturation and intensity) color model. The HSI color model is used to get the color information of the given image. The boundary of the image is extracted by using edge detection algorithm, whereas, the image regions are filled where the boundaries make the closure. Both HSI color information and edge detection are applied separately and simultaneously. The color segmented image is obtained by taking the union of HSI color information and edge detection. The performance of the proposed algorithm is evaluated and compared with existing region-growing algorithm by considering three parameters, precision (P), recall (R) and F1 value. The accuracy of the proposed algorithm is also measured by using precision-recall (PR) and receiver operator characteristics (ROC) analysis. The efficiency of the proposed algorithm has been tested on more than 1500 images from UCD (University College Dublin) image dataset and other resources. The experiment results show that the efficiency of proposed algorithm is found very significant. MATLAB is used to implement the proposed algorithm.

Index Terms: Color · Edge detection · Image processing · Image segmentation · MATLAB

1 Introduction

Image segmentation is the basic step to understand and analysis the given image. It divides the image into several constituent regions in such a way that any two adjacent regions may not necessarily be homogeneous. There are plenty of algorithms which have been developed for gray-scale images over a few decades. But, unfortunately, scientific community has been less concentrated on the development of algorithms for color images due to their complexities [1]. Color images are difficult to process and time-consuming. But, when color images have been segmented, they provide more information as compare to monochrome images. The reason is that three primary colors, namely, red (R), green (G) and blue (B) are processed separately and then, they are combined together to obtain the color segmented image [2, 3]. An edge or boundary of an image is the discontinuity in the intensity level of the image. This

© Springer Nature Singapore Pte Ltd. 2017
D. Singh et al. (Eds.): ICAICR 2017, CCIS 712, pp. 130–144, 2017.
DOI: 10.1007/978-981-10-5780-9_12

helps us to achieve the high-level task such as recognition of object and interpretation of a scene [4].

Researchers have evaluated the different methods for segmentation algorithms [5, 6]. Reference [7] shows the proposed fuzzy-based watershed algorithm which has been combined with region based classical watershed algorithm using HSV color space. Researcher have performed the extensive survey and compared the various image segmentation algorithms such as k-mean clustering, edge-based, thresholding, neural network and region-based algorithms [8–11]. Reference [12] shows survey the theory of edge detection for image segmentation using soft computing approach based on fuzzy logic, genetic algorithm and neural network. The researchers compared the various edge detectors like Sobel, Canny, Prewitt, Robert etc. They have obtained the better results in case of Canny operator [13–15]. Reference [16] shows the development of the graph-based algorithms to segment the image and extract the visual objects. Reference [17] shows the performance of the system level evaluation, subjective, unsupervised and supervised segmentation algorithms. Reference [18] shows the proposed generic framework for the evaluation of segmentation algorithms by taking the multiple regions in the segment partitions Reference [19] represents the framework to evaluate the image segmentation techniques by considering three factors namely, accuracy (validity), precision (reliability) and efficiency (viability). Reference [20] presents the evaluation criterion based on measurement of precision of boundary segmentation. The human segmentation results have compared and tested with automatic segmentation algorithms. Reference [21] shows the proposed statistical objective performance analysis and detector parameter selection by different detector parameters. The results have been derived using receiver operating characteristic (ROC) analysis and chi-square test.

This paper is organized as: Sect. 2 shows the proposed algorithm. Section 3 describes the algorithm. Section 4 explains the performance criteria for the algorithm. Authors compared and evaluate the performance of proposed algorithm with the existing region-growing algorithm in Sect. 5. Finally, Sect. 6 concludes the paper.

2 Proposed Algorithm

In the proposed color image segmentation algorithm, the color information of the image is represented by hue (H), saturation (S) and intensity (I) components. The HSI components are calculated by setting the threshold which is based on the hue, saturation and intensity separately. The HSI component has been used to analyze the color because hue, saturation and intensity can process the image separately. The H, S and I are independent of each other. So, there is no need to correlate them while processing the image. On the other hand, if RGB components have been used, the color of the segmented image will change on modifying the value of few pixels. When an image is segmented by the HSI component, there may be lack of boundaries present in the image. To compensate this, an algorithm has been used to extract the boundaries of the segmented image [22]. The flowchart of proposed algorithm is shown in Fig. 1.

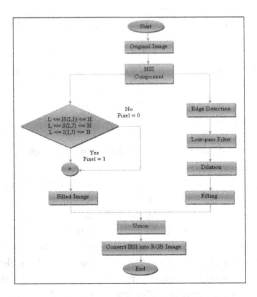

Fig. 1. Flowchart of proposed algorithm (Color figure online)

3 Algorithm

```
Step 1:  Select an image of size 256 × 256.
Step 2:  Extract the color information by taking hue (H), saturation (S) and
         intensity (I) separately from the given image. This is   done by set up
         the threshold which is based on the pixel values of H, S and I.
Step 3:  Extract the boundary of the image by using edge detection algorithm.
Step 4:  Perform the morphology operation to connect the disconnected boundaries.
Step 5:  Take the union of step 2 and step 4 so that both color information and
         boundary information could be combined together.
Step 6:  Finally, perform the morphology operation to remove the noise present in
         the image.
```

3.1 Working of Proposed Algorithm

The color RGB images have been taken from the UCD (University College Dublin) image dataset [23]. First, the given RGB image has been converted into HSI image by using the formula as given by Eq. (1–3).

$$H = cos^{-1}\left[\frac{\frac{1}{2}(R - G) + (R - B)}{[(R - G)^2 + (R - B)(G - B)]^{\frac{1}{2}}}\right], 0° \ll H \ll 180° \qquad (1)$$

$$S = 1 - \frac{3}{(R + G + B)}[min(R, G, B)], S \in [0, 1] \qquad (2)$$

$$I = \frac{1}{3}(R + G + B), I \in [0, 1] \qquad (3)$$

The edges of the given image have been obtained by using the edge detection algorithm. Then, segmentation operation has been performed on the image. Both edge and segmented image are combined together. Both edge and HSI image are also combined together. Morphology operation has been performed to connect the disconnected boundaries. Finally, the obtained segmented image is merged with the original image to get the color segmented image. This is shown in Fig. 2.

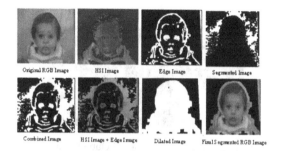

Fig. 2. Working of proposed algorithm (Color figure online)

3.2 Results

The authors have selected 290 images from UCD (University College Dublin) Image dataset and other resources. These images are partially segmented from the original image. The input and corresponding output images are shown in Figs. (3, 4, 5, 6 and 7).

Fig. 3. (a) Input image 1 (b) output image 1

Fig. 4. (a) Input image 2 (b) output image 2

Fig. 5. (a) Input image 3 (b) output image 3

Fig. 6. (a) Input image 4 (b) Output image 4

Fig. 7. (a) Input image 5 (b) output image 5

4   Evaluation Criterion of Proposed Algorithm

As the number of developed algorithms have been increased in the past decade, there is need to evaluate the algorithms which are based on some criterions. There are experimental and analytical methods which have been used for the objective evaluation about the quality of color segmented images. The experimental methods are used to evaluate, interpret and comparison of color image segmentation algorithms. The analytical methods are used to find the complexity, robustness and analysis of the algorithms.

In this research work, the authors have been used three evaluation criterions, namely, Precision (P), Recall (R) and F1 value to evaluate the performance of the proposed algorithm with the existing one. The parameters P, R and F1 value are used to characterize the efficiency of the proposed algorithm. Authors have also been used

Receiver Operator Characteristics (ROC) curves and Precision-Recall (PR) curves to show the performance of the proposed algorithm.

ROC curves are generally used for binary decision problems in machine learning. However, in the case of image databases, PR curves provide more information about the performance of the algorithms. The ROC space and PR space are closely related such that a curve dominates in ROC space if and only if it also dominates in PR space. The ROC curves represent how correctly classified positive examples vary with the incorrectly classified negative examples. On the other hand, PR curves are used for retrieval of information. The ROC and PR space differ in visually representation of the curves.

The parameters P, R and F1 value are used as evaluation criterions to evaluate and compare the proposed algorithm with the existing region-growing algorithm. These evaluation criterions are applied on the color images of UCD database. These parameters compare the boundaries of the color images which have been segmented by proposed algorithm and region-growing algorithm. It has been shown in Fig. 8.

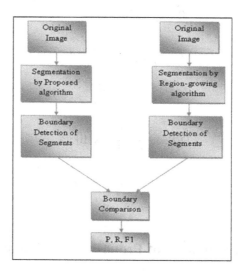

Fig. 8. Principal block diagram of evaluation criterion. (Color figure online)

In the binary decision problem, the classifiers label the examples either positive or negative. The decision given by classifier is represented by a structure which is known as contingency table or confusion matrix. The contingency table has four categories: True Positives (TP) refers to examples correctly labeled as positives. False Positives (FP) are examples incorrectly labeled as positives. True Negatives (TN) refers to examples correctly labeled as negatives. False Negatives (FN) are examples incorrectly labeled as negatives. A contingency table or confusion matrix has been shown in Table 1.

The contingency table is used to construct a point either in PR space or ROC space. In ROC space, False Positive Rate (FPR) and True Positive Rate (TPR) are plotted as

Table 1. Contingency table or confusion matrix

	Actual positives	Actual negatives
Predicted positives	TP	FP
Predicted negatives	FN	TN

X-axis and Y-axis respectively. FPR calculates the fraction of negative examples which are classified as positive, while, TPR calculates the fraction of positive examples which are correctly labeled. On the other hand, in PR space, Recall (R) and Precision (P) are plotted on the X-axis and Y-axis respectively. Precision (P) calculates the fraction of positive examples which are truly positive, while, Recall (R) is same as TPR. Table 1 provides the definition for each metric. The contingency table is used as a function which defines a point either in PR or in ROC space. For example, given a matrix A, RECALL (A) returns the Recall associated with A. The P, R, F1 value, TPR and FPR are given by Eqs. (4–8).

$$R = \frac{TP}{TP + FN} \times 100\% \tag{4}$$

$$P = \frac{TP}{TP + FP} \times 100\% \tag{5}$$

$$F1 = \frac{2PR}{P + R} \tag{6}$$

$$TPR = \frac{TP}{TP + FN} \times 100\% \tag{7}$$

$$FPR = \frac{FP}{FP + TN} \times 100\% \tag{8}$$

5 Performance Evaluation of Proposed and Region-Growing Algorithm

The performance of proposed algorithm and existing region-growing algorithm are evaluated and compared by taking more than 1500 color images from UCD image dataset and other resources. Authors have used two different methods for comparative analysis. In the first methods, receiver operator characteristics (ROC) analysis and precision-recall (PR) analysis have been consider. In the other method, the evaluation parameters namely, precision (P), recall (R) and F1 value are taken.

5.1 Performance Measurement of Proposed and Existing Region-Growing Algorithm by Precision-Recall (PR) and Receiver Operator Characteristic (ROC)

The authors have measured and compared the performance of both algorithms by taking parameters precision (P), true-positive rate (TPR) and false-positive rate (FPR). TPR measures the fraction of positive examples which have been correctly labeled, while, FPR measures the fraction of negative examples which have been misclassified as positive. This is shown in Table 2.

Table 2. Comparison of proposed and existing region-growing algorithm by taking parameters P, TPR and FPR

Image	Precision (P)		True-positive rate (TPR)		False-positive rate (TPR)	
	Proposed method	Region-growing	Proposed method	Region-growing	Proposed method	Region-growing
1	0.5329	0.6956	0.6620	0.6799	0.4190	0.3576
2	0.4853	0.6708	0.6451	0.5220	0.4389	0.4362
3	0.3975	0.6157	0.6865	0.6852	0.4336	0.3762
4	0.5123	0.7577	0.7495	0.7349	0.4299	0.3428
5	0.4272	0.6663	0.6927	0.5888	0.4268	0.3969
6	0.4716	0.5864	0.7696	0.5483	0.3905	0.4145
7	0.6139	0.7758	0.7691	0.6947	0.4097	0.3711
8	0.4703	0.8052	0.6924	0.6880	0.4098	0.3002
9	0.4031	0.7025	0.6195	0.5794	0.4702	0.4158
10	0.5680	0.6349	0.7788	0.7533	0.2659	0.2474

The graph of above image dataset has been shown in Figs. (9, 10, 11, 12, 13, 14, 15, 16, 17 and 18).

The experiment results have been shown that the proposed algorithm detected true pixel 8.45% more than existing region-growing algorithm. But, unfortunately, it also detect false pixel 9.77% more than existing algorithm.

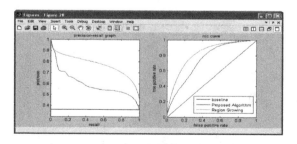

Fig. 9. PR and ROC curve of image 1

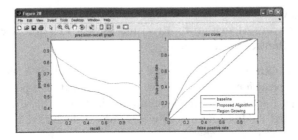

Fig. 10. PR and ROC curve of image 2

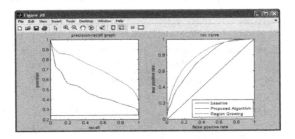

Fig. 11. PR and ROC curve of image 3

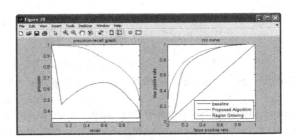

Fig. 12. PR and ROC curve of image 4

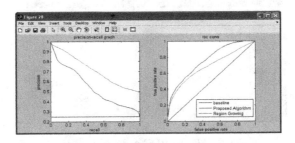

Fig. 13. PR and ROC curve of Image 5

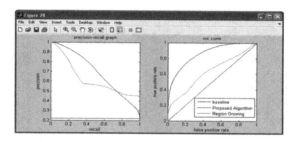

Fig. 14. PR and ROC curve of image 6

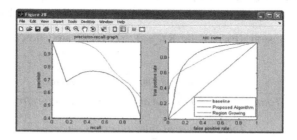

Fig. 15. PR and ROC curve of image 7

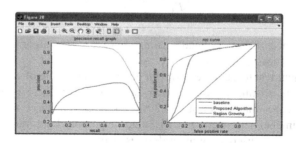

Fig. 16. PR and ROC curve of image 8

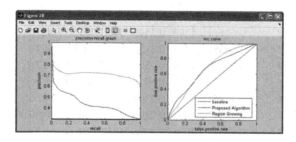

Fig. 17. PR and ROC curve of image 9

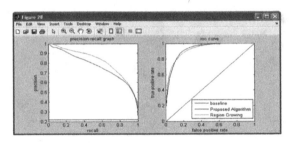

Fig. 18. PR and ROC curve of image 10

5.2 Performance Measure of Proposed Model and Existing Region-Growing Algorithm by Precision (P), Recall (R) and F1 Value

The value of precision (P), recall (R) and F1 value are shown in Eqs. (9–11) respectively.

$$P = \frac{Total\ number\ of\ relevant\ pixels\ retrived}{Total\ number\ of\ relevant\ and\ irrelevant\ pixels\ retrived} \tag{9}$$

$$R = \frac{Total\ number\ of\ relevant\ pixels\ retrieved}{Total\ number\ of\ relevant\ pixels} \tag{10}$$

$$F_1 = \frac{2PR}{P+R} \tag{11}$$

The performance of proposed and existing region-growing algorithm are evaluated and compared by measuring P, R and F1 value in Tables 3 and 4 respectively.

The experiment results have been shown that precision value of proposed model is 1.11% better than existing region-growing algorithm when there is less number of people present in the image. But, it is 3.29% less in case of large number of people presents in the image. The recall and F1 value of proposed algorithm is 8.36% and 4.25% better than region-growing algorithm respectively.

Table 3. Measurement of proposed model by Precision (P), recall (R) and F1 value

Image	TP	FN	FP	P	R	F1
1	0.6620	0.4190	0.3380	61.24	66.20	63.63
2	0.6451	0.4389	0.3549	59.51	64.51	64.76
3	0.6865	0.4336	0.3135	61.29	68.65	64.78
4	0.7495	0.4299	0.2505	63.55	74.95	68.78
5	0.6927	0.4268	0.3073	61.88	69.27	65.36
6	0.7696	0.3905	0.2304	66.34	76.96	71.26
7	0.7691	0.4097	0.2309	65.24	76.91	70.60
8	0.6924	0.4098	0.3076	62.82	69.24	65.87
9	0.6195	0.4702	0.3805	56.85	61.95	59.29
10	0.7788	0.2659	0.2212	74.55	77.88	76.18

Table 4. Measurement of existing region-growing algorithm by Precision (P), recall (R) and F1 value

Image	TP	FN	FP	P	R	F1
1	0.6799	0.3576	0.3201	65.53	68	66.74
2	0.5220	0.4362	0.4780	54.48	52.20	53.31
3	0.6852	0.3762	0.3148	64.56	68.52	66.48
4	0.7349	0.3428	0.2651	68.20	73.49	70.47
5	0.5888	0.3969	0.4112	59.73	58.88	59.30
6	0.5483	0.4145	0.4517	56.95	54.83	55.87
7	0.6947	0.3711	0.3053	65.18	69.47	67.26
8	0.6880	0.3002	0.3120	69.62	68.80	69.21
9	0.5794	0.4158	0.4206	58.27	57.94	58.10
10	0.7533	0.2474	0.2467	75.28	75.33	75.30

The Fig. 19 shows the comparison of precision value of proposed model and existing region-growing algorithm on MATLAB 7.4 [24]. The graph of precision, recall and F1 value over the given image dataset is shown in Figs. (20, 21 and 22).

The experiments results have been shown that over a large image dataset, the proposed model has perform better than region-growing algorithm in case of recall and F1 value. But, unfortunately, when the precision value over the large image dataset has been calculated, it has been given indeterminate results. It highly depended on the individual image.

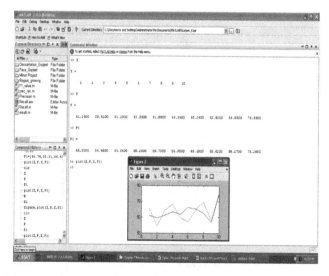

Fig. 19. Comparison of proposed model and existing region-growing algorithm by plotting Precision (P) value in MATLAB 7.4.

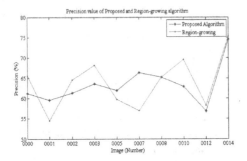

Fig. 20. Comparison of proposed model and existing region-growing algorithm by Precision

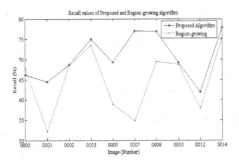

Fig. 21. Comparison of proposed model and existing region-growing algorithm by Recall

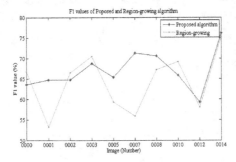

Fig. 22. Comparison of proposed model and existing region-growing algorithm by F1 value

6   Conclusion

In this research work, the authors developed the color image segmentation algorithm by using color information and edge extraction. The color information of the image is obtained by using HSI color model. The color information is used to get the texture information of the output image, while, the extracted edge detected the boundaries present in the output image. The proposed algorithm obtained the color information and edge extraction separately and simultaneously. Then, union of both color information and edge extraction are combined together. Finally, the noise present in the image is removed. The color images are taken from the UCD (University College Dublin) image dataset and other resources.

The authors have considered three parameters namely, precision (P), recall (R) and F1 value for evaluating and comparing the performance of proposed algorithm with existing region-growing algorithm. The precision-recall (PR) analysis against the receiver operator characteristic (ROC) analysis are used to measure the accuracy of the proposed algorithm. The experiment results have been shown that precision value of proposed algorithm is 1.11% better than existing region-growing algorithm. The recall and F1 value of proposed algorithm is 8.36% and 4.25% better than existing algorithm respectively. The proposed algorithm has been detected more true pixels, but, it detected more false pixels also. In case of recall and F1 value, the proposed algorithm has been performed better as compare to existing algorithm over a large image dataset. But, unfortunately, it has been shown indeterminate results when the precision value has been calculated over the large image dataset. It highly depended on the quality of the individual image. In short, it has been concluded that the proposed algorithm obtained the better results as compare to existing one.

Acknowledgment. The first author (R.K.) is grateful to the Management, the Dean, the HOD and all staff members of Faculty of Computing department, Botho University, Gaborone, Botswana for their valuable support. The work of the second author (S.M.) was supported and encouraged by the Management, the Director, the Dean and the Principal of BNMIT, Bangalore, India.

References

1. Hosea, S.P., Ranichandra, S., Rajagopal, T.K.P.: Color image segmentation an approach. Int. J. Sci. Eng. Res. **2**(3) (2011). http://citeseerx.ist.psu.edu/viewdoc/download?doi=10.1.1.301. 5431&rep=rep1&type=pdf

2. Gonzalez, R.C., Woods, R.E.: Digital Image Processing, 3rd edn. Prentice Hall, Upper Saddle River (2008)

3. Gonzalez, R.C., et al.: Digital Image Processing using MATLAB. Pearson Education, Upper Saddle River (2004)

4. Solomon, C., Breckon, T.: Fundamentals of Digital Image Processing: A Practical Approach with Examples in MATLAB. Wiley-Blackwell, Hoboken. ISBN: 978-0-470-84472-4

5. Aly, A.A., Deris, S.B., Zaki, N.: Research review for digital image segmentation techniques. Int. J. Comput. Sci. Inf. Technol. (IJCSIT) **3**(5), 99–106 (2011). doi:10.5121/ijcsit.2011. 3509

6. Khan, W.: Image segmentation techniques: a survey. J. Image Graph. **1**(4), 166–170 (2013). doi:10.12720/joig.1.4.166-170

7. Bora, D.J., Gupta, A.K., Khan, F.A.: Color image segmentation using an efficient fuzzy based watershed approach. Sig. Image Process.: Int. J. (SIPIJ) **6**(5), 15–34 (2015). doi:10. 5121/sipij.2015.6502

8. Burdescu, D.D., Brezovan, M., Ganea, E., Stanescu, L.: A new method for segmentation of images represented in a HSV color space. In: Blanc-Talon, J., Philips, W., Popescu, D., Scheunders, P. (eds.) ACIVS 2009. LNCS, vol. 5807, pp. 606–617. Springer, Heidelberg (2009). doi:10.1007/978-3-642-04697-1_57

9. Estrada, F.J., Jepson, A.D.: Benchmarking image segmentation algorithms. Int. J. Comput. Vis. **85**, 167–181 (2009). doi:10.1007/s11263-009-0251-z. Springer

10. Kumar, M.J., Raj Kumar, G., Vijay Kumar Reddy, R.: Review on image segmentation techniques. Int. J. Sci. Res. Eng. Technol. (IJSRET) **3**(6), 992–997 (2014)

11. Sharma, N., Mishra, M., Shrivastava, M.: Colour image segmentation techniques and issues: an approach. Int. J. Sci. Technol. Res. **1**(4), 9–12 (2012)

12. Senthilkumaran, N., Rajesh, R.: Edge detection techniques for image segmentation and a survey of soft computing approaches. Int. J. Recent Trends Eng. **1**(2), 250–254 (2009)

13. Srinivas, B.L., Hemalatha, Jeevan, K.A.: Edge detection techniques for image segmentation. Int. J. Innov. Res. Comput. Commun. Eng. **3**(7), 288–292 (2015). ISSN (Online) 2320-9801, ISSN (Print) 2320-9798

14. Bhardwaj, S., Mittal, A.: A survey on various edge detector techniques. Procedia Technol. **4**, 220–226 (2012). doi:10.1016/j.protcy.2012.05.033. C3IT-2012, Elsevier

15. Das, S.: Comparison of various edge detection technique. Int. J. Process. Image Process. Pattern Recogn IJSIP **9**(2), 143–158 (2016). ISSN 2005-4254. http://dx.doi.org/10.14257/ijsip.2016.9.2.13

16. Iancu, A., Popescu, B., Brezovan, M., Ganea, E.: Quantitative evaluation of color image segmentation algorithms. Int. J. Comput. Sci. Appl. **8**(1), 36–53 (2011). Techno mathematics Research Foundation

17. Zhang, H., Fritts, J.E., Goldman, S.A.: Image segmentation evaluation: a survey of unsupervised methods. Comput. Vis. Image Underst., 260–280 (2008). Elsevier. doi:10.1016/j.cviu.2007.08.003110. http://www.elsevier.com/locate/cviu/

18. Cardoso, J.S., Corte Real, L.: Toward a generic evaluation of image segmentation. IEEE Trans. Image Process. **14**(11), 1173–1782 (2005). doi:10.1109/TIP.2005.854491

19. Udupa, J.K., et al.: A framework for evaluating image segmentation algorithms. Comput. Med. Imaging Graph. **30**, 75–87 (2006). doi:10.1016/j.compmedimag.2005.12.001. Elsevier. http://www.ncbi.nlm.nih.gov/pubmed/16584976/

20. Lukac, P., et al.: The evaluation criterion for color image segmentation algorithms. J. Electr. Eng. **63**(1), 13–20 (2012). ISSN 1335-3632 c 2012 FEI STU. http://www.degruyter.com/view/j/jee.2012.63.issue-1/v10187-012-0002-1/v10187-012-0002-1.xml

21. Yitzhaky, Y., Pel, E.: A method for objective edge detection evaluation and detector parameter selection. IEEE Trans. Pattern Anal. Mach. Intell. **25**(10), 1027–1033 (2003). doi:10.1109/TPAMI.2003.1217608

22. Zaitoun, N.M., Aqel, M.J.: Survey on image segmentation techniques. In: International Conference on Communication, Management and Information Technology (ICCMIT 2015), vol. 65, pp. 797–806 (2015). Procedia Comput. Sci. Elsevier

23. University College Dublin (UCD) database: http://www.wudapt.org/create-lcz-classification

24. http://www.mathworks.com/products/matlab/

Electroencephalography Based Analysis of Emotions Among Indian Film Viewers

Gautham Krishna G, Krishna G, and Bhalaji N[✉]

Department of Information Technology, SSN College of Engineering,
Kalavakkam, Chennai 603 110, India
gauthkris@gmail.com, smartkrish95@gmail.com,
bhalajin@ssn.edu.in

Abstract. The film industry has been a major factor in the rapid growth of the Indian entertainment industry. While watching a film, the viewers undergo an experience that evolves over time, thereby grabbing their attention. This triggers a sequence of processes which is perceptual, cognitive and emotional. Neurocinematics is an emerging field of research, that measures the cognitive responses of a film viewer. Neurocinematic studies, till date, have been performed using functional magnetic resonance imaging (fMRI); however recent studies have suggested the use of advancements in electroencephalography (EEG) in neurocinematics to address the issues involved with fMRI. In this article the emotions corresponding to two different genres of Indian films are captured with the real-time brainwaves of viewers using EEG and analyzed using R language.

Keywords: EEG · Indian film · Neurocinematics · Cognitive review · BCI

1 Introduction

The advancements in functional neuroimaging procedures have enabled researchers to measure the activities of brain when viewers watch a film, leading to increased research focus in the area of neuroscience. The term neurocinematics was coined by Hasson et al. [1, 2], they used functional magnetic resonance imaging (fMRI) to capture the viewer's emotion during viewing of films. A new method called inter-subject correlation (ISC) was introduced by them [1, 2], which highlighted the simultaneous activation of similar brain regions for different people. This method (ISC) was considered as a new way of reviewing films to get better responses. Even though the functional magnetic resonance (fMRI) based method offered a new dimension of reviewing a film, the method has its own drawback when considered for practical implementation of neurocinematics. Firstly, the environment where the fMRI based reviewing method is carried out is entirely different from the environment in which viewers watch film in theatre. In Hasson et al.'s study, the viewers were lying inside a MRI scanner, which has a small amount of space compared to normal viewing conditions and hence expressing their natural responses would have been difficult. Secondly, a viewer's emotion might vary based on the number of people they are watching a film with, for instance, a viewer watching a comedy clip alone would express lesser emotions as

© Springer Nature Singapore Pte Ltd. 2017
D. Singh et al. (Eds.): ICAICR 2017, CCIS 712, pp. 145–155, 2017.
DOI: 10.1007/978-981-10-5780-9_13

compared to one who is viewing the same clip with partners. Thirdly, fMRI is an expensive procedure among all neuroimaging techniques and experimenting this procedure for a large number of subjects can be considered only after measuring the reliability of the experiment. Finally, EEG has the capability to detect changes within a millisecond timeframe, which is excellent considering the fact that movie scenes change quickly.

Synchronized neural activities in the brain give rise to EEG signals, which can be studied by placing the EEG electrodes near the scalp or on the scalp (Non-invasive method) [3] or by implanting the EEG electrodes in the skull (Invasive method). Mostow et al. [4] noted that development, mental state, and cognitive activity influenced the synchronized neural activity, and the variations in neural activity could be measurably detected by EEG signals. For instance, within particular frequency bands, the EEG signals undergo rhythmic fluctuations, each frequency band correlates with different emotional states of brain like concentration, anxiety and anger, as observed in various tasks and characteristics [5–7].

Hospitals and laboratories have been using multi-electrode EEG systems for a long time, but the trending EEG devices which are economical, have made it possible to use the concept of EEG for large-scale purposes. For example, the Neurosky Mindwave Mobile, Fig. 1 (used in this experiment). The device consists of a headset, an ear clip and a sensor arm.

Fig. 1. The Mindwave Mobile, picture taken from [8]

The headset's reference and ground electrodes are on the ear clip and the EEG electrode is on the sensor arm, which rests on the forehead above the eye (Fp1) [8], as shown in Fig. 2. Moreover, this device requires no gel or saline for recording as compared to other devices in lab, along with noise-cancellation [10]. Bluetooth/BLE is used for integration between the computer and Mindwave Mobile.

The Mindwave, though constrained with having a single, dry sensor, and studied with untrained users, gave an accuracy of 86% while differentiating various states [10]. Secondly, the Mindwave is also found to be more resistant to noise than the Biopac

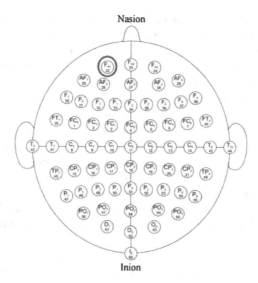

Fig. 2. The ten-twenty 64-electrode system of the International Federation [9], picture was taken from [11]. The red circle at the top indicates Fp1. (Colour figure online)

system since Mindwave uses shorter wires for EEG signal transmission. Thus, the device has been used in this experiment.

The rest of the paper is methodized as follows. Section 2 deals with the Literature Review of previous articles related to this field. Section 3 showcases the Wave Graph and Power Spectrum of two volunteers watching two movies each. In the same section, further, the data is loaded and analyzed using R language. Section 4 concludes the article. Finally, in Sect. 5, Future works and research scope of this field are discussed, followed by References.

2   Literature Review

The proposals in this article are alternate versions of functional magnetic resonance imaging (fMRI), which is a neuroimaging procedure that detects the changes in blood flow to track brain activities. The fact that the cerebral blood flow and neuronal activations are coupled, is used in this technique. When an area of brain is active, the blood flow to that region of the brain increases.

The output of the MRI scanner is reprogrammed to get three dimensional images of the brain varying continuously with time. If there is an increase in neural activity in a certain region of brain, then the intensities of images at that part of the brain increases. It was also observed that cinema viewing involves high spatiotemporal complexity, hence the conventional fMRI methods were not found to be useful, therefore a new method known as intersubject correlation [2] was devised, which measured the similarities in the brain activities among all cinema viewers.

While Hasson et al. [1, 2] used ISC method for neurocinematic experiments, the model of Narrative Nowness for neurocinematic experiments was proposed by Janne et al. [12], they highlighted the fact that the fMRI experiment by Hasson et al. showed significant inter-subjective correlation between the brain responses of viewers of a Hitchcock film, but that did not hold for those watching a random surveillance video footage. Therefore Janne et al. suggested that the similarity of brain behavior between viewers was likely due to the way their attention was trapped, guided, and tricked by the narrative design that was a system of temporal contexts.

Janne et al. [12] also pointed out that, the mere comparison of context annotation of features present at a given moment with the synchronized brain responses may not alone provide a sufficient basis for naturalistic neurosciences to understand higher levels of cognitive functions, they suggested that neuroscientific studies that neglected the viewer's temporal situatedness with respect to continuous narrative just fell short of meeting the attribute 'naturalistic.' They proposed another layer of representing the narrative to relate it to the brain activity.

These published articles have lot of merits, as they provided a breakthrough for taking the live responses of films and also traced the brain activities of different viewers, capturing the live responses, hence giving an overall precise review for each section of a film. The disadvantage with these methods is that, every MRI scan is time consuming and tedious.

3 Observing Brainwaves During Film Viewing

In this experiment performed to study the brainwaves during film viewing, two volunteers, each were asked to view the opening 15 min of two different genres of Indian films - Maya, a well known horror film by Ashwin Saravanan (2015) and Thillu Mullu, a well known comedy film by K. Balachander (1981). The volunteers were scanned by using EEG devices. High definition video and audio were supplied to the subjects. The High definition video was presented in a laptop. Sound was delivered through earphones. The volunteers were allowed to watch the movie without any hindrance. The raw EEG data was analyzed using the NeuroView software and simultaneously raw waves were converted to digital data, which was analyzed using R language to get a final value of frequencies (corresponding to different emotions) for a specified time interval for each movie.

The x-axis on each of the raw wave graphs, shows one second at a time. Each second gives 512 data points. The y-axis shows values that are simply called Neuro-View units and are not defined in a more specific way [13].

In the histogram, the x-axis represents time interval and the y-axis represents frequency.

It is to be noted that the Raw Brainwaves and Power Spectrum observed, are similar for volunteers watching the same genre of films, as shown in Figs. 3 and 4 for the comedy genre, and Figs. 5 and 6 for the horror genre. This conveys the fact that the movies of various genres had a similar effect on both the viewers.

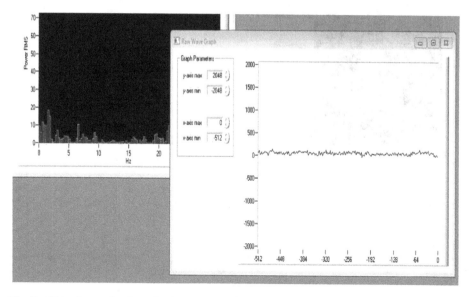

Fig. 3. This shows the Raw Brainwave and Power Spectrum (as viewed in NeuroView) of volunteer 1 watching the film Thillu Mullu. The genre of movie is comedy, the subject is a male in the age category 20–25.

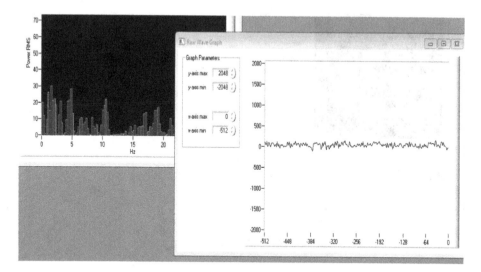

Fig. 4. This shows the Raw Brainwave and Power Spectrum (as viewed in NeuroView) of volunteer 2 watching the film Thillu Mullu. The genre of movie is comedy, the subject is a male in the age category 20–25.

The values obtained from the graph are broadly classified into 4 regions, namely, alpha, beta, theta and delta. The delta waves occur in the region of 0–4 Hz, the theta waves occur in the region of 4–8 Hz, the alpha waves occur in the frequency range of

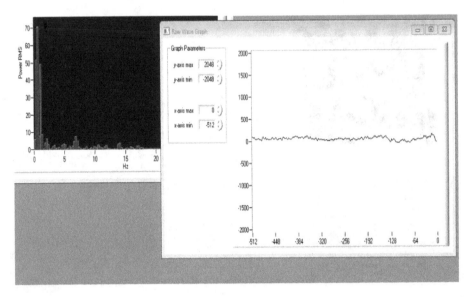

Fig. 5. This shows the Raw Brainwave and Power Spectrum (as viewed in NeuroView) of volunteer 1 watching the film Maya. The genre of movie is horror, the subject is a male in the age category 20–25.

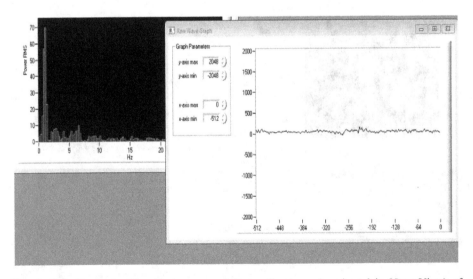

Fig. 6. This shows the Raw Brainwave and Power Spectrum (as viewed in NeuroView) of volunteer 2 watching the film Maya. The genre of movie is horror, the subject is a male in the age category 20–25.

8–14 Hz, the beta waves occur in the frequency range of 14–30 Hz, and the gamma waves occur in the region of 30–50 Hz. Each wave has a set of emotions associated with them. Beta waves are associated with attentiveness, alertness and engagement in mental activity. Alpha waves are associated with calmness, relaxed, anti–depressed states. Theta waves are associated with vivid imagery, and where we hold our fears, troubled history and nightmares. Delta waves are associated with deep dreamless sleep and are found wane with rise in age, while gamma waves are very high frequencies and involve rapid processing of information. Therefore the latter two waves are ignored in this study, as it does not correspond to any specific emotion in Neurocinematics.

3.1 Using R Language to Analyze the Obtained Dataset

The R language is used to perform analysis on the large data set that is obtained. The data is loaded into R studio in the form of a CSV file, the obtained data set consists of the powers of brainwaves across all frequencies at a time gap of one second, as shown in Fig. 7. Using R programming the mean value at a particular second is calculated for each power spectrum, the highest value among all values is considered as the final value for that particular time interval.

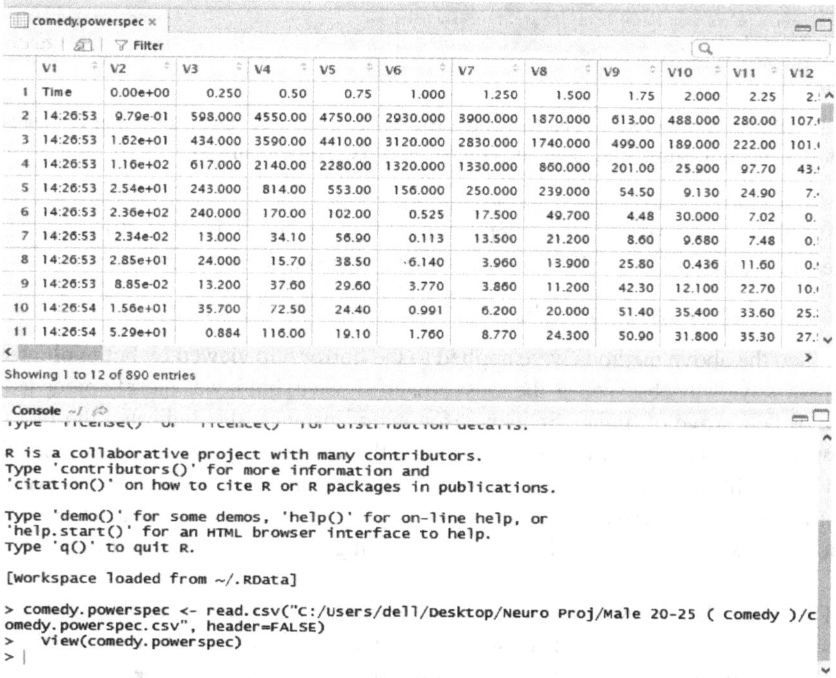
comedy.powerspec

	V1	V2	V3	V4	V5	V6	V7	V8	V9	V10	V11	V12
1	Time	0.00e+00	0.250	0.50	0.75	1.000	1.250	1.500	1.75	2.000	2.25	2.
2	14:26:53	9.79e-01	598.000	4550.00	4750.00	2930.000	3900.000	1870.000	613.00	488.000	280.00	107.
3	14:26:53	1.62e+01	434.000	3590.00	4410.00	3120.000	2830.000	1740.000	499.00	189.000	222.00	101.
4	14:26:53	1.16e+02	617.000	2140.00	2280.00	1320.000	1330.000	860.000	201.00	25.900	97.70	43.
5	14:26:53	2.54e+01	243.000	814.00	553.00	156.000	250.000	239.000	54.50	9.130	24.90	7.
6	14:26:53	2.36e+02	240.000	170.00	102.00	0.525	17.500	49.700	4.48	30.000	7.02	0.
7	14:26:53	2.34e-02	13.000	34.10	56.90	0.113	13.500	21.200	8.60	9.680	7.48	0.
8	14:26:53	2.85e+01	24.000	15.70	38.50	6.140	3.960	13.900	25.80	0.436	11.60	0.
9	14:26:53	8.85e-02	13.200	37.60	29.60	3.770	3.860	11.200	42.30	12.100	22.70	10.
10	14:26:54	1.56e+01	35.700	72.50	24.40	0.991	6.200	20.000	51.40	35.400	33.60	25.
11	14:26:54	5.29e+01	0.884	116.00	19.10	1.760	8.770	24.300	50.90	31.800	35.30	27.

Showing 1 to 12 of 890 entries

Console ~/

```
R is a collaborative project with many contributors.
Type 'contributors()' for more information and
'citation()' on how to cite R or R packages in publications.

Type 'demo()' for some demos, 'help()' for on-line help, or
'help.start()' for an HTML browser interface to help.
Type 'q()' to quit R.

[Workspace loaded from ~/.RData]

> comedy.powerspec <- read.csv("C:/Users/dell/Desktop/Neuro Proj/Male 20-25 ( Comedy )/c
omedy.powerspec.csv", header=FALSE)
>   View(comedy.powerspec)
> |
```

Fig. 7. This shows sample data loaded in R Studio, the first row in data set represents time shows and the first column represents frequency.

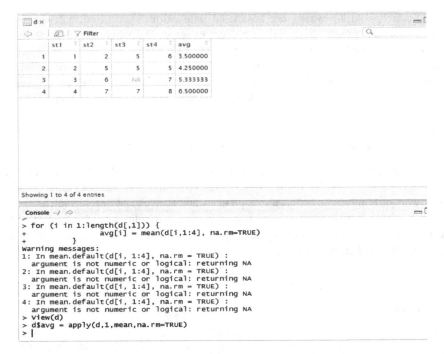

Fig. 8. This shows sample values for which row-wise mean was calculated using R language, and the maximum value in the average column is taken as the final value.

Mean is calculated row-wise across suitable frequencies (e.g., 4–8 Hz for Theta wave) as shown in Fig. 8. The mean is calculated using R language as follows,

```
data_frame$means <- apply(data_frame, 1, mean)
```

When the above methods were applied to the horror clip viewed by both volunteers, the theta wave was observed as the most powerful wave, but it was closely preceded by alpha or beta wave of higher frequencies at every instance, this indicated the fact that volunteers were constantly oscillating between the states of anxiety and relaxation. This shows that the film has captured viewers' attention at every second. Whenever the ghost appears, theta wave spikes. It then returns to a normal state in a few seconds, while alpha wave is observed for a scene involving the peaceful scenes of protagonist (Fig. 9).

The result data set was totally different for comedy film, where, alpha wave was observed almost every second, indicating the fact that volunteer was constantly in a state of anti-depression (was happy) during the movie. Moreover, beta wave is also showing the engagement of the viewer into the comedy movie. The observation of alpha and beta waves throughout has indicated that the viewer was completely engrossed in the film (Fig. 10).

5.82E-14	5.60E-14	5.74E-14	5.33E-14	5.08E-14	5.06E-14	4.95E-14	4.86E-14	4.81E-14	4.77E-14	2.041634	
1.60E-14	1.76E-14	1.07E-14	1.14E-14	8.78E-15	7.76E-15	6.51E-15	5.53E-15	4.87E-15	4.47E-15	0.054425	
3.94E-15	4.12E-15	1.73E-15	2.91E-15	1.70E-15	1.83E-15	1.52E-15	1.37E-15	1.25E-15	1.18E-15	1.06E-08	
1.28E-13	1.26E-13	1.34E-13	1.29E-13	1.25E-13	1.25E-13	1.23E-13	1.22E-13	1.21E-13	1.21E-13	19.486	
4.83E-15	2.12E-15	2.09E-15	1.71E-15	1.60E-15	1.62E-15	1.52E-15	1.44E-15	1.40E-15	1.37E-15	2.082765	theta
5.73E-14	5.70E-14	5.61E-14	5.05E-14	4.97E-14	4.86E-14	4.69E-14	4.57E-14	4.49E-14	4.44E-14	1.626667	
3.28E-14	2.05E-14	2.67E-14	2.28E-14	2.41E-14	2.40E-14	2.39E-14	2.38E-14	2.38E-14	2.38E-14	0.93828	
3.00E-14	3.56E-14	3.76E-14	3.07E-14	3.25E-14	3.11E-14	3.04E-14	2.99E-14	2.96E-14	2.93E-14	0.612124	
6.33E-14	6.18E-14	6.35E-14	5.30E-14	5.57E-14	5.24E-14	5.13E-14	5.00E-14	4.93E-14	4.88E-14	0.2579	
2.25E-14	1.46E-14	1.21E-14	8.53E-15	7.28E-15	4.81E-15	3.11E-15	1.74E-15	7.75E-16	1.96E-16	0.00622	
1.87E-13	1.61E-13	1.68E-13	1.65E-13	1.65E-13	1.63E-13	1.62E-13	1.61E-13	1.61E-13	1.60E-13	2.37E-09	
2.30E-14	1.25E-14	1.61E-14	1.27E-14	1.21E-14	1.16E-14	1.06E-14	1.01E-14	9.74E-15	9.52E-15	21.21271	
3.41E-13	2.97E-13	3.24E-13	2.98E-13	3.09E-13	3.00E-13	2.99E-13	2.97E-13	2.96E-13	2.95E-13	4.9217	theta
2.22E-13	1.73E-13	1.37E-13	1.21E-13	8.79E-14	7.08E-14	5.33E-14	4.04E-14	3.11E-14	2.56E-14	1.412111	
1.17E-14	8.66E-15	6.79E-15	8.41E-15	6.61E-15	5.88E-15	5.47E-15	5.03E-15	4.75E-15	4.57E-15	2.191333	
9.14E-14	8.97E-14	9.34E-14	8.82E-14	8.53E-14	8.63E-14	8.51E-14	8.42E-14	8.38E-14	8.34E-14	1.6037	
2.90E-13	2.62E-13	2.68E-13	2.61E-13	2.58E-13	2.58E-13	2.51E-13	2.51E-13	2.50E-13	2.49E-13	0.601647	
3.98E-14	3.12E-14	3.09E-14	2.78E-14	2.62E-14	2.43E-14	2.36E-14	2.24E-14	2.18E-14	2.14E-14	0.007578	
2.54E-13	2.20E-13	2.11E-13	2.09E-13	2.07E-13	1.99E-13	1.98E-13	1.95E-13	1.93E-13	1.92E-13	4.30E-09	
7.36E-14	4.96E-14	5.27E-14	5.15E-14	4.97E-14	4.87E-14	4.74E-14	4.66E-14	4.60E-14	4.56E-14	126.2689	
5.47E-14	7.65E-14	5.40E-14	4.66E-14	3.80E-14	3.16E-14	2.57E-14	2.13E-14	1.80E-14	1.61E-14	2.660224	theta
1.40E-13	1.01E-13	1.11E-13	1.04E-13	1.05E-13	1.02E-13	1.03E-13	1.02E-13	1.01E-13	1.01E-13	1.766333	
1.50E-14	2.44E-14	1.72E-14	1.48E-14	1.12E-14	8.79E-15	7.02E-15	5.43E-15	4.31E-15	3.65E-15	1.615489	
1.44E-13	1.21E-13	1.12E-13	1.21E-13	1.16E-13	1.16E-13	1.15E-13	1.15E-13	1.14E-13	1.14E-13	0.672832	
2.73E-14	2.37E-14	2.26E-14	1.69E-14	1.45E-14	1.20E-14	1.02E-14	8.70E-15	7.65E-15	7.00E-15	0.730269	
6.21E-14	6.96E-14	5.93E-14	6.19E-14	6.12E-14	6.08E-14	6.06E-14	6.02E-14	6.01E-14	6.00E-14	0.013078	
1.01E-14	1.19E-14	6.93E-15	7.03E-15	6.88E-15	5.96E-15	5.42E-15	5.07E-15	4.79E-15	4.63E-15	4.68E-09	
1.18E-13	1.26E-13	1.12E-13	1.14E-13	1.08E-13	1.08E-13	1.07E-13	1.06E-13	1.05E-13	1.05E-13	74.14176	
1.02E-14	1.03E-14	8.32E-15	4.73E-15	4.43E-15	2.82E-15	1.90E-15	1.12E-15	5.50E-16	2.11E-16	5.163347	theta
6.69E-14	4.51E-14	4.59E-14	4.42E-14	4.31E-14	4.05E-14	4.01E-14	3.91E-14	3.84E-14	3.80E-14	1.1016	
5.48E-14	5.75E-14	4.27E-14	3.84E-14	3.94E-14	3.94E-14	3.83E-14	3.81E-14	3.79E-14	3.78E-14	1.095356	
3.98E-15	3.89E-15	1.99E-15	2.05E-15	1.29E-15	1.06E-15	5.58E-16	3.38E-16	1.51E-16	3.85E-17	0.870308	
1.57E-14	1.52E-14	1.31E-14	1.45E-14	1.32E-14	1.35E-14	1.28E-14	1.28E-14	1.26E-14	1.26E-14	0.575435	
7.08E-14	6.13E-14	6.32E-14	6.15E-14	6.12E-14	6.22E-14	6.06E-14	6.09E-14	6.06E-14	6.05E-14	0.00633	

Fig. 9. The right most column is the final calculated value for the horror movie (Maya), and it is observed that theta waves are observed mostly, while alpha and beta waves (higher frequencies just above theta) precede theta waves.

8.49E-14	1.18E-13	8.48E-14	1.16E-13	1.15E-13	9.19E-14	9.96E-14	9.65E-14	9.47E-14	9.42E-14	9.30E-14	9.24E-14	9.20E-14	162.9638	
1.55E-13	1.17E-13	1.13E-13	1.22E-13	9.87E-14	1.10E-13	9.73E-14	9.38E-14	8.89E-14	8.62E-14	8.35E-14	8.17E-14	8.06E-14	2.992588	
1.18E-13	2.71E-14	5.79E-14	3.29E-14	5.45E-14	4.30E-14	4.44E-14	4.34E-14	4.22E-14	4.14E-14	4.10E-14	4.07E-14	4.05E-14	4.774333	l.alpha
1.87E-13	4.90E-13	4.04E-13	3.98E-13	3.61E-13	3.77E-13	3.72E-13	3.66E-13	3.58E-13	3.57E-13	3.55E-13	3.53E-13	3.52E-13	1.733333	
1.30E-13	3.39E-13	2.64E-13	1.96E-13	2.74E-13	2.27E-13	2.22E-13	2.31E-13	2.25E-13	2.24E-13	2.23E-13	2.22E-13	2.22E-13	2.03164	
7.40E-14	5.26E-14	3.01E-15	5.82E-15	6.55E-15	3.78E-15	2.51E-15	3.88E-15	2.85E-15	3.11E-15	2.96E-15	2.90E-15	2.88E-15	1.207727	
3.17E-13	9.53E-14	9.31E-14	1.09E-13	9.26E-14	9.66E-14	9.36E-14	9.11E-14	9.21E-14	8.91E-14	8.89E-14	8.83E-14	8.80E-14	0.031313	
1.30E-13	3.65E-13	2.32E-13	2.51E-13	1.85E-13	2.23E-13	2.17E-13	2.10E-13	2.10E-13	2.08E-13	2.06E-13	2.06E-13	2.05E-13	3.71E-08	
1.18E-13	4.32E-14	5.64E-14	8.69E-14	7.14E-14	7.17E-14	7.40E-14	6.97E-14	6.93E-14	6.93E-14	6.90E-14	6.87E-14	6.86E-14	10.42471	
2.43E-13	3.28E-13	3.61E-13	2.30E-13	3.13E-13	2.70E-13	2.85E-13	2.74E-13	2.73E-13	2.69E-13	2.68E-13	2.67E-13	2.66E-13	1.205624	
1.93E-13	1.21E-13	1.32E-13	1.17E-13	1.28E-13	1.03E-13	1.18E-13	1.11E-13	1.09E-13	1.10E-13	1.09E-13	1.09E-13	1.09E-13	2.203356	l.alpha
3.79E-14	1.89E-14	4.40E-14	7.41E-15	1.30E-14	1.81E-14	1.15E-14	1.38E-14	1.24E-14	1.24E-14	1.22E-14	1.21E-14	1.20E-14	1.967556	
2.41E-13	1.15E-13	6.62E-14	1.20E-13	9.32E-14	1.09E-13	9.52E-14	1.01E-13	9.76E-14	9.82E-14	9.75E-14	9.72E-14	9.71E-14	1.473608	
1.08E-13	7.28E-14	2.90E-14	4.43E-14	5.85E-14	4.67E-14	4.78E-14	4.74E-14	4.49E-14	4.54E-14	4.47E-14	4.43E-14	4.41E-14	1.101501	
2.71E-12	1.99E-12	2.34E-12	2.14E-12	2.05E-12	2.06E-12	2.06E-12	2.05E-12	2.03E-12	2.02E-12	2.01E-12	2.00E-12	2.00E-12	0.02485	
2.51E-14	1.55E-14	9.12E-17	1.36E-14	4.31E-15	3.41E-15	3.49E-15	3.48E-15	3.16E-15	2.93E-15	2.79E-15	2.70E-15	2.65E-15	1.33E-08	
2.82E-12	2.60E-12	2.44E-12	2.50E-12	2.31E-12	2.34E-12	2.30E-12	2.26E-12	2.25E-12	2.22E-12	2.21E-12	2.20E-12	2.19E-12	11.81306	
5.15E-12	4.98E-12	5.26E-12	4.49E-12	4.82E-12	4.59E-12	4.59E-12	4.54E-12	4.52E-12	4.48E-12	4.46E-12	4.44E-12	4.43E-12	5.376294	
6.76E-14	1.92E-13	1.95E-13	8.66E-14	1.05E-13	1.31E-13	1.14E-13	1.10E-13	1.08E-13	1.07E-13	1.06E-13	1.05E-13	1.05E-13	3.492889	
6.07E-13	2.83E-13	2.91E-13	2.98E-13	2.32E-13	2.89E-13	2.71E-13	2.60E-13	2.63E-13	2.60E-13	2.59E-13	2.58E-13	2.58E-13	8.048889	
1.71E-13	1.39E-13	1.50E-13	5.04E-14	1.30E-13	9.92E-14	9.70E-14	9.70E-14	9.70E-14	9.72E-14	9.71E-14	9.67E-14	9.66E-14	7.472884	
2.74E-13	2.85E-14	7.17E-14	1.40E-13	3.66E-14	7.96E-14	5.50E-14	5.34E-14	5.03E-14	4.72E-14	4.50E-14	4.36E-14	4.27E-14	8.345857	h.beta
1.20E-14	2.43E-14	1.75E-14	3.95E-14	1.12E-14	1.15E-14	1.11E-14	7.33E-15	6.33E-15	5.43E-15	4.53E-15	3.96E-15	3.61E-15	0.135347	
1.06E-13	2.50E-13	9.72E-14	1.49E-13	1.17E-13	9.29E-14	9.88E-14	9.63E-14	9.10E-14	8.75E-14	8.51E-14	8.33E-14	8.22E-14	3.58E-08	
6.65E-14	1.07E-14	5.18E-16	3.86E-15	9.01E-16	2.90E-16	3.66E-16	4.16E-16	4.36E-16	4.39E-16	4.32E-16	4.32E-16	4.36E-16	19.28682	
5.40E-13	1.18E-13	2.09E-13	2.15E-13	2.06E-13	1.95E-13	1.95E-13	1.93E-13	1.90E-13	1.90E-13	1.89E-13	1.88E-13	1.87E-13	3.176176	
6.08E-14	1.64E-14	1.98E-14	1.33E-14	1.08E-14	1.59E-14	1.26E-14	1.26E-14	1.19E-14	1.23E-14	1.21E-14	1.21E-14	1.20E-14	4.039111	l.alpha
5.04E-13	3.51E-13	2.40E-13	2.99E-13	2.58E-13	2.95E-13	2.76E-13	2.69E-13	2.71E-13	2.68E-13	2.67E-13	2.66E-13	2.66E-13	2.745778	
1.34E-13	1.46E-13	1.13E-13	1.15E-13	1.28E-13	1.02E-13	9.54E-14	9.38E-14	8.59E-14	8.32E-14	7.99E-14	7.76E-14	7.63E-14	1.959896	
2.70E-14	8.96E-14	5.22E-14	8.86E-14	7.66E-14	6.82E-14	6.68E-14	6.32E-14	5.93E-14	5.89E-14	5.74E-14	5.64E-14	5.58E-14	1.489582	
3.98E-13	2.72E-13	2.49E-13	1.94E-13	2.33E-13	2.26E-13	2.17E-13	2.16E-13	2.16E-13	2.13E-13	2.12E-13	2.11E-13	2.11E-13	0.05145	
3.02E-14	1.51E-13	1.56E-13	7.03E-14	7.06E-14	7.93E-14	5.49E-14	5.00E-14	4.17E-14	3.79E-14	3.34E-14	3.04E-14	2.86E-14	4.13E-08	
1.39E-13	1.63E-13	5.48E-14	6.29E-14	4.05E-14	4.78E-14	2.84E-14	2.18E-14	1.57E-14	1.01E-14	6.09E-15	3.15E-15	1.40E-15	43.95118	
8.18E-14	3.39E-13	9.78E-14	5.71E-14	9.30E-14	5.86E-14	4.80E-14	3.54E-14	2.31E-14	1.55E-14	8.55E-15	3.81E-15	9.75E-16	4.448182	theta

Fig. 10. The right most column is the final calculated value for the comedy movie (Thillu Mullu), and it is observed that alpha waves are observed mostly along with beta waves, indicating that viewer is mostly engaged and in an anti-depressed state (happy).

4 Conclusion

In this article, a new statistical approach to study the emotions in brain was explored for measuring the viewer's brain activity and observing patterns for an effective output. This paper proposes that latest EEG devices like Neurosky Mindwave Mobile (used in this experiment), can offer a cheaper and more affordable means for analyzing emotions effectively and easily. This study does not claim that it is the central measure to analyze emotions, and the experiment has been done, only to analyze the emotions among Indian Film viewers. The emotions of two different viewers for two different genres of Indian films - Comedy and Horror, were successfully captured and analyzed, and the results have matched with the intended emotions (which was determined based on the released movie's IMDb reviews), making this experiment a success.

5 Future Works

In the field of Neurocinematic studies, research could pave the way to huge developments, since it is still in its nascent stages. While one method has been explored here, for measuring the volunteers' activities in brain, there are also advancements in the field of fMRI which offer good analysis of various emotions displayed by the viewer. There are also better EEG devices with higher costs which provide near-accurate brainwave analysis. All these studies together might provide a breakthrough in accurate emotion analysis. An advanced version of this experiment, analyzing the emotions of viewers among different age groups, for all genre of films, for a longer duration could open the scope for newer reviewing techniques for movies using EEG, but as of now, this is beyond the scope of this experiment.

References

1. Hasson, U., Landesman, O., Knappmeyer, B., Vallines, I., Rubin, N., Heeger, D.J.: Neurocinematics: the neuroscience of film. Projections 2(1), 1–26 (2008). doi:10.3167/proj.2008.020102
2. Hasson, U., Nir, Y., Levy, I., Fuhrmann, G., Malach, R.: Intersubject synchronization of cortical activity during natural vision. Science 303(5664), 1634–1640 (2004). doi:10.1126/science.1089506
3. Donoghue, J.P., Nurmikko, A., Black, M., Hochberg, L.R.: Assistive technology and robotic control using motor cortex ensemble-based neural interface systems in humans with tetraplegia. J. Physiol. 579(Pt. 3), 603–611 (2007). doi:10.1113/jphysiol.2006.127209
4. Mostow, J., Chang, K., Nelson, J.: Toward exploiting EEG input in a reading tutor. In: Biswas, G., Bull, S., Kay, J., Mitrovic, A. (eds.) AIED 2011. LNCS, vol. 6738, pp. 230–237. Springer, Heidelberg (2011). doi:10.1007/978-3-642-21869-9_31
5. Berka, C., Levendowski, D.J., Lumicao, M.N., Yau, A., Davis, G., Zivkovic, V.T., Olmstead, R.E., Tremoulet, P.D., Craven, P.L.: EEG correlates of task engagement and mental workload in vigilance, learning, and memory tasks. Aviat. Space Environ. Med. 78(5 Suppl.), B231–B244 (2007)

6. Lutsyuk, N.V., Eismont, E.V., Pavlenko, V.B.: Correlation of the characteristics of EEG potentials with the indices of attention in 12-to 13-year-old children. Neurophysiology **38**(3), 209–216 (2006). doi:10.1007/s11062-006-0048-4

7. Marosi, E., Bazan, O., Yanez, G., Bernal, J., Fernandez, T., Rodriguez, M., Silva, J., Reyes, A.: Narrow-band spectral measurements of EEG during emotional tasks. Int. J. Neurosci. **112**(7), 871–891 (2002)

8. Neurosky: Neurosky's eSense™ Meters and Detection of Mental State. http://www.neurosky.com/

9. Klem, G.H., Luders, H.O., Jasper, H.H., Elger, C.: The ten-twenty electrode system of the international federation. The international federation of clinical neurophysiology. Electroencephalogr. Clin. Neurophysiol. **52**(Suppl.), 3–6 (1999)

10. Oyama, K., Takeuchi, A., Chang, C.K.: Brain lattice: concept lattice based causal analysis of changes in mental workload. In: IEEE International Multi-Disciplinary Conference on Cognitive Methods in Situation Awareness and Decision Support (CogSIMA), San Diego, CA, pp. 59–66 (2013). doi:10.1109/CogSIMA.2013.6523824

11. Sharbrough, F., Chatrian, C.E., Lesser, R.P., Luders, H., Nuwer, M., Piction, T.W.: American electroencephalographic society guidelines for standard electrode position nomenclature. J. Clin. Neurophysiol. **8**(2), 200–202 (1991)

12. Kauttonen, J., Kaipainen, M., Tikka, P.: Model of narrative narrowness for neurocinematic experiments. In: Proceedings of the 5th Workshop on Computational Models of Narrative (CMN 2014). Open Access Series Informatics (Germany: Schloss Dagstuhl - Leibniz - Zentrum für Informatik, Dagstuhl Publishing), pp. 77–87 (2014)

13. Guðmundsdóttir, K.: Improving players' control over the neurosky brain-computer interface. Research report (2011). http://hdl.handle.net/1946/9187

Fuel Assembly Height Measurements at the Nuclear Power Plant Unit Active Zone

Konstantin E. Rumyantsev$^{(\boxtimes)}$ ⓘ, Sergey L. Balabaev ⓘ,
and Irina Yu. Balabaeva ⓘ

Southern Federal University, Taganrog, Russian Federation
{rumyancev, sbalabaev, ibalabaeva}@sfedu.ru

Abstract. The article studies the system of fuel assembly (FA) height measurement by single CCD camera. The algorithm of FA height measurement involves camera moving around the circle of radius 3 m and forming the images from six locations. Suspension height of the camera provides simultaneous observation of the cell with 7 fuel assemblies. Optical axis of camera in each location passes through the gravity center of the central FA upper surface. The camera mathematical model and developed software allows to register discrete pixel coordinates, that display the gravity centers of FA heads upper surfaces. The paper gives the detailed analysis for three stereo pairs of images, got as combinations of measurements from four camera locations: two adjacent locations, two locations in one from each other, and two opposite locations. Algorithm analysis gives minimum height measuring error and reasonable camera locations selection for obtaining most precise measurement results. The paper proves possibility of restriction to measurements from pairs of opposite camera locations to reach the maximum FA height measurement precision.

Keywords: CCD camera · Contactless measurement method · Fuel assembly · Height measurement · Methodical error

1 Introduction

Development of reliable complexes for technological process control is one of the modern trends in atomics. The regular procedures at nuclear power plants with nuclear water reactors include the determining of the height of the nuclear reactor fuel assembly heads. The basic quality criteria for this measurement is the measurement error minimization [1, 2].

To raise the safety one can use the contactless system of FA height measurement on the base of TV image processing by the vidicon system [3]. The operated system uses only one video camera. The camera moves successively to various points in space to form a 3D image [4]. The object images from video camera in two adjacent positions form the stereo pair of images (SPI). The image processing includes its quality

The research was supported by the Russian Foundation for Basic Research (project № 16-08-00752) and by the Russian Scientific Foundation (project № 17-19-01078).

© Springer Nature Singapore Pte Ltd. 2017
D. Singh et al. (Eds.): ICAICR 2017, CCIS 712, pp. 156–163, 2017.
DOI: 10.1007/978-981-10-5780-9_14

estimation based on luminance probability distribution histogram, elimination on small elements, FA upper surfaces borders selection, FA upper surfaces ellipse approximation, and, finally, determining 3D coordinates of FA upper surfaces centers of gravity [5, 6]. The method [7, 8] is provided with the mathematical model of stereo system and the algorithm of the determining 3D coordinates of FA upper surfaces centers of gravity for six positions (angles) of vidicon camera.

This research aims at the precision increase of the contactless FA head height measurement on the base of 3D-scene reconstruction from the image stereo pairs series obtained by the single CCD camera in various locations.

2 Problem Description

The studied algorithm of FA head height measurement provides the movement of camera optical center while cell inspection along the circle of radius with formation of images from six angles (in positions CL1...CL6 in Fig. 1 with numbering clockwise).

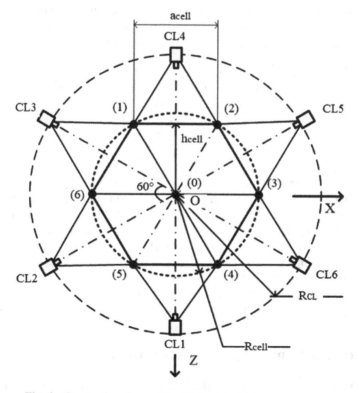

Fig. 1. Camera locations while FA head height measurement

The distance a_{cell} between upper surfaces centers of gravity of any two adjacent FA in the model of CCD camera height measurement is constant. So, a cell is a regular hexagon.

The hexagon vertices (points (1) … (6) in Fig. 1) lay in the gravity centers of FA upper surfaces. The vertices are located at the circle of radius $R_{cell} = a_{cell}$. The hexagon gravity center coincides with the gravity center of the central FA upper surface (point (0)).

Suspension height of the camera H_{CL} should provide an opportunity to observe the entire cell (entire hexagon). The optical axis of camera in each location must pass through the cell center of gravity (point (0)).

The FA head height in the global coordinate system (GCS) of the cell OXYZ corresponds to its coordinate on the axis OY. The GCS origin coincides with the hexagon gravity center (point (0) in Fig. 1). The OY axis of GCS is perpendicular to the plane formed by the camera locations CL1 … CL6. The OZ axis is perpendicular to one of the hexagon sides (line segment 4–5 in Fig. 1).

The mathematical model of camera [9, 10] allows to register the discrete coordinates of pixels (photocells in CCD), that images the FA upper surface gravity centers. 30 discrete coordinates are registered for each of seven gravity centers of FA upper surfaces. For example, for point (1) in Fig. 1 the system will register pixel coordinates from two cameras in the following 15 stereo pairs of images from camera locations:

$$CL1 - CL2, \; CL1 - CL3, \; CL1 - CL4, \; CL1 - CL5, \; CL1 - CL6,$$
$$CL2 - CL3, \; CL2 - CL4, \; CL2 - CL5, \; CL2 - CL6,$$
$$CL3 - CL4, \; CL3 - CL5, \; CL3 - CL6,$$
$$CL4 - CL5, \; CL4 - CL6,$$
$$CL5 - CL6.$$

In total, after round observation of the cell the system will register 210 coordinates for all gravity centers of FA upper surfaces.

Such great number of coordinates is caused by the image stereo pair feature. Camera axes in two locations are non-parallel both to each other and to the axis of the stereo pair. Here the term "stereo pair axis" describes a virtual line, which is perpendicular to the stereo base and passes through its middle. According to the photogrammetry principles, registered local coordinates from left and right cameras are independently translated into GCS.

In such conditions the problem of feasibility and necessity of the whole set of 210 registered coordinates of FA upper surfaces gravity centers comes natural and evident.

3 FA Height Control System Parameters

The CCD camera system observes the cell, where the distance between the gravity centers of adjacent FA upper surfaces is equal to 234 mm. The suspension height of the camera of 2,6 m and radius of camera locations of 3 m guarantees observation of the entire cell. The camera optical axis passes through point (0). The inclination angle of camera to OY axis is 49,1°.

If all FAs have the height of 3 mm, the 3D coordinates $(X_{CAMk}, Y_{CAMk}, Z_{CAMk})$ of the center and the vertices of regular hexagon (points (0) ... (6) in Fig. 1) in the cell GCS OXYZ can be specified by the 7×3 matrix $\|M\| = \|M_{ij}\|_{7,3}$. Here index i is a point number (0...6), and index j corresponds to the axes OX, OY и OZ, relatively. Their values in millimeters are as follows:

$$M_{01} = M_{03} = M_{33} = M_{63} = 0;$$
$$M_{02} = M_{12} = M_{22} = M_{32} = M_{42} = M_{52} = M_{62} = 3;$$
$$M_{11} = M_{51} = -117;$$
$$M_{21} = M_{41} = 117;$$
$$M_{31} = 234;$$
$$M_{61} = -234;$$
$$M_{13} = M_{23} = -203;$$
$$M43 = M53 = 203.$$

The system is supposed to use CDR 3223 Baxall camera with lens focal length 24 mm and CCD resolution 800×600. Its pixel size is 9×8, 8 µm.

The 3D points projection onto the CCD plane has continuous coordinates

$$x_{CAMk} = f \frac{X_{CAMk}}{Z_{CAMk}}; \quad y_{CAMk} = f \frac{Y_{CAMk}}{Z_{CAMk}}; \quad k = \overline{1, 6}.$$

The image description requires expressing the two-dimensional continuous points coordinates in CCD plane (x_{CAMk}, y_{CAMk}) by the two-dimensional discrete coordinates (u_{CAMk}, v_{CAMk}).

Let $u_0 = 0$ and $v_0 = 0$ be the discrete coordinates of point (0) relative to the origin expressed in the numbers of CCD cells along rows and columns (axes 0x and 0y). Then

$$u_{CAMk} = \left[\frac{x_{CAMk}}{K_{0x}}\right]; \quad v_{CAMk} = \left[\frac{y_{CAMk}}{K_{0y}}\right]; \quad k = \overline{1, 6},$$

where $K_{0x} = 9 \, \mu m \, per \, pixel$ and $K_{0y} = 8,8 \, \mu m \, per \, pixel$ are the scale factors for the distances between CCD cells in rows and columns (axes 0x and 0y).

These equations allow to calculate the pixel numbers for images of FA heads upper surfaces gravity centers.

Article [11] shows that 3D scene information construction requires 15 stereo pairs of images which are obtained as combinations of images in six camera locations. Only three stereo pairs of images, got as combinations of measurements from four camera locations (CL1...CL4 in Fig. 1) are of theoretical interest:

- stereo pair of images SPI1 is a combination of images from two adjacent locations (CL1−CL2);
- stereo pair of images SPI2 is a combination of images from two locations (CL1−CL3) which are in one of each other;
- stereo pair of images SPI3 is a combination of images from two opposite locations (CL1−CL4).

The following equations gives the calculation method for 3D coordinate vectors in four camera locations

$$\begin{bmatrix} Z_1 \\ Z_2 \end{bmatrix} = \begin{bmatrix} \vec{v_1^T} \cdot A_1^{-T} \cdot A_1^{-1} \cdot \vec{v_1} & -\vec{v_1^T} \cdot A_1^{-T} \cdot R^T \cdot A_2^{-1} \cdot \vec{v_1} \\ \vec{v_1^T} \cdot A_1^{-T} \cdot R^T \cdot A_2^{-1} \cdot \vec{v_2} & \vec{v_2^T} \cdot A_2^{-T} \cdot A_2^{-1} \cdot \vec{v_2} \end{bmatrix} \cdot \begin{bmatrix} \vec{v_1^T} \cdot A_1^{-T} \cdot R^T \\ \vec{v_2^T} \cdot A_2^{-T} \end{bmatrix} \cdot |t|,$$

where:

Z_1 and Z_2 are OZ-axis coordinates of one cell vertex for two analyzed camera locations;

$|t|$ is a translation matrix, which determines the position of camera optic center in the second location in the local coordinate system of the first camera location;

$\vec{v_1}$, $\vec{v_2}$ are vectors of homogeneous internal coordinates of the first and the second camera locations;

A_1, A_2 are matrices of internal camera location parameters, containing parameters of the camera optic system and of the photodetector.

This expression allows to calculate 3D coordinates of $\overrightarrow{M_{CAMk-SPIs}}$ vector for camera location k ($k = \overline{1, 4}$) based on stereo pair of images SPIs ($s = \overline{1, 3}$).

The developed mathematical model of CCD camera allows to make the reverse translation of coordinates in the camera discrete coordinate system into the observed cell GCS. Then, taking into account internal camera parameters and camera locations, it is possible to calculate FA upper surface gravity centers coordinates for the stereo pair of images and estimate the methodical error of FA heights measurement [12].

4 FA Height Measurement

4.1 FA Height Measurement Based on SPI from Two Adjacent Camera Locations CL1 - CL2

As established, points (5), (0) and (2) on the stereo pair axis have the same absolute FA height measurement error both from the location CL1 and from the location CL2. The error for point (5) is equal to −295 µm, for point (0) it is −865 µm, and for point (2) the error is 669 µm. The points (4) and (6) are located symmetrically relative to the stereo pair axis and at the same distance from it. But the coordinates of these points translated to the cell GCS are different as they are in different distance from the camera locations.

The difference in height measurement results for the points (4) and (6) is 149 µm. The measurement of the nearest camera location is expedient and preferable: location CL2 for point (6) and location CL1 for point (4).

The height measurement results for the points (1) and (3) prove this conclusion. Point (1) is closer to CL2 location than to CL1 location. Consequently, the height in the coordinate system of the camera in the location CL2, will have less error.

In contrast, the point (3) is closer to CL1, than to CL2. So, the error for CL1 is less than for CL2. Since the distance from the locations CL1 and CL2 to the points (1) and (3) differ less markedly, than for the points (4) and (6), the error in GCS for locations CL1 and CL2 will differ from each other less. The difference here is 56 µm only.

The points (5), (0) and (2) are equidistant from the CL1 and CL2 locations. Therefore, the results of any camera location measurement in GCS can be taken as a result for the points positioned on the stereo pair axis.

For points, that are located outside the stereo pair axis the height measurement from the closest location should be taken as a result.

4.2 FA Height Measurement Based on SPI from the Camera Locations CL1 - CL3

Here the point (0) lays on the stereo base axis and is equidistant from CL1 and CL3 locations. Therefore, it is the only point, where the object height measurement error is equal for both camera locations.

The distance from the point (1) to the camera location CL1 is equal to distance from the point (4) to the location CL3. Consequently, the error of measurement by the camera in the location CL1 for the point (1) is equal to the error of measurement by the camera in the location CL3 for the point (4) (147 µm). Similarly, the points (1) and (4) are equidistant from the camera in the locations CL1 и CL3, respectively. So, the error of the camera in the location CL3 (−95 µm) for the point (1) is equal to the error for the point (4) in the location CL1.

The relative error reaches 30% while height measurement for the cell center. The minimum relative error 3,2% is provided for FAs number (1) and (4), that are the least remote from the camera locations CL3 and CL1.

4.3 FA Height Measurement Based on SPI from the Camera Locations CL1 - CL4 with the Maximum Base of Stereo System

The points (0), (3) and (6) lay on the axis of stereo pair, therefore, the measurement of camera in any location can be chosen as a result. Moreover, these points are equidistant from the camera locations CL1 and CL4. The height measurement errors for the points (0), (3) and (6) are the same and equals to −865 µm.

The points (1) and (2) are positioned at the same distance from the camera in the location CL4. Similarly, this distance is equal to the distance from the points (4) and (5) to the camera in the location CL1. So, the height measurement error is the same and reaches 71 µm.

The error of height measurement for the points (1) and (2) (points (4) and (5)) in the location CL1 (CL4) is estimated as 78 µm.

The relative measurement error is up to 30% for the points (0), (3) and (6) on the axis of stereo pair. The minimum relative error 2,4% is provided for the other points in the camera locations, that are the closest to FAs.

5   Comparative Analysis of the FA Height Measurement Results

In all analyzed cases, any camera location and stereo pair of images can be chosen for the point (0). The FA height measurement error is maximum (865 μm) for any camera location combinations. High error is obtained while height measuring of the points (6) 689 μm and (3) 203 μm, as well.

Minimum error of FA height measurement is achieved for the points (1), (2), (4) and (5), when stereo pair of images SPI is formed from the opposite-directed camera positions (CL1−CL4).

Hence, minimum FA height measurement error (71 μm, 2,4%) can be provided by the stereo pair of images from the camera locations:

CL1 − CL4 for the points (1), (2), (4) and (5);

CL2 − CL5 for the points (2), (3), (5) and (6);

CL3 − CL6 for the points (1), (3), (4) and (6).

The result height value should be taken from the measurement of the camera in the closest position to the observed point.

6   Summary

The study of a fuel assembly height measurement algorithm, involving the movement of the camera around the circle forming the images from six positions, is presented in the article. Suspension height of the camera provides simultaneous observation of the cell with 7 FAs. The article proves that the minimum FA height measurement error can be achieved from the opposite located camera positions for the points beyond the stereo pair axis (when the stereo base is maximum and equals to 6 m). The result for each point should be taken from the closest camera location to the observed point. Therefore, measurements of the fuel assemblies head height from the opposite camera locations are sufficient for achievement of maximum measurement precision.

References

1. Makeev, V.V., Povarov, V.P., Korobkin, V.V., Lebedev, O.V.: Contactless height measurement system for fuel assembly heads in the nuclear reactor active zone. University News. North Caucasian Region. Technical Sciences Series, vol. 16, pp. 37–41 (2006)
2. Lozovskaya, E.G., Balabaev, S.L., Rumyantsev, K.E.: Error estimation for the height difference measurement for strictly geometrically arranged objects by the digital video system. In: Proceedings I Russian Scientific Confence of Young Scientists, Post-Graduates and Students Fundamental and Applied Aspects of Computer Technologies and Information Security, Taganrog, pp. 213–217 (2015)

3. Kalyaev, I.A., Korobkin, V.V., Kuharenko, A.P., Makeev, V.V., Povarov, V.P., Rumyantsev, K.E.: Innovations of Southern research center of RAS in control system development for atomics. Innovations **10**, 62–65 (2006)
4. Rumyantsev, K.E., Zibrov V.A., Balabaev S.L. (2004) Contactless measurement of rolling and metallurgical product dimensions. Shakhty
5. Kalyaev, I.A., Rumyantsev, K.E., Makeev, V.V., Balabaev, S.L., Korobkin, V.V., Korovin, J.S., Kuharenko, A.P., Radetzky, V.G.: Non-contact method for determining of the height of the heads nuclear reactor fuel assemblies on the basis of three-dimensional reconstruction images. Izv. SFedU. Eng. Sci. **80**(3), 126–131 (2008)
6. Balabaev, S.L., Kornilova, T.A., Lozovskaya, E.G., Rumyantsev, K.E.: Stereoscopic system for fuel assembly heads height monitoring in the nuclear reactor. In: Proceedings of XVI International Conference Complex objects control and modelling, Samara, pp. 673–677 (2014)
7. Balabaev, S.L., Radetzky, V.G., Rumyantsev, K.E.: Telemetry control method of the height of the cylindrical objects. Izv. SFedU. Eng. Sci. **80**(3), 94–110 (2008)
8. Lozovskaya, E.G., Balabaev, S.L., Rumyantsev, K.E.: The mathematical model of the recording video camera for the height measurement of the regularly situated objects. In: Materiały X Międzynarodowej naukowi-praktycznej konferencji Strategiczne pytania światowej nauki – 2014, vol. 31. pp. 27–34 (2014)
9. Balabaev, S.L., Lozovskaya, E.G., Rumyantsev, K.E.: Estimates of the error in the height of the strict geometric order of objects based on digital television systems on the CCD. Izv. SFedU. Eng. Sci. **157**(8), 227–241 (2014)
10. Rumyantsev, K.E., Balabaev, S.L., Lozovskaya, E.G.: Mathematical model of registering video camera for the fuel assembly head height measurement. Certificate of software official registration № 2015663359 RF (2015)
11. Balabaev, S.L., Lozovskaya, E.G., Rumyantsev, K.E.: Methods estimating uncertainty of measurement height of objects in strict geometrical order using the digital video systems. In: Proceedings of International Scientific - e-Symposium Physico-Mathematical Methods and Information Technology in Science, Technology and the Humanities. Kirov, pp. 61–76 (2015)
12. Balabaev, S.L., Lozovskaya, E.G.: The choice of camera position to minimize the measurement error of the fuel assembly head. Izv. SFedU. Eng. Sci. **169**(8), 58–76 (2015)

A Novel Approach to Segment Nucleus of Uterine Cervix Pap Smear Cells Using Watershed Segmentation

Sanjay Kumar Singh[1,2(✉)] and Anjali Goyal[3]

[1] IKG-Punjab Technical University, Jalandhar, Punjab, India
sanjayksingh.012@gmail.com
[2] Department of Computer Science and Engineering,
Lovely Professional University, Phagwara, Punjab, India
[3] Department of Computer Applications, GNIMT, Ludhiana, Punjab, India
anjali.garg73@gmail.com

Abstract. This paper presents an approach for segmentation of nuclei of uterine cervix pap smear cells using watershed segmentation. The proposed approach consists of manly three steps: preprocessing of pap smear images, formation of improved binary image and application of watershed segmentation to extract nucleus part of pap smear images. The novelty of proposed approach is that it has introduced systematic way to create improved binary image using thresholding and series of morphological operations as explained in proposed methodology Sect. 2. Each single cell image is segmented in three regions namely nucleus, boundary between nucleus and background and background of image.

Keywords: Pap smear · Watershed segmentation · Morphological operations · Thresholding · Nuclei detection

1 Introduction

Discovery of cervical cancer is one of the most alarming and feared health problems in women. Cancer of cervical uterine was the second most widespread type of cancer that affected women in 2012. In that year, the 230131 cases of cervical cancer and 117780 deaths due to cervix cancer were noted only in India [1]. Figure 1 shows the prediction of cervical cancer incidence in India with age group less than 65 year and above 65 years.

Figure 1 highlights that approximately 57% incidence will increase with respect to 2012 in 2035. Today's major issue that affects women's health is cancer of cervix, most particularly in the countries under development [2].

Three datasets were used [3] for removing debris by segmentation of cervical cell include cell nuclei and debris. Here after removing unwanted objects, the classifier is applied to make classification. Accurate nuclei detection [4] using segmentation algorithms to extract the inflammatory cells by combination of gray level thresholding and distance rule. Semiautomatic computer based cellular image analysis system proposed [5], which is intended to segment nuclear and cytoplasm contours and use

© Springer Nature Singapore Pte Ltd. 2017
D. Singh et al. (Eds.): ICAICR 2017, CCIS 712, pp. 164–174, 2017.
DOI: 10.1007/978-981-10-5780-9_15

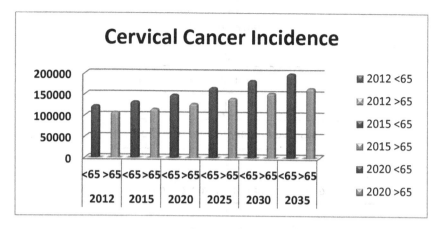

Fig. 1. Prediction of cervical cancer incidence in India

morphometric and textual features to train support vector machine (SVM) to classify different types of cells.

Morphological approach for image segmentation combined both region growing and edge detection [6] includes grouping of image pixels near minima region of image and boundaries of groupings are located along crest lines of the gradient image. An edge-based watershed technique [7] used to segment remote sensing images and over segmentation of watershed is controlled by spectral marker and morphological marker that are extracted automatically by the data.

2   Proposed Methodology

Proposed approach for segmentation of nuclei of cervix pap smear cells involved various steps includes removal of noise, converting to binary image, obtaining improved binary image using threshold and filling holes after that apply watershed transformation on distance transform of improved binary image. Figure 2 shows the approach used in the proposed work.

2.1   Database Preparation

For this work a 500 single cells pap smear image [8] has been used. The database includes 200 normal pap smear cell images and 300 dysplastic pap smear cell images. For this work we have only considered 250 squamous cells with different categories as shown in Table 1.

2.2   Pre-processing

Pre-processing of cervical cells involved mainly two tasks, first task is to smooth the image with Gaussian low pass filter of size 5×5 and standard deviation having value 0.5, filter matrix is given in Eq. 1 and second task is to convert in binary image [9].

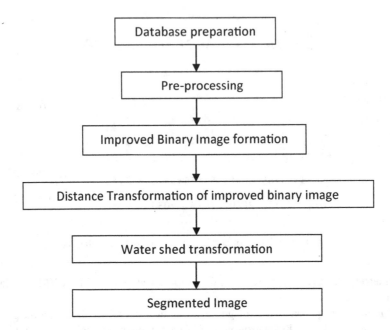

Fig. 2. Proposed approach for segmentation

Table 1. Types of cells used for segmentation

Class (N/D)	Cell type	No. of single cell image
Normal (N)	Superficial squamous epitheelial cells (SSE)	50
Normal (N)	Intermediate squamous epitheelial cells (ISE)	50
Dysplastic (D)	Mild squamous dysplastic cells (MSD)	50
Dysplastic (D)	Severe squamous dysplastic cells (SSD)	50
Dysplastic(D)	Squamous Carcinoma in situ cells (SCS)	50

Figure 3 shows the filtered image by applying low pass filter and binary image by Otsu algorithm [9].

$$H = \begin{bmatrix} 0 & 0 & 0.0002 & 0 & 0 \\ 0 & 0.0113 & 0.0837 & 0.0113 & 0 \\ 0.0002 & 0.0837 & 0.6187 & 0.0837 & 0.0002 \\ 0 & 0.0113 & 0.0837 & 0.0113 & 0 \\ 0 & 0 & 0.0002 & 0 & 0 \end{bmatrix} \tag{1}$$

2.3   Improved Binary Image

This is the main work of this paper which involves the following steps:

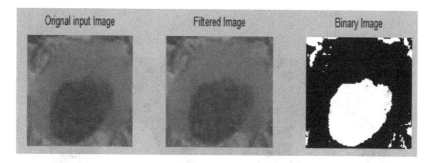

Fig. 3. Filtered and binary image

Thresholed Binary Image

Binary image formed by Otsu method [9] has more outliers or contain objects, which is not the part of nucleus. So using thresholding technique to convert in binary image, removes some unwanted objects from image. For this purpose we have used threshold value which is the mean of smallest gray value and highest gray value of image. Figure 4 shows the binary image by Otsu algorithm and output of threshold image.

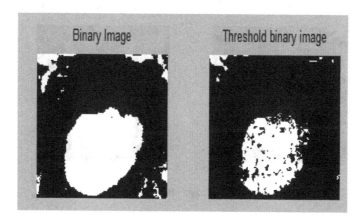

Fig. 4. Threshold binary image

Fill Holes

As threshold output binary image contain holes hence it required to fills the holes in order to complete the object. For this purpose we have use the algorithm proposed in paper [10]. Figure 5 shows the output after filling the holes.

Remove Small Object from Binary Image

Here the basic step required is, to determine the connected components of binary image and then compute the area of each component. After computing the area of each component remove the small object that looks like outlier or not the part of nucleus using threshold techniques. We have used the threshold value as half of total number of pixels involved in object. Figure 6 shows the output after removing of small objects.

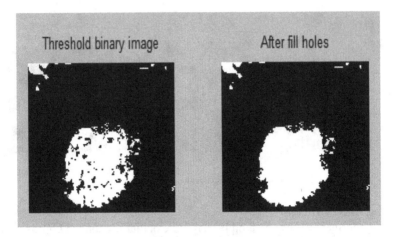

Fig. 5. Binary image after filling holes

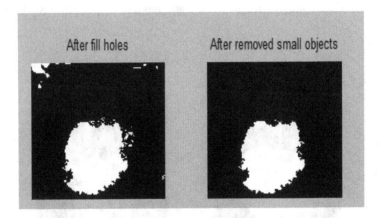

Fig. 6. Improved binary image after removing of small object

2.4 Distance Transformation of Improved Binary Image

It involves first step as to computation of the Euclidean distance transformation of complement of improved binary image. Second step is to complement the distance transformation and then force the pixel that not belongs to the object as $-\infty$.

2.5 Watershed Transformation

Watershed lines can be used as basic tool in segmenting an image using mathematical morphology [11]. We have used algorithm to compute watershed transformation proposed by Fernand Meyer [11]. This algorithm uses mainly gradient image that detects the catchments basins of all minimum in gradient images.

3 Result and Discussion

Results of proposed algorithm of segmentation are shown in Tables 2 and 3. Table 2 contains normal cells of superficial squamous epitheelial cells (SSE) and intermediate squamous epitheelial cells (ISE). Table 3 contains dysplastic cells of mild squamous

Table 2. Result for normal cells using proposed approach

Sr. No.	Cell Type	Result of Watershed transform for nucleus using proposed approach
1	SSE	
2	SSE	

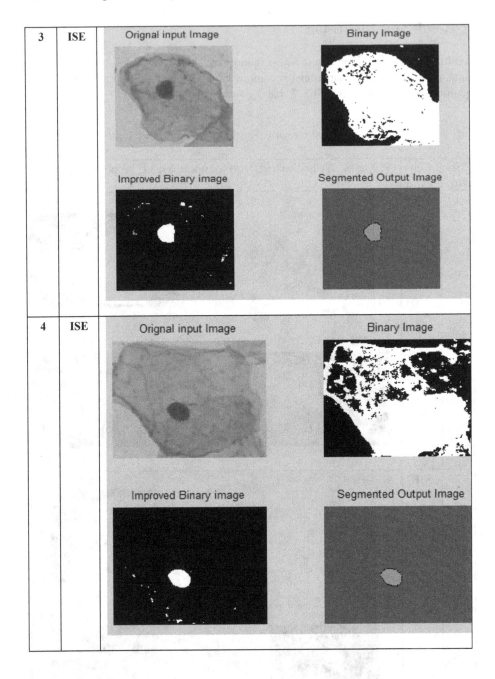

dysplastic cells (MSD), severe squamous dysplastic cells (SSD) and squamous Carcinoma in situ cells (SCS).

Table 3. Result for dysplastic cells using proposed approach

Sr. No.	Cell Type	Result of Watershed transform for nucleus using proposed approach
1	MSD	
2	MSD	

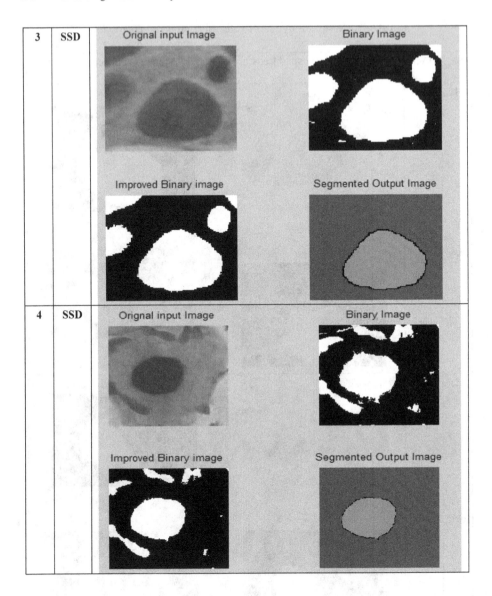

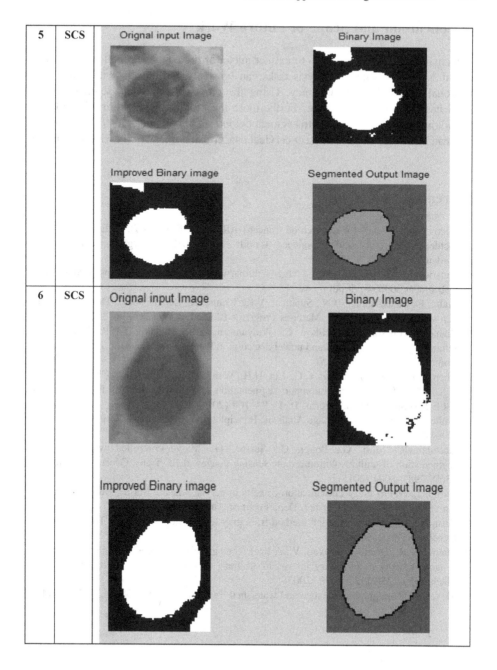

From the results, it is emphasized that watershed transformation can easily be used to segment nuclei of pap smear cell images. The boundary represented by black color, background represented by red color and nuclei represented by green color respectively.

4   Conclusion and Scope of Future Work

Segmentation is considered here to extract nuclei of the pap smear cell images; based on which, more advanced analysis tasks can be easily carried out, with lower computational cost and better accuracy. Using the proposed approach, segmentation of nuclei has been accurately done. Furthermore the proposed algorithm with different thresholding values can be used to segment cytoplasm of cell nuclei also. The proposed work can also be extended to detect cervical cancer using image processing techniques.

References

1. International Agency for research on Cancer (IARC) GLOBOCAN 2012: Estimated Cancer Incidence, Mortality and Prevalence Worldwide in 2012. http://globocan.iarc.fr/Pages/burden_sel.aspx
2. American Cancer Society, Inc. http://www.cancer.org/acs/groups/cid/documents/webcontent/003094-pdf.pdf
3. Malm, P., Balakrishnan, B.N., Sujathan, V.K., Kumar, R., Bengtsson, E.: Debris removal in Pap smear images. Comput. Methods Programs Biomed. 3(1), 128–138 (2013)
4. Riana, D., Plissiti, M.E., Nikou, C., Widyantoro, D.H., Mengko, T.L.R., Kalsoem, O.: Inflammatory cell extraction and nuclei detection in Pap smear images. Int. J. E-Health Med. Commun. 6(2), 27–43 (2015)
5. Chen, Y.F., Huang, P.C., Lin, K.C., Lin, H.H., Wang, L.E., Cheng, C.C., Chen, T.P., Chan, Y.K., Chiang, J.Y.: Semi-automatic segmentation and classification of Pap smear cells. IEEE J. Biomed. Health Inform. 18(1), 94–108 (2014)
6. Soille, P.: Morphological Image Analysis: Principles and Applications. Springer, Heidelberg (2004)
7. Gaetano, R., Masi, G., Poggi, G., Scarpa, G.: Marker-controlled watershed based segmentation of multiresolution remote sensing images. IEEE Trans. Geosci. Remote Sens. 53(6), 2987–3004 (2015)
8. Byriel, J.: Neuro-fuzzy classification of cells in cervial smears. Master's thesis, Technical University of Denmark, Oersted. Department of Automation (1999)
9. Otsu, N.: A threshold selection method from gray-level histograms. IEEE Trans. Syst. Man Cybern. 9(1), 62–66 (1979)
10. Maurer, C.R., Qi, R., Raghavan, V.: A linear time algorithm for computing exact Euclidean distance transforms of binary images in arbitrary dimensions. IEEE Trans. Pattern Anal. Mach. Intell. 25(2), 265–270 (2003)
11. Meyer, F.: Topographic distance and watershed lines. Sig. Process. 38, 113–125 (1994)

Parametric Study of Various Direction of Arrival Estimation Techniques

Dharmendra Ganage[1](✉) and Y. Ravinder[2]

[1] Department of E&TC, Sinhgad College of Engineering, Pune, India
dgganage@gmail.com
[2] Department of E&TC, Pune Institute of Computer Technology, Pune, India
yerramravi@yahoo.com

Abstract. The adaptive antenna array system consists of a number of an antenna array element with the signal processing unit, which can adapt its radiation pattern to provide maxima towards the desired user and null towards the interferer. Hence to locate the desired user Direction of Arrival (DOA) of the signal needs to be estimated. This paper presents a parametric study of various DOA estimation algorithms on the uniform linear array (ULA) and also a comparative performance regarding resolution, Signal-to-Noise Ratio (SNR), the number of snapshots, separation angle, etc. It starts with traditional methods of Minimum Variance Distortionless Response (MVDR) algorithm. The subspace-based techniques use the eigenstructure of data covariance matrix. The different subspace-based techniques are Multiple Signal Classification (MUSIC), Root-MUSIC, and Estimation of Signal Parameters via Rotational Invariance Technique (ESPRIT). However, simulation results show that the antenna array elements, SNR, the snapshots, coherent nature of signals, and separation angle between the two sources can affect the DOA estimation results. The result shows that MUSIC algorithm has comparatively better resolution than MVDR, Root-MUSIC and ESPRIT algorithms.

Keywords: DOA · MVDR · MUSIC · Root-MUSIC · ESPRIT

1 Introduction

The Direction of Arrival (DOA) estimation techniques are the emerging applications of many actual domains, such as radar, speech signal processing, mobile communication and so on [1–3]. DOA estimation technique is an essential part of Smart Antenna. The antenna array which collects data from impinging signals on it with a combination of spatial information by receiving signals, this received data used to estimate the angle of arrival with higher resolution algorithms [1, 4].

There are four different types of DOA estimation technique conventional, maximum likelihood, subspace based and integrated techniques [2, 5]. Beamforming techniques were used in conventional methods, and it requires a large number of the antenna element for getting better resolution. Maximum likelihood technique requires large computation. The integrated technique is a combination of property restoral technique and subspace-based technique. The sum and delay or Bartlett and MVDR or

© Springer Nature Singapore Pte Ltd. 2017
D. Singh et al. (Eds.): ICAICR 2017, CCIS 712, pp. 175–184, 2017.
DOI: 10.1007/978-981-10-5780-9_16

Capon etc. are spatial correlation type method. The DOA estimation techniques such as MVDR, MUSIC, Root-MUSIC, and ESPRIT have been analyzed.

The paper is organized as follows. The uniform linear array structure is presented in Sect. 2 with mathematical formulation required for DOA estimation algorithms. Section 3 details explanation of various DOA estimation algorithms. Next Sect. 4 shows the simulation result and discussion. Section 5 presents conclusion on the basis of simulation results.

2   Array Sensor System

Figure 1 shows the system consists of Uniform Linear Array (ULA) [1, 3]. Consider the D-number of signals impinges on ULA antenna elements, the received input data vector at M-elements, separated by a distance d can be represented as a combination of the D-incident signals and noise $n(t)$. The signal vector $u(t)$ is defined as

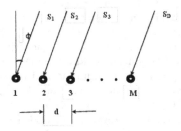

Fig. 1. Uniform linear array

$$u(t) = \sum_{l=0}^{D-1} a(\phi_1)s_1(t) + n(t) \tag{1}$$

$$u(t) = [a(\phi_0)...a(\phi_{D-1})] \begin{bmatrix} s_1(t) \\ \vdots \\ s_l(t) \end{bmatrix} + n(t) \tag{2}$$

$$u(t) = As(t) + n(t) \tag{3}$$

Where, $s(t)$ is the vector of incident signals, $n(t)$ is the noise vector, and $a(\phi_j)$ is the array steering vector. In terms of the above data model, the input covariance matrix R_{uu} expressed as [3].

$$R_{uu} = AE[ss^H]A^H + E[nn^H] \tag{4}$$

Where R_{ss} is the signal correlation matrix of $E[ss^H]$.

3 DOA Estimation Algorithms

3.1 MVDR Algorithm

The concept of MVDR algorithm is to minimize the received power in all direction of every impinging signal to nullify the effect of interference, also maintain a unity gain in desired direction [6, 7]. The condition apply on this algorithm is given as

$$\min_w E\left[|y(k)|^2\right] = \min_w w^H R_{uu} w \text{ subject to } w^H a(\phi_0) = 1 \qquad (5)$$

By solving (5), the obtained w weight vector is (MVDR) beamformer weights. Applying Lagrange multiplier to Eq. (5) which is a constraint optimization,

$$w = \frac{R_{uu}^{-1} a(\phi)}{a^H(\phi) R_{uu} a(\phi)} \qquad (6)$$

The output power spectrum of MVDR for DOA estimation is given as,

$$P_{MVDR}(\phi) = \frac{1}{a^H(\phi) R_{uu}^{-1} a(\phi)} \qquad (7)$$

3.2 MUSIC Algorithm

The Multiple Signal Classification algorithm was proposed by Schmidt [8] in 1979. The array correlation matrix R_{uu} is given as follows,

$$R_{uu} = A R_{ss} A^H + \sigma_n^2 I \qquad (8)$$

Next step is to find the correlational matrices eigenvalues and their associated eigenvectors. Then produce D and $M - D$ eigenvectors associated with the signals and noise respectively. Select the eigenvectors having smallest eigenvalues [9, 12]. Then construct the $M \times (M - D)$ dimensional subspace composed of the noise eigenvectors such that,

$$V_n = [q_1, q_2 \ldots q_{M-D}] \qquad (9)$$

The steering vectors of array and eigenvectors of noise subspace are orthogonal to each other, $a^H(\phi) V_n V_n^H a(\phi) = 0$ at an angle of arrival. Hence the MUSIC spectrum can be calculated as

$$P_{music}(\phi) = \frac{1}{a^H(\phi) V_n V_n^H a(\phi)} \qquad (10)$$

The condition of orthogonality will give rises to peaks in the spectrum of MUSIC defined in Eq. (10) by minimizing the denominator.

3.3 Root-MUSIC Algorithm

To increase resolution performance and decrease the computational complexity various modifications have been proposed to the MUSIC algorithm. The Root-MUSIC algorithm developed by Barabell [10] which is based on an idea of polynomial rooting giving higher resolution, but it works only if a uniform spaced linear array is present. For the case of a uniform linear array with the spacing between each element is d, the Mth element of the antenna steering vector $a(\phi)$ which can expressed as,

$$a_m(\phi) = \exp\left(j2\pi\left(\frac{d}{\lambda}\right)\cos\phi\right); m = 1, 2, \ldots M. \tag{11}$$

The MUSIC spectrum is given by

$$P_{music}(\phi) = \frac{1}{a^H(\phi)C\,a(\phi)}, \text{ Where } C = V_n V_n^H \tag{12}$$

$$P_{MUSIC}^{-1}(\phi) = \sum_{l=-M+1}^{M+1} C_1 \exp\left(-j2\pi\left(\frac{dl}{\lambda}\right)\cos\phi\right) \tag{13}$$

$$D(z) = \sum_{l=-M+1}^{M+1} C_1 Z^{-1} \tag{14}$$

Evaluating the MUSIC spectrum becomes equivalent to evaluating the roots of the polynomial given by $D(z)$ on the unity circle, and therefore peaks of the spectrum [13]. In true sense, for the noiseless condition, the roots of the polynomial at the denominator of the function is called as poles and will be expressed on the unity circle which will determine DOA of impinging signal. In other words, a pole of $D(z)$ at $z = z_1 = |z_1| \exp(j \arg(z_1))$ will leads to obtain a peak in the Root-MUSIC spectrum at

$$\cos\phi = \left(\frac{\lambda}{2\pi d}\right) \arg(z_1) \tag{15}$$

3.4 ESPRIT Algorithm

Estimation of Signal Parameters via Rotational Invariance Technique (ESPRIT) algorithm involves decomposing an N element array into two identical subarrays each with S element [11]. The objective of ESPRIT algorithm is to estimate the direction of arrival by determining the rotation operator. The relation of $u_0(t), u_1(t)$ are received signals, and $n_0(t), n_1(t)$ are additive noise is given as:

$$u_0(t) = As(t) + n_0(t) \quad \text{and} \quad u_1(t) = A(\phi)s(t) + n_1(t) \tag{16}$$

and, $\phi = diag\{e^{j\psi_1}, e^{j\psi_2}, \ldots, e^{j\psi_M}\}$; where $\psi = kd\sin\theta_m$ and $m = 1, 2, \ldots, M$ (17)

$$\therefore u(t) = \begin{bmatrix} u_0(t) \\ u_1(t) \end{bmatrix} = \bar{A}s(t) + n(t) \tag{18}$$

As per input covariance matrix given in Eq. (8), the Eigen decomposition becomes:

$$\hat{R}_{uu} = V \wedge V^H \tag{19}$$

Where $\wedge = diag\{\lambda_0 \ldots \lambda_{M-1}\}$ and $V = [q_0 \ldots q_{M-1}]$ represent the eigenvalues and eigenvectors. Estimation of the number of signals $\hat{D}$, by using the theorem of multiplicity, K of the smallest eigenvalue $\lambda_{\min}, \hat{D} = M - K$. Obtain, the estimation of the signal subspace $\hat{V}_s = \lfloor \hat{V}_0 \ldots \hat{V}_{L-1} \rfloor$ and decomposes it into sub-array matrix, and compute the eigendecomposition $(\lambda_0 \ldots \lambda_{2i})$ and partition V into $\hat{D} \times \hat{D}$ sub-matrices,

$$\hat{V}_{01}^H \hat{V}_{01} = \begin{bmatrix} \hat{V}_0^H \\ \hat{V}_1^H \end{bmatrix} \begin{bmatrix} \hat{V}_0^H & \hat{V}_1^H \end{bmatrix} \tag{20}$$

$$V = \begin{bmatrix} V_{11} & V_{12} \\ V_{21} & V_{22} \end{bmatrix} \tag{21}$$

Calculate the eigenvalues of $\psi_1 = -V_{12}V_{22}^{-1}$ as,

$$\hat{\phi}_K = \text{eigenvalues of} \left(-V_{12}V_{22}^{-1} \right), \text{Where } K = 0 \ldots \hat{L} - 1 \tag{22}$$

ESPRIT gives the DOA estimation in terms of the eigenvaluee, therefore estimate the DOA as,

$$\theta_K = \cos^{-1}\left[\frac{\arg\left(\hat{\phi}_K\right)}{\beta d} \right] \tag{23}$$

4 Simulation Results

DOA estimation techniques simulated using Matlab 2014a. In these simulations, 30 antenna elements of ULA are considered which are equally separated by the distance of $\lambda/2$. The noise is ideal Gaussian white noise. The simulation has been run for two independent narrow band signals with equal amplitude, and 1000 numbers of snapshots. The performance has been analyzed with different values array elements, and Signal to Noise ratio. The closely spaced and coherent type of nature of signals, also considered for the evaluating the performance of theses algorithms.

4.1 MVDR Algorithm

Case 1: Effect of signal to noise ratio and number of array elements on MVDR

The effect of changing the signal to noise ratio with three different values $SNR_1 = 10$,

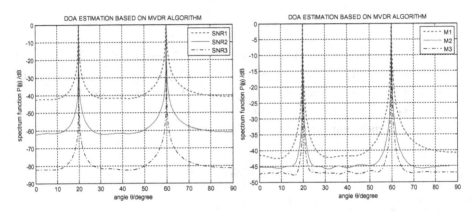

Fig. 2. MVDR spectrum (a) Effect of SNR; (b) Effect of antenna elements

$SNR_2 = 20$ and $SNR_3 = 30$, with the DOA is 20^0 and 60^0, it is clear from Fig. 2(a), as the value of SNR increases, the beamwidth of power spectrum becomes narrower. The resolution of DOA estimation can be increased by increasing SNR. Now, the three different values of the number of array elements are $M_1 = 10$, $M_2 = 50$, $M_3 = 100$. It is found that the width of the spectral beam becomes narrower as the number of array elements increases as shown in Fig. 2(b).

Case 2: Effect of closely spaced in resolution and coherent signals on MVDR

The effect of closely spaced signals on MVDR algorithm with DOA is 20^0 and 24^0 i.e. with 4^0 resolution of the signals. It is clear from Fig. 3(a), as the signals are very close, MVDR gets fails to resolve the signal and observes very poor beamwidth in power spectrum. Now, if the two narrow band signals has large resolution with coherent in nature, and processes by MVDR. It is clear from Fig. 3(b), spectrum becomes oscillating. The auto covariance matrix rank degrades effectively when the signals are coherent in nature as well as in closely spaced in nature, and the MVDR shows poor performance.

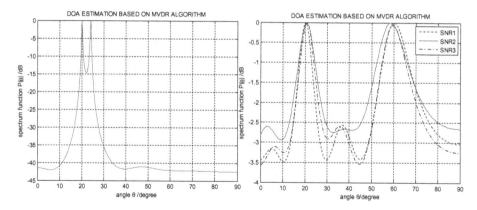

Fig. 3. MVDR spectrum (a) Closely spaced signals; (b) Effect of coherent signals

4.2 MUSIC Algorithm

Case 1: Effect of signal to noise ratio and number of array elements on MUSIC

The effect of changing the signal to noise ratio with three different values $SNR_1 = 10$, $SNR_2 = 20$ and $SNR_3 = 30$, with the DOA is 20^0 and 60^0, it is clear from Fig. 4(a), value of SNR increases, the spectral beam width becomes narrower the direction of the signal becomes clearer. The accuracy of DOA estimation can be increased by increasing SNR. Also, the three different values of the number of array elements are $M_1 = 10$, $M_2 = 50$, $M_3 = 100$. Figure 4(b), shows that as the value of array elements increases, the spectral beam width becomes narrower.

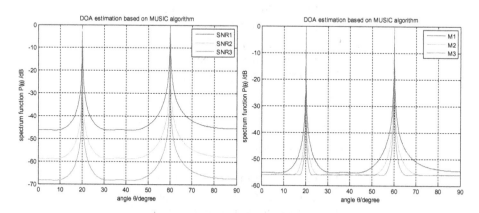

Fig. 4. MUSIC spectrum (a) Effect of SNR; (b) Effect of antenna elements

Case 2: Effect of closely spaced in resolution and coherent signals MUSIC

The effect of closely spaced signals on MUSIC algorithm with DOA is 20^0 and 24^0 i.e. with 4^0 resolution of the signals. It is clear from Fig. 5(a), as the signals are very close, MUSIC gets resolve the signal but with less spectral beamwidth and observes

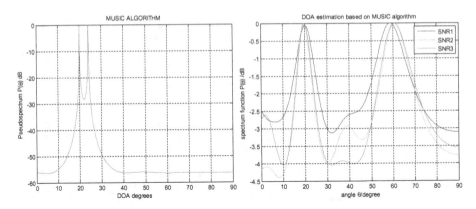

Fig. 5. MUSIC spectrum (a) Closely spaced signals; (b) Effect of coherent signals

satisfactorily performance in upper power levels in output spectrum. Now, if the two narrow band signals has large resolution with coherent in nature processes by MUSIC with the different values of SNR. It is clear from Fig. 5(b), spectrum becomes oscillating. The auto covariance matrix rank degrades effectively, when the signals are coherent in nature, and the MUSIC shows poor performance. It requires the computation of the matrix inverse which can be expensive for large arrays.

Table 1. Root-MUSIC spectrum: DOA vs. number of snapshots

DOA	Number of snapshots →			
	10	50	100	200
14^0	13.8917	13.9186	13.9987	13.9989
23^0	23.1703	22.9479	22.9857	22.9998
35^0	34.8885	35.0784	34.9882	34.9991
55^0	55.4278	54.8934	54.9763	54.9983

Table 2. Root-MUSIC spectrum: DOA vs. SNR

DOA	Signal to noise ratio in dB →			
	0	10	20	30
14^0	13.8917	13.9186	13.9987	13.9989
23^0	23.1703	22.9479	22.9857	22.9998
35^0	34.8885	35.0784	34.9882	34.9991
55^0	55.4278	54.8934	54.9763	54.9983

4.3 Root-MUSIC Algorithm

The simulation has been carried out for four independent narrow band signals with a DOA of 14^0, 23^0, 35^0, and 55^0. The performance of each independent signal has been analyzed for different values of snapshots (10, 50, 100, and 200) expressed in Table 1. Also, the performance of each independent signal has been analyzed for different values of SNR in dB (0, 10, 20, and 30) expressed in Table 2.

As the value of number of snapshots and signal to noise ratio increases the Root-MUSIC gives an accurate estimation of the direction of arrival.

Table 3. ESPRIT spectrum: DOA vs. number of snapshots

DOA	Number of snapshots →			
	10	50	100	200
14^0	14.0265	13.9676	13.9223	14.0080
23^0	22.9250	22.9413	22.9494	23.0563
35^0	34.9665	35.0124	35.0710	35.0144
55^0	54.9639	55.1145	54.9493	54.9963

Table 4. ESPRIT spectrum: DOA vs. SNR

DOA	Signal to noise ratio in dB →			
	0	10	20	30
14^0	13.8917	13.9186	13.9987	13.9989
23^0	23.1703	22.9479	22.9857	22.9998
35^0	34.8885	35.0784	34.9882	34.9991
55^0	55.4278	54.8934	54.9763	54.9983

4.4 ESPRIT Algorithm

The simulation has been carried out for four independent narrow band signals with a DOA of 14^0, 23^0, 35^0, and 55^0. The performance of each independent signal has been analyzed for different values of snapshots (10, 50 100, and 200) expressed in Table 3. Also, the performance for different values of SNR in dB (0, 10 20, and 30) expressed in Table 4.

Hence, the number of snapshots and SNR can be increased for accurate DOA estimation of the signal. As seen from simulation results of various DOA estimation techniques, as a number of snapshots, signal to noise ratio and a number of antenna elements increases, the resolution goes on increasing and results are more sharpen. The reason is that simulation environment is ideal i.e. 30 antenna elements, 1000 snapshots, and positive value of SNR. In practical situations, such as multiple signal receptions, aliasing, zero or negative value of SNR, with less number of snapshots, and fewer number of an antenna elements was degraded the performance of these algorithms. The remedy and scope for future modifications of these existing techniques are to develop the pre-processing as well as post-processing techniques to inherit the performance in real and practical environment.

5 Conclusions

This paper presents comparative performance simulation study of various DOA estimation techniques and their dependence of various parameters. The different DOA estimation techniques are MVDR, MUSIC, Root-MUSIC and ESPRIT algorithms. The algorithms were found to be responsive to the array elements, snapshots, SNR. The simulation result also shows that the resolution of the algorithm increases with increasing the number of array elements, the number of snapshots, SNR. The MUSIC algorithm is accurate as compared to the MVDR, Root-MUSIC, and ESPRIT algorithm, but has wide radiation pattern. The MUSIC algorithm is showing good performance in closely spaced signals compared to the MVDR, Root-MUSIC, and ESPRIT algorithm. Also, for coherent sources, MUSIC algorithm is not as efficient as Root-MUSIC and ESPRIT algorithm.

References

1. Balanis, C.A.: Antenna Theory Analysis and Design. Wiley, Hoboken (2005)
2. Liberti, J.C., Rappaport, T.S.: Smart Antenna for Wireless Communications. Prentice Hall PTR, Upper Saddle River (1999)
3. Gross, F.: Smart Antennas for Wireless Communications: With MATLAB. McGraw-Hill, New York City (2005)
4. Godara, L.A.: Application of antenna arrays to mobile communications, Part I: performance improvement, feasibility, and system considerations. Proc. IEEE **85**, 1031–1060 (1997)
5. Capon, J.: High-resolution frequency-wave number spectrum analysis. Proc. IEEE **57**(8), 1408–1418 (1969)
6. Schmidt, R.: Multiple emitter location and signal parameter estimation. IEEE Trans. Antennas Propag. **34**(3), 276–280 (1986)
7. Barabell, A.: Improving the resolution of eigen structure-based direction-finding algorithms. In: IEEE International Conference on Acoustics, Speech and Signal Processing, vol. 8, pp. 336–339 (1983)
8. Roy, R., Kailath, T.: ESPRIT Estimation of signal parameters via rotational invariance techniques. IEEE Trans. Acoust. Speech Sig. Process. **37**(7), 984–995 (1989)
9. Xiao-guang, W., Tian-wen, G.: Direction of arrival parametric estimation and simulation based on MATLAB. J. Comput. Inf. Syst. **6**(14), 4723–4731 (2010)
10. Abdalla, M.M., Abuitbel, M.M., Hassan, M.: Performance evaluation of direction of arrival estimation using MUSIC and ESPRIT algorithms for mobile communication systems. In: Proceedings of the IEEE (2013)
11. Sanudin, R., Noordin, N.H., El-Rayis, A.O., Haridas, N., Erdogan, A.T., Arslan, T.: Capon-like DOA estimation algorithm for directional antenna arrays. In: IEEE International Conference on Antennas and Propagation (2011)
12. Mohanna, M., Rabeh, M.L., Zieur, E.M., Hekala, S.: Optimization of MUSIC algorithm for angle of arrival estimation in wireless communications. NRIAG J. Astron. Geophys. **2**, 116–124 (2013)
13. Waweru, N.P., Konditi, D.B.O., Langat, P.K.: Performance Analysis of MUSIC. Root-MUSIC ESPRIT DOA Estimation Algorithm **8**, 212–219 (2014)

Deep CNN-Based Method for Segmenting Lung Fields in Digital Chest Radiographs

Simranpreet Kaur[1(✉)], Rahul Hooda[2], Ajay Mittal[1], Akashdeep[1], and Sanjeev Sofat[2]

[1] UIET, Panjab University, Chandigarh, India
simranpreetkaur0905@gmail.com,
{ajaymittal,akashdeep}@pu.ac.in
[2] PEC University of Technology, Chandigarh, India
r89hooda@gmail.com

Abstract. Lung Field Segmentation (LFS) is an indispensable step for detecting austere lung diseases in various computer-aided diagnosis. This paper presents a deep learning-based Convolutional Neural Network (CNN) for segmenting lung fields in chest radiographs. The proposed CNN network consists of three sets of convolutional-layer and rectified linear unit (ReLU) layer, followed by a fully connected layer. At each convolutional layer, 64 filters retrieve the representative features. Japanese Society of Radiological Technology (JSRT) dataset is used for training and validation. Test results have 98.05% average accuracy, 93.4% average overlap, 96.25% average sensitivity, and 98.80% average specificity. The obtained results are promising and better than many of the existing state-of-the-art LFS techniques.

Keywords: Lung Field Segmentation (LFS) · Convolutional Neural Network (CNN) · Deep learning · Chest radiography

1 Introduction

Chest radiography is still the most commonly used imaging modality for diagnosing various pulmonary diseases. Nowadays, digital chest radiographs (DCRs) have completely replaced the conventional screen film radiographs due their reduced radiation dose, better image quality, and lesser acquisition time. Moreover, automatic interpretation of these DCRs by computer-aided diagnosis (CADx) systems have significantly reduced the diagnosis time, inter- and intra-observer variability, and have greatly helped the clinical practitioners in effective decision making.

A chest radiographic CADx system firstly segments an anatomical structure such as lungs, heart, clavicles, mediastinum, and rib-cage to define the region- of-interest (RoI), and then search for specific kind of patterns in the defined RoI to detect abnormalities. Lungs being largest amongst various anatomical structures in the thoracic region, most of the CADx systems for lung cancer, tuberculosis, chronic obstructive pulmonary disease (COPD), and pneumonia firstly segment the lung fields. In context of CADx systems, lung fields include the air cavities in the lung region, and exclude the area obscured by the pleural fluid, mediastinum, heart, and aorta.

© Springer Nature Singapore Pte Ltd. 2017
D. Singh et al. (Eds.): ICAICR 2017, CCIS 712, pp. 185–194, 2017.
DOI: 10.1007/978-981-10-5780-9_17

Although, lung field segmentation (LFS) problem has been extensively researched during the last four decades, it has not been completely solved being complex and extremely challenging in nature. The various challenges involved in segmenting lung fields involve (i) overlapping anatomical structures such as heart, clavicles, rib-cage, and mediastinum, (ii) variations in shape and size due to factors such as age, gender, and physical structure of subject, (iii) highly dynamic range of DCR image intensities depending upon radiation dose, and other parameters of x-ray machine, (iv) presence of foreign objects such as buttons, brassier clips, and catheters, and (v) varied pathological indications and radiologic artifacts.

This paper presents a deep CNN based method for segmenting lung fields in digital chest radiographs. The proposed CNN architecture consists of 7 layers organized as three sets of convolutional and ReLU layers, followed by a fully connected layer. The deep CNN is trained over 4960 128 × 128 images obtained by augmenting 124 resized images from JSRT dataset.

The rest of the paper is organized as follows. Section 2 presents a brief overview of various LFS methods presented till date. An introduction to CNNs is provided in Sect. 3. The proposed methodology is presented in detail in Sect. 4, followed by results and discussions in Sect. 5. Section 6 concludes the work.

2 Related Work

As illustrated in Fig. 1, van Ginneken *et al.* [1] classified LFS methods into four broad categories (i) rule-based methods, (ii) pixel classification-based methods, (iii) deformable model-based methods, and (iv) hybrid methods.

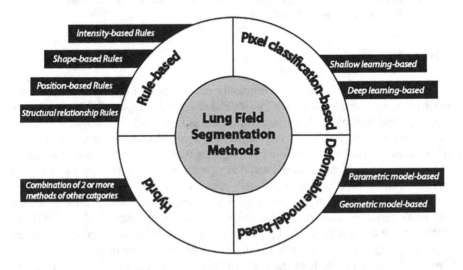

Fig. 1. Classification of LFS methods

Rule-based LFS methods use heuristic rules formulated from the prior knowledge of lung anatomy and its imaging characteristics to segment the lung field. A number of rule-based LFS methods [2–5] have been proposed that segments the lung fields on the basis of intensity, position, shape, texture, and their structural relationship with other anatomical structures. Generally, a number of rules are applied in sequence to obtain the desired result. The rule-based LFS methods are fragile, and tend to have poor performance when a portion of lung fields is missing, or highly deformed.

Pixel classification-based LFS methods use different machine learning techniques to classify each pixel of a DCR as either belonging to lung or non-lung region. In 1993, McNitt-Gray *et al.* [6] presented a method that uses 59 gray-level based, local difference-based, and local texture-based features, and three different classifiers namely k-nearest neighbor (kNN), linear discriminant analysis (LDA), and feed-forward backpropagation neural network (FFBPNN) to classify each pixel of DCR as lung or non-lung pixel. The FFBPNN gave the best performance by classifying 76% of the pixels correctly. In the later pixel classification-based LFS methods, various combination of features and classifiers such as adaptive-sized hybrid neural network (ASHNN) [7], modified kNN [8], Markov random field (MRF) modeling in conjunction with iterative conditional modes (ICM) [9] have been explored, and the best reported accuracy has reached 96.9% [8]. Unlike rule-based LFS methods, these methods exhibit stable performance even when a portion of lung fields is missing or highly deformed, provided the classifier is properly trained. However, proper training of classifier is far from easy. Apart from the difficulties in obtaining sufficient annotated medical training data of good quality and variety, the process of extracting relevant features is excessively adhoc and cumbersome. The deep CNNs have alleviated the feature extraction problem by automatically extracting the features at multiple levels of abstractions. Each successive layer of deep CNN uses the features from the previous layer to learn more complex features. Although deep CNNs have given promising results in computer vision, image classification, and image retrieval, their use for LFS has been unexplored. The recently presented encoder-decoder CNN (ED-CNN)-based LFS method [10] is the only representative work in this category.

Deformable model-based LFS methods [11–16] represent lungs as flexible 2D curves that can be deformed and iteratively evolved under the influence of internal forces, external forces, and user-defined constraints. These methods firstly initialize an abstract lung model either interactively, using average lung shape, or using population-based and patient-specific statistics, then use optimization techniques to minimize the internal and external energy of the model. The energy minimized lung model best represents the lung boundary. Active shape model (ASM) and active appearance models (AAM) are the two deformable methods that have been commonly used in most of LFS methods. Although deformable model-based LFS methods give promising results even under tremendous variability in lung shape; they have some limitations as well. The performance of a method is highly dependent upon the initial model, and it may get trapped at local minima due to strong ribcage edges.

Hybrid LFS methods combine the merits of two or more methods of other categories to segment the lung field. The usual combinations are of rule-based and pixel classification-based methods; and pixel classification-based and deformable model-based methods. Candemir *et al.* [17] proposed a hybrid LFS method in which content-based image retrieval approach is used to find training images similar to the patient's image, and to create a lung atlas. The initial lung model is then created using the patient-specific lung atlas, and then graph cuts discrete optimization technique with modified energy function is used to obtain the final segmented result. Ginneken *et al.* [18] fuse the results of ASM, AAM, and pixel classification-based method by majority voting. The result of pixel classification-based is used to initialize the lung model in AAM and ASM methods. As of now, hybrid LFS methods are state-of-the-art, and have given best results till date.

3 Deep Convolutional Neural Networks

Machine learning is traditionally used for intelligent decision making, but is restricted due to limited number of handcrafted features. Deep learning overcomes this limitation by exploring millions of features which are automatically extracted by the underlying network. Amongst the different types of deep networks, Convolutional Neural Networks (CNNs), which are based on weight sharing architecture, are most commonly applied deep networks for image processing. Hubel and Wiesel proposed these layered networks, whereby different layers share the weights [19]. They were inspired by the rectangular topology of cells in visual cortex of cat. CNNs are computationally more powerful and efficient than other neural networks since they are not fully connected and remove neurons that do not contribute to the performance of the network. Moreover, neural networks process the input without sharing the weights whereas CNNs share weights among various layers. CNNs can extract different characteristics or features of the objects which are translation invariant. The popularity of CNNs can be understood by diving deep into the layers of CNN architectures and understanding the process to train the networks for learning weights.

CNNs are composed of various layers out of which convolutional layer are the core of the network. It detects various patterns across the image by using rectangular grids of neurons called kernels or filters. The features are extracted by convolving the data stream with these filters (see Fig. 2). For $M \times M \times P$ dimensional input, k filters of $N \times N \times P$ dimension produces a feature map of $Q \times Q \times k$ size, where $M > N$ and $Q = M - (N - 1)$, when stride = 1 and padding = $(N - 1)/2$. After convolution is applied, translation and rotational invariant characteristics are induced in the CNNs. Linear translations are modeled by pooling layer using max or average pool operation, whereas non-linearity is gained by applying non-linear activation layer. Different layers in a network have different purpose and adds distinct characteristic while extracting new features. In the end, it is required to link all these extracted features. Fully-connected layer does so to compute the final results. The hierarchy and functionality of CNNs depends upon the training of the network. For this, a special layer named loss layer is applied which computes the training error by comparing the output of the network with the desired output. The error is then back propagated to update the weights. Different arrangements of these layers can produce different CNNs for specific tasks.

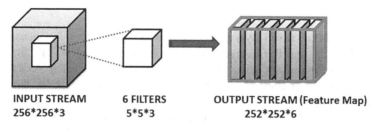

INPUT STREAM   6 FILTERS   OUTPUT STREAM (Feature Map)
256*256*3   5*5*3   252*252*6

Fig. 2. Convolutional layer

The deep-learning based CNN architectures are very powerful in nature. The have the power to drive the high-level information starting from very low-level details. They understand the patterns along with the flow of data. Hence, they have wide applications such as object detection, semantic segmentation, video classification, speech processing and text documentation. CNNs have improved the state-of-the art in these domains and are proving to be very promising for various unexplored fields. This work is an effort to use the hierarchically developed and trained deep features for segmenting lung fields.

4 Proposed Method

The proposed methodology consists of data augmentation, creation of network architecture, and selecting the training parameters. The formation of the required dataset is explained in Sect. 4.1. Section 4.2 presents the proposed CNN along with the details of the training parameters.

4.1 Data Augmentation

Data play a crucial role in the development of a deep learning-based LFS method. A large set of DCR images is required for its training, validation, testing, and performance comparison. Annotated medical data being scarce and costly, the available small datasets are generally augmented using techniques such as mirroring, rotation, contrast adjustment, and random cropping, to meet the data requirements of a deep network.

The present work uses images from JSRT dataset and their ground truth segmentation from Segmentation in Chest Radiographs (SCR) dataset for training and testing of the proposed network. Out of 247 JSRT images, 124 images are randomly selected, resized to 128×128 using uniform bi-linear scale down transformation, and subjected to histogram equalization, horizontal flip, vertical flip, and 5-random crops of 32×32 and their subsequent scaling to 128×128 using bi-cubic interpolation, to create $124 \times 2 \times 2 \times 2 \times 5 = 4960$ training images. The rest 123 JSRT images are used for testing.

4.2   Method

The proposed CNN is a seven layer architecture as shown in Fig. 3. It consists of three sets of convolutional and ReLU layer, and a fully connected layers. The first convolutional layer extracts features using 64 filters of $5 \times 5 \times 1$ dimension. As a result, 64 low-level features are retrieved and represented by $128 \times 128 \times 64$ dimensional feature map. For non-linear translations, the feature map is activated by the ReLU layer. The second set of layers exhibits same behavioral pattern. In this set, 64 filters of $5 \times 5 \times 64$ dimensions fetch higher level features derived from the previous details. The third set replicates the second set producing same spatial dimensions. At last, the fully connected layer links all previously yielded features. Table 1 demonstrates the details of each layer.

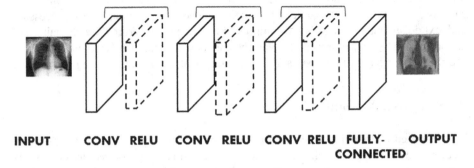

INPUT   CONV RELU   CONV RELU   CONV RELU FULLY-   OUTPUT
CONNECTED

Fig. 3. The proposed CNN

Table 1. Description of the layers of Proposed CNN

LAYER	TYPE	INPUT SIZE	OUTPUT SIZE	NO. OF FILTERS	FILTER SIZE	PAD VALUE
1.	conv	128×128×1	128×128×64	64	5×5×1	2
2.	relu	128×128×64	128×128×64	----	----	----
3.	conv	128×128×64	128×128×64	64	5×5×64	2
4.	relu	128×128×64	128×128×64	----	----	----
5.	conv	128×128×64	128×128×64	64	5×5×64	2
6.	relu	128×128×64	128×128×64	----	----	----
7.	conv	128×128×64	128×128×1	1	5×5×64	2

The output of CNN highly depends upon the training process. Stochastic gradient descent (SGD) optimization technique in association with backpropagation algorithm trains the network. The proposed CNN is trained for 1200 epochs by gradually reducing the learning rate up to 0.001. Before training, histogram equalization adjusts image intensities to enhance contrast. The output requires further processing to improve the results. The binary segment contains a few black patches within the lung region. These patches are removed by calculating the connected components and applying smoothing operation.

5 Result and Discussion

In order to evaluate the results of the proposed method, accuracy and overlap are used as key metrics. The average accuracy of 98.05% with maximum and minimum values of 99.07% and 93.84%, respectively, and average overlap of 93.4% is obtained with the maximum overlapping value of 97.04%. Other metrics used to evaluate the proposed algorithm are sensitivity and specificity. The proposed method exhibits 96.25% average sensitivity and 98.80% average specificity. The proposed CNN architecture was selected after trying different network architectures. Amongst them, a network which downsamples the images from 512×512 to 128×128 was also evaluated. It took a long time to train that network and the results were also poor. Likewise, other network arrangements also did not gave promising results. The present network with 64 filters gave the best performance. These filters extract various features. Figure 4 demonstrates the 64 features extracted by a convolutional layer. Similarly, other convolutional layers also fetch these kinds of features. Table 2 lists results of few sample cases where blue edge boundary delineates the desired segment and red boundary defines the obtained output segment.

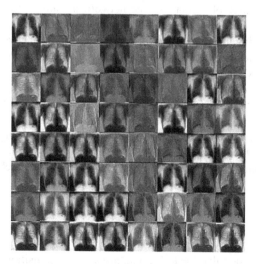

Fig. 4. Features extracted by convolutional layer

Table 2. Experimental Results

S. NO.	ACQUIRED RESULT	ACCURACY (%)	OVERLAP (%)
1.		98.792	96.195
2.		99.072	97.048
3.		98.358	94.868
4.		98.853	96.489

After using deep learning-based method for segmenting lung fields in chest radiographs, it is found that automated extracted deep features are more reliable than limited handcrafted features. The technique is appropriate to tackle the present challenges in LFS in radiographic images. The network is entirely responsible to extract features and learn weights with the help of training images. Deep networks exhibit the feasibility of extracting features based upon training of the network. It takes lesser efforts as compared to the machine learning-based and other methods in the state-of-the-art. The proposed network with 5 hidden layers is still better than a traditional shallow network for segmenting the region of interest. This is so because CNN reduces the node redundancies while extracting low level information, and thus needs lower computational power than fully connected traditional neural network. Another challenge for LFS is the non-availability of a large dataset for training the network. By augmenting 124 chest radiographic images, a dataset is formed with 4960 images in the training set. Overcoming these gaps, deep learning-based CNN architecture is proven to be more reliable and accurate for segmenting lung fields in chest radiographs.

6   Conclusion

Chest radiographs are popular due to low expenses, easy acquisition and low dosage of radiation as compared to other imaging modalities. Various CADx systems have been developed to diagnose interstitial lung diseases, lung nodules, lung cancer, tuberculosis and emphysema. Prior to diagnosis, it is important to segment the region of interest to specify the processing area. LFS is an elementary step for many CADx systems and this paper develops a reliable deep learning-based technique for LFS in chest radiographs. A 7-layer CNN architecture is designed to perform LFS, which extracts hierarchical features maintaining high level of abstraction in each layer. The average accuracy of 98.05%, average overlap of 93.4%, average specificity of 98.80% and average sensitivity of 96.25% are enough to reveal that deep CNNs are promising for LFS. The proposed lung segmentation technique is significant for specifying the processing region to develop more accurate and efficient CADx systems for screening lung diseases. Data augmentation is also performed to meet the CNN requirement to have large training dataset. The results reported in this study allow concluding that deep learning is a promising technique for further improving state-of-the-art LFS performance. The automated segmentation approach developed in this work is robust, but can still be improved in many ways. The future work suggests the use of different optimization approaches to train the network, developing different CNN architectures to fetch the information and testing the network on other benchmark datasets.

References

1. Van Ginneken, B., ter Haar Romeny, B.M., Viergever, M.A.: Computer-aided diagnosis in chest radiography: a survey. IEEE Trans. Med. Imaging 20(12), 1228–1241 (2001)
2. Li, L., Zheng, Y., Kallergi, M., Clark, R.A.: Improved method for automatic identification of lung regions on chest radiographs. Acad. Radiol. 8(7), 629–638 (2001)
3. Duryea, J., Boone, J.M.: A fully automated algorithm for the segmentation of lung fields on digital chest radiographic images. Med. Phys. 22(2), 183–191 (1995)
4. Armato, S.G., Giger, M.L., MacMahon, H.: Automated lung segmentation in digitized posteroanterior chest radiographs. Acad. Radiol. 5(4), 245–255 (1998)
5. Ahmad, W.S.H.M.W., Zaki, W.M.D.W., Fauzi, M.F.A.: Lung segmentation on standard and mobile chest radiographs using oriented Gaussian derivatives filter. Biomed. Eng. Online 14(1), 1 (2015)
6. McNitt-Gray, M.F., Sayre, J.W., Huang, H.K., Razavi, M.: Pattern classification approach to segmentation of chest radiographs. In: Medical Imaging 1993, pp. 160–170. International Society for Optics and Photonics (1993)
7. Tsujii, O., Freedman, M.T., Mun, S.K.: Automated segmentation of anatomic regions in chest radiographs using an adaptive-sized hybrid neural network. In: Medical Imaging 1997, pp. 802–811. International Society for Optics and Photonics (1997)
8. Van Ginneken, B., ter Haar Romeny, B.M.: Automatic segmentation of lung fields in chest radiographs. Med. phys. 27(10), 2445–2455 (2000)
9. Vittitoe, N.F., Vargas-Voracek, R., Floyd Jr., C.E.: Markov random field modeling in posteroanterior chest radiograph segmentation. Med. Phys. 26(8), 1670–1677 (1999)
10. Kalinovsky, A.A., Kovalev, V.: Lung image segmentation using deep learning methods and convolutional neural networks (2016)
11. van Ginneken, B., Frangi, A.F., Staal, J.J., ter Haar Romeny, B.M., Viergever, M.A.: Active shape model segmentation with optimal features. IEEE Trans. Med. Imaging 21(8), 924–933 (2002)
12. Xu, T., Mandal, M., Long, R., Basu, A.: Gradient vector flow based active shape model for lung field segmentation in chest radiographs. In: Proceedings of Annual International Conference of the IEEE Engineering in Medicine and Biology Society, vol. 2009, p. 3561. IEEE Engineering in Medicine and Biology Society (2009)

13. Lee, J.-S., Wu, H.-H., Yuan, M.-Z.: Lung segmentation for chest radiograph by using adaptive active shape models. Biomed. Eng.: Appl. Basis Commun. **22**(02), 149–156 (2010)
14. Tao, X., Mandal, M., Long, R., Cheng, I., Basu, A.: An edge region force guided active shape approach for automatic lung field detection in chest radiographs. Comput. Med. Imaging Graph. **36**(6), 452–463 (2012)
15. Candemir, S., Jaeger, S., Palaniappan, K., Antani, S., Thoma, G.: Graph-cut based automatic lung boundary detection in chest radiographs. In: IEEE Healthcare Technology Conference: Translational Engineering in Health and Medicine, pp. 31–34 (2012)
16. Shi, Y., Qi, F., Xue, Z., Chen, L., Ito, K., Matsuo, H., Shen, D.: Segmenting lung fields in serial chest radiographs using both population-based and patient-specific shape statistics. IEEE Trans. Med. Imaging **27**(4), 481–494 (2008)
17. Candemir, S., Jaeger, S., Palaniappan, K., Musco, J.P., Singh, R.K., Xue, Z., Karargyris, A., Antani, S., Thoma, G., McDonald, C.J.: Lung segmentation in chest radiographs using anatomical atlases with nonrigid registration. IEEE Trans. Med. Imaging **33**(2), 577–590 (2014)
18. van Ginneken, B., Stegmann, M.B., Loog, M.: Segmentation of anatomical structures in chest radiographs using supervised methods: a comparative study on a public database. Med. Image Anal. **10**(1), 19–40 (2006)
19. Hubel, D.H., Wiesel, T.N.: Receptive fields, binocular interaction and functional architecture in the cat's visual cortex. J. Physiol. **160**(1), 106–154 (1962)

Quality Assessment of a Job Portal System Designed Using Bout Design Pattern

G. Priyalakshmi[1(✉)], R. Nadarajan[1], Hironori Washizaki[2],
and Smriti Sharma[1]

[1] Department of Applied Mathematics and Computational Sciences,
PSG College of Technology, Coimbatore, India
priya.venky2001@gmail.com, nadarajan_psg@yahoo.co.in,
smrit.bhav@gmail.com
[2] Waseda University, Tokyo, Japan
washizaki@waseda.jp

Abstract. Design Patterns provide solutions to problems that are notably prevailing in software engineering. The paper targets the importance of design patterns, but also aims on how design patterns uncover and fortify good object oriented principles. A design pattern called Bout was discovered to maintain sessions for a specific period of time. The design is a generic solution to implementing web portals by storing session data of clients on the server. The Bout pattern comprises the design principle of Singleton and Prototype patterns, thus guaranteeing a more reusable design. The Bout pattern is documented in the Gang of Four pattern description template. The Bout pattern was tested with a Job Portal system with additional patterns, Factory Method, Decorator and Observer, with significant improvement in object oriented design metrics. Metrics which showed a significant enhancement were Depth of Inheritance Tree and McCabe Cyclomatic Complexity. The reusability of black box components was analyzed for the Job Portal system which shows a momentous rise in the metrics. The source code was analyzed for modularity traits such as size, complexity, cohesion and coupling, which in turn determines the class quality, package quality and hence the modularity index. These quality metrics showed a symbolic upswing with Bout pattern and supporting patterns. Thus software designers can enhance the quality of distributed systems with the exercising of Bout pattern.

1 Introduction

In software engineering, a design pattern is a solution to a problem within a given context [2]. Design patterns figure out many of the day-to-day problems object-oriented designers face. The problem contemplated in this work is storage of client data in distributed systems with n-tier or cloud architectures. The pattern documented in the paper is Bout, which can be applied to all distributed applications and two-tier, three-tier and scale out to n-tier web architectures. The Bout pattern can also be offered as a design solution to systems which scale up to cloud technology. The research work comprises of describing the pattern in the GOF pattern template [2], which facilitates the software developers to skillfully adopt the new design solution.

© Springer Nature Singapore Pte Ltd. 2017
D. Singh et al. (Eds.): ICAICR 2017, CCIS 712, pp. 195–205, 2017.
DOI: 10.1007/978-981-10-5780-9_18

Bout design pattern provides a communicative storage object between any two nodes in a distributed architecture and it comprises of multiple request and response between the two networked systems. The pattern maintains session data with a single access point used to store secured data in a stash for a defined time. Session is a conversional state between client and server and it consists of multiple request and response between client and server [17]. The session variable consists of two pieces, a very small session identifier which is stored on the client usually identified as SessionId and stored as a cookie. The second piece of a session is the actual data, and it is stored on the server. Each session is identified by that SessionId and the client sends it with every request.

The Session object stores information about, or change settings for a user session in the form of an associative HashMap containing session variables available to the current user and their corresponding values. Variables stored in a Session object hold common information about one single user, and are available to all pages in one application. For each new user the server assigns a new user id and creates a new Session object by using Prototype pattern which clones the previous session object and returns it with respective changes in its values. The Singleton ClientSession Object holds user id and the user's respective Session object mapped to it. The server creates a new entry in ClientSession object for each new user and maps the new user id with its created Session object, and destroys the Session object along with user id when the session expires.

The Bout pattern is documented in the well-formed GOF template [2], which is very familiar to object oriented designers and hence can be tailored suitably. The Bout design pattern is applied to job portal system along with Factory Method, Decorator and Observer patterns. The important reusability metrics along with black box component reusability is tabulated [4]. The modularity index, class and package quality [5] shows improvement when Bout pattern was applied. The other metrics which were calculated to distinguish between the two implemented systems; with patterns and without patterns; were Number of Abstract Methods, Number of Object Fields, Number of Private Constructors, etc. Thus the authors have emphasized on the usage of Bout pattern along with few other GOF patterns to improve the software quality.

Section 2 discusses the similar work done by researchers in the evaluation of quality of systems implemented with design patterns. Section 3 gives an elaborate pattern description of the Bout design pattern in GOF template. Section 4 lists the other GOF design patterns used along with the Bout pattern. Section 5 describes the class design of Job Portal System. Section 6 details on the experiments done and tabulates the results. Finally, Sect. 7 provides a recap of the work.

2   Related Work

The assessment of quality of systems constructed with design patterns has been evolved since many years. These experiments help object oriented designers in modeling systems with higher reusability and easier refactoring. Christopher Alexander in 1977, analyzed occurrence of problems recurrently in our environment, and proposed a general solution to similar problems. Gamma et al. in the year 1994, endeavored the concept of design patterns, since then there has been a constant rise in the design of systems using software design patterns [2]. There is a large number of literature work done in the area of software engineering, analyzing the impact of patterns on the design quality. Ampatzoglou et al. [11] summarized the state of research related to design patterns existed till 2013. After a thorough literature review, Ampatzoglou et al. have projected that the quality characteristics that take a major role in determining the system reusability are Cohesion, Coupling, Inheritance, Size, Messaging, and Complexity [13]. Ampatzoglou et al. in 2012, discovered an approach to compare designs with and without patterns [12].

Turnu et al. [3] have examined varied releases of the open source Eclipse and NetBeans systems measuring the entropy of Response for Class and Coupling between Object for each release analyzed. They also showed that the number of bugs in Eclipse and NetBeans were proportional to the entropy of CBO and RFC. Wendorff has proved that improper practice of patterns can perhaps be unsuccessful during software reengineering [10]. A detailed Systematic Literature Review was made by Jabangwe et al. [14] to relate object oriented measures and external quality attributes. They have concluded their work by asserting the research community that the important indicators for reliability and maintainability are complexity, cohesion, coupling and size. Al Dallal introduced a cohesion metric to quantify the discriminative power of class cohesion [9]. The reuse-proneness of classes [15] can be augmented by internal quality attributes. This concept was experimentally proven by Al Dallal's team further in 2014. In 2008, Khomh and Gueheneuc [7] made contradictory statements proving that design patterns are not persistent in improving the quality of software systems. Hence their study substantiated the need for research in this direction. A hierarchical model QMOOD was developed [8] by Bansiya and Davis, whose outcome was a quality tool QMOOD++ to evaluate real time applications.

Sorensen in 2002 wrote a pattern language for state-full multi-user systems [17]. In 2016, a new pattern with the name Shuffler was brought to the knowledge of software practitioners [1]. Uchiyama et al. have worked on design pattern detection by using software metrics and published two papers in 2011 and 2014. In 2013, Pop presented a content ontology design pattern for the representation of software metrics, in software engineering ontologies, called OOP Metrics [6].

3 Bout Design Pattern

3.1 Pattern Name and Classification

Bout, Creational Pattern.

3.2 Intent

Store information about a single client and maintain the data till the client session expires. A single entry will be stashed corresponding to a client.

3.3 Also Known as

Dossier.

3.4 Motivation

Sometimes in a two-tier or n-tier distributed environment or cloud architecture, the client session details are not stored with strong integrity and security constraints. To overcome this, a class ApplicantSession is created to store a HaspMap with session details of the active users as shown in the Fig. 1.

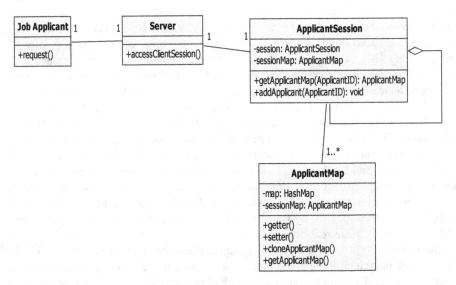

Fig. 1. Class diagram of job portal system with Bout pattern

Consider an online job portal system with applicants applying for jobs. Companies registered with that portal can view the applicants querying for jobs with criteria like preferred location, job type and work profile. The storage object is a HashMap which is maintained throughout the session, till the particular client is active.

The system provides a class ApplicantSession, which stores a HashMap, which is an object of class ApplicantMap. If the Server class gets a request from a client entering into the system with a new session, the addApplicant() method is invoked. If the client is already interacting with the system, the getApplicantMap() method is invoked, which returns the existing client session details as an object of ApplicantMap. To maintain high integrity and security, the ApplicantSession class is a Singleton, so that irrespective of the number of clients or sessions, the same HaspMap is updated.

3.5 Applicability

Use the Bout Pattern when

1. Distributed systems or systems with cloud architecture are designed.
2. The client request must be encapsulated in an object for security purposes.
3. The client request must be stashed for further reference, during the same session.

Don't use the Bout pattern when

1. Systems under consideration are standalone, with no networking.

3.6 Structure

The structure of Bout Design Pattern is depicted in Fig. 2.

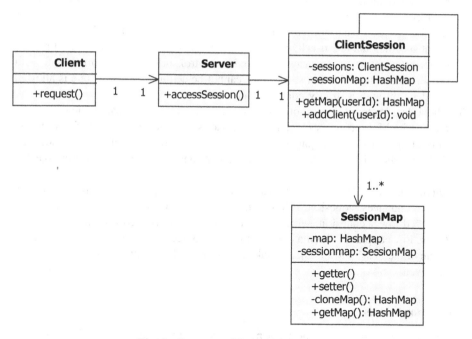

Fig. 2. Structure of Bout design pattern

3.7 Participants

1. Client – The client when needs a service, calls the *request()* method in the Client class. The Client places a request for a Session object from the Server.
2. Server – The Server invokes the *addClient()* method of *ClientSession* class to register any client placing a request.

3. ClientSession – This class is a Singleton. If the client is opening a new session, a new entry is inserted into the *sessionmap* data member. The *SessionMap* is cloned and obtained by this class and stored in *sessionmap*. If the client is accessing an existing session, the client's session data stored in the *sessionmap* is returned.
4. SessionMap – The *SessionMap* class returns a clone of itself when requested. It also updates a clone with the new client specific information.

3.8   Consequences

The Bout pattern provides the following benefits and liabilities:

1. It provides centralized single point access. The ClientSession class provides centralized storage stored on the server. In high availability and virtualized environments, when two or more servers need access to the same data, the pattern is remarkably superior. The benefits of centralized data storage are several-fold like, reduced expenditure and risk, redundancy, disk performance, reliability, disaster recovery and data consistency.
2. It offers secured data storage. The SessionMap class has a HaspMap to store the client specific data like userID and other client sensitive data. Thus the Bout pattern offers data protection, security, and version control. Information is made safe with proper access authorization such that it cannot be acquired lest someone is allowed privilege through a strictly controlled process.
3. Client data is stored throughout the session. When an authenticated client signs in, the SessionMap object is cloned and a clone is provided for each client to access through a series of web pages. His/her session details are stored throughout the time, the client is active. When once the client logs off, the ClientSession object is dumped into the garbage.
4. Offers high cohesion. The ClientSession and SessionMap classes are put separately, which enhances cohesion. These classes when coupled together would have achieved lower cohesion, which leads to poor object oriented design.
5. Offers low coupling. When a client signs in, an object of ClientSession is created, a clone of the SessionMap object is taken and sent to the server. Thus low coupling is achieved.

3.9   Known Uses

Perhaps the first example of the Bout pattern was in J2EE Session Façade [16].

3.10   Related Patterns

- Façade Pattern can be used to encapsulate business tier components and expose a coarse-grained service to remote clients [16].
- Session Patterns is a small pattern language for state-full multi-user systems [17].
- Designs that exploit the use of Bout pattern will have the advantage of Prototype and Singleton as well.

4   Patterns Hatched

Pattern hatching is coined as the process of designing a system with other patterns along with the main pattern to produce better design metrics [18]. The design patterns which can be combined with Bout pattern are Factory method pattern, Decorator pattern, and Observer pattern. The job portal system is analyzed for design metrics like cohesion, coupling, component level metrics, and modularity. The above mentioned metrics show a significant improvement when the Bout pattern is applied along with the other three design patterns.

5   Job Portal System

The system studied for this research work is a client server system for companies and candidates exploring for a relevant job matching to their skills set. The client, who in this system is an applicant searching for an appropriate job, must register and apply online. He/she accesses the service of the ApplicantFactory class (denoted as c in the Fig. 3) by calling the factory method getApplicant(). The applicant is provided with a user interface or Viewer object, showing the list of companies. The Viewer class, which is the UI shown to the applicant, may be decorated with two behaviors for signing in and signing up (denoted as a in the Fig. 3). The Company and the Viewer (Applicant) behaves like a Subject in the Observer pattern. The DBUpdate class acts like an Observer, which updates the domain of an applicant or the web page of a company (denoted as b in the Fig. 3). If any change in the requirements of the company, all the applicants will get notified, or if any change in the domain of the applicant, all the companies will be notified. Thus Decorator pattern plays a significant role in this system. Next, the Bout pattern handles the storage of the applicant details in a

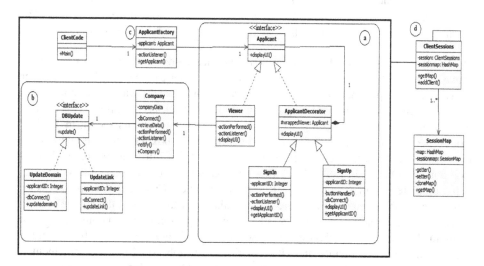

Fig. 3. Class diagram of job portal system with design pattern implemented on it.

consistent manner (denoted as (d) in the Fig. 3). The component denoted as (a) is Decorator pattern, (b) is Observer pattern, (c) is Factory pattern and (d) is Bout pattern.

6   Results

To analyze the health of object oriented code and to compare quality metrics of the system, the Metrics Plug-in of Eclipse tool is used. There are 23 metrics analyzed on every system, given as input, by this open source eclipse plug-in. The results tabulated in Table 1, are obtained directly from the Metrics plug-in run on the Job Portal system, with and without design patterns.

Table 1. Comparison of object oriented metrics

Metric	Without pattern				With pattern			
	Total	Mean	Std. Dev	Max	Total	Mean	Std. Dev	Max
Number of attributes	47	3.357	4.79	16	48	2.667	4.57	
Number of children	0	0	0	0	2	0.111	0.458	2
Method lines of code	498	20.75	27.511	103	502	12.872	21.976	93
Nested block depth		1.708	0.978	4		1.513	0.873	4
Depth of inheritance		3.429	2.441	6		2.5	2.192	6
Number of interfaces	0	0	0	0	2	2	0	2
McCabe cyclomatic complexity		2.333	1.929	9		2	1.826	9
Number of parameters		0.875	0.599	3		0.692	0.821	4
Lack of cohesion of methods		0.222	0.426	1.111		0.172	0.387	1.118
Number of static methods	7	0.5	0.5	1	4	0.222	0.533	2
Normalized distance		0	0	0		0.143	0	0.143
Abstractness		0	0	0		0.143	0	0.143
Number of static attributes	56	0.357	1.042	4	7	0.389	0.951	4

To measure the reusability of various fine grained components of the system and to prove the effective reuse of components, a reusability metric combining five metrics for measuring a component's understandability, adaptability, and portability is considered [4]. This metrics suite for measuring the reusability of black-box components is applied on the source code of the components. These experimental results shown in Table 2 would be of great help to effectively identify black-box components with high reusability. The five metrics are EMI: Existence of Meta-Information, RCO: Rate of Component Observability, RCC: Rate of Component Customizability, SCCr: Self-Completeness of Component's Return Value and SCCp: Self-Completeness of Component's Parameter. To measure the modularity of the system, the source code is analyzed for modularity traits such as size, complexity, cohesion, and coupling, which helps in determining the class quality and package quality [5]. The Tables 3 and 4 compare the function quality and class quality of the job portal system implemented with and without design patterns. The metrics are NLOC: number of non-commenting lines of code, LCOM: lack of cohesion of methods, F: number of functions, FQ: function quality value, CQ: class quality value and PQ: package quality value. The total package quality for code implemented without patterns is 0.4225 and for code implemented with patterns is 0.7228. A few other important metrics was analyzed in order to distinguish between the two systems. These metrics are tabulated in Table 5, which show an enrichment in the system implemented using design patterns.

Table 2. Comparison of component's reusability metrics

Class	With pattern					Without pattern				
	EMI	RCO	RCC	SCCr	SCCp	EMI	RCO	RCC	SCCr	SCCp
Viewer class	1	0	0.69	1	0	0	0	0.5	1	0
SignIn class	1	1	0.67	0.75	0.33	0	0	0.5	1	0
SignUp class	1	1	1	0.75	0.75	0	0	0.5	1	0
Company class	0	0	1	1	0.33	0	0	0.5	1	0

Table 3. Modularity metrics applied on system without design pattern

Class	NLOC	LOCq	F	Fq	LCOM	Cq
Start class	111	0.00022	2	1.611	1	0.8
Login class	26	0.7	1	0.343	1	0.52
Signin class	102	0.00031	3	0.687	1	0.34
Signup class	154	0.000075	2	0.515	1	0.26
View class	73	0.00045	3	0.687	0.5	0.13
Company class	129	0.00031	2	0.515	0.5	0.13
Display class	102	0.00031	3	0.687	1	0.34
Hyperlink class	47	0.96	3	0.687	1	0.82

Table 4. Modularity metrics applied on system with design pattern

Class	NLOC	LOCq	F	Fq	LCOM	Cq
Factory class	121	0.00016	3	0.687	0.5	0.69
Applicant decorator class	8	0.475	1	0.343	1	0.41
Signinwindow class	8	0.475	1	0.343	1	0.41
Signupwindow class	8	0.475	1	0.343	1	0.41
Signin class	78	0.0011	5	1.031	0.875	0.59
Signup class	164	0.000062	4	0.859	1.084	0.4
View class	87	0.00062	4	0.859	0.56	0.77
Company class	137	0.00011	5	1.031	0.75	0.69
Sessionmap class	54	0.059	14	0.0023	0.54	0.057
Hyperlink class	47	0.96	3	0.687	1	0.82
Updatedomain class	47	0.96	2	0.515	1	0.74
Updatelink class	47	0.96	2	0.515	1	0.74
Clientsession class	22	0.65	3	0.687	0.25	2.67

Table 5. Comparison of additional metrics

Metric	With pattern	Without pattern
NOAM (Number of abstract methods)	1	0
NORM (Number of overridden methods)	7	0
NOPC (Number of private constructors)	1	0
NOTC (Number of constructors with argument of object type)	1	0
NOOF (Number of object fields)	5	0
NCOF (Number of other classes with field of own type)	2	0
NMGI (Number of methods to generate instances)	8	9

7 Conclusion

The authors have catalogued Bout design pattern for the benefit of a large number of software practitioners seeking for low coupled and high cohesive systems. The pattern gets the aid of two other widely used creational patterns Singleton and Prototype. Any distributed client server system per se, will show improvement in the object oriented metrics tabulated in the results section. But the authors have dealt with a Job Portal system showing satisfactory results. The other patterns interweaved were Factory Method, Observer and Decorator patterns. The Eclipse Metrics plug-in showed meaningful ascent in metrics like Depth of Inheritance Tree and McCabe Cyclomatic Complexity and ideal reduction in Lack of Cohesion of Methods. The reusability of components was measured without source code, which also showed increase in EMI, RCO, RCC and SCC_p. Also the function quality, class quality and package quality computations show good variations. Hence these results must give a major drive to software evangelists to use design solutions like Bout and other GOF patterns. As future work, the authors have planned to extend their work by applying the Bout pattern to other distributed systems with cloud servers. These results may encourage developers to use Bout pattern to improve the reusability and modularity of systems. Another direction which researchers can work is to determine the decrease in the time taken to refactor systems, if Bout design pattern is adopted.

References

1. Priyalakshmi, G., Nadarajan, R., Anandhi, S.: Software reuse with shuffler design pattern In: SEAT (2016)
2. Gamma, E., Helm, R., Johnson, R., Vlissides, J.: Design patterns: elements of reusable object-oriented software. ACM Digital Library (1995)
3. Turnu, I., Concas, G., Marchesi, M., Tonelli, R.: Entropy of some CK metrics to assess object-oriented software quality. Int. J. Softw. Eng. Knowl. Eng. **23**, 173–188 (2013)
4. Washizaki, H., Yamamoto, H., Fukazawa, Y.: A metrics suite for measuring reusability of software components. IEEE Xplore (2003)

5. Emanuel, A.W.R., Wardoyo, R., Istiyanto, J.E., Mustofa, K.: Modularity index metrics for java-based open source software projects. Int. J. Adv. Comput. Sci. Appl. 2(11) (2011)
6. Pop, I.V.: A content ontology design pattern for software metrics. Informatica 58(1), 71–80 (2013)
7. Khomh, F., Gueheneuc, Y.-G.: Do design patterns impact software quality positively? IEEE Xplore (2008)
8. Bansiya, J., Davis, C.G.: A hierarchical model for object-oriented design quality assessment. IEEE Trans. Softw. Eng. 28, 4–17 (2002)
9. Al Dallal, J.: Measuring the discriminative power of object-oriented class cohesion metrics. IEEE Trans. Softw. Eng. 37, 788–804 (2011)
10. Wendorff, P.: Assessment of design patterns during software reengineering: lessons learned from a large commercial project. IEEE Xplore (2002)
11. Ampatzoglou, A., Charalampidou, S., Stamelos, I.: Research state of the art on GoF design patterns a mapping study. J. Syst. Softw. 86, 1945–1964 (2013)
12. Ampatzoglou, A., Frantzeskou, G., Stamelos, I.: A methodology to assess the impact of design patterns on software quality. Inf. Softw. Technol. 54, 331–346 2012
13. Ampatzoglou, A., Kritikos, A., Kakarontzas, G., Stamelos, I.: An empirical investigation on the reusability of design patterns and software packages. J. Syst. Softw. 84, 2265–2283 (2011)
14. Jabangwe, R., Börstler, J., Smite, D., Wohlin, C.: Empirical evidence on the link between object-oriented measures and external quality attributes: a systematic literature review. Empirical Softw. Eng. 20, 640–693 (2015)
15. Al Dallal, J., Morasca, S.: Predicting object-oriented class reuse-proneness using internal quality attributes. Empirical Softw. Eng. 19, 775–821 (2014)
16. Deepak, A.: Core J2EE Patterns Best Practices and Design Strategies. Pearson Education, Upper Saddle River (2001)
17. Sorensen, K.E.: Session Patterns, Security Pattern Repository (2002)
18. Vlissides, J.: Pattern Hatching: Design Patterns Applied. Addison Wesley, Boston (1998)

Analyzing Factors Affecting the Performance of Data Mining Tools

Balrajpreet Kaur$^{(\boxtimes)}$ and Anil Sharma

School of Computer Application, LPU, Phagwara, Punjab, India
balrajpreetkaur2@gmail.com, anil.19656@lpu.co.in

Abstract. Data mining is the key technique for finding interesting patterns and hidden information from huge volume of data. There is a wide range of tools available with different algorithms and techniques to work on data. These data mining tools provide a generalized platform for applying machine learning techniques on dataset to attain required results. These tools are available as open source as well as on payment mode which provide more customizable options. Every tool has its own strength and weakness, but there is no obvious consensus regarding the best one. This paper focuses on three tools namely WEKA, Orange and MATLAB. Authors compared these tools on some given factors like correctly classified accuracy, in-correctly classified accuracy and time by applying four algorithms i.e. Support Vector Machine (SVM), K Nearest Neighbour (KNN), Decision Tree and Naive Bayes for getting performance results with two different datasets.

Keywords: Data mining · Data mining tools · WEKA · Orange · MATLAB · SVM · KNN · Decision tree · Naive Bayes

1 Introduction

Data Mining is a process of extracting information from huge amount of data. It is used for performing task on sales, market, responses and profits. Now a days, Automated Artificial Intelligence methods are also used in data mining [1]. The standard model of data mining include regression, classification, clustering and association rules [2]. It is expanded rapidly for the business benefits. There are many applications area where data mining is used such as Retail, Banking, Credit Card Management, Insurance and Telecommunication etc. Data Mining is used in two contexts i.e. Data Understanding and Business Understanding [3]. The new work in data mining is generating results from larger datasets and deal with more complex forms of data. Research continues to get results from massive datasets [4].

The Data Mining tools provide the facility to apply different data mining techniques on different kinds of datasets. There are three different types of data mining tools i.e. Traditional data mining tools, Application data mining tools and Web based data mining tools [5]. The traditional data mining tools are the tools used by various companies for decision making process. These tools support windows as well as UNIX Operating Systems. Some of these tools are Rapid Miner [6], KNIME [7], WEKA [8] and R Tool [5]. Application based tools are business oriented tools which provide data performance results. These are mostly use and help in administrative kind of works. Web based tools are used in text mining and it has ability to mine various forms of texts

© Springer Nature Singapore Pte Ltd. 2017
D. Singh et al. (Eds.): ICAICR 2017, CCIS 712, pp. 206–217, 2017.
DOI: 10.1007/978-981-10-5780-9_19

through web sources. Some of these tools are Orange [9], NLTK [10] etc. These various types of tools need to be capable of accurately predicting results, scalable and capable of automatic implementation. Scalable tools are needed for handling huge amount of data and some analytical are also needed for critical datasets [5].

Rapid Miner is an open source data mining tool. This provides application for data analysis, data transformation, visualization, predictive analytics and business analytics. The user can easily select charts and visualization. It is having advanced analytics by giving interface for big data handling [1, 6]. WEKA is a collection of machine learning algorithms. The main advantage of this tool is that it is directly applied to datasets. WEKA provides pre-processing tools, classification, clustering, association and visualization. There are different algorithm provided in each categories. In classifier output the results are in the form of numerical values [2, 8]. Orange is an open source for data visualization and data analytics for an expert and novice. It provides interactive graphical interface and workflow. The orange is having machine learning algorithm and it is mostly used for bioinformatics and text mining. It has scoring feature and cross validation process [2, 9]. The KNIME GUI provides a platform to create data flows, data analysis and review the results and models. KNIME is written in JAVA and built on Eclipse. There are different applications of KNIME such as image mining, text mining, time series analysis and many more [2, 7]. Natural Language Tool Kit basically used for sentiment analysis and various languages processing task. It is written in python. It can divide the sentences into tokens and also provide the tokenization. It is mostly used for analyzing the customer behaviour [2, 10].

2 Related Work

There are some review of paper which include comparative analysis of data mining for evaluating the performance. In [11], the author give description about data mining and data mining tools. The data mining tools include WEKA, Rapid Miner, KNIME, Orange and Net Tools Spider. The performance evaluation of data mining tools based on parameters i.e. Application Program Interface, Database system support, Visualization capabilities, Predictive Model Mark-up Language support and statistical Analysis capabilities. The paper give the description about the uses and importance of each tool in various aspects. In [12] the analysis is done on the medical data for finding the results. There are nine dataset used for finding the accuracy based on Decision tree, SVM, KNN, ANN, GKK classifier. The GKNN provide good accuracy result on datasets as compared to other dataset. The paper includes a comparative table for classification results with property, overall accuracy and dataset used by different researchers. This comparative analysis provide information regarding the improvement of classifier in medical field. In [13], the author do the classification comparison based on some classifier such as M5P, MLP, K-star and M5Rule. The parameters taken for the comparison are execution time and accuracy. Two types of dataset are used i.e. sequential and parallel. According to the result K-star show the accurate results as compared to other algorithms. In [14], the author test the diabetes dataset on various classification methods use in this paper are Naive Bayes, J48, Random Forest, REP Tree, KNN and Bayes. The comparison is based on some parameters such as sensitivity, specificity, Accuracy, positive precision, negative precision and error rate. The KNN give the best results in classification and give zero error rate.

In [15], the author discussed about the data mining techniques. For comparative analysis three data mining techniques used i.e. classification, clustering and association rule mining. For testing the WEKA tool is used. The paper describe the different windows of WEKA such as explorer, experimenter, knowledge flow and simple CLI. The main reason for using WEKA is that it is easy to use without having any programming skills. The author take different classification and clustering algorithm for comparison and get variation in results based on some parameters. In [16], the author give description about classification algorithms and data mining tools. The two classification algorithm i.e. Decision tree algorithm and K-means are explained with advantages and disadvantages as well as the optimization of these algorithms are given in the paper. Orange and WEKA are discussed with the advantages and disadvantages and also give the comparative analysis of tools based on some features. In [17], the author do the comparison of data mining tools for lung cancer patients. Dataset of 350 patients is used for finding the results. The comparison is based on the decision tree. The two parameters taken for comparison are accuracy and efficiency. The WEKA take 0.5 s to build a model and Rattle R take 0.2 s. The accuracy of WEKA is 60% and R-rattle is 56%. As per results the R-rattle is good in efficiency and WEKA is good in accuracy. The classification result provide the results regarding the correlation between patients and symptoms and the treatment to be used.

In [18], the author discussed about the data mining and data mining tools. The paper includes the description about type of data based on period of time such as Vedic period data, Medieval year of data and many more. The different type of Information extraction techniques with pros and cons described in the form of table. There is a comparative table for different type of data mining tools with their strength and weakness. The paper also include the improved and new algorithm for handling large amount of data with different parameters. In [19], the author check the comparative analysis of classification algorithm on web videos. For comparison the parameters taken are metadata, length, view count, comments for finding the knowledge. The J48 and Naive Bayes classification algorithm chosen for predicting classes. From comparative analysis Naive Bayes give more efficient result than J48. In [20], the author used classification techniques for predicting chronic kidney disease. The author take 400 patients data from UCI repository. The Rapid Miner tool is used for getting the results of classification. The two algorithm are used for comparison i.e. Naive Bayes and Artificial neural network. From the result the Naive Bayes give most accurate result and ANN having 72.7% accuracy. The factors considered in this paper is age, diabetes, blood pressure and RBC count.

3 Methodology

In methodology, authors have chosen three data mining tools and apply two different datasets on them. The datasets do have different values in context to size. The first dataset is adult dataset which contains the census data of 1994 to predict task that determines the person over 50 K a year. This dataset contain the missing values. The second dataset is the ionosphere dataset which contain 34 attributes. The targets were free electrons in the ionosphere. "Good" radar returns are those showing evidence of some type of structure in the ionosphere. "Bad" returns are those that do not their signals pass through the iono-sphere. There are no missing values in the this dataset. The comparison is based on some factors for comparing the results in each tool. There is a wide range of tools in data mining. Authors have selected tools on the basis of availability and knowledge.

The WEKA, Orange and MATLAB2016 are used. WEKA is the mostly used tool for classification and it is easy to understand the functions of tool. Orange is good with many widgets. One can use orange widgets for performing different tasks. MATLAB2016 is having new app i.e. classifier learner. It is added in 2015 version of MATLAB. This application having some classification algorithm and provide results in the form of accuracy, execution time and many more. The different parameters used by authors give result to find which algorithm is best for which dataset between the three tools.

4 Implementation and Results

We have taken three tools i.e. Orange, WEKA and MATLAB (R2016a). The below table represent the technical evaluation of these tools. There are some features which is only present in Matlab2016 and not in WEKA and Orange (Table 1).

Table 1. Technical evaluation of tool

		WEKA	Orange	MATLAB2016
Platform support	Windows	✓	✓	✓
	MAC	✓	✓	✓
	LINUX	✓	✓	✓
Output	Classification Tree	✓	✓	✓
	Scatter Plot	✓	✓	✓
	3D Images	--	---	✓
Interface	Text	--	---	---
	GUI	--	---	✓
	Interactive GUI	✓	✓	✓
Supported	Decision Tree	✓	✓	✓
	SVM	✓	✓	✓
	Naive Bayes	✓	✓	✓

4.1   Result Table

There are different table of results with each dataset and each algorithm on WEKA, Orange and MATLAB. The dataset authors used are taken from UCI repository [21].

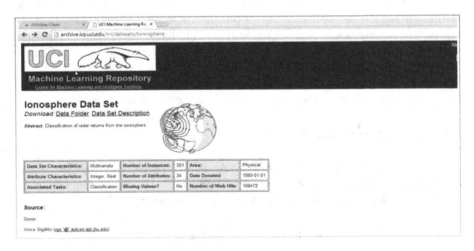

Fig. 1. Screenshot of dataset

WEKA Result Table on Adult Dataset

Table 2. Result of WEKA on adult dataset

Parameters	Naive Bayes	J48	KNN	SVM
Correctly classified	83.492%	85.9306%	75.9183%	84.9447%
Incorrectly classified	16.508%	14.0694%	24.0817%	15.0553%
Time taken	0.18 sec	5.62 sec	0.04 sec	1275.82 sec
Recall	83.5%	85.9%	75.9%	84.9%
Precision	82.6%	85.4%	57.6%	84.2%
F-measure	82.5%	85.5%	65.5%	84.3%

According to the above table, KNN take less time for classification as compared to other algorithms and SVM take highest value in time in this classification. The accuracy in classification is higher in J48 and SVM also give good accuracy result as compared to others.

The KNN give the highest incorrectly classified result as compared to others. According to the above table J48 is better as compared to SVM.

Table 3. Result of WEKA on ionosphere dataset

Parameters	Naive Bayes	J48	KNN	SVM
Correctly classified	82.6211%	89.74%	64.1026%	88.604%
Incorrectly classified	17.3789%	10.25%	35.8974%	11.396%
Time taken	0.01 sec	0.09 sec	0.02 sec	0.038%
Recall	82.6%	89.7%	64.1%	88.6%
Precision	84.2%	89.7%	41.1%	89.1%
F-measure	82.9%	89.6%	50.1%	88.3%

According to the above table, Naive Bayes takes less time for classification as compared to other algorithms and SVM take highest time for classification. The accuracy in classification is highest in J48 and SVM as compared to others.

Results on Orange with Adult Dataset

Table 4. Result of Orange on ionosphere dataset

Parameters	Naive Bayes	KNN	SVM	J48
Classification accuracy	88.31%	85.47%	88.32%	88.61%
Precision	88.98%	82.22%	88.33%	90.75%
Recall	93.33%	98.67%	94.22%	91.56%
Time taken	0.04 sec	0.02 sec	0.05 sec	0.03 sec
F-measure	91.11%	89.70%	91.18%	91.15%
Sensitivity	93.33%	98.67%	94.22%	91.56%

According to the above table J48 give the highest accuracy than others. KNN and SVM both are having second highest accuracy. KNN takes the less time as compared to others. The precision value is highest in J48. According to the above result J48 give efficient result in classification on ionosphere dataset.

Table 5. Result of Orange on adult dataset

Parameters	Naive Bayes	KNN	SVM	J48
Classification accuracy	84.27%	80.06%	No result	82.58%
Precision	71.56%	59.08%	No result	64.72%
Recall	57.56%	55.94%	No result	60.82%
Time taken	16 sec	254.8 sec	No result	36 sec
F-measure	63.80%	57.46%	No result	62.71%
Sensitivity	57.56%	55.94%	No result	60.82%

According to the above table Naive Bayes give the highest accuracy than other algorithms. SVM don't give any result on this dataset. The time taken is less in Naive Bayes as compared to others. For this dataset Naive Bayes give best result in classification.

Result of MATLAB on Ionosphere Dataset

Table 6. Result of MATLAB on ionosphere dataset

Parameters	Naive Bayes	KNN	SVM	J48
Accuracy	82.1%	89.7%	92.0%	90.9%
Execution time	3.87 sec	2.581 sec	9.98 sec	5.56 sec
Incorrectly classified	17.9%	10.3%	08.0%	9.1%
Observation speed	2300 ob/sec	2000 ob/sec	1500 ob/sec	2100 ob/sec

According to the Table 6 SVM gives the highest accuracy as compared to others algorithms. J48 also give good classification result. The KNN take less time as compared to SVM, Naive Bayes and J48. The number of observation is highest in Naive Bayes.

Table 7. Result of MATLAB on adult dataset

Parameters	Naive Bayes	KNN	SVM	J48
Accuracy	No result	No result	69.1%	70.5%
Execution time	No result	No result	818.26 sec	15.607 sec
Incorrectly classified	No result	No result	40.9%	29.5%
Observation speed	No result	No result	5200 ob/sec	9700 ob/sec

According to the above table J48 give highest accuracy as compared to other algorithms. The Naive Bayes and KNN give no result on this dataset. The execution time is less in J48 as compared to SVM. The number of observation is high in J48 than SVM.

Comparison Table of Tools Based on Algorithm with Adult Dataset

Table 8. Result of tools on adult dataset with Naive Bayes algorithm

Tool (Naive Bayes Algorithm)	Correctly classified	Incorrectly classified	Time
WEKA	83.492%	16.508%	0.18 sec
MATLAB	No Result	No Result	No Result
Orange	84.27%	15.73%	16 sec

Table 9. Result of tools on adult dataset with SVM algorithm

Tool (SVM Algorithm)	Correctly classified	Incorrectly classified	Time
WEKA	84.9447%	15.0553%	1275.82 sec
MATLAB	69.1%	40.9%	818.26 sec
Orange	No result	No result	No result

Table 10. Result of tools on adult dataset with KNN algorithm

Tool (KNN Algorithm)	Correctly classified	Incorrectly classified	Time
WEKA	**75.9183%**	**24.0817%**	**0.04 sec**
MATLAB	No result	No result	No result
Orange	80.06%	19.94%	254.8 sec

Table 11. Result of tools on adult dataset with J48 algorithm

Tool (J48 Algorithm)	Correctly classified	Incorrectly classified	Time
WEKA	85.9306%	14.0694%	5.62 sec
MATLAB	70.5%	29.5%	15.607 sec
Orange	82.58%	17.42%	36 sec

Comparison Table of Tools Based on Algorithm with Ionosphere Dataset

Table 12. Result of tools on adult dataset with Naive Bayes algorithm

Tool (Naive Bayes Algorithm)	Correctly classified	Incorrectly classified	Time
WEKA	82.6211%	17.3789%	0.01 sec
MATLAB	82.1%	17.9%	3.57 sec
Orange	88.31%	11.69%	0.04 sec

Table 13. Result of tools on adult dataset with SVM algorithm

Tool (SVM Algorithm)	Correctly classified	Incorrectly classified	Time
WEKA	88.604%	11.396%	0.38 sec
MATLAB	92.0%	8.0%	9.98 sec
Orange	88.32%	11.68%	0.05 sec

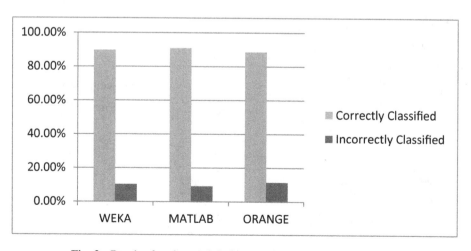

Fig. 2. Result of tools on adult dataset with Naive Bayes algorithm

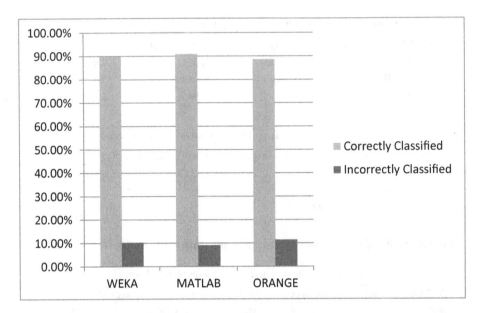

Fig. 3. Result of tools on adult dataset with SVM algorithm

Table 14. Result of tools on adult dataset with KNN algorithm

Tool (KNN Algorithm)	Correctly classified	Incorrectly classified	Time
WEKA	64.1026%	35.8974%	0.02 sec
MATLAB	89.7%	10.3%	2.581 sec
Orange	85.47%	14.53%	0.02 sec

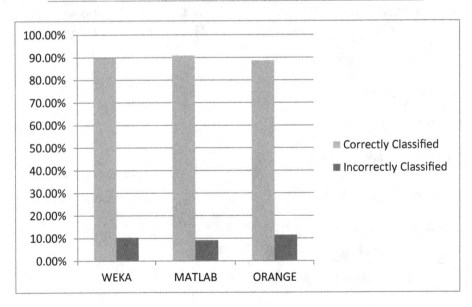

Fig. 4. Result of tools on adult dataset with KNN algorithm

Table 15. Result of tools on adult dataset with J48 algorithm

Tool (J48 Algorithm)	Correctly classified	Incorrectly classified	Time
WEKA	89.74%	10.256%	0.09 sec
MATLAB	90.9%	9.1%	5.56 sec
Orange	88.61%	11.39%	0.03 sec

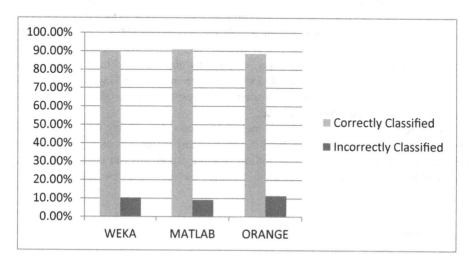

Fig. 5. Result of tools on adult dataset with J48 algorithm

As per the Tables 2, 3, 4, 5, 6, 7, 8, 9, 10, 11, 12, 13 and 14 and Figs. 1, 2, 3 and 4 shown above, According to the results on adult dataset with missing value, WEKA has given the better results than orange and MATLAB in accuracy with SVM and J48. On the other side orange has shown better accuracy than MATLAB and WEKA is performing better in accuracy with KNN and Naive Bayes algorithms. The time taken is less in WEKA as compared to others (Table 15 and Fig. 5).

In second dataset i.e. ionosphere the MATLAB has shown better results in SVM, KNN and J48 than WEKA and Orange but the time taken is less in WEKA. The accuracy result is best in MATLAB with this dataset.

The Factors that Affect the performance of data mining tools are

1. **Type of data set**
2. **Size of dataset**
3. **Type of Algorithm used**
4. **No. of attributes**
5. **Type of Techniques**
6. **Graphical interface**

5 Conclusion and Future Work

Data mining is the process of finding patterns from large amount of data. Most of the companies use the data mining techniques and tools for their benefits. This is used for analyzing and finding information. The data mining tools provide the automatic interface for users to analyze the data. These tools provide many data mining techniques. The major issue in data mining tools is in context of performance. The handling of data and to provide accurate results are two main requirements of good data mining tools. In the thesis, we describe about data mining and discussed about the performance of some of the data mining tools. In the thesis authors provided the comparative analysis of three tools namely WEKA, Orange and MATLAB on the basis three parameters (correctly classified accuracy, in-correctly classified and time) by applying four algorithms namely SVM, KNN, Decision Tree and Naive Bayes. From these results we have found the variations in accuracy of result and time taken by each data mining tool with respect to each dataset.

In future work authors propose the inclusion of new data mining tools along with few more parameters. Testing can be done on the same parameters as well as on new parameters by applying the same algorithms or more algorithms can also be explored. This will be really interesting to find the changing patterns with new additions.

References

1. Rnageri, B.: Data mining techniques and applications. Indian J. Comput. Sci. Eng. (2010)
2. Agrawal, H., Agrawal, P.: Review on data mining tools. IJISET **1**, 52–56 (2014)
3. Kumar, R., Verma, R.: Classification algorithm for data mining: a survey. IJIET **1**, 7–14 (2012)
4. Joshi, A., Pandey, N., Chawla, R., Patil, P.: Use of data mining techniques to improve the effectiveness of sales and marketing. IJCSMC **4** (2015)
5. Patel, S., Desai, S.: A comparative study on data mining tools. IJATCSE (2015)
6. Krstevski, J., Mihajlove, D., Chorbev, I.: Student data analysis with rapid miner. In: ICT Innovations (2011)
7. Berthold, M., et al.: KNIME: the Konstanz Information Miner. In: Preisach, C., Burkhardt, H., Schmidt-Thieme, L., Decker, R. (eds.) Data Analysis, Machine Learning and Applications. Studies in Classification, Data Analysis, and Knowledge Organization, pp. 319–326. Springer, Heidelberg (2008). doi:10.1007/978-3-540-78246-9_38
8. Hall, M., Frank, E., Holmes, G.: The WEKA data mining software: an update. SIGKDD Explor. (2009)
9. Demšar, J., Zupan, B.: Orange: data mining fruitful and fun - a historical perspective (2012)
10. Loper, E., Bird, S.: NLTK: The Natural Language Toolkit (2002)
11. Hirudkar, A., Sherebar, S.: Comparative analysis of data mining tools and techniques for evaluating performance of database system. Int. J. Comput. Sci. Appl. (2013)
12. Lashari, A., Ibrahim, R.: Comparative analysis of data mining techniques for medical data classification. In: 4th International Conference on Computing and Information (2013)
13. Sharma, R., Kumar, S., Maheshwari R.: Comparative analysis of classification technique in data mining using different dataset. Int. J. Comput. Sci. Mob. Comput. (2015)

14. Joshi, S., Shetty, S.: Performance analysis of different classification methods in data mining for diabetes dataset using WEKA tool. IJRITCC **3**, 1168–1173 (2015)
15. Singh, P., Grag, R., Singh, S., Singh, D.: Comparative study of data mining algorithm through WEKA. Int. J. Emerg. Res. Manag. Technol. (2015)
16. Patel, J.: Classification algorithm and comparison in data mining. Int. J. Innov. Adv. Comput. Sci. (2015)
17. Khan, A., Ahmed, S.: Comparative analysis of data mining tools for lung cancer patients. J. Inf. Commun. Technol. (2015)
18. Verma, A., Kaur, I., Arora, N.: Comparative analysis of information extraction techniques for data mining. Indian J. Comput. Sci. Technol. (2016)
19. Algur, S., Bhat, P.: Web video mining: metadata predictive analysis using classification techniques. Indian J. Inf. Technol. Comput. Sci. (2016)
20. Kunwar, V., Chandal, K., Sabitha, A., Bansal A.: Chronic kidney disease analysis using data mining classification technique. IEEE (2016)
21. UC Irvine Machine Learning Repository. http://archive.ics.uci.edu/ml/

Privacy Preserving Data Mining Using Association Rule Based on Apriori Algorithm

Shabnum Rehman[✉] and Anil Sharma

Lovely Professional University, Phagwara, India
shabnum148@gmail.com, anil.19656@lpu.co.in

Abstract. Data mining is a process of extracting knowledge from the large databases. This has made data mining a significant and functional emerging trend. Association rule is one of the most used data mining techniques that discover hidden correlations from huge data sets. There are several mining algorithms for association rules Apriori is one of the most popular algorithm used for extracting frequent item sets from databases and getting the association rule for knowledge discovery. The time required for generating frequent item sets plays an important role. Based on this algorithm we are performing comparison of sanitized data and existing data based on number of iterations and the execution time. The experimental results shows that the number of iteration is reduced in sanitized data than that of existing data also the time is reduced in sanitized data. The association rule generation leads to ensure privacy of the dataset by creating items so, in this way privacy of association rules along with data quality is well maintained.

Keywords: Data mining · Data privacy · Association rule mining · Apriori algorithm

1 Introduction

1.1 Data Mining

Data mining is a promising and the fastest developing fields in computer science and engineering. In the middle 1990's, data mining appeared as a strong tool [1] with the aim of examining the data stored in the databases from different perspectives by performing various operations so that interesting patterns and hidden knowledge is uncovered from the large data sets that is further used to predict the future benefits and trends with the help of different data mining techniques. Sometimes data mining is referred as knowledge hub or knowledge discovery in databases although data mining is a part of knowledge discovery process [2, 3].

The main reason that attracted a lot of consideration in information technology the innovation of important information from huge databases towards the area of data mining is because the impression of "we are information rich however data poor". There are huge volumes of data but however, we are not able to turn them into valuable information and knowledge for making decision in business. To make valuable information we may require huge collection of data. In order to take absolute advantage

© Springer Nature Singapore Pte Ltd. 2017
D. Singh et al. (Eds.): ICAICR 2017, CCIS 712, pp. 218–226, 2017.
DOI: 10.1007/978-981-10-5780-9_20

of data, different tools and techniques are required for extraction of data, summarization of data, and the detection of patterns from raw data. Data mining is one of the powerful technologies that assist business organizations to focus on most valuable information stored in their data warehouse. Data mining helps in predicting future patterns and also businesses can make out convenient knowledge driven decision [4]. Data mining tools can respond queries that traditionally were extremely tedious, making it impossible to determine. Different tools organize databases for uncovering unknown knowledge; discovering analytical information that specialist may neglect since it lies outside their prospects. Beside the effective utilization of data mining tools and techniques, there are numerous threats to privacy. By using different data mining techniques one can easily reveal others private data or knowledge. So, before discharging database, private data of an individual or an organization must be hidden from any un-authorization access. Privacy is mainly essential because it may have harm full consequences on someone's life. There are several data mining techniques used in different data mining projects like for example: association rule, clustering, classification, prediction, sequential patterns and decision tree. We will briefly examine one of the technique i.e. association rule mining.

1.2 Association Rule

Association is one of the most widely used data mining technique in which interesting patterns are obtained on the basis of relationship between items in the same transactions [5]. Association technique is sometimes called as relation technique. Association is usually used in market basket analysis in order to find out the products that customers purchase together frequently. The unearthed correlations are represented in the form of association rules or set of frequent items. In [6] presented association rule for identifying consistency between items in large transaction data verified by point of scale systems in supermarkets. For example, on the basis of historical data stored in the databases retailers can identify the customers buying habits like if customer is buying diapers then it's obvious the customer will also purchase beer along with the diapers therefore; they put diapers and beer together. Hence the rule recommends that there is a robust correlation between the beer and diapers, using these rule retailers can try to identify the innovative chances for selling products to the customers [7, 8]. Other than retailer data, analysis of association is pertinent to many application spaces for example bioinformatics, medicinal analysis, and web mining, systematic analysis. While performing analysis of earth science data, for instance the relationship examples may uncover interesting correlation between sea, land and the atmospheric processes. Association rules generally are if/then statements used to identify relationship between data in the data repositories. There are two main steps involved in association rule mining i.e. support and confidence to recognize the associations and also some rules are identified by analyzing data from frequent sets. Association rules generally require convincing a user precise minimum support and a user specific minimum confidence at the equivalent time. Support specifies how frequently items are appearing in the database and the confidence specifies the quantity of times the if/then statement are found to be true. During association rule, information pattern should be analyzed and also the data structure of database so that we may be able to find out the preferred plans to keep the stability between the accuracy of database and the privacy or private information [9]. There are algorithms like Apriori and Eclate used for generating frequent item sets so that association rules are mined proficiently.

1.3 Apriori Algorithm

Apriori algorithm is one of the classical and the most popular association rule mining algorithm used to identify all the frequent individual items in the database. It continues by recognizing the individual items that occur frequently in database and expand them to larger and larger item set as extensive as those item sets become visible adequately frequently in the database. Frequent item sets recognized through Apriori also decide association rules which emphasize common patterns in the database for example, market basket analysis. Apriori algorithm employs the breadth first search and data structure of Apriori algorithm is very simple, clear and easy to understand [10]. Apriori algorithm follows Apriori property which states that if an item set occurs frequently, then all of its subsets must also be frequent. If the item set are not frequent, then none of its superset is frequent [11, 12]. Apriori algorithm follows two steps: first one is generate phase, in this phase candidate (K + 1) item set is generated using K-item set; or we can simply say that this phase is responsible for generating CK candidate set. Another is prune phase here the candidate set is pruned and large frequent item set are generated using "minimum support" so, that these large frequent items can be used as the pruning parameter.

2 Related Work

There are some existing systems or techniques for privacy preserving in data mining on which we will take a brief look on:

In [13] proposed a genetic algorithm for hiding sensitive rules, which investigates how sensitive rules must be guarded against malicious data miner. In this algorithm, a fitness function is computed, transactions are selected on the basis of this value, and the private items in these transactions are transformed by crossover and some mutation operations without facing any loss of data. Using this method, sensitive rules are hidden, fake rules can't be generated and non sensitive rules are not changed. In [14] some limitations of existing Apriori algorithm like wasting time in scanning the entire database identifying on the frequent item sets. An improved Apriori is presented that helps in reducing the time depending on scanning only some transactions. The time consumed by improved Apriori in each and every one value of minimum support is lesser than the original Apriori. In [15] an algorithm decrease support rule cluster is used to maintain privacy of sensitive association rules in database. Sensitive association rules are clustered on the basis of certain criteria by changing some transactions and hide several rules at a time. Besides it offer privacy for sensitive rules at certain level while ensuring database quality. The performance of this algorithm is better than other existing approaches.

In [16] describes about Apriori algorithm and how it's used for discovering nearby frequent patterns. It's one of the most suitable algorithm used for transactional data-bases. Apriori can be applied to different applications like telecommunication, network analysis, banking, market analysis and many more. In [17] presented a simple solution for preserving privacy association rule mining which states that some filter can be used to weed out or hide restricted association rules after mining phase is done. This way a balance between privacy and knowledge discovery in association rule is well main-tained. In [18] a Homomorphic encryption scheme solution is proposed for privacy preserving outsourced frequent item set mining for vertically partitioned database. To protect data owner's raw data from other data owners and the cloud this solution can be used. They also compared their proposed solution to existing solutions and observed that proposed solution leaks less information and is very efficient.

In [19] designed MDSRRC algorithm and a matrix Apriori algorithm, MDSRRC hides sensitive association rules by performing modification on database for main-taining transaction database quality and also provides security to data by encryption policy. Whereas matrix algorithm generates frequent patterns and reduces the number of sets when compared to other algorithms also helps in maintaining efficiency. In [20] proposed Apriori based distributed privacy preserving frequent item set mining algo-rithm. When there are more than two parties involved this algorithm can be fit in the secure multiparty computations model of privacy preserving computation. In [21] a fast hiding sensitive association rule algorithm is designed, idea behind the algorithm is to decrease the execution time while hiding sensitive rules during one database scan. Relation between association rules and transactions in this algorithm are evaluated to proficiently pick the suitable items to modify. In [22] introduced an efficient sliding window algorithm which maintains balance between sensitive data and knowledge discovery. Proposed algorithm is helpful for sanitizing transactional databases based on disclosure threshold controlled by a database owner. It has the lowest cost among the other sanitized algorithms also there are no chances of generating original database from the sanitized data. In [23] to protect sensitive rules against disclosure there are two approaches mentioned. In first step, group of transactions are scanned and rules are sanitized. Second approach groups sensitive rules are grouped into clusters that share the same itemsets. The advantage of using this algorithm is that it allows database owners to put a definite disclosure threshold for each sensitive rule.

3 Proposed Work

Improved Apriori algorithm is designed in such a way that it reduces the time and takes a reduction number of scans to generate the frequent itemsets. The improved Apriori algorithm is as follows:

Procedure: intersect TID sets (T, D)
Input: T is available as horizontal data base

Output: list of frequent item sets

1. Initialize: P= {<1j, t (1j)> for all 1 item set in T

2. For each item set A with < A, t (A)> in P do

PA<Q

3. For each item set < Y, t(Y)> in P such that Y is

Lexicographically > A do

4. Nay = XA U Y

5. T (Nay) = t (A) U t(Y)

6. If support of Nay >= D

7. Then PA <- PA <- {<Nay, t (Nay)>}

8. End

9. End

10. Intersect TID sets (PA, D)

End

Improved Apriori algorithm, initially generates the minimum support count = 2, after that it searches the items that occur frequently with the given itemsets. The next step of this algorithm is to create association rules such as C1, L1, C2, L2, C3, L3, and mining of these rules based on the support count, that is the frequent itemsets occurrences in transaction is greater than or equal to the given support count. Authors have considered market basket data with a set of Item ID and Transaction ID. An improved Apriori algorithm is implemented on MATLAB 2013 Tool, which finds the most frequent item sets that are based on minimum support threshold. The framework of proposed work is shown in Fig. 1.

Authors have generated some frequent item sets from source database after that association rules are created rules such as C1, L1, C2, L2, C3, and L3, based on the minimum support which ensure encryption policy. When association rules are created maximum number of items gets processed from the data this is because instead of accessing single items per transaction multiple itemsets are accessed which reduces the number of iterations the rules created ensure certain privacy for the specified rules and maintains data quality.

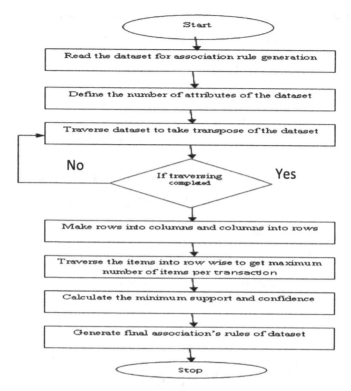

Fig. 1. Flowchart of proposed work

4 Experimental Results

For determining privacy, association rule algorithm such as improved Apriori is implemented by using parameters like number of iterations and time it takes to mine the rules, this algorithm is implemented on Market Basket data consisting of attributes like Item ID and Transaction ID. Improved Apriori algorithm is assessed by performance metrics as time (time is required to find out the frequent itemsets) and number of iterations (required to check the transactions for association rules occurrences). Comparison of itemsets generated from original data set and the sanitized data is performed on the basis of Apriori algorithm. The result generation section consists of a user interface it displays the association rules generated, and the iterations in sanitized data and existing data. Also time executed by iterations is displayed in both sanitized data and existing data (Tables 1 and 2).

Results showed that the number of iterations in sanitized data is less than that of the data which are generated from original data. So if any one mines the sanitized data will not get appropriate results in terms of frequent itemsets and strong association rules. So this way privacy of association rule and data quality is well maintained (Figs. 2 and 3).

Analysis shows that the time taken by iteration in sanitized data is less than the time taken by the original data.

Table 1. Comparison of iterations in original data and sanitized data

Levels	Existing iterations	New iterations
C1	2.025%	1.568%
L1	1.640%	1.186%
C2	3.486%	3.029%
L2	3.798%	4.255%
C3	4.222%	2.851%
L3	4.070%	2.243%

Table 2. Comparison of time taken by iterations in original data and sanitized data

Levels	Existed time calculated	New time calculated
C1	3.395 s	2.938 s
L1	4.381 s	3.924 s
C2	4.857 s	4.400 s
L2	5.169 s	4.712 s
C3	6.506 s	6.049 s
L3	4.070 s	3.614 s

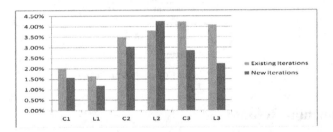

Fig. 2. Comparison of iterations in existing data and new data

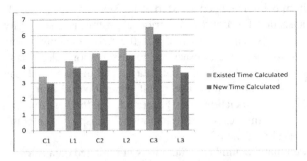

Fig. 3. Comparison of time taken by iterations in existing data and new data

5 Conclusion and Future Work

Preserving Privacy in data mining is a latest body of study focusing on the implications that originate from the application of data mining algorithms to large public databases. Apriori algorithm is implemented for generating the itemsets from the market basket data and thus some rules are created in the form of association rules which ensure privacy. A comparison framework has been developed between existing itemsets and the new item sets. In the existing itemsets no privacy is ensured while in new itemsets encryption policy is ensured. Comparison is performed on the basis of number of iteration and the execution time authors conclude that the number of iterations and their execution time in sanitized data is less than that of the data which are generated from original dat. So, this way privacy of association rule and data quality is well maintained. Proposed approach is using Apriori algorithm which tends to be slow with huge amount of data. In future an improved Apriori can be implemented to deal with the scalability of data.

References

1. Tekieh, M.H., Raaheni, B.: Importance of data mining in healthcare: a survey. In: International Conference on Advances in Social Networks Analysis and Mining IEEE (2015)
2. Himel, D., Tanmoy, S., Madhusudan, B., Mohammad, E.A.: An approach to protect the privacy of cloud data from data mining based attacks, pp. 1106–1115. IEEE (2013). doi:10.1109/SC.Companion.2012.133
3. Dileep, K.S., Vishnu, S.: Data security and privacy in data mining: research issues & preparation. Int. J. Comput. Trends Technol. 4(2), 194–200 (2013)
4. Padhy, N., Mishra, P., Panigrahi, R.: The survey of data mining applications and future scope. Int. J. Comput. Sci. Eng. Inf. Technol. 2(2), 43–58 (2012). doi:10.5121/ijcseit.2012.2303
5. Domadiya, N.H., Rao, U.P.: Hiding sensitive association rules to maintain privacy and data quality in database. In: 3rd IEEE International Advance Computing Conference (2013)
6. Agarwal, R., Imielinski, T., Swami, A.: Mining association rules between sets of items in large databases. In: International Conference on Management of Data – SIGMOD, pp. 207–216 (1993)
7. Modi, C.N., Rao, U.D., Patel, D.R.: Maintaining privacy and data quality in privacy preserving association rule mining. In: 2nd International Conference on Computing Communication and Networking Technologies IEEE (2010)
8. Zheng, J., Yan, L.: Research on the improvement of Apriori algorithm and its application in intrusion detection system. IEEE, pp. 105–108 (2015)
9. Wu, S., Wang, H.: Research on privacy preserving algorithm of association rule mining in centralized database. In: International Symposium on Information Processing IEEE, pp. 131–134 (2008). doi:10.1109/ISIP.2008.11
10. Zhang, K., Liu, J., Chai, Y., Zhou, J., Li, Y.: A method to optimize Apriori algorithm for frequent items mining. In: 7th International Symposium on Computational Intelligence and Design IEEE, pp. 71–75 (2014). doi:10.1109/ISCID.2014.233
11. Ingle, G., Suryavanshi, N.Y.: Association rule mining using improved Apriori algorithm. Int. J. Comput. Appl. 112(4), 37–42 (2015)

12. Yabing, J.: Research of an improved Apriori algorithm in data mining association rules. Int. J. Comput. Commun. Eng. **2**(1), 25–27 (2013)

13. Narmadha, S., Vijayarani, S.: Protecting sensitive association rules in privacy preserving data mining using genetic algorithms. Int. J. Comput. Appl. **33**(7), 37–43 (2011)

14. Maolegi, M.A., Arkok, B.: An improved Apriori algorithm for association rules. Int. J. Nat. Lang. Comput. **3**(1), 21–29 (2014). doi:10.5121/ijnlc.2014.3103.21

15. Aniket, Y.J., Virendra, R.D., Sagar, S.B., Hardik, P.K.: Privacy preserving association rule mining in retail industries. Int. J. Adv. Res. Comput. Commun. Eng. **4**(3) (2015). doi:10.17148/IJARCCE.2015.4320

16. Afzali, G.A., Shahriar, M.: Privacy preserving big data mining: association rule hiding. J. Inf. Syst. Telecommun. **4**(2), 70–77 (2016)

17. Shaofei, W., Hui, W.: Research on the privacy preserving algorithm of association rule mining in centralized database. In: International Symposium on Information Processing IEEE, pp. 131–134 (2008). doi:10.1109/ISIP.2008.11

18. Linchun, L., Rongxing, L., Kim, K.R.C., Anwitaman, D., Jun, S.: Privacy preserving outsourced association rule mining on vertically partitioned databases. IEEE (2016). doi:10.1109/TIFS.2016.2561241

19. Pravin, R.P., Jagade, S.M.: Privacy preserving by hiding association rule mining from database. IOSR J. Comput. Eng. **16**(5), 25–31 (2014)

20. Adrian, C., Szilvia, L., Andres, L.: Efficient Apriori based algorithm for privacy preserving frequent itemset mining. In: 5th International Conference on Cognitive Info Communications IEEE, pp. 431–435 (2014)

21. Chih, C.W., Shan, T.C., Hung, C.L.: A novel algorithm for completely hiding sensitive association rules. In: 8th International Conference on Intelligent Systems Design & Applications IEEE, pp. 202–208 (2008). doi:10.1109/ISDA.2008.180

22. Stanly, R.M.O., Osmar, R.Z.: Protecting Sensitive Knowledge by Data Sanitization

23. Janakiramaiah, B., RamaMohan, R.A., Kalyani, G.: An approach for privacy preserving in association rule mining using data restriction. Int. J. Eng. Sci. Invention **2**(1), 27–34 (2013)

Stable Feature Selection with Privacy Preserving Data Mining Algorithm

Mohana Chelvan P[1(✉)] and Perumal K[2]

[1] Department of Computer Science, Hindustan College of Arts and Science,
Chennai, India
pmohanselvan@rediff.com
[2] Department of Computer Applications, Madurai Kamaraj University,
Madurai, India
perumalmala@gmail.com

Abstract. Data mining extracts previously not known and valuable type of patterns and information procured from large storage of data that is archived. In the last few decades, the advancements in internet technologies results in enormous increase in the dimensionality of the dataset concerned with data mining. Feature selection is an important dimensionality reduction technique as it improves accuracy, efficiency and model interpretability of data mining algorithms. Selection of feature and its stability may be perceived to be the robustness of the algorithm for feature selection which helps selecting similar or the same subset of features for small perturbations in the dataset. The essential purpose of data mining that is used for the preservation of privacy is the modification of original datasets by means of a method to preserve privacy of the individuals and work out subsequent data mining algorithm to get information from it. This perturbation of the dataset will affect the feature selection stability. There will be a correlation between privacy preserving data mining and feature selection stability. This paper explores on this problem and also introduces a privacy preserving algorithm which has less impact on feature selection stability as well as accuracy.

Keywords: Data mining · Privacy preservation · Feature selection · Selection stability · Kuncheva Index

1 Introduction

1.1 Feature Selection Stability

Data mining may be defined as the analysis of archived datasets of organizations for the purpose of extracting potentially useful, previously unknown, non-trivial, implicit and interesting patterns or knowledge. Data mining is indispensable for organizations for getting edge over their competitors. The collected data of individuals by the online systems are mostly high dimensional because of the advancements in the internet throughput technologies which will makes the data mining tasks very difficult and is in common terms denoted as "the curse of dimensionality" [1]. Feature selection is known to be a dimensionality reduction technique in which relevant features forming a small subset is chosen from among the dataset that is original in accordance to convinced

© Springer Nature Singapore Pte Ltd. 2017
D. Singh et al. (Eds.): ICAICR 2017, CCIS 712, pp. 227–237, 2017.
DOI: 10.1007/978-981-10-5780-9_21

criteria of evaluation that is relevant [2, 3]. Feature selection process results in better learning recital such as lower computational cost, higher learning precision, better model interpretability and reduced storage space. Further, the high dimensional data that has background information or public information can identify the record owners that are underlying and that in turn can pose a threat for their privacy.

Stability of feature selection is the insensitivity of the algorithm of feature selection for the selection of similar or the same features that are subsets in subsequent iterations of the algorithms for selection of features for the addition or deletion of few tuples from the dataset [4]. Unstable feature selection will result in confusion in the researcher's mind about their research conclusions and the experimental results become unreliable [5–7]. Now-a-days, the importance of feature selection stability is realised by the researchers as it decrease their confidence on their research work. And also selection stability is considered as an important criterion of feature selection algorithms as it becomes an emerging topic of research [6, 8]. The change in the characteristics of the dataset will influence the feature selection stability but it is not completely algorithmic independent [9–11]. The factors that affect the selection stability consist of number selected features [12], dimensionality, sample size [5] and different data distribution across different folds.

1.2 Privacy Preserving Data Mining

The data mining techniques for the preservation of privacy may be divided into two prime types known as the techniques of masking and the techniques for synthetic generation of data. In the techniques for masking they preserve confidentiality of respondents by which the original dataset is altered in such a way that it produces new datasets that are suitable for analysis of statistical data. The techniques for masking may be divided into two types i.e., non-perturbative and perturbative. In non-perturbative masking technique, the original dataset remains intact, but certain types of data are concealed and sometimes certain details are detached. Examples of the non-perturbative techniques can be Generalization, Bottom coding, Top coding, Sampling, Local suppression and Global recoding. In the case of the technique of perturbative masking, the original data are modified. Examples for the perturbative masking techniques are Resampling, Rounding, Lossy compression, Random noise, MASSC, PRAM, Swapping, Rank swapping and Micro-aggregation. In the techniques of generation of synthetic data, the tuples in a set of data is replaced with the tuples of a new set but the original data's main statistical properties are however preserved. Those microdata that is released is duly mixed with that of the original or is kept entirely synthetic.

Data mining for preservation of privacy indicates that branch of mining that aims at protection of information that is privacy-sensitive of individuals belonging to unsanctioned and sometimes unsolicited revelation and so defending the tuples of dataset along with their privacy. In data mining for preservation of privacy, the sensitive raw data and also the sensitive knowledge of mining results are protected in some way by the perturbation of the original dataset using the developed algorithm [13]. Using this technique, privacy of the individuals is preserved and at the same time useful knowledge is extracted from the dataset [14]. The major obligation of good privacy preserving techniques is high data quality with privacy. In order to protect the person's records from being re-identified, these techniques perturb the collected dataset by some form of transformation or modification before its release [15]. Due to these perturbations, the selection stability will be affected as it is mostly dataset dependent. More changes to the dataset will results in unstable feature selection which will also leads to less data utility. It has been found that there has been no valuable research effort put relevant to the topic i.e., the relationship between perturbation of data for data mining for preservation of privacy and feature selection stability.

2 Methodology

2.1 Proposed Methodology

Most of the methods of data mining for preservation of privacy are affected by the inevitable curse known as the curse of dimensionality of datasets in occurrence of civic information. The attributes in microdata are generally grouped as identifiers, quasi identifiers, and confidential attributes or sensitive attributes [16]. Identifiers are those aspects that exclusively recognize a microdata respondent. For example, social security number and employee number are the attributes that will uniquely identify the tuple with which they are associated. The ones known as quasi identifiers are the grouping of aspects can be linked along with outside data for the purpose of re-identifying those respondents that are referred in the information. For instance, attributes like birth date, pin code and sex are termed as quasi identifiers and can be connected duly to outside information on civics and can be used to identify the identity of those respondents that match or even to the uncertainty of a particular group of respondents that can be brought down. The sensitive or confidential attributes are those attributes where microdata contain confidential information. For instance, attributes like salary or result of disease test can be considered as confidential.

The proposed methodology is shown in Algorithm 1. The feature selection algorithm Information Gain IG was used to identify the quasi identifier attributes of the datasets taken for the particular experiment. The IG gives a list of ranks of attributes based on their significance. From the ranked list of attributes, quasi identifier attributes are selected. The boundary between sensitive attributes and quasi identifiers may become blurred due to the curse of dimensionality particularly when the adversaries may have substantial background information. The identified attributes known as quasi identifiers and the attributes that are sensitive are perturbed by the algorithm for mining of data for the preservation of privacy and is also shown in Algorithm 2. The algorithm for feature selection which is Correlation-based Feature Selection CFS is being applied on the datasets both before and after the perturbation by the privacy preserving algorithm. From the chosen feature subsets, selection of features and their stability is calculated by making use of the stability measure called Kuncheva Index KI. The privacy preserved datasets are duly tested for identifying their data mining utility.

Step 1: Quasi identifiers are selected using Information Gain ranking method.

Step 2: Statistical properties, i.e., mean, standard deviation and variance are calculated for experimental datasets.

Step 3: Feature selection algorithm CFS has applied on the experimental datasets.

Step 4: Accuracy for selected features is calculated before privacy preserving perturbation.

Step 5: Quasi identifier attributes and sensitive attributes are perturbed using privacy preserving algorithm.

Step 6: Statistical properties, i.e., mean, standard deviation and variance are calculated for privacy preserved datasets.

Step 7: Feature selection algorithm CFS has applied on the privacy preserved datasets.

Step 8: Feature selection stability values of the privacy preserved datasets are calculated using Kuncheva Index KI.

Step 9: Accuracy for selected features is calculated after privacy preserving perturbation.

Step 10: Statistical properties, feature selection stability and accuracy are analysed for the privacy preserved datasets and hence for the privacy preserving algorithm.

Algorithm 1. Proposed methodology

2.2 Privacy Preserving Algorithm

The proposed privacy preserving algorithm used in the experiments is shown in the Algorithm 2. The data alteration can be done in different ways including suppression, perturbation, data swapping, data shuffling, microaggregation, rounding or coarsening and noise addition. In this algorithm, calculated noise was added for numerical attribute domain values while generalization technique was applied for categorical attribute domain values pertaining to the identified attributes of quasi identifiers as well as attributes that are sensitive. The algorithm so proposed for the data mining for preservation of privacy protects the data that is sensitive with good feature selection stability and accuracy which will creates a model for better data utility.

Input   :   Experimental dataset
Output   :   Perturbed dataset for attributes of quasi identifiers as well as
                  sensitive

1.   Let the dataset D includes T tuples as D = {T1, T2...Tn}. In every
         tuple of T contains an attribute set T =   {A1, A2,...Ap} in which
         Ai ε T and Ti ε D
2.   Select attributes that are ranked high based on the method of
         Information Gain IG ranking technique as the attribute for Quasi
         Identifier A_Q
3.   For Each Sensitive Attribute or Quasi Identifier Attribute A_Q of
         Tuple T where A_Q ε T
         Repeat Step 4 to Step 20
4.   If selected attribute A_Q =Numeric
         Then Go to Step 5
         Else Go to Step 17
5.   The domain values of the attributes are divided into ranges
6.   Assign N = Original value of attribute A_Q
7.   Assign L = Lowest value of the range to which A_Q belongs
8.   Compute R = L / N
9.   If R <= 0.5
         Then Go to 10
         Else Go to 11
10.   Compute R1 = 1 − R
11.   Compute R1 = R
12.   Assign X = Number of Digits of N
13.   Compute R2 = R1 * (10 ^ X)
14.   If N < mean
         Then Go to Step 15
         Else Go to Step 16
15.   Numeric attribute perturbation: N1 = N + Noise of value R2
         Go to Step 20
16.   Numeric attribute perturbation: N1 = N − Noise of value R2
         Go to Step 20
17.   If selected attribute A_Q = Categorical
         Then Go to Step 18
         Else Go to Step 20
18.   An attribute perturbation in case of categorical : N1 = perturb of
         the attribute's original value by a process of generalization of
         the value of the attribute and allocation of a number
19.   The number assigned for N1 is mapped to a range.
20.   End

Algorithm 2. Proposed privacy preserving algorithm

2.3   Information Gain IG

The entropy is the impurity training set condition S. It is described as a reflecting measures more data regarding Y presented by X which symbolizes the actual amount of the entropy of that of Y decreases [17]. This type of measure is called Information Gain and is given in (1).

$$IG = H(Y) - H(Y/X) = H(X) - H(X/Y) \qquad (1)$$

A symmetrical measure that is derived once the information on X on observing Y is equal to the information that is derived on Y on observing X is known as IG. This IG is normally balanced towards those features that have some additional values even in case of not being useful. The gain of information with regard to class is calculated on the basis of the worth of the evaluated attribute. The independence existing between the class label and the feature is duly assessed by means of IG on taking into consideration the divergence that exists among entropy of the particular feature as well as conditional entropy of the class label as according to (2).

$$IG\,(Class, Attribute) = H(Class) - H(Class \mid Attribute) \qquad (2)$$

2.4   Correlation-Based Feature Selection CFS

The respective attributes and their subset values are evaluated through CFS by taking into account the redundancy degree among them together with the individual predictive ability of each feature. Features subsets that are including low inter-correlation between the classes but that are highly correlated within the class are preferred [5]. The search strategies including genetic search, best-first search, backward elimination, forward selection and bi-directional search can be combined with CFS for determining the best feature subset which is given in (3).

$$r_{zc} = \frac{k\,r_{zi}}{\sqrt{k + (k-1)r_{ii}}} \qquad (3)$$

in which r_{zc} denotes the actual correlation that exist in the class variable and also the subset features that are summed, where k denotes the number of features of subset, r_{zi} denotes the average of correlations in the class variable along with the subset features and here r_{ii} denotes the average of inter-correlation in the subset features [5].

2.5   Kuncheva Index KI

In most of the stability measures, there will be overlap between the two subsets of the features due to chance. The larger cardinality of the selected features' lists positively correlated with the chance of overlap. To overcome this drawback, the Kuncheva Index KI is proposed in [18] which contains correction term to avoid the intersection by chance. KI is the only measurement that obeys all the requirements appeared in [18] i.e., Monotonicity, Limits and Correction for chance. The correction for chance term was introduced in KI and so it becomes desirable. Unlike the other measurements, the larger value of cardinality will not affect the stability value in KI.

$$KI\,(F'_1, F'_2) = \frac{|F'_1 \cap F'_2| \cdot m - k^2}{k\,(m-k)} \qquad (4)$$

In (4), F'_1 and F'_2 are subset of features selected in subsequent iterations of feature selection algorithms, k is number of features in the subsets and m is the total number of features in experimental dataset. KI's results bound between the ranges of $[-1, 1]$, where -1 means $k = m/2$, i.e., there is no intersection between the two subsets of features. KI becomes 1 when the cardinality of the intersection set equals k, i.e., F'_1 and F'_2 are identical. KI becomes close to zero for dissimilarly drawn lists of subset of features.

3 Experimental Results

The two datasets used in the experiments are Census-Income (KDD) dataset and Insurance Company Benchmark (COIL 2000) dataset. The datasets are obtained from the KEEL dataset repository [19]. Table 1 shows the characteristics of the datasets. In the listed datasets, the Census dataset has both categorical and numeric values while the Coil 2000 dataset has only numeric values.

Table 1. Characteristics of datasets Census and Coil 2000

S.No.	Datasets characteristics	Datasets	
		Census	Coil 2000
1	Type	Classification	Classification
2	Origin	Real World	Real World
3	Instances	142521	9822
4	Features	41	85
5	Classes	3	2
6	Missing values	Yes	No
7	Attribute type	Numerical, categorical	Numerical

The ranked attributes are obtained by evaluating the significance of an attribute by measuring the information gain with reverence to the class. This was done by the feature selection algorithm Information Gain IG. Based on the obtained ranked attributes, the quasi identifiers are identified and selected for privacy preserving perturbation. The quasi identifiers and sensitive attributes are perturbed using the privacy preserving algorithm which is shown in Algorithm 2. Each and every domain value of the selected attribute has modified for 100% privacy preservation and so an intruder or malicious data miner even with considerable background information cannot be sure about the precision of a re-identification.

The feature selection algorithm CFS has been used to select attributes from both original and privacy preserved datasets and the search method used in the experiment is BestFirst. CFS algorithm is filter-based, so it does not engage any classifier in the selection process. Overfitting is reduced by using 10-fold cross validation. BestFirst uses greedy hillclimbing for searching the space of attribute subsets and is improved with a backtracking facility. BestFirst may search backward after starting with the full set of attributes or search forward after starting with the empty set of attributes or search in both directions after starting at any point by taking into account all possible single attribute additions and deletions at a specified point. The number of selected features was kept at optimum number as selection stability will improve up to the optimum number of relevant features and then decreases.

The statistical properties, i.e., mean, variance and standard deviation for the numerical attributes of original dataset and modified dataset have been calculated. The experiments for statistical performances have been conducted on the privacy preserved datasets for verification. The Fig. 1 shows that privacy preserving perturbation has formed almost the identical statistical results after the alteration also.

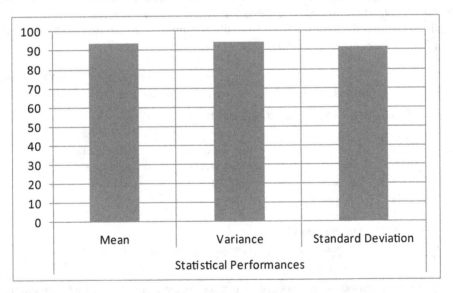

Fig. 1. Statistical performances of the privacy preserving algorithm

Feature selection stability values of the privacy preserved datasets Census and Coil 2000 are calculated using the stability measure Kuncheva Index KI and the result is shown in the Fig. 2. In the case of KI, the larger value of cardinality will not affect the selection stability and so it is used in the experiments as a stability measure. Selection stability is negatively correlated with the variation of the dataset i.e., perturbation of the training samples. The privacy preserving algorithm has produced almost stable feature selection results because of the statistical properties for the numerical attributes of the perturbed datasets are consistent. The dataset Coil 2000 has all the attributes as numeric while the dataset Census has both categorical and numerical attributes. And so from the results, it has been seen the dataset Coil 2000 is more stable than the dataset Census as it contains only numeric attributes.

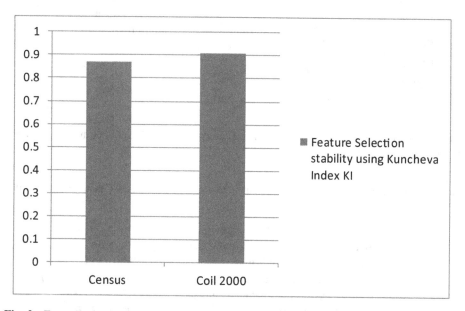

Fig. 2. Feature selection stability using Kuncheva Index KI for the datasets Census and Coil 2000 after privacy preserving perturbation

Feature selection stability and data utility are positively correlated. As the feature selection stability results for the privacy preserving algorithm are good, the accuracy of the privacy preserved datasets are almost same as before perturbation. The accuracy results are shown in the Fig. 3.

Thus, the proposed privacy preserving algorithm has been tested using two different experimental datasets for its performance in privacy preservation, feature selection stability and data utility. The experimental results have proved that the application of the algorithm on experimental datasets result in stable feature selection with almost consistent accuracy. The Table 2 summarises the statistics of the conducted experiment on the datasets in relation with feature selection stability and accuracy.

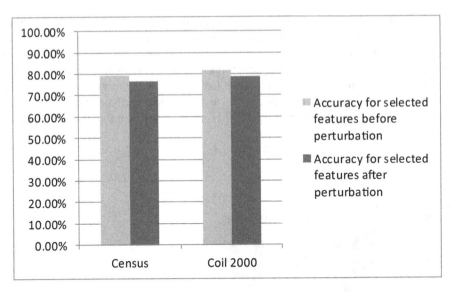

Fig. 3. Accuracy for selected features for the datasets Census and Coil 2000 before and after privacy preserving perturbation

Table 2. Summary of feature selection stability and accuracy for datasets Census and Coil 2000

Experimental results	Datasets	
	Census	Coil 2000
Feature selection stability using Kuncheva Index KI	0.87	0.91
Overall accuracy before perturbation	73.48%	75.91%
Overall accuracy after perturbation	70.85%	72.61%
Accuracy of selected features before perturbation	79.31%	81.72%
Accuracy of selected features after perturbation	76.52%	78.72%

4   Conclusion

Defending the privacy-sensitive data of individuals and also extracting useful information from microdata is a very complicated problem. There will be tradeoffs between privacy preservation, feature election stability and accuracy. From the experimental results, it has been concluded that the proposed privacy preserving algorithm which is used to perturb the quasi identifier attributes and sensitive attributes of the experimental datasets will preserve the privacy of the individuals. For the numerical attributes of the original and modified datasets, the statistical measures of mean, variance and standard deviation gave almost similar results. The experiments have proved that the proposed privacy preserving algorithm gave almost stable feature selection results. At the same time there will be minimum change in the accuracy due to the perturbation of the datasets. So, the proposed privacy preserving algorithm used in the experiments has preserved the privacy of the individuals and at the same time gave good feature selection stability and also the decrease in accuracy is almost negligible.

References

1. Hastie, T., Tibshirani, R., Friedman, J.: The Elements of Statistical Learning. Springer, New York (2001)
2. Guyon, I., Elisseeff, A.: An introduction to variable and feature selection. J. Mach. Learn. Res. **3**, 1157–1182 (2003)
3. Liu, H., Motoda, H.: Feature Selection for Knowledge Discovery and Data Mining. Kluwer Academic Publishers, Boston (1998)
4. Davis, C.A., Gerick, F., Hintermair, V., Friedel, C.C., Fundel, K., Küffner, R., Zimmer, R.: Reliable gene signatures for microarray classification: assessment of stability and performance. Bioinformatics **22**(19), 2356–2363 (2006)
5. Hall, M.A.: Correlation-based feature selection for machine learning. Department of Computer Science, University of Waikato (1998). http://www.cs.waikato.ac.nz/~mhall/thesis.pdf
6. Kalousis, A., Prados, J., Hilario, M.: Stability of feature selection algorithms: a study on high-dimensional spaces. Knowl. Inf. Syst. **12**(1), 95–116 (2007)
7. He, Z., Yu, W.: Stable feature selection for biomarker discovery (2010)
8. Kalousis, A., Prados, J., Hilario, M.: Stability of feature selection algorithms, p. 8, November 2005
9. Alelyani, S., Liu, H.: The effect of the characteristics of the dataset on the selection stability. In: IEEE International Conference on Tools with Artificial Intelligence (2011). doi:10.1109/ICTAI.2011.167. 1082-3409/11
10. Alelyani, S., Zhao, Z., Liu, H.: A dilemma in assessing stability of feature selection algorithms. In: IEEE International Conference on High Performance Computing and Communications (2011). doi:10.1109/HPCC.2011.99. ISBN 978-0-7695-4538-7/11
11. Alelyani, S.: On feature selection stability: a data perspective. Doctoral dissertation, Arizona State University, AZ, USA. ACM Digital Library (2013). ISBN 978-1-303-02654-6
12. Kalousis, A., Prados, J., Hilario, M.: Stability of feature selection algorithms: a study high-dimensional spaces. Knowl. Inf. Syst. **12**, 95–116 (2007)
13. Veryhios, V.S., Bertino, E., Fovino, I.N., Provenza, L.P., Saygin, Y., Theodoridis, Y.: State-of-the-art in privacy preserving data mining. SIGMOD Rec. **33**(1) (2004)
14. Xiniun, Q., Zong, M.: An overview of privacy preserving data mining. Procedia Environ. Sci.**12** (2012). doi:10.1016/j.proenv.2012.01.432. ISSN 1878-0296
15. Agarwal, R., Srikant, R.: Privacy preserving data mining. In: Proceedings of the ACM SIGMOD Conference of Management of Data, pp. 439–450. ACM Press, May 2000
16. Ciriani, V., De Capitani di Vimercati, S., Foresti, S., Samarati, P.: Micro data protection. In: Yu, T., Jajodia, S. (eds.) Secure Data Management in Decentralized Systems. Advances in Information Security, vol. 33, pp. 291–321. Springer, Heidelberg (2007). doi:10.1007/978-0-387-27696-0_9
17. Hall, M.A., Smith, L.A.: Practical feature subset selection for machine learning. In: McDonald, C. (ed.) Proceedings of the 21st Australian Computer Science Conference, pp. 181–191. Springer, Heidelberg (1998)
18. Kuncheva, L.I.: A stability index for feature selection. In: Proceedings of the 25th Conference on IASTED International Multi Conference: Artificial Intelligence and Applications, Anaheim, CA, USA, pp. 390–395. ACTA Press (2007)
19. Alcalá-Fdez, J., Fernández, A., Luengo, J., Derrac, J., García, S., Sánchez, L., Herrera, F.: KEEL data-mining software tool: data set repository, integration of algorithms and experimental analysis framework. J. Multiple-Valued Log. Soft Comput. **17**(2), 255–287 (2010)

Process Mining in Intrusion Detection-The Need of Current Digital World

Ved Prakash Mishra[1](✉) and Balvinder Shukla[2]

[1] Department of Computer Science and Engineering, Amity University,
Dubai, UAE
mishra.ved@gmail.com, vmishra@amityuniversity.ae
[2] Amity University, Noida, India

Abstract. In the current age of digital world, all users of Internet/Network as well as organizations are suffering from intrusions which results into data/information are theft/loss. In the present manuscript concept of intrusion detection system (IDS) were discussed along with its types and basic approaches. It is found that signature analysis, expert system, data mining etc. still using for IDS. Survey was given related to cybercrime incidents across various industry sectors. After analyzing the attacks on networks of organizations in different industry sectors it is found that still attacks like DDoS are not preventable. Comparison of data mining algorithms used for intrusion detection was also done. Various methods to implement the algorithm along with the advantages and disadvantages were also discussed in detail. Because of the disadvantages like over fitting, slow testing speed, unstable algorithms etc., intruders in the network are still active. To avert these shortcomings there is a need to develop real-time intrusion detection and prevention system through which data/information can be protected and saved in real-time basis before a severe loss is experienced. The real-time prevention is possible only if alerts are received instantly without delays. For this purpose, process mining could be used. This technique gives instant time alerts with real time analysis so as to prevent intrusions and data loss.

Keywords: Process mining · Data mining · Intrusion · Audit trails/event logs · Security

1 Introduction

Commonly users think that firewall can recognize the intruders and block them, but firewall only restricts the users to access the designated points. Intrusion meaning when someone is attempting to compromise the integrity, availability and confidentiality for any network or computer [1]. To detect this type of activity we need strong Intrusion detection system (IDS). It works as a monitor and analyzer of the processes and events occurs in IT systems and networks for identifying the intrusions [2]. Till now various methods for Intrusion detection systems have been used such as Signature Analysis, Colored Petri Nets, Expert Systems, Neural Networks, Machine Learning and Data Mining. However, none of these systems are able to provide real time intrusion detection and prevention. The existing Intrusion Detection Systems are even not able to

© Springer Nature Singapore Pte Ltd. 2017
D. Singh et al. (Eds.): ICAICR 2017, CCIS 712, pp. 238–246, 2017.
DOI: 10.1007/978-981-10-5780-9_22

fulfill the need of business organizations. The Monitoring and analysis of the event logs on a real time basis is required for detection of Intrusions in real time. Therefore, it is required to monitor the logs for every event occurrence. In current IDS, sensors are sending a lot of false positive results and gives a challenge to reduce the rate of false positive results. Furthermore, the IDS are still reactive rather than proactive, giving a challenge to be proactive. Hence, to fulfill these gaps process mining may prove to be useful. The Process Mining is basically focused to improve the IDS by latest tools and techniques for discovering best process, control, organizational, data and hierarchy structure of the organization from event logs/Audit trails [3]. The concept of Process Mining is to discover new processes and monitor them on real time and if there is any need of improve them, then improve it on real time basis with currently available event logs [4]. This technique provides the link between the process model and the actual processes i.e. between data-oriented analysis and model-based analysis. The policies of security covers from the role based access control and cryptography to auditing and four eye principle. Basically audit trail can be used for Computer security and auditing [1]. The security violations can be identified via analysis of behavioral patterns using audit trails. The event log mainly contains about the events referring a case and an activity. It also contains the information about the person or system components also called an actor, executing or initiating event. Process mining is useful for at-least two reasons: firstly process mining can be used as a tool to find out how procedure/people really work and secondly comparison can be done easily with some predefined process and actual process i.e. also called Delta Analysis.

Therefore, based on the needs and challenges of IDS and the importance of process mining technique, the present manuscript is organized in the following format. The concept of IDS along with the types and basic approaches is given in Sect. 2. Section 3 includes the percentage data of significant detected cybercrime incidents across the industries in recent years. The comparison of data mining algorithms used for intrusion detection is mentioned in Sect. 4. Advantages and limitations of different methods are also discussed. It is found that the slow speed of algorithms is still the problem of concern. To overcome these difficulties, Sect. 5 introduces the concept of process mining and benefits of process mining over data mining. Section 6 concludes the results. It is found that the process mining technique IDS can be more effective and proactive.

2 Intrusion Detection System

Attempt to compromise with confidentiality, availability and integrity or to bypass the security mechanism of network or computer is called intrusion. In current business scenario where everyone is talking about digital world, our main challenge is to protect the intrusion from the network [5]. Therefore, a strong system is needed which can protect from unauthorized access to system resource and data [6]. The work of IDS is to continuously monitor the system/network and giving the alert immediately if any suspicious/malicious event or activity is entering. The IDS collects the information of the system or network. After processing and analyzing, it makes the decision that whether the activity is violating the security rules or not [7–9] and generates the immediate alarm to the administrator if gets some unusual activity. Using IDS following activities can be performed:

- Analysis and Monitoring of user and system activity.
- Auditing of system configurations and vulnerabilities.
- Assessing the integrity of critical system and data files.
- Statistical analysis of activity patterns based on the matching to known attacks.
- Abnormal activity analysis.
- Operating system audit.

2.1   Types of Intrusion Detection Systems

There are three main types of Intrusion Detection System on basis of information source:

- Network Based System - The network based Intrusion Detection System detects the attack by analyzing the network packets. This type of system is placed on the network nearby the system or systems being monitored. It examines the network traffic and determines whether it falls within acceptable boundaries or not. This system is not able to detect encrypted messages. In current world, virtual private network is increasing and to detect an encrypted message is considered as a big challenge.
- Host Based System - Host based Intrusion Detection System works on the information collected from the individual computer. This type of system actually runs on the system being monitored and examines the system to determine whether the activity on the system is acceptable or not. Host based system generally utilizes the two types of information sources; (i) System logs and (ii) Operating system audit trails. Even host based system can also be disabled by DOS attacks.
- Application Based System - Application based Intrusion Detection System is the subset of host based IDS. It analyses the events within the software applications. Application based systems are not able to detect Trojan horse or other software tampering. Therefore it is always used in the combination with either host based or network based IDS.

2.2   Basic Approaches for IDS

Approaches for Intrusion detection systems can be broadly classified as:

Signature based (Knowledge-based) IDS - Signature based IDS works with the reference of data, which previous attacks have left. When intrusion enters in to the system, it lefts some footprints e.g. failed attempt to run an application, nature of data packet, failed login, folder/file accesses etc. These footprints are called signature. The signature based IDS uses these footprints to identify and prevents the same type of attack in the future. In knowledge based IDS, the data base must be continuously maintained and updated, otherwise it may fail to identify unique attacks and the same is considered as the basic limitation of this approach.

Behavior-based (Anomaly-based) IDS - Behavior based Intrusion Detection System references a learned pattern or baseline of a normal system activity to identify active intrusion attempts [10]. Deviations from this baseline or pattern, cause an alarm to be triggered and relates behavior-based IDS to higher false alarm.

2.3 Data Processing Techniques Used for IDS

Based on the approaches discussed in previous subsection, following data processing techniques are being used till now for IDS:

- Signature Analysis.
- Colored Petri Nets.
- State transition analysis.
- Statistical analysis approach.
- Expert Systems.
- Neural Networks.
- User Intention Identification.
- Machine Learning.
- Computer Immunology.
- Data Mining.

3 Significant Detected Cybercrime Incidents Across Various Industry Sectors

(See Fig. 1).

3.1 Details of DDoS Attacks on Companies with Different Sizes (in Terms of Employees)

As per the report of US cybercrime "Rising risks, reduced readiness Key findings from the 2014 US State of Cybercrime Survey" following are the DDoS attack percentage for different size of companies (Table 1):

4 Comparison of Data Mining Algorithm Used for Intrusion Detection

Following algorithms [11, 12] have been used for Intrusion detection system using Data Mining Techniques: Artificial neural Network, K Nearest Neighbor, Support Vector Machine, Decision Tree and Bayesian Method [13]. Each algorithm has some advantages and disadvantages given in Table 2.

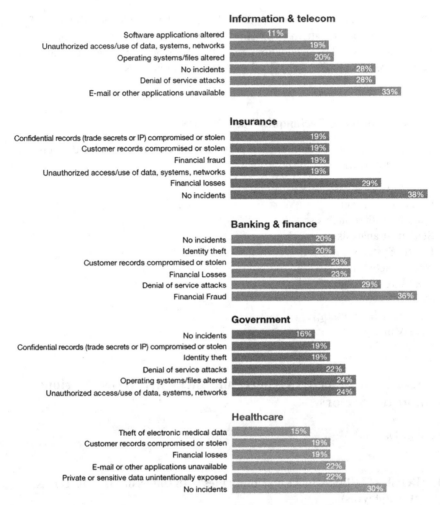

Fig. 1. Illustrates the most frequent types of cybercrime in various sectors are: Spyware, Network interruption, Malware, Phishing and Denial of Service attacks (As per the report of US cybercrime "Rising risks, reduced readiness Key findings from the 2014 US State of Cybercrime Survey").

Table 1. Company size vs DDoS attack (in percentage).

Company size (In terms of employees)	DDoS attack (in percentage)
250–499	19%
500–999	26%
1000–4999	27%
5000–9999	12%
10000 or more	17%

Table 2. Comparison of data mining algorithms used for intrusion detection

Algorithm name	Method	Advantage	Disadvantage
Artificial Neural Network	1. This algorithm is adaptive in nature and change the structure on the basis of internal and external information pass through the network/system during initial phase 2. It measure how far the particular solution is from optimal solution. The concept is used in ANN is called Cost function	1. High tolerance to noisy data 2. It has high degree of accuracy to recognize known suspicious events 3. It has the ability to learn the characteristics of misuse attacks and identify instances, which have been observed before by the network 4. It is used to learn complex nonlinear input-output relationships	1. Over fitting 2. More computation is required 3. Black box in nature
K-Nearest Neighbor	1. This is instance based learning to classify objects based on closest training examples in the feature space 2. By majority vote of its neighbors, an object classified and most common amongst its K-nearest neighbors, object being assigned to the class 3. To find the locally optimal hypothesis function, uses the similarity based search	1. Use the local information and because of this it may be adaptive in behavior 2. Can be used for parallel implementation	1. When we need to classify the test tuple, it's very slow 2. Storage problem (need large storage)
Support Vector Machine	1. It makes the set of hyper planes which can be used for regression, classification etc 2. Through linear programming, Support vector machine algorithm maps the real valued feature vector to Higher dimension feature space	1. Less chances of over fitting in comparison to other algorithms 2. More accurate	1. Testing speed is slow 2. Kernel choice is difficult
Decision Tree	1. Mainly used for the classification in data mining 2. It uses the value of its attributes for the classification of data. Initially decision tree constructed from pre-defined data 3. Firstly it selects the attributes and then it divides the data items into classes	1. This algorithm is able to handle all types of data 2. No need of any particular domain knowledge for construction	1. Algorithms are unstable 2. Need of categorical output attribute

(*continued*)

Table 2. (*continued*)

Algorithm name	Method	Advantage	Disadvantage
Bayesian Method	1. Bayesian method encodes the probabilistic relationships in variable of interest 2. This is generally used with the combination of statistical schemes for intrusion detection	1. In large database accuracy and speed is more 2. Computation is simple in comparison to others	1. Probability data is not available easily 2. The main disadvantage of Bayesian method is that the results are similar to those derived from threshold-based systems, while considerably higher computational effort is required

After comparison of the data mining algorithms used till date for intrusion detection system, still many limitations are found in each data mining algorithms used for IDS. The most common problem found is slow speed and more computation is required. Slow speed of data mining algorithm unable to detect and prevent the intrusions in real time. Though Bayesian method has overcome the slow speed but still has disadvantages. In Bayesian method the results are similar to those derived from threshold-based systems, while considerably higher computational effort is required.

5   Process Mining

Prevention from cybercrime on social network websites, networks and system is possible if any abnormal activity could be detected on real time basis. In recent times, organizations prefer to use process mining because of the fact that the processes move and change the data in information system [14]. The aim of process mining is to discover new processes, monitor and improve real processes using the knowledge gained after analysis of event logs. Process models are very important in larger organizations. Generally two types of process models are used; (i) Informal and (ii) Formal (executable) [3, 15, 16]. Informal models are used for the documentation and the formal models are used for enactment and analysis. The three main types of process mining's are: Discovery, Conformance and Enhancement. Discovery technique takes the event logs and produces a model without using any prior information [17, 18]. Most common algorithm used for this is α-algorithm. The α-algorithm constructs Petri-Net automatically without any additional knowledge. Conformance technique compares the event log and existing process model for same process. Using conformance techniques, we can design the IDS which could work on real time basis [19–21]. The Enhancement technique is to improve existing process models using the processes created with the actual event logs. Security issues like access control violations, fraud, privacy violation and denial of service attacks could be taken care with the process mining. Current virus detectors are based on signature scanner, file authentication and activity monitor. Analysis of Audit trail is one of the important approach to secure the computers. Currently process mining is used to inspect audit trails for certain pattern using α- algorithm and WF-nets [3, 22–24]. Intrusion Detection using fixed-Length

Audit Trail Patterns and Intrusion Detection Using Variable-Length Audit Trail Patterns are currently in use.

5.1   Benefit of Process Mining Over Data Mining

The benefits of process mining are two folds:

- It combines the strengths of Process modeling as well as Data Mining.
- Process mining can automatically create the process models on the basis of IT Logs and businesses are connected lively and updated on real time basis.
- Using Process mining we get real time process execution model that help us to track how data is generated and how it moves from one point to next and who handles the data.

6   Conclusion

In the present manuscript the limitations of algorithms used in IDS are discussed and the key findings are concluded as follows: Data Mining algorithms are being used for intrusion detection but still it is unable to monitor the intrusion on real-time and various types of attacks are still active like DDoS in the organization networks. These limitations can be overcome using process mining technique. This technique gives the real-time process execution model that would help to track how data is generated and how it moves from one point to next and who handles the data. The implementation of process mining concept in IDS is very useful for developing an automatic system to monitor process and event logs with low false alarms and prevent the systems/networks from intrusions. Using process mining one can monitor the host based systems in real time. Some real time work has been done using the expert system only for Network based IDS. IDS using Process mining can be implemented on network as well as host based systems.

References

1. Fekolkin, R.: Intrusion detection & prevention system: overview of snort & suricata. Internet Security, A7011N, Lulea University of Technology, pp 1–4, 06 January 2015
2. Mukkamala, S., Janoski, G., Sung, A.: Intrusion detection using neural networks and support vector machines. In: International Joint Conference on Neural Networks (IJCNN), vol. 2, pp. 1702–1707. IEEE (2002)
3. Van der Aalst, W.M.P., De Medeiros, A.K.A.: Process mining and security: detecting anomalous process executions and checking process conformance. Electron. Notes Theor. Comput. Sci. **121**(4), 3–21 (2005)
4. Ambre, A., Shekokar, N.: Insider threat detection using log analysis and event correlation. Procedia Comput. Sci. **45**, 436–445 (2015). Elsevier, Science Direct

5. Pawar, M.V., Anuradha, J.: Network security and types of attack in network. Procedia Comput. Sci. **48**, 503–506 (2015). Elsevier, Science Direct
6. Salama, S.E., Marie, M.I., El-Fangary, L.M., Helmy, Y.K.: Web server logs preprocessing for web intrusion detection. Comput. Inf. Sci. **4**(4), 123–133 (2011). Canadian Center of Science & Education
7. Vijayarani, S., Maria, S.S.: Intrusion detection system- a study. IJSPTM **4**(1), 31–44 (2015)
8. Amiri, E., Hassan, K., Heidari, H., Mohamadi, E., Hossein, M.: Intrusion detection system in MANET: a review. Procedia-Soc. Behav. Sci. **129**, 453–459 (2014)
9. Hassan, M.M.M.: Current studies on intrusion detection system, genetic algorithm and fuzzy logic. Int. J. Distrib. Parallel Syst. (IJDPS) **4**(2), 35–47 (2013)
10. Bezerra, F., Wainer, J.: Anomaly detection algorithms in business process logs. In: Proceedings of the Tenth International Conference on Enterprise Information Systems, ICEIS 2008. AIDSS (2008)
11. Patel, R., Thakkar, A., Ganatra, A.: A survey and comparative analysis of data mining techniques for network intrusion detection systems. IJSCE **2**(1), 265–271 (2012). ISSN 2231-2307
12. Adebowale, A., Idowu, S.A., Amarachi, A.: Comparative study of selected data mining algorithms used for intrusion detection. IJSCE **3**(3), 237–241 (2013). ISSN 2231-2307
13. Lee, W., Stolfo, S., Mok, K.: A data mining framework for building intrusion detection model. In: Proceedings of the IEEE Symposium Security and Privacy, pp. 120–132 (1999)
14. Van der Aalst, W.M.P.: Process Mining: Discovery, Conformance and Enhancement of Business Processes. Springer, New York (2011)
15. Claes, J., Poels, G.: Merging event logs for process mining: a rule based merging method and rule suggestion algorithm. Expert Syst. Appl. **41**(16), 7291–7306 (2014)
16. Weijters, A.J.M.M., Van der Aalst, W.M.P., Alves de Medeiros, A.K.: Process mining with the heuristics miner algorithm. In: BETA Working Paper Series, WP 166. Eindhoven University of Technology, Eindhoven, pp. 1–30 (2006)
17. Weijters, A.J.M.M., Van der Aalst, W.M.P.: Process mining discovering workflow models from event-based data. In: Proceedings of the 13th Belgium. Citeseer (2001)
18. Corney, M., Mohay, G., Clack, A.: Detection of anomalies from user profiles generated from system logs. In: CRPIT - Information Security 2011, AISC 2011, Perth Australia, vol. 116, pp. 23–31 (2011)
19. Bae, J., Liu, L., Caverlee, J., Rouse, W.B.: Process mining, discovery, and integration using distance measures. In: IEEE International Conference on Web Services (ICWS 2006) (2006)
20. Bezerra, F., Wainer, J.: Anomaly detection algorithms in logs of process aware systems. In: Proceedings of the 2008 ACM Symposium on Applied Computing, SAC 2008, pp. 951–952. ACM Press (2008)
21. Park, S., Kang, Y.S.: A study of process mining-based business process innovation. Procedia Comput. Sci. **91**, 734–743 (2016)
22. Van der Aalst, W.M.P., Van Dongen, B.F., Herbst, J., Maruster, L., Schimm, G., Weijters, A.J.M.M.: Workflow mining: a survey of issues and approaches. Data Knowl. Eng. **47**(2), 237–267 (2003)
23. Bose, R.P.J.C., Van der Aalst, W.M.P., Žliobaite, I., Pechenizkiy, M.: Dealing with concept drifts in process mining. IEEE Trans. Neural Netw. Learn. Syst. **25**(1), 154–171 (2014)
24. Su, M.Y., Jong, G., Chun, Y., Lin, Y.: A real-time network intrusion detection system for large-scale attacks based on an incremental mining approach. Comput. Secur. **28**(5), 301–309 (2009). Elsevier

Security and Privacy

Public Network Security by Bluffing the Intruders Through Encryption Over Encryption Using Public Key Cryptography Method

Vishu Madaan[1], Dimple Sethi[1], Prateek Agrawal[1(✉)], Leena Jain[2], and Ranjit Kaur[1]

[1] Lovely Professional University, Phagwara, Punjab, India
vishumadaan123@gmail.com, dimplesethi153@gmail.com,
prateek061186@gmail.com, reetbansal09@gmail.com
[2] Global Institute of Management and Emerging Technologies,
Amritsar, Punjab, India
leenajain79@gmail.com

Abstract. Cryptography and network security is the concept of protecting the network and data transmission. Security of data is important, as data is transferred over unreliable network. Public-key cryptography provides optimal solutions to many of the existing security issues in communication systems. In our proposed algorithm we have used some of these secure algorithms in order to generate a highly secured algorithm which can deal with the various flaws of these algorithms. RSA, Reil-fence algorithm, substitution and transposition algorithms has been used in the proposed algorithm. Encryption over encryption is done in order to confuse the intruder. The proposed algorithm is used to provide multilevel security.

Keywords: RSA algorithm · Reil-fence algorithm · Public key cryptography · Encryption over encryption

1 Introduction

Growth of e-commerce and internet has brought various privacy issues in electronic communications. Huge amount of important, sensitive and personal information is transmitted and stored daily in electronic communication. The data from simple social networking sites to data of military is being transmitted through the electronic communication. Even the details of bank account, details of transactions is also transferred and stored in electronic communication. Is there any guarantee that whatever the data we are sending to another person will be a secure one? There are so many ways to get this data. Someone can easily intercept your message, can modify it, can do anything with the information you are sending to another person. In previous era, there were tools to ensure the confidentiality and privacy of paper-based communication. Similarly in electronic communication arena there are so many tools and techniques available which ensure the confidentiality and privacy of the information.

D. Singh et al. (Eds.): ICAICR 2017, CCIS 712, pp. 249–257, 2017.
DOI: 10.1007/978-981-10-5780-9_23

To make the communication private and secure the one of the standard method used is Encryption. The person, who wants to send message to another person, will simply encrypt the message before transmitting it over the network. Only the person who is having key or access to decrypt the message will be available to read or modify the message using the decryption techniques [1]. Even if someone steals the message over the network will not be able to understand the message, because the encrypted message will not make any sense to them.

There are so many encryption and decryption tools and techniques available for encryption and decryption of data. Simply, these algorithms can be called as cryptographic algorithms [2].

The most common and well known cryptographic algorithms are:

DES: Data Encryption Standard, this is an algorithm which is very popular and operated of 64-bit blocks of data. The key used in this algorithm is of 56-bit. Basically, the key is also of 64-bit but every 8th bit is ignored so the size of key is considered as 56-bit.

RSA: RSA is basically Rivest-Shamir-Adleman algorithm, which is one of the most used and popular secure public key encryption algorithm [3]. According to this algorithm, if message is of large size, then it can be broken into number of blocks. The message should be represented as an integer between 0 and (n-1) then you need to encrypt the message by raising the values to the pth power modulo n. The resultant is cipher-text message, represented by C. Once the encryption is done, the decryption of the message is required at the receiver end [4]. To decrypt the cipher-text message C, we need to raise it to the power d modulo n.

HASH: Hash algorithm is sometimes known as "fingerprint" or "message digests" algorithm. It is used for encrypting a fixed length message/file.

MD5: It is 128 bit message digest function and was developed by Ron Rivest.

SHA-1: It is a hashing algorithm. The structure and functionality of algorithm is same as that of MD5 but it produces a digest of 160 bits [5]. This scheme has been proposed such that no two messages will have the same message digest generated by SHA-1.

Substitution Cipher: This cipher make changes in one piece of plaintext at a time. Figure 1 shown below is representing the encryption of "VOYAGER" with substitution method.

Transposition Ciphers: In these types of ciphers the alphabets are not substituted by other alphabets instead this position will be changed. As an example, every two letters can be switched with each other.

So, above mention are the important and wide used techniques or tools for encryption and decryption [6]. In our proposed algorithm we have used some of these secure algorithms in order to generate a highly secured algorithm which can deal with the various flaws of these algorithms. RSA, Reil-fence algorithm, substitution and transposition algorithms has been used in the proposed algorithm [7]. Above discuss algorithm are having their own limitations and advantages. Every algorithm will have some limitations, so to cope with those limitations a new algorithm has been proposed which will result in highly secure electronic communication. The proposed algorithm is

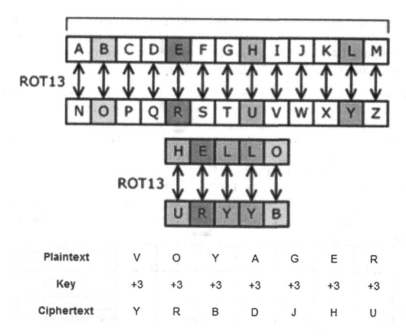

Fig. 1. Showing substitution cipher

going to provide high level of security because the multiple level encryption is their in the algorithm.

2 Background Details

There are few terms which need to be cleared before implying any technique for encryption and decryption. For network security following terms are useful, they need to be understood first. Some important definitions to be considered:

i. **Plaintext:** The simple message to be converted into encrypted form.
ii. **Cipher-text:** The message which we obtain after performing encryption is known as cipher-text.
iii. **Encryption:** The process of converting plaintext into cipher-text using some defined techniques is known as encryption.
iv. **Decryption:** The process of converting cipher-text back to plaintext is known as decryption.
v. **Key:** Key is a parameter that is used in the process of encryption and decryption.
vi. **Cryptography:** Study of cryptosystem is known as cryptography.
vii. **Cryptosystem:** To encrypt or decrypt the information, the system used is known as cryptosystem.
viii. **Symmetric Cryptosystem:** System which uses the same key to encrypt and decrypt the information is considered as a symmetric cryptosystem.

ix. **Asymmetric Cryptosystem:** System which used different key for encryption and different key for decryption is considered as an Asymmetric Cryptosystem.

x. **Crypto-analysis:** The study to breaking the system of encryption and decryption (Cryptosystem) is known as Crypto-analysis.

We have used some of the important algorithms and techniques in our proposed system. RSA is one of the algorithms which we have used in our study. RSA is basically Rivest-Shamir-Adleman algorithm is one of the most used and popular secure public key encryption algorithm. According to this algorithm, if message is of large size, it can be broken into number of blocks. The message should be represented as an integer between 0 and (n-1). Then you need to encrypt the message by raising the values to the pth power modulo n [8, 12] (Fig. 2). The resultant is cipher-text message, represented by C. Once the encryption is done, the decryption of the message is required at the receiver end. To decrypt the cipher text message C, we need to raise it to the power d modulo n.

The encryption key can be made public but the decryption key will remain private to the user. In figure we have shown the algorithm for RSA.

1. Choose two very large (100+digit) prime numbers. Denote these numbers as p and q.
2. Set n equal to p*q.
3. Choose any large integer,d,such that GCD(d,((p-1)*(q-1)))=1.
4. Find e such that e*d=1(mod((p-1)*(q-1))).

Fig. 2. Algorithm for RSA.

Reil-Fence Cipher: This cipher is one of the transposition ciphers. Reil-fence cipher is also considered as a zigzag cipher. It is easy to apply. It works by writing your message in zigzag form [9]. The example is shown in figure below:

D		F		N		T		E		A		T		A		L
	E		E		D		H		E		S		W		L	

Fig. 3. Showing working of Reil-fence cipher

After writing the message in zigzag form, you need to read each-line in turn. The cipher-text then read off will be "DFNTEATALEEDHESWL". Figure 3 showing Reil-Fence cipher, which is writing a simple message i.e. "DEFEND THE EAST WALL" in a zig-zag form. When going to perform encryption the message will be read in row wise direction. First read the first row, then read the second row and together they will form a single row, which is an encrypted form.

These algorithms are used in the proposed algorithm. Any of the above given methods/algorithms can be used in our algorithm, the main concept is of level, where multi-level encryption will be generated.

3 Methodology

Many existing security problems can be resolved with the help of Public-key cryptography in communication systems. Still, too much computational demands like speed, size of code and memory, have restricted the use of public key cryptography, specifically in wireless communication [1]. Hardly, we face any issues at the time of execution of public-key cryptography on server side and client side platforms due to the availability of high-speed processors and large memory space [10].

The conventional way to classify encryption mechanisms is purely based on the type of key i.e. symmetric (like: DES) or asymmetric (like: RSA). *Stream* key generation mechanism adds another dimension by involving key generation time to form *dynamic* keys, one per each data record [10, 11].

History of encryption and decryption techniques is gathered for the purpose of cryptanalysis and thus they values of used encrypted key can be obtained. If the key is obtained once, then the entire decrypted content can be encrypted and security will be compromised [11]. Hence privacy of data will be violated. But with dynamic encryption method even if one of the key is obtained or cipher-text record is broken it, the security and privacy will not be compromised.

3.1 Proposed Algorithm

1. Calculate length of key "n".
2. Encrypt the key by using any encryption algorithm, say RSA method.
3. Again implement RSA algorithm over resulted encrypted key after each "n" unit time interval.
4. Repeat step 3 upto "n" times.
5. Repeat step 2 to 4

Figure 4 shows a flowchart for proposed algorithm is showing step by stp security that will be provided by the given algorithm.

According to our algorithm we are first going to calculate the length of the key and denote it with "n".

After calculating the length of key, we will encrypt the key using some encryption method. The encryption method can be any like RSA, DSA. Let's take RSA algorithm.

After getting encrypted output using RSA Algorithm, again implement RSA Algorithm over resulted encrypted key "n" unit time interval.

Last step will be repeated again and again upto "n" times.

Suppose if the length of key is 7 then we are going to encrypt it 7 times using the same algorithm.

Again repeat 2 and 4 steps.

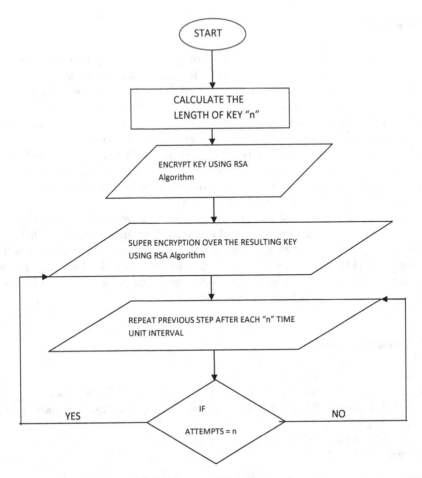

Fig. 4. Proposed algorithm.

4 Results

After applying the proposed algorithm, following data has been obtained. In the following figures we have shown step by step encryption on the input data i.e. "dfre". The output encrypted data is shown in following figures.

Figure 5 shows the first level of encryption, the message is "dfre", first length is calculated and then encryption is done with the help of RSA algorithm.

Figure 6 shows encryption at second level, which is done on the output obtained from the first level.

As the key length was four, so four times we need to perform the encryption using RSA Algorithm. Figure 7 shows the encryption at third level, the input for this level was output obtained at second level.

The result obtained at level 3 will be further encrypted in fourth level. Figure 8 shows 4th level of encryption and is the final encrypted output.

```
Enter text to enter :dfre
lenght of text value =4
Encrypted =cMq7g3D1ubEfueIgBoxUfA==
lenght of encrypted value =24
Encrypted Data in RSA (counter1-4):
Encrypted Data in RSA (counter2-4):
156 98 243 176 91 217 79 128 42 161 242 26 34 179 134 240 225 76 233 183 209 33
170 46 59 159 133 185 141 148 86 183 47 144 41 17 120 212 238 179 114 205 168 86
 217 136 119 64 173 40 134 253 8 168 100 250 22 78 141 52 53 235 22 202 36 17 24
5 254 21 112 189 218 101 13 93 218 78 171 49 68 69 116 253 115 219 24 20 163 70
60 102 158 220 206 46 107 122 78 234 239 76 75 113 223 178 95 209 227 106 139 12
5 114 185 24 173 183 251 241 225 238 126 206 3 84 169 180 79 104
```

Fig. 5. Output window 1

```
Encrypted Data in RSA (counter1-3):
Encrypted Data in RSA (counter2-3):
85 232 62 130 143 88 155 69 148 88 157 71 191 58 221 115 242 79 158 140 116 40 1
16 93 127 108 54 191 70 184 36 241 225 84 27 95 109 127 37 173 186 20 100 210 15
 200 179 23 179 89 250 201 250 249 235 59 254 180 140 164 88 194 78 183 68 225 3
8 29 116 10 120 169 62 121 70 2 45 69 185 210 106 196 71 126 184 37 74 181 32 17
 73 83 27 143 225 17 182 96 138 59 6 220 150 179 15 0 255 37 191 186 128 198 14
92 63 217 197 204 4 144 173 51 145 67 194 246 77 78
```

Fig. 6. Output window 2

```
Encrypted Data in RSA (counter1-2):
Encrypted Data in RSA (counter2-2):
39 213 166 219 214 252 102 15 4 17 233 241 179 254 202 158 242 14 78 147 217 30
20 184 1 159 81 171 86 85 16 148 185 104 230 150 125 210 155 221 130 42 80 32 32
 50 185 116 246 77 155 156 186 232 215 192 40 243 125 98 143 77 255 6 210 64 227
 251 110 3 245 128 119 215 150 45 194 255 72 178 239 53 23 119 41 36 157 92 169
215 214 37 37 206 231 166 104 80 64 78 230 114 97 182 68 217 109 219 201 106 179
 54 229 228 251 235 92 250 160 46 45 186 139 211 159 14 179 85
```

Fig. 7. Output window 3

```
Encrypted Data in RSA (counter1-1):
Encrypted Data in RSA (counter2-1):
19 191 94 41 138 254 106 154 141 189 66 113 23 59 161 224 5 165 34 72 254 16 218
 215 121 109 209 71 52 161 236 97 251 10 201 103 142 146 146 39 161 118 163 37 8
9 166 170 197 228 79 170 220 164 8 237 97 161 139 170 103 58 159 116 29 78 60 24
8 225 49 42 60 71 125 196 125 98 130 91 23 215 173 112 18 111 55 96 249 147 144
99 14 57 133 188 86 142 154 27 7 65 174 153 132 173 142 249 220 55 151 249 114 1
12 83 11 217 72 246 215 180 225 201 213 159 194 207 102 179 216
```

Fig. 8. Output window 4

Figure 9 shows simple decryption of the encrypted text and the length of decrypted value.

```
Decrypted =dfre
lenght of decrypted value =4
```

Fig. 9. Decrypted text.

Each window is shows step by step encryption. As in the given example we are taking a string "dfre". RSA is applied at the first step, then the first output is generated. As we are having key is of 4 length, so 4 times encryption is done on "dfre". Four encryption steps are shown in the above shown figures and along with this last window is showing decryption part.

5 Conclusion and Future Scope

Further work can be done by making encryption stronger. We have applied RSA algorithm for super encryption. Other type of stronger algorithms can also be joined in a proper way to make the data more secure. This is one approach that we have implied. Furthermore algorithm can be join together to generate a strong algorithm. This algorithm is providing multilevel security. Algorithm containing multilevel and multiple security can be implied such that to provide a very strong algorithm, which will be difficult to hack or break. The network is growing at a faster rate so security issues are also arising. DES, Transposition, RSA may also be combined together in a manner to get a strong encrypted output.

References

1. Appadwedula, S., Veeravalli, V.V., Jones, D.L.: Energy-efficient detection in sensor networks. IEEE J. Sel. Areas Commun. **23**(4), 693–702 (2005)
2. Bertsekas, D.: Dynamic Programming and Optimal Control, vol. I and II. Athena Scientific, Belmont (1995)
3. Hernández-Lerma, O., Lasserre, J.B.: Discrete-Time Markov Control Processes: Basic Optimality Criteria. Springer, New York (1996)
4. Lehmann, E.L., Casella, G.: Theory of Point Estimation. Springer, New York (1998)
5. Prasanthi, V.K., Kumar, A.: Optimizing delay in sequential change detection on ad hoc wireless sensor networks. In: IEEE SECON, VA, USA, pp. 306–315, September 2006

6. Rago, C., Willet, P., Bar-Shalom, Y.: Censoring sensors: a low communication-rate scheme for distributed detection. IEEE Trans. Aerosp. Electron. Syst. **32**(2), 554–568 (1996)
7. Shiryaev, A.N.: Optimal Stopping Rules. Springer, New York (1978)
8. Veeravalli, V.V.: Decentralized quickest change detection. IEEE Trans. Inf. Theory **47**(4), 1657–1665 (2001)
9. Wu, Y., Fahmy, S., Shroff, N.B.: Energy efficient sleep/wake scheduling for multi-hop sensor networks: non-convexity and approximation algorithm. IEEE Infocom **07**, 1568–1576 (2007)
10. Zacharias, L., Sundaresan, R.: Decentralized sequential change detection using physical layer fusion. IEEE Trans. Wirel. Commun. **7**(12), 4999–5008 (2007)
11. Omari, M.: An efficient application of a dynamic crypto system in mobile wireless security. In: IEEE International Conference on Wireless Communications and Networking, pp. 837–842 (2004)
12. Rivest, R.L., Shamir, A., Adleman, L.: A method for obtaining digital signatures and public-key cryptosystems. Commun. ACM **21**(2), 120–126 (1978)

Network Services

Happiness Index in Social Network

Kuldeep Singh[(⊠)], Harish Kumar Shakya, and Bhaskar Biswas

Department of Computer Science and Engineering,
Indian Institute of Technology (BHU),
Varanasi, India
{kuldeep.rs.cse13,hkshakya.rs.cse,
bhaskar.cse}@iitbhu.ac.in

Abstract. Happiness index in social networking sites shows the happiness of human being. For this dataset is collected from social network, Twitter and applied various sentiment analysis techniques to the data set. Positive Sentiment and Negative Sentiment is calculated based on the tweets. Tweets were retrieved based on location-wise (latitude and longitude) and country-wise. Consequently, maps are plotted based on these sentiments location-wise and country-wise. Individual users are also track, and their happiness is monitored over time to get an idea of how frequent their mood changes and their general happiness pattern. Proposed algorithm finds a change of the pattern of happiness. A user's past tweets are also monitored and applied topic detection and the subjectivity extraction technique to get a more concrete idea of this pattern.

Keywords: Twitter · Social network · Sentiment analysis · Happiness index

1 Introduction

Happiness is something which everyone wishes for and is the primary goal of life for all. Happiness is something which is of utmost to everything we do. The best part of happiness is that it can be indexed, that is we can calculate happiness and scale it. For instance, the index associated with happiness is more when a person wins a lottery than when he wins a little Counter-Strike match. Thus, this property of index in happiness, we have harnessed and used in our method.

We have concentrated our efforts on finding happiness index in Social Networks [1]. The prime reason for this is ease of data collection. Collecting data from the Social Networking sites is rather easy. Also, the growth in people using these sites and remaining active with them for the most of the day has motivated us to take up this field. It is a growing trend of expressing oneself on social networks and updating each and every information of the day to day activity. We have used Twitter to get the data set. We did not use Facebook for various reasons which are details in coming sections.

Twitter [2] is used to get the datasets because the length of tweets is not high and fewer slangs words. A tweet can have at most 140 characters.

A user tweeting about some event, product, etc. can be used as a right source of his happiness. We monitors past tweets of the person to find various information about the person like his happiness over a span of time, mood swings, topics of interest, his

© Springer Nature Singapore Pte Ltd. 2017
D. Singh et al. (Eds.): ICAICR 2017, CCIS 712, pp. 261–270, 2017.
DOI: 10.1007/978-981-10-5780-9_24

subjectivity, etc. This can have multiple uses in diverse fields like psychology, online product portals, behavioral monitoring, etc.

The Happiness Index in Social Networking sites is quite popular nowadays. Various techniques are being used to give a proper idea of this index and use it in different areas. Happiness Index though is not limited to, Social Networks and in the past, before the advent of social networks a similar study has been done around 1998 and a latest report on HPI is published in 2016 [3].

A. Happiness Index

Happiness Index means all the criteria and metrics which can be used to describe happiness. Happiness is a rather relative term and to quantize happiness as either happy or sad is quite difficult. But devising a scale on which happiness can be measured, is the way through which happiness indexing can be achieved.

We have used the concept of Sentiment Analysis to find the sentiments associated with each data (tweet). Finding a positive and negative sentiment of each tweet and then finding the effective sentiment can be used for subjective tweets. For tweets which are rather objective, we determine if the net sentiment is positive or negative based on the words used in the tweet. Subjectivity Analysis and topic detection are the other helping techniques for calculating happiness index.

B. Happiness Index Uses

Happiness Index has been in use for quite some time. Though the calculating happiness index in social networking sites is a rather new concept. In the past happiness, index has found its use as Happy Planet Index (HPI).

HPI [4] is an associate index of human well-being and environmental impact, introduced in July 2006 by the New Economics Foundation. The index is weighted to administer increasingly higher scores to nations with lower ecological footprints. Currently, in 2016, HPI measured for the whole world. Figure 1 shows the happy planet index score of the world. Red color shows unhappy countries and hard green color shows fully happy countries. And other colors shows happiness in between these boundary (Fully happy to unhappy).

The index is intended to challenge well-established indices of countries' development, like Gross Domestic Product (GDP) and also the Human Development Index (HDI). However, these are not seen property. Therefore, GDP is not considered to be appropriate, as the common final aim of the majority is to be Happy and healthy, not to be rich. Furthermore, to pursue these goals a notion of property development needs a measure of the environmental costs.

Though the criteria and metrics employed in this case are quite completely different from that would be using however still the spirit of scheming happiness index is nearly the same.

C. Happiness Index in Social Networking?

Getting data in real life will involve great volunteers and would be very tedious. Getting this kind of data from each country would further cause problems. With social networking, we have a medium where people from different part of the world share opinions, thoughts, and ideas on a common platform. Retrieving data, in this case, is quite simple.

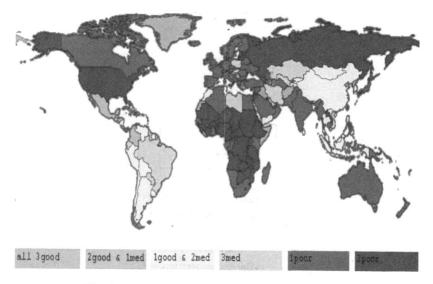

Fig. 1. Happy planet index score (Color figure online)

D. Choose Twitter to Get Dataset

We decided to use data from Twitter instead of Facebook because of the following reasons. Tweet length in Twitter is limited so, processing such small tweets is easier. Also, in most cases, tweets are subjective hence we could get a better Net Sentiment score.

In Facebook with the use of graph search API's we can get posts, but posts are vast, and Topic Detection, as well as Sentiment Analysis technique, wouldn't yield decent results. In Facebook, the posts are varied a lot consisting of the different type of pictures and posts are not subjective.

In Twitter, the use of hashtags, trending topics, etc. helps in retrieving data. One can also filter tweets based on location, language, topic, words, etc. This combined with the recent trends helps in finding events that were happening in the past and their outcomes. For these and various other reasons, we decided to use data from Twitter instead of Facebook.

2   Proposed Method

We have devised certain algorithms that use the results from these techniques and give more practical and scalable results. The flowchart in Fig. 2 shows the main steps of proposed method.

A. Dataset Collection

Twitter provided various data feeds for research purposes. We collected tweets as a dataset over a three weeks period. Our dataset includes of around ten thou-sand tweets posted by over thousand individual users. Every tweet delivered by Twitter was accompanied by a core set of informational attributes. User location is available for a few

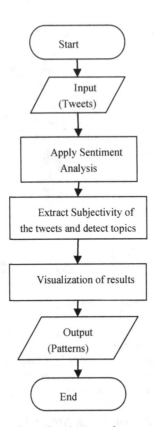

Fig. 2. Flowchart of mainsteps of proposed agorithm

tweets within the type of either current latitude and longitude, as reported as an example of a smart-phone, or a static, free text entry of a hometown at the side of state and country. For measures of social interactions. Against the numerous advantages of employing a data source like Twitter, there are many cognitive issues to be raised, notably representativeness. First, concerning primary sampling, tweets allotted to knowledge feeds by Twitter were excellently chosen every which way from all tweets. Our observation of this apparent absence of bias in no method dismisses the way stronger issue that the entire assortment of tweets could be a non-uniform sub sampling of all utterances created by a non-representative universe of all individuals. Our interest is finding suggestions of universal patterns. Moreover, we tend to note that like several different social networking services, Twitter accommodates organizations as users, significantly news services. Twitter's user population is such a mix of people, teams of people, organizations, media retailers, and automatic services like bots, representing a sort of disaggregated; crowd sourced media. In conclusion, the two most important statements for pursuing the Twitter as a stream dataset [2]:

- Potential for describing universal human patterns, whether or not they are social and emotional.

- A current and growing importance of Twitter to have correct data storage like a database to produce a quick answer to the queries.

Twitter data can be categories into two types based on design and access method based mostly.

REST architecture based REST APIs are the widely used for developing the web APIs. It uses pull strategy for retrieval of data. To get the information a user need poses explicitly request [5].

Streaming based APIs provides a continuous access the data stream. It is also uses the push strategy for retrieval of data. After posting the request for information, it provides an uninterrupted access the stream of data without taking further inputs [5].

We used MySQL [6] database to store the tweets by using locking mechanism for maintaining atomicity of transactions. It is one of the relational database management system based, open-source software that used widely in the universe.

B. Sentiment Analysis

Sentiment Analysis looks to automatically associate a bit of text data with a score based on their sentiment such as positive or negative score. he gathered sentiment can offer a plan of how individuals are responding to a corporation, product, and topic. The sentiment analysis algorithm is predicated on a Naive Bayes Classifier. It classifies a data by comparing each word with the class attribute and labeled the words as positive or negative. The phrase within the data is used additional in positive data; hence the Tweet is with positive label. If the phrase within the data is used additional in negative data, hence the Tweet is with negative label.

A naive Bayes classifier [7] is an easy and straightforward probabilistic classifier with naive Bayes' independence assumptions. A further descriptive term for the underlying probability model would be "independent feature model." In simple, it assumes that for given the class variable, the value of a specific feature is orthogonal to the presence or absence of any other feature.

For score, the sentiment SentiWordNet [8] is employed. It is a lexical analyzer for mine the opinions. SentiWordNet assigns three scores based on their sentiment to every synset of WordNet: positivity, negativity, objectivity. In Sentiment Classification, many subtasks can be identified and need to do for tagging the text:

- Determining text Subjective Objective Polarity (SO-polarity) [8], to decide that given text feature has a factual nature or not. (i.e. describes a given state of affairs or event, while not expressing a positive or a negative opinion on it) or conveys an associate opinion on its subjective. To perform binary text categorization classes Subjective and Objective are used.
- Determining text PN-polarity(Positive-Negative Polarity) [8], to decide the given Subjective text expresses a Positive or a Negative opinion on its subject.
- Determining the strength of text PN-polarity, as to decide e.g. whether or not the Positive opinion expressed by a text on its subject matter is infirm Positive, gently Positive, or strongly Positive

We have broadly classified the topics as Computers and Technology, Arts, Business & Economy, Health, Home and Domestic Life, News, Recreation & Activities,

Reference and Education, Science, Shopping, Society, Sports. With each of this topic, we associate two variables α (alpha) & β (beta). α is the positive sentiment quotient while β is negative sentiment quotient. We assign these values to α & β depending on the topic detected. Thus we have if the statement is subjective then:

$$\text{Net Sentiment} = \alpha * (\text{Positive Sentiment}) - \beta * (\text{Negative Sentiment})$$

Otherwise, the statement is objective then:

$$\text{Net Sentiment} = \text{Positive Sentiment} - \text{Negative Sentiment}.$$

We can change the values for each topic like for Health $\alpha = 0.5$ while $\beta = 1$. For Shopping $\alpha = 0.5$, $\beta = 0.3$. Similarly, for other topics, we can assign different quotients. For objective tweets, we have $\alpha = 1$ and $\beta = 1$.

In last of this step, we used tweet modeling for user-centric data. When we needed to compare tweets of the past between users we couldn't map them time wise. Reason being time don't coincide. Hence we model the tweets as tweets belonging to a time frame or time window. We capture tweets in that window, find a mean of the Positive Sentiment and Negative Sentiment, the Net Sentiment and model the score for that time frame. In this way, we have a comparable data and this same data we will be using in finding trends and patterns in past tweets of a single user.

C. Pattern Finding (Topic Detection)

We find the pattern in tweets of one user by using Topic Detection. Each topic could be an aggregation of words. Every topic has all of the words within the dataset with the probability of the word happiness to its topic. Whereas all words within the topic are same, the weight given differs for each topic. For example, we find a topic related to sports that are up of 40% of basketball, 35% of football, 15% of baseball, 0.02% of Congress, and 0.01% of Obama. Another topic related to politics could be made up of 35% of Congress, 30% of Obama, 1% of football, 0.1% of baseball, 0.1% of basketball. Only top words have been taken inspecting to a topic because each topic can have every word. Latent Dirichlet Allocation (LDA) [9] do the work of finds the probable words for a topic that is correlated with each topic.

In LDA could be a generative model that permits sets of observations to be explained by unobserved teams that designate why some elements of the data are similar. For example, if observations are that the words collected into documents, it posits that every document could be a mixture of a little number of topics which each word's creation is attributable to one of the document's topics. In LDA, every document is also viewed as a mix of various topics. The subject distribution is assumed to own a Dirichlet prior. In following, this leads to additional affordable mixtures of topics in a document. It's been noted. However, the pLSA model resembles the LDA model beneath a uniform Dirichlet prior distribution.

Also, we can find how frequently the mood of a person swings by finding the tangent. Also, we can find how often the mood of a person turns by finding the tangent.

The Height (a) is ΔNet Sentiment while Base (b) is ΔTime. We find the tangent simply by doing a/b.

$$Tan\ \theta = Sin\ \theta/Cos\ \theta$$

$$Tan\ \theta =\ Height/Base$$

Greater the value of tangent means there is a more drastic change in the mood of the person. Accompanied with α (Positive Sentiment Quotient) and β (Negative Sentiment Quotient) we calculate the mood swing pattern.

D. Visualization of Results

For visualization of results, Google Chart [10] has been used. Google Charts provides a right way to visualize data. We have used two types of maps to visualize the sentiment. Heat Map [11] and Intensity Map [12].

The Google Maps API Utility Library includes a heatmap utility, which you can use to add one or more heatmaps to a Google map in your application. Heat-maps create it straightforward for viewers to know the distribution and relative intensity of data points on a map. Instead of putting a marker at every location, Heatmaps use color to represent the distribution of the data.

Intensity map is used to highlights the regions or countries based on their relative values.

3   Experimental Results

Experimental results of the various components along with their features, screenshots, and flow of control are shown in this section. A HeatMap in Fig. 3, shows the Net Sentiment based on location (latitude & longitude) and the Intensity Map in Fig. 4 shows the Net Sentiment country wise. These can be used as global happiness index. The comparison graphs in Fig. 5 compare different users and their past modeled tweets.

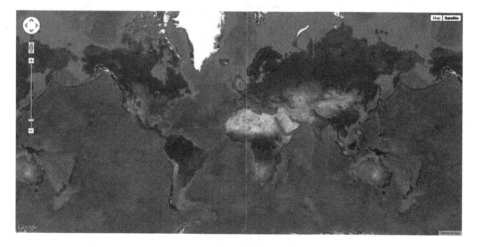

Fig. 3. Heat map

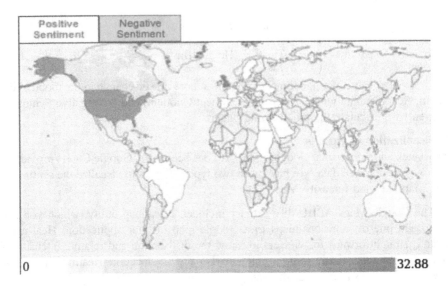

Fig. 4. Intensity map

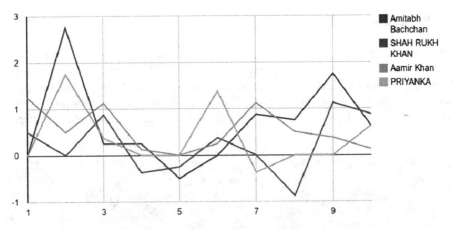

Fig. 5. Happiness index comparison graph of users.

The user-centric graph in Fig. 6 plots the tweet sentiment at the time of a particular user. With the pattern finding techniques and after finding tangents we reach various conclusions.

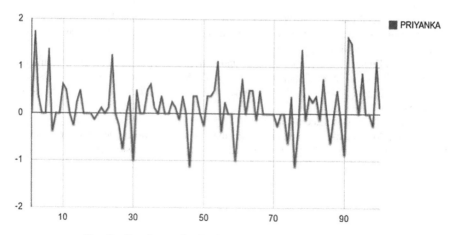

Fig. 6. Centric graph of Priyanka chopra's happiness index

4 Conclusion

Twitter a social site was used as a dataset to find the happiness index of people. Dataset (Tweets) were retrieved based on latitude and longitude. Then sentiment analysis techniques have been applied to retrieved dataset. Positive Sentiment and Negative Sentiment is being computed of Tweets. Maps were plotted based on these sentiments, location wise and country wise, accordingly. The proposed algorithm, tracked individual users and their happiness was monitored over time to get an idea of how frequent their mood changes and their general happiness pattern. We followed this change of the pattern of happiness. A user's past tweets were monitored and applied topic detection and the subjectivity extraction technique to get a more concrete idea of this pattern.

References

1. Dodds, P.S., Harris, K.D., Kloumann, I.M., Bliss, C.A., Danforth, C.M.: Temporal patterns of happiness and information in a global social network: hedonometrics and Twitter. PLoS ONE **6**(12), 2011. doi:10.1371/journal.pone.0026752
2. https://dev.twitter.com/docs/api/streaming
3. http://worldhappiness.report/
4. http://happyplanetindex.org/
5. Kumar, S., Morstatter, F., Liu, H.: Twitter Data Analytics. Springer, New York (2014). doi:10.1007/978-1-4614-9372-3. Series ISSN -2191-5768
6. https://www.mysql.com/
7. Narayanan, V., Arora, I., Bhatia, A.: Fast and accurate sentiment classification using an enhanced naive bayes model. In: Yin, H., Tang, K., Gao, Y., Klawonn, F., Lee, M., Weise, T., Li, B., Yao, X. (eds.) IDEAL 2013. LNCS, vol. 8206, pp. 194–201. Springer, Heidelberg (2013). doi:10.1007/978-3-642-41278-3_24

8. Esuli, A., Sebastiani, F.: SENTIWORDNET: a publicly available lexical resource for opinion mining. In: Proceedings of 5th Conference on Language Resources and Evaluation (LREC 2006), pp. 417–422 (2006)
9. Bolelli, L., Ertekin, Ş., Giles, C.L.: Topic and trend detection in text collections using latent dirichlet allocation. In: Boughanem, M., Berrut, C., Mothe, J., Soule-Dupuy, C. (eds.) ECIR 2009. LNCS, vol. 5478, pp. 776–780. Springer, Heidelberg (2009). doi:10.1007/978-3-642-00958-7_84
10. https://developers.google.com/chart/
11. https://developers.google.com/maps/documentation/javascript/examples/layer-heatmap
12. https://developers.google.com/chart/interactive/docs/gallery/intensitymap

An Efficient Routing Protocol for DTN

Aikta Arya[✉] and Awadhesh Kumar Singh

Department of Computer Engineering, National Institute of Technology,
Kurukshetra, India
aiktarya@gmail.com, aksingh@nitkkr.ac.in

Abstract. Delay Tolerant Networks (DTNs) are different from the conventional ad hoc networks as they support information exchange in the presence of long latency in end to end path availability. Hence, they use store-carry-forward approach for message exchange unlike other ad hoc networks that use carry-forward approach. As DTNs have evolved from MANETs, they inherit many properties of MANETs, like sparse structure, mobility, network partitioning etc. However, route discovery in DTNs is more challenging because of above mentioned difference. Therefore, routing in DTNs is an interesting topic of research. As end to end path availability is not guaranteed the nodes communicate in opportunistic manner. The performance of store carry forward approach is heavily dependent on the probability of availability of path and storage space at the node. Therefore, we have proposed a probabilistic method of routing using efficient buffer management. The performance of proposed protocol has been evaluated with the help of simulation experiments.

Keywords: Delay Tolerant Networks (DTN) · Buffer management · Routing · Disruption tolerant networks · Queue management

1 Introduction

In last few years, much research activity has been done in wireless, mobile, and ad hoc networks (MANETs). In MANETs, if nodes enter in each other's communication range they can directly communicate with each other. A node can serve as a relay (forward packets) or terminate packets. Hence, a packet traverses by being forwarded from one node to another, unless it reaches its destination. As nodes are mobile and since the topology of the network is constantly changing, this becomes a challenging task that how to insure robust and reliable communication in the face of constantly changing topology, how to find destination, how to route packets to destination, in mobile ad hoc networks.

Routing in mobile ad hoc networks is deeply-studied topic. Many routing protocols have been proposed recently To accommodate the constantly changing topology of mobile ad hoc networks. In all of these proposed routing protocols, there stays an implicit assumption that there exists an opportunistic end-to-end path between any of the source and destination pair and the network is connected always. But, this assumption may not be true always in physically existing ad-hoc networks.

In MANETs, events like mobility of nodes, links disturbed by intervening objects, periodical shut down of links, and conservation of power at nodes can result in

© Springer Nature Singapore Pte Ltd. 2017
D. Singh et al. (Eds.): ICAICR 2017, CCIS 712, pp. 271–282, 2017.
DOI: 10.1007/978-981-10-5780-9_25

Intermittent connectivity. At any instant network partition occurs if there does not exists any path between source and destination. Thus, there exists maximum possibility of two nodes not being part of same connected portion of the network. Hence these type of networks are called intermittently connected ad hoc networks (ICNs) or Delay tolerant networks (DTNs). DTNs tolerates delays beyond the bounds of conventional IP forwarding delays.

There are many research challenges in DTNs such as congestion control, application layer design, routing, convergence layer design, flow control, security etc. In this paper we have proposed an approach for routing in DTNs. But then another questions that arises is, as DTNs are evolved from MANETs, why can't we use existing protocols of MANETs in DTNs. The Routing Protocols of MANETs are not applicable to DTNs as in routing protocols of MANETs when a packet arrives at a node, for a specific destination and for which there does not exists any opportunistic end-to-end path, the packet is dropped. Hence new system architectures and routing protocols must be developed for DTNs (Table 1).

Table 1. Difference between routing in MANETs and DTNs

Attributes	Routing in MANETs	Routing in DTNs
Delivery delay	Less	High
End-to-end connectivity	Contemporaneous	Less frequently connected
Routing behavior	Symmetric	Asymmetric
Transmission reliability	High	Low

The traditional internet has some implicit well known assumption-

- Very low propagation delay
- Contiguous connectivity
- Reasonably low packet loss rate.

DTNs sometimes doesn't satisfies any of these assumptions. There are many challenges in developing efficient protocols for DTNs such as opportunistic connections, frequent disconnection, and extremely long delay (up to days). Also, the existing protocols of wired networks will not work properly for DTNs. For an instant if TCP/IP protocol is used for DTNs, the packets for which end-to-end path doesn't exists will be dropped eventually. TCP usually ends the session, if the packet dropping rate is too high. Also UDP can't provide 'hold and forward' service and is not much reliable.

Considerable amount of effort has been made by researchers for designing an approach for routing in DTNs but the issues related to buffer management is not given that much attention even if it has direct impact on performance of routing protocol. Mostly the routing protocols assume for infinite buffer space and during simulation they consider to have FIFO replacement policy with finite buffer space. But most of the DTN applications have constrained amount of storage and energy resources that degrades the performance of underlying routing protocol in terms of decrements in delivery ratio and increments in delivery delay.

Also, Many of the routing protocols in DTNs doesn't have any kind of message scheduling which has directly impact on performance of routing protocol. The Basic reason for this is, they assume for infinite bandwidth without any kind of interruption which is not favorable for real time applications. In this paper we have proposed an approach for routing in DTNs that acquires efficient buffer management strategy along with reliable message forwarding.

In this paper Sect. 2 discusses state of the art routing protocols in DTNs. Later Sect. 3 discusses the proposed routing protocol having efficient buffer management strategy along with reliable message forwarding. Section 4 verifies the efficiency of proposed protocol with the help of simulation results. Later Sects. 5 and 6 gives the conclusion and discusses future scope.

2 Related Work

The State-of-the-art of Routing Protocols in DTNs can be broadly be classified as given below (Table 2).

Table 2. Routing Protocols in DTNs

Deterministic approaches	Stochastic approaches
- Tree based approaches	- Epidemic/random spray approaches
- Space time routing	- Coding based approaches
- Modified shortest path approaches	- Model based approaches
	- Control based approaches
	- History or predication based approaches

All the previous work on Routing in DTNs has solely been based on different assumptions regarding availability of knowledge of environment, control on environment and connectivity of entire network. Many routing algorithms proposed for DTNs are widely applicable as they make fewer assumptions. Conventionally, these algorithms are based on there decision of dropping a message in case of maximum buffer occupacy and forwarding a message in case of meeting with a given relay node.

2.1 Deterministic Approaches

In Deterministic approaches there stays a basic assumption that we have complete knowledge about all future connectivity and mobility of every node. in other words, we are known to entire topology of network ahead of time.

In the article [1], Ferreira explains a combinatorial model that describes most common behaviors of time varying networks. In [2] based on the availability of knowledge about mobility of nodes, algorithms presented selects a path for message delivery. Based on the knowledge available about the traffic and topology of the network, some routing algorithms are presented in [3].

In [4], a space-time graph is constructed to model the dynamics of the network over a specific time interval. Using shortest path algorithms and dynamic programming, routing algorithms are designed for constructed space time graph.

In all the deterministic approaches firstly an end-to-end path is find out before the actual message transmission takes place. But, in some cases entire network topology is not known ahead of time. In those cases many other routing protocols are designed that falls under the category of stochastic approaches.

2.2 Stochastic Approaches

In stochastic cases, the network behavior is considered to be random. For these cases new routing protocols must be designed as entire topology of network is not known ahead of time. Basically these protocols are only based on there decisions of when and where to transmit the packets. The simplest way to make the decision is to broadcast the packets to nodes within its range, other ways are based on the availability of information about mobility patterns, history data etc.

Epidemic Routing Based Approaches
In this category, without any prediction on link transmitting probability messages received at a relay node is transmitted to all or some part of the neighboring nodes. Epidemic routing is most simplest way of transmitting packets to its destination when there is no information available about link transmission probability or mobility patterns.

An Epidemic routing protocol for ICNs was developed by Vahdat and Becker in [5]. Other routing protocols that falls under this can be found in [6, 7]. To limit the extent to which broadcast is done Spraying protocol was proposed in [8]. [9, 10] presents the overall analysis of the delay present in various epidemic routing protocols.

Coding Based Approaches
In this category, researchers have basically concentrated on wireless channel losses. To get rid of these losses researchers gave techniques like network coding and erasure coding for DTNs and wireless ad-hoc networks.

In erasure coding basically the original message is encoded into larger no of blocks before transmission of the original message. In erasure coding, the original message can be correctly decoded if out of m, p blocks are already received (m > p) given that original message was encoded into m blocks before transmission. Network coding can be used to enhance throughput of the system.

The State-of-the-art of routing protocols that falls under this category can be found in [11, 12].

Model Based Approaches
In stochastic approaches it is basically assumed that there stays a random movement of nodes throughout the network. But in real life there exists some known patterns through which devices move such as driving through the road, walking along a streets etc. Model based approaches take advantage of these mobility patterns. Once we have the mobility patterns of nodes, the relay nodes can have accurate estimation that which node is having highest probability for moving towards the destination node.

In Model Based Routing protocol proposed in [13], real world models, such as building charts and road maps, are used for accurately selecting the relay node and avoiding flooding entire network with a specific message. Basically in this protocol it has been taken into account that the mobile device in the network are carried out by human beings and they are not following the motion patterns of random walks.

The State-of-the-art of routing protocols that falls under this category can be found in [14, 15].

Control Based Approaches

All the previous approaches discussed in previous sections allows the nodes of the network to wait passively for their re-connection to the network. This may result in unavoidable transmission delays that may be unacceptable for some real time applications. Some researchers have developed approaches that constraints these delays occurring due to number of re-connections by controlling and exploiting movement of nodes in the network. Basically in control based approaches movement of some selected nodes is contained so that the overall system performance is enhanced.

The State-of-the-art of routing protocols that falls under this category can be found in [16, 17].

History or Prediction Based Approaches

In some of the previous approaches the messages were blindly transmitted to all or some of the neighboring nodes. In this way entire network gets flooded with the same messages. In history or prediction based approaches rather than blindly forwarding packets the relay nodes computes the likelihood of each outgoing link for ultimately forwarding the packets to the destination. Based on this estimated likelihood, the relay nodes make some decisions such as to which node message should be forwarded or whether to store the message into buffer and wait for a better estimated likelihood.

The very first abstract work done on estimation of link was proposed in [18]. Later, some routing protocols take transmitting decision per encounter based on the moderate end to end metrics, while other routing protocols take transmitting decision per encounter based on the information available with the next hop.

Vahdat's work given in [5] is extended in [19] so that it gets applicable to the situation where resources are limited. Identical to the work in [19], PROPHET protocol was proposed in [20].

The PROPHET (Probabilistic Routing Protocol using History of Encounters and Transitivity) protocol is a probabilistic routing protocol which requires two neighboring nodes to exchange routing information on encountering each other. The PROPHET protocol proposed in [20] considered infinite buffer space at every node. As usual for Simulating the work they have used finite buffer space with FIFO queue management. But still the results shown by the simulation were percent better than Epidemic routing protocol in case of packet delivery ratio.

The State-of-the-art of routing protocols that falls under this category can be found in [21–23].

During the entire literature survey of routing protocols for DTN we have found many shortcomings in many different protocols. In this paper we have tried to improve the routing performance of PROPHET protocol that was lacking due to absence of an efficient buffer management strategy in the original protocol. Instead of using conventional FIFO queue management as buffer management strategy, we have used our proposed buffer management strategy to overall improve the routing performance of the proposed routing protocol.

3 The Proposed Protocol

In this section we have discussed the detailed protocol itself and some of the assumptions related to the applicability of the proposed protocol. Although DTNs can operate perfectly in many environments like underwater sensors, hand-held devices, zebras, pedestrians, or vehicles but we have considered that our existing DTN is consists of vehicles, hand-held devices and desktop hardware.

Also, we have assumed non-randomness in mobility of nodes in the network. This is because in real world rather than having random movements, real users do move in a predictable fashion for example if a location is visited by a node for considerable on of times then there exists more likelihood for that node visiting that specific location again.

3.1 Model

We assume that-

- There is no *a priori* knowledge of connectivity of network available with the nodes.
- Environment doesn't consists of any node that is always stationary.
- There stays limited amount of opportunity to transfer in terms of both bandwidth and duration.
- Nodes don't have any kind of control on their movements in the network.
- Every node has infinite buffer for the packets originated by them but there satays a finite buffer space for having the packets transmitted by other nodes.

Basically, the procedure done by a routing protocol in DTN can be performed in three stages as follows:

1. **Neighboring Nodes Discovery:** Before the beginning of transmission opportunity nodes must discover each other as they do not have any knowledge about when will the next transmission opportunity will be available.
2. **Transmission of Data:** After two nodes discover each other, they tend towards exchanging packets with each other frequently as there is limited amount of data that can be transferred in a specific transmission opportunity. Nodes do not have any knowledge about the duration of transmission opportunity.
3. **Management of Buffer Space:** As the new packets are received by the node from its neighboring node, it starts managing its finite buffer by sorting the packets already present in its buffer, deleting some packets from its buffer in order to free some buffer space according to some buffer management scheme. The packets that have receiving node as their destination are passed on to application layer and then are removed out from the buffer space.

When low bandwidth radios are used or when there is short duration trans- mission opportunity bandwidth can stay a limited resource. When hand-held devices are used storage can be a limited resource.

To improve the performance of routing and by observing a non randomness in the mobility patterns of nodes in the network we have considered probabilistic approach for message forwarding and hence PROPHET (Probabilistic ROuting Protocol using History of Encounters and Transitivity) is exercised for forwarding messages.

Firstly, PROPHET estimates a *delivery predictability* metric $P_{(x,y)} \in [0, 1]$ which is a probabilistic metric for each known destination y and is defined at every node x. This *delivery predictability* metric $P_{(x,y)}$ indicated the likelihood of a node x for delivering the packets to a known destination node y.

Whenever two nodes discover each other they exchange some important information with each other such as delivery predictability vectors and summary vectors containing the information about the destinations known by the nodes. Up-gradation of internal delivery predictability vectors occurs with the help of additional information which is described later. After this, the forwarding mechanism decides which messages to request from the new discovered node with the help of information available in summery vectors.

Computation of Delivery Predictability Metrics

The computation of delivery predictability is carried out in three sections. Firstly the delivery predictability metric is updated whenever two nodes meet each other so that the nodes that meet with each other more frequently have higher delivery predictability values. This computation is presented in Eq. 1, here initialization constant is P_{init} initialized to some value in $P_{\text{init}} \in (0, 1]$.

$$P_{(x,y)} = P_{(x,y)\,\text{old}} + \left(1 - P_{(x,y)\,\text{old}}\right) \times P_{\text{init}} \tag{1}$$

If two nodes haven't met with each other from a longer period of time then there is less likelihood of being a good message forwarders to each other anymore. Hence there must be some concept of aging in delivery predictability metric values for practicing this type of cases. This computation is presented in Eq. 2, aging constant is γ having values in the range $\gamma \in (0, 1)$ and t is the amount of units of time Passed since this metric was updated or aged last time.

$$P_{(x,y)} = P_{(x,y)\,\text{old}} \times \gamma^t \tag{2}$$

The delivery predictability probabilistic metric is considered to be transitive in nature i.e.. if x and y are good forwarders of packets destined for node y and if y and z are good forwarders of packets destined for node z then the node z can be considered as a good forwarder of packets destined for node x. This computation is presented in Eq. 3, here scaling constant is α having values in the range $\alpha \in [0, 1]$.

$$P_{(x,z)} = P_{(x,z)\text{old}} + \left(1 - P_{(x,z)\text{old}}\right) \times P_{(x,y)} \times P_{(y,z)} \times \alpha \tag{3}$$

3.2   Forwarding Mechanism

It is very simple task in some of the traditional routing protocols to select a node from all the nodes within its range to forward a packet. They simply forward the packets to the neighboring node which has the shortest path to the destination of the packets or has the lowest cost path. Also, in traditional routing protocols, the message gets forwarded to single node as the path selected is highly reliable. But while designing routing protocols for DTNs things changes completely here as compared to traditional routing protocols.

In the very starting nodes when packets starts arriving at nodes, they may have to store the messages into their buffer as the path to the destination node may not be available. whenever two nodes discover each other they must have to the decision that whether to store the message in its buffer or to transfer it to newly discovered node. It may also be considered as a practical decision to forward the packets to many no of nodes to increase the probability of the packets to get delivered to its destination. Unfortunately, these are some imperative decisions on which performance of routing protocols depends.

One way of taking this decision in some cases can be to set a fixed threshold on delivery predictability metric values of nodes and a node x will only transmit the packets to node y if and only if the delivery predictability metric value on node y is more than the fixed threshold. In other cases, while ignoring the nodes with low delivery predictability metric values there is no certainly of a node with higher delivery predictability metric values than the fixed threshold will be encountered soon. hence, in those cases we might not stick to the fixed threshold and can also transmit the packets to the nodes with lower values for the time being.

Broadcasting or multi-casting a message to a considerable no of nodes definitely increases the probability of the node for being delivered to it destination but also wastes some of the important network resources such buffer space, bandwidth etc. However, if we forward the packets to lesser no of nodes to conserve our network resources, the probability of node getting being delivered to its destination gets compromised and it also increases the transmission delays.

The simple Forwarding mechanism adapted by PROPHET can be described as follows- whenever two nodes x and y encounter each other, a message m gets transmitted from x to y if and only if the delivery predictability probabilistic metric value for the destination of message m is greater at node y as compared to the value at node x. Even after the transmission of message m to node y, the node x doesn't deletes the message m until enough buffer space is available as it may be a possibility that node x may encounter a node with more better delivery predictability probabilistic metric value or even the destination node of message m itself.

3.3   Buffer Management Strategy

In this section have proposed an efficient buffer management strategy for PROPHET protocol that improves the routing performance of PROPHET. In the original protocol they have used FIFO queue management scheme, in case if the buffer space gets fully occupied, to drop the packets.

As the new packets are received by the node from its neighboring node, it starts managing its finite buffer by sorting the packets already present in its buffer and deleting some packets from its buffer in order to free some buffer space according to some buffer management scheme. The packets that have receiving node as their destination are passed on to application layer and then are removed out from the buffer space.

Basically in the proposed buffer management strategy firstly, the logical partitioning of entire buffer space is performed on the basis of threshold on Time-to-Live (TTL) values. The messages that are having Time-to-Live (TTL) value lower than the set threshold are sorted according to their TTL and the messages that are having higher TTL than the set threshold are sorted according to their Hop-count values.

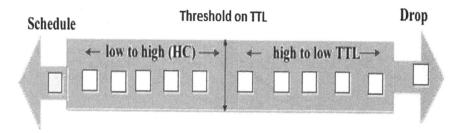

Fig. 1. Logical partitioning of buffer space

The sorting and logical partitioning of entire buffer space is carried out in the way shown in above Fig. 1. The message having the TTL value greater than the set threshold and the least value of hop count is transmitted first as it has not proceeded much far from its source (shown by its low hop count value) and has long way to travel to its destination as compared to other messages in this partition. Hence, these messages are scheduled first to have low delivery delay and high delivery rate.

The message having lowest TTL value and higher hop count is selected to be dropped first as from this specific node it has lower likelihood of reaching to its destination (shown by it low TTL value). And it can be assumed that copy of this message is already available at some other nodes (shown by its higher hop count value) and from those nodes the message can be forwarded to the destination and hence we can afford to drop this packet for now.

4 Results

We have used ONE (Opportunistic Network Environment) Simulator [24] for implementing the proposed idea. PROPHET protocol is one of the best known probabilistic routing algorithm for DTN. One of the best key points of this protocol is its way of estimating the delivery predictability. Only the side where it was lacking is the buffer management policy adapted which is purely removed by our proposed buffer management protocol. The proposed Buffer management strategy is also applicable to other routing protocols to improve their performance lacking due to efficient buffer management.

The results shown by the simulation is depicted in Fig. 2. It shows the comparative study of PROPHET protocol with and without the proposed buffer management strategy in terms of Delivery ratio. We can observe in the figure that the delivery ratio also increases as the buffer space increases. This is due to the availability of more buffer space to carry and store more messages as the buffer space increases, hence enhances the overall routing performance lacking due to unavailability of buffer space. The simulation settings of the proposed protocol can be found in Table 3.

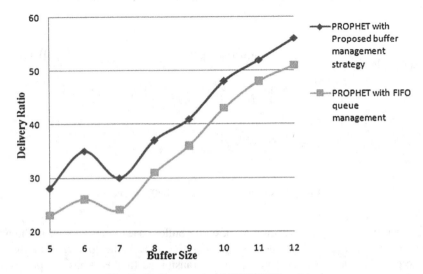

Fig. 2. Delivery ratio of PROPHET protocol

Table 3. Simulation settings

Parameter	Value
Hosts	150
Hosts speed (m/s)	1.5–14.5
Buffer capacity	5–12 MB
Message TTL	4 h
Message inter-arrival time	30–40 s
Message size	1–1.5 MB
World size (meters)	4500X3400
Transmission speed	4 Mbps
γ	0.98
α	0.25
P_{init}	0.75

5 Conclusions

Any DTN routing protocol primarily goals at maximizing the delivery ratio of the packets and minimizing the latency between source and destination. Our proposed routing protocol for Delay Tolerant Networks applies an efficient buffer management along with a reliable message forwarding approach. The prediction technique used forwards the packets according to their delivery predictability so that the packet is forwarded to least no. of nodes. Hence, reduces the buffer occupancy and bandwidth consumption without compromising the probability of packets to be forwarded to their destination. With the help of proposed buffer management strategy message scheduling and message drop policy is used to efficiently utilize the available buffer space. Together, these above approaches helped in enhancing the performance of proposed Routing protocol.

6 Future Scope

Considerable amount of effort has been made by researchers in recent years for designing an approach for routing in DTNs but the issues related to buffer management is not given that much attention even if it has direct impact on performance of routing protocol. Hence, the proposed Buffer management strategy can be used by other routing protocols to improve their performance lacking due to efficient buffer management. Instead of considering FIFO message replacement policy the proposed buffer management policy can be used to improve the simulation results.

References

1. Ferreira, A.: Building a reference combinatorial model for MANETs. IEEE Netw. **18**(5), 24–29 (2004). doi:10.1109/MNET.2004.1337732
2. Handorean, R., Gill, C., Roman, G.-C.: Accommodating transient connectivity in ad hoc and mobile settings. In: Ferscha, A., Mattern, F. (eds.) Pervasive 2004. LNCS, vol. 3001, pp. 305–322. Springer, Heidelberg (2004). doi:10.1007/978-3-540-24646-6_22
3. Jain, S., Fall, K., Patra, R.: Routing in a delay tolerant network, vol. 34, no. 4, pp. 145–158. ACM (2004). doi:10.1145/1030194.1015484
4. Merugu, S., Ammar, M., Zegura, E.: Routing in space and time in networks with predictable mobility. Technical report, Georgia Institute of Technology (2004)
5. Vahdat, A., Becker, D.: Epidemic routing for partially connected ad hoc networks. Technical report, Department of Computer Science, Duke University, Durham, NC (2000)
6. Small, T., Haas, Z.: The shared wireless infostation model: a new ad hoc networking paradigm (or where there is a whale, there is a way). In: Proceedings of the 4th ACM International Symposium on Mobile Ad Hoc Networking & Computing, pp. 233–244. ACM, June 2003
7. Nain, D., Petigara, N., Balakrishnan, H.: Integrated routing and storage for messaging applications in mobile ad hoc networks. Mob. Netw. Appl. **9**(6), 595–604 (2004)

8. Tchakountio, F., Ramanathan, R.: Tracking highly mobile endpoints. In: Proceedings of the 4th ACM International Workshop on Wireless Mobile Multimedia, pp. 83–94. ACM, July 2001

9. Spyropoulos, T., Psounis, K., Raghavendra, S.: Spray and wait: an efficient routing scheme for intermittently connected mobile networks. In: Proceedings of the 2005 ACM SIGCOMM Workshop on Delay-Tolerant Networking. pp. 252–259. ACM, August 2005

10. Spyropoulos, T., Psounis, K., Raghavendra, S.: Single-copy routing in intermittently connected mobile networks. In: 2004 First Annual IEEE Communications Society Conference on Sensor and Ad Hoc Communications and Networks, IEEE SECON 2004, pp. 235–244. IEEE, October 2004

11. Widmer, J., Le Boudec, J.: Network coding for efficient communication in extreme networks. In: Proceedings of the 2005 ACM SIGCOMM Workshop on Delay-Tolerant Networking, pp. 284–291. ACM, August 2005

12. Liao, y.: Combining erasure-coding and relay node evaluation in delay tolerant network routing. Technical report, Microsoft (2006)

13. Becker, C., Schiele, G.: New mechanisms for routing in ad hoc networks through world models. In: Proceedings of the 4th CaberNet Plenary Workshop, Pisa, Italy, pp. 1–4, October 2001

14. Chen, D., Kung, T., Vlah, D.: Ad hoc relay wireless networks over moving vehicles on highways. In: Proceedings of the 2nd ACM International Symposium on Mobile Ad Hoc Networking & Computing, pp. 247–250. ACM, October 2001

15. Li, Q., Rus, D.: Communication in disconnected ad hoc networks using message relay. J Parallel Distrib. Comput. 75–86 (2003). Chicago

16. Burns, B.: MV routing and capacity building in disruption tolerant networks. In: IEEE INFOCOM 2005, Miami, FL (2005)

17. Zhao, W., Ammar, M., Zegura, E.: A message ferrying approach for data delivery in sparse mobile ad hoc networks. In: Proceedings of the 5th ACM International Symposium on Mobile Ad Hoc Networking and Computing, pp. 187–198. ACM, May 2004. doi:10.1145/989459.989483. 989483

18. McDonald, A., Znati, T.: A mobility-based framework for adaptive clustering in wireless ad hoc networks. IEEE J. Sel. Areas Commun. **17**(8), 1466–1487 (1999). doi:10.1109/49.780353

19. Davis, J., Fagg, A., Levine, B.: Wearable computers as packet transport mechanisms in highly-partitioned ad-hoc networks. In: Proceedings of Fifth International Symposium on Wearable Computers, pp. 141–148. IEEE (2001). doi:10.1109/ISWC.2001.962117

20. Lindgren, A., Doria, A., Schelen, O.: Probabilistic routing in intermittently connected networks. ACM SIGMOBILE Mob. Comput. Commun. Rev. **7**(3), 19–20 (2003). doi:10.1145/961268.961272

21. Musolesi, M., Hailes, S., Mascolo, C.: Adaptive routing for intermittently connected mobile ad hoc networks. In: Sixth IEEE International Symposium on a World of wireless mobile and multimedia networks 2005, WoWMoM 2005, pp. 183–189. IEEE, June 2005. doi:10.1109/WOWMOM.2005.17

22. Shen, C., Borkar, G., Rajagopalan, S., Jaikaeo, C.: Interrogation-based relay routing for ad hoc satellite networks. In: Global Telecommunications Conference 2002, GLOBECOM 2002, vol. 3, pp. 2920–2924. IEEE, November 2002. doi:10.1109/GLOCOM.2002.1189163

23. Burns, B.: MV routing and capacity building in disruption tolerant networks. In: IEEE INFOCOM 2005, Miami, FL (2005). doi:10.1109/INFCOM.2005.1497909

24. Keranen, A., Ott, J., Karkkainen, T.: Simulating mobility and DTNs with the ONE. J. Commun. **5**(2), 92–105 (2010)

Impact of Higher Order Impairments on QoS Aware Connection Provisioning in 10 Gbps NRZ Optical Networks

Karamjit Kaur[1](✉), Hardeep Singh[2], and Anil Kumar[3]

[1] EIED, Thapar University, Patiala, Punjab, India
karam_sekhon@yahoo.co.in
[2] ECED, Thapar University, Patiala, Punjab, India
[3] Amity University Haryana, Gurgaon, Haryana, India

Abstract. Invent of the optical amplifier has increased the data traffic being carried by each fiber such that even a brief disruption could result in enormous data loss. As we are moving towards transparent networks, connection provisioning is becoming quite challenging task due to additive nature of physical layer impairments and decreased O-E-O conversions taking place inside the routes. In static connection provisioning, the cost function representing the signal quality must consider not only the linear impairments but also, the effect of higher order impairments as they significantly influence the quality of transmission. Present work describes the design of a system with capability to consider the effect of higher order impairments on OSNR (optical signal to noise ratio) and BER (bit error rate) for connection provisioning in optical networks with the focus on comprehensiveness, transparency, and scalability of the system. The processing is carried out in time domain by offline digital signal processing using eye diagram analysis.

Keywords: Lightpath · Connection provisioning · Propagation constant · Eye diagram

1 Introduction

Optical fiber communication system has emerged swiftly to meet the requirements of today's telecommunication networks. The great revolution in the field of optical fiber communication has taken place since 1990, when optical amplifier became commercially available, making it possible to transmit hundreds of Gbps over thousands of kilometers without electronic repeaters. Because of such an enormous amount of data traffic carried by each fiber, even a brief disruption could result in enormous data loss. Thus, for the proper operation and management of these networks, it is vital to have the capability of monitoring the parameters affecting network's performances. Examples of functions that require monitoring include switching components like add drop multiplexers, wavelength convertors, amplifier control, channel identification and component alarms.

The present optical networks are point-to-point opaque network where O-E-O conversion takes place at almost every node. With the introduction of optical components like add drop multiplexers, wavelength convertors, optical amplifiers, these

© Springer Nature Singapore Pte Ltd. 2017
D. Singh et al. (Eds.): ICAICR 2017, CCIS 712, pp. 283–293, 2017.
DOI: 10.1007/978-981-10-5780-9_26

networks will be replaced by translucent and transparent network where the signal will remain in the optical domain only. In opaque networks, since the regeneration of signals take place at almost every node, the quality of transmission is maintained. But in all optical (transparent) and translucent networks, signal has to transverse through the plenty of network elements, making the data susceptible to network malfunctions, misconfigurations and signal impairments. As most of the degradation effects are additive in nature, they tend to accumulate along the lightpath thereby degrading the signal quality by the time it reach at the destination end. Thus, connection provisioning will be quite challenging task for future networks. Considering the importance of signal quality during transmission, connection provisioning in optical networks will not only calculate the shortest path for each request, but will have to consider the different impairments present in the proposed lightpath that would otherwise result in network failure and enormous data loss [1–8]. The connection provisioning may be static or dynamic depending on the methodology of route calculations [9]. In static routing, it is assumed that the traffic patterns are known at the stage of network design only. So for any path request between a source node to destination, set of network resources like fiber links, waveband, electrical/optical components to be utilized are predefined and whenever there is request for lightpath setup, the path is followed as per the network design parameters. In dynamic routing, whenever the connection request arrives, the path computation is done depending upon the current state of the networks [10]. The static routing emphasize on minimum resource utilization for path setup while dynamic routing focus on minimum blocking probability of network. Since dynamic routing requires a lot of computations making it complex and time consuming, the present state networks employ static routing for connection provisioning. For calculating the signal quality during transmission, these networks consider the fixed cost function representing the different impairments. Since the non-linear impairments are intensity dependent and will change with the network state, it is impossible to estimate them at the stage of network design. Instead, static routing algorithms consider linear impairments as they can be easily determined from the type of fiber, wavelength/waveband, amplifier, environmental conditions. It will reduce the computational complexity and processing time without losing any important information regarding signal quality. In the present scenario, the impact of dispersion on OSNR [11–13], ASE (Amplified Spontaneous Emission) [14], Dispersion and ASE [15] has been taken into consideration. It is important that effect of higher order impairments must be considered while calculating this cost function as they significantly influence the quality of transmission.

Present work describes the design of a system with capability to study the effect of higher order impairments on connection provisioning for optical networks with the focus on comprehensiveness, transparency and scalability of the system. Since in point to point networks, O-E-O conversion takes places at almost every node, the processing may be easily carried out in time domain using offline digital signal processing. Eye diagram analysis is used to calculate the amount of higher order impairments present in the network links. Among the different linear impairments, higher order dispersion is the parameter which most affects the OSNR and BER. So in the present work, mathematical modeling of higher order dispersion is being carried out and the equations obtained are simulated in OPTSIM. The disparaging effect of higher order dispersion is studied in form of time delay, eye opening, eye closure, OSNR and BER. This information is then used by routing algorithm for connection provisioning. The algorithm is designed based on best fit routing. The performance of routing algorithm is studied in the form of blocking probability.

2 Mathematical Modeling

Dispersion is the pulse broadening effect causing neighboring pulses to overlap thereby decreasing the bit error rate. Since single mode fibers are considered in the present work, group velocity dispersion and polarization mode dispersion (PMD) are taken in to account. Polarized mode dispersion can be characterized by PMD vector using Principle State Model as [16]

$$\tau = \Delta\tau\hat{p}$$

Where,

τ - PMD vector in 3-D Strokes space
$\Delta\tau$ - Differential group delay
$\hat{p}$ -unit vector pointing toward slower PSP

Using Principle State Model and variation of PMD with angular frequency ω, through a Taylor series expansion of T(ω) with $\Delta\omega$ about the carrier frequency ω_0 may be calculated for large signal bandwidths, in order to obtain higher order PMD's.
Second order PMD is given by:

$$\Delta\omega\frac{d\tau}{d\omega} = \Delta\omega\left(\frac{d\Delta\tau}{d\omega}\hat{p} + \frac{d\hat{p}}{d\omega}\Delta\tau\right)$$

Graphical representation of the same is shown in Fig. 1.

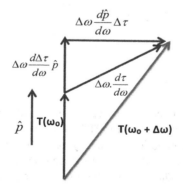

Fig. 1. Graphical representation of 2nd order PMD

Third order PMD is given by:

$$\left\{\frac{1}{2}\left(\Delta\omega^2\frac{d^2\tau}{d\omega^2}\right)\right\} = \frac{\Delta\omega^2}{2}\left\{\hat{p}\frac{d^2\Delta\tau}{d\omega^2} + \frac{d\hat{p}}{d\omega}\left(\frac{d\Delta\tau}{d\omega} + \frac{d^2\Delta\tau}{d\omega^2}\right) + \frac{d^2\hat{p}}{d\omega^2}\Delta\tau\right\}$$

Similarly, equations for further higher order may be obtained through Taylor series expansion.

Group Velocity dispersion parameter β_2 may be expressed as

$$\beta_2 = -D\frac{\lambda^2}{(2\pi c)}$$

Where, D-dispersion parameter

and $D = \frac{d\left(v_g\right)^{-1}}{d\lambda}$

Third order dispersion parameter

$$\beta_3 = \frac{\lambda^2}{(2\pi c)^2}\left(\lambda^2 S + 2\lambda D\right)$$

Where, S-dispersion slope parameter

and $S = \frac{dD}{d\lambda}$

Fourth order Dispersion parameter

$$\beta_4 = -\frac{\lambda^4}{(2\pi c)^3}\left(4\lambda S + \lambda^2\frac{dS}{d\lambda} + 2D\right)$$

Fifth order Dispersion parameter

$$\beta_5 = \frac{\lambda^6}{(2\pi c)^4}\left(6S + 6\lambda\frac{dS}{d\lambda} + \lambda^2\frac{d^2S}{d\lambda^2}\right)$$

3 Network Design

For analyzing the effect of higher order dispersion, a simple source to destination node link as shown in Fig. 2 is designed in OPTSIM. In the designed system, a CW Lorentzian laser with central emission frequency of 1550 nm is used as light source. 10 Gbps NRZ signal is generated by using different Pseudo-random binary sequence (PRBS) generator and modulated on the optical fiber through Amplitude Dual

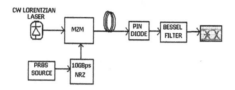

Fig. 2. Set up for monitoring 10 Gbps NRZ signal

Arm MZM. At the receiver end, PIN diode is used for O-E conversion. The electrical output is filtered using forth order Bessel filter.

The output of this Bessel filter is shared with connection provisioning algorithm using electrical read/write function of OPTSIM. The algorithm is based on basic principle of Dijkstra shortest path computation algorithm with small modifications. In the presented algorithm, cost function representing the quality of signal being transmitted is used along with path length for selecting a particular route. The detailed description of this algorithm is described in [17]. To calculate set of nodes to be used between a source and destination for any connection request, a nine node network model as shown in Fig. 3 is used.

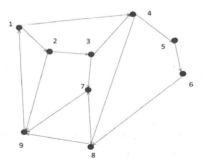

Fig. 3. Nine node network

The direction that a signal may transverse between two connecting nodes is represented by the arrowhead (links are not bidirectional). Between every pair of nodes (x, y) ∈ {1, 2, 3...9}, there exist matrices representing path length, cost function for quality of lightpath, and status of link between x, y (whether already occupied or free). Depending on priority of connection request (low, high or medium), all the possible paths with corresponding path length and quality is calculated and final route is selected based on best fit principle. If No path is available, Request is aborted at this stage only. The flow chart of algorithm developed is shown in Fig. 4.

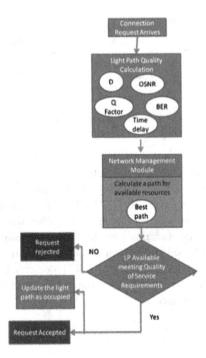

Fig. 4. Flow chart of route finding algorithm

4 Result and Conclusion

The electrical output at the receiver end is used to generate the eye diagrams. These eye diagrams are further processed and analyzed to calculate the effect of higher order impairments on the signal quality. Some of the dominant results are presented here. Figure 5 represents the eye diagram of system with second order dispersion parameter value −7.84, −15.68 and −23.52 is represented by blue, green and brown color respectively. The corresponding propagation constant, BER, eye opening, eye closing and time delay introduced is summarized in Table 1.

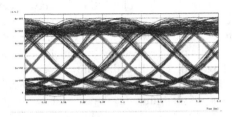

Fig. 5. Eye diagram of system with second order propagation constant

Table 1. Response of simulated network for different values of propagation constant

S.No	β	BER	Q factor (dB)	Eye opening (a.u)	Eye closure (dB)	Time delay (ns)
1.	10	1e−040	25.4	4.26331e−005	0.562150	ref
2.	20	2.59741e−023	19.9	3.85621e−005	1.078671	0.024
3.	30	1.48001e−013	17.3	3.37964e−005	1.376975	0.064

In order to study the effect of higher order dispersions, the different combinations of β_2, β_3, β_4 and β_5 are used as summarized in Fig. 6 the corresponding eye diagrams are shown in Fig. 7. The image is obtained by superimposing Eye Diagram obtained for network with no higher order dispersion present and over the presence of (a) fifth order only (b) forth order only (c) Third order only (d) Second order only (e) Third and Fifth order (f) Third, fourth and fifth order (g) second and fourth order (h) All orders. The eye diagram obtained after superimposing all the possible states is represented by Fig. 8. The Q-value, eye opening, eye closure, OSNR and optical power received has been summarized in Table 2(a, b) and Fig. 9(a–d).

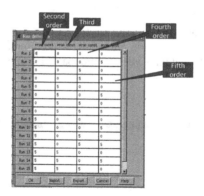

Fig. 6. Values of different orders of beta for different runs

Using these results, path satisfying the requested quality condition, if it exists, is calculated successfully. On the other hand, if none of the available path satisfies the minimum quality condition, the connection request is aborted. The blocking probability curve so obtained is shown in Fig. 10. From the diagram it may be seen that blocking probability increase with increase in load. Although, it has been found that as the higher order impairments are included, the probability of connection failure does increase. But this helps in set up of connection more accurately in accordance with service level agreement with the users.

Thus, it has been demonstrated that presence of multiple orders of dispersion in the network may introduce delay, decrease the optical power of the signal and have disparaging effect in overall quality of signal being transmitted. Hence they must be cautiously dealt with for routing and wavelength assignment issues as the effects may

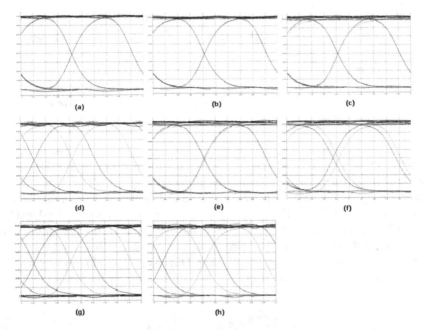

Fig. 7. Superimposition of eye diagram obtained for network with no higher order dispersion present and over the presence of (a) fifth order only (b) forth order only (c) third order only (d) second order only (e) third and Fifth order (f) third fourth and fifth order (g) second and fourth order (h) all orders

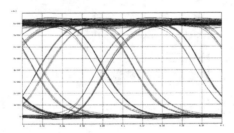

Fig. 8. Eye diagram obtained considering propagation constant till fifth order

be dominant for long and ultra long haul optical networks. For further research, the impact may be calculated for dynamic routing of optical networks. The computational complexities may arise as non linear impairments are network state dependent and have cancellation effect w.r.t linear impairments. Suitable compensation techniques may be proposed for these networks with optimal resource utilization and regenerator placements keeping in mind the amount of information that needs to be collected and processed so as to reduce the blocking probability, computational complexity and processing time.

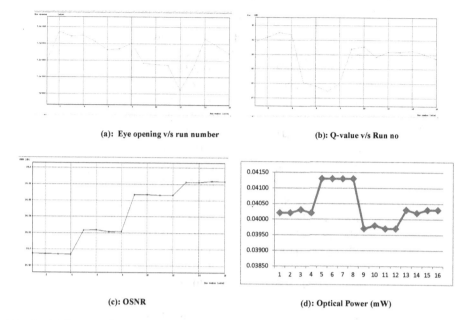

Fig. 9. (a) Eye opening v/s run number, (b) Q-value v/s run no, (c) OSNR, (d) optical power (mW)

Table 2. (a) Q-value and eye diagram parameters for different runs (b) optical power received in different runs

(a) Q-value and eye diagram parameters for different runs			
Run	Q-value (dB)	Q-value linear)	Eye closure (dB)	Eye opening
1	30.8945	35.05303	0.33999	0.72061E−04
2	31.1886	36.26017	0.22964	0.73727E−04
3	31.5371	37.74461	0.26470	0.73454E−04
4	31.3767	37.05423	0.22582	0.73503E−04
5	28.0840	25.36310	0.35115	0.73131E−04
6	27.8355	24.64755	0.37969	0.72638E−04
7	27.4611	23.60783	0.36684	0.72700E−04
8	27.9999	25.11871	0.34756	0.73042E−04
9	30.4065	33.13806	0.30276	0.71844E−04
10	30.5655	33.74998	0.31434	0.71768E−04
11	29.8403	31.04668	0.27850	0.71728E−04
12	30.1950	32.34059	0.36079	0.70218E−04
13	30.1884	32.31602	0.35600	0.71505E−04
14	30.2730	32.63247	0.25432	0.73302E−04
15	30.04503	31.78716	0.29189	0.72896E−04
16	29.72864	30.65012	0.32276	0.72430E−04

(continued)

Table 2. (*continued*)

(b) Optical power received in different runs

Run no.	Optical power (dB)	Optical power (mW)
1	−13.953	0.402E−01
2	−13.958	0.402E−01
3	−13.950	0.403E−01
4	−13.956	0.402E−01
5	−13.841	0.413E−01
6	−13.840	0.413E−01
7	−13.840	0.413E−01
8	−13.838	0.413E−01
9	−14.007	0.397E−01
10	−14.007	0.398E−01
11	−14.011	0.397E−01
12	−14.010	0.397E−01
13	−13.952	0.403E−01
14	−13.953	0.402E−01
15	−13.950	0.403E−01
16	−13.950	0.403E−01

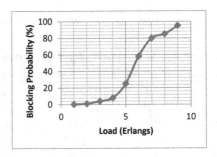

Fig. 10. Blocking probability curve for different loads

References

1. Saradhi, C.V., Subramaniam, S.: physical layer impairment aware routing (PLIAR) in WDM optical networks: issues and challenges. IEEE Commun. Surv. Tutor. **11**(4), 109–130 (2009)
2. Azodolmolky, S., Klinkowski, M., et al.: A survey on physical layer impairments aware routing and wavelength assignment algorithms in optical networks. Comput. Netw. **53**, 926–944 (2009)
3. Georgakilas, K.N., Katrinis, K., et al.: Performance evaluation of impairment-aware routing under single- and double-link failures. IEEE J. Opt. Commun. Netw. **2**(8), 633–641 (2011)

4. Martnez, R., et al.: Challenges and requirements for introducing impairment-awareness into the management and control planes of ASON/GMPLS WDM networks. IEEE Commun. Mag. **44**(12), 76–85 (2006)

5. Berthold, J., Saleh, A.A.M., et al.: Optical networking: past, present, and future. IEEE J. Lightwave Technol. **26**(9), 1104–1118 (2008)

6. Manousakis, K., Christodoulopoulos, K., et al.: Offline impairment-aware routing and wavelength assignment algorithms in translucent WDM optical networks. IEEE J. Lightwave Technol. **27**(12), 1866–1877 (2009)

7. Ramamurthy, B., Datta, D., et al.: Impact of transmission impairments on the teletraffic performance of wavelength-routed optical networks. J. Lightwave Technol. **17**(10), 1713–1723 (1999)

8. Rangnekar, A., Sivalingam, K.M.: QoS aware multi-channel scheduling for IEEE 802.15.3 networks. J. Mob. Netw. Appl. **11**, 47–62 (2006)

9. Mohan, G., Siva Ram Murthy, C., Somani, A.K.: Efficient algorithms for routing dependable connections in WDM optical networks. IEEE/ACM Trans. Netw. **9**(5), 553–566 (2001)

10. Zang, H., Jue, J.B., Mukherjee, B.: A review of routing and wavelength assignment approaches for wavelength-routed optical WDM networks. Opt. Netw. Mag. **1**(1), 47–60 (2000)

11. Tomkos, I., Sygletos, S., et al.: Impairment constraint based routing in mesh optical networks. In: OSA Conference on Optical Fiber Communication and National Fiber Optic Engineers, March 2007, paper OWR1 (2007)

12. Zulkifli, N., Okonkwo, C., Guild, K.: Dispersion optimised impairment constraint based routing and wavelength assignment algorithms for all-optical networks. In: Proceedings of ICTON 2006, paper We.A3.5 (2006)

13. Huang, Y., Heritage, J.P., Mukherjee, B.: Connection provisioning with transmission impairment consideration in optical WDM networks with high-speed channels. J. Lightwave Technol. **23**(3), 982–993 (2005)

14. Pavani, G.S., Zuliani, L.G., et al.: Distributed approaches for impairment-aware routing and wavelength assignment algorithms in GMPLS networks. Comput. Netw. **52**, 1905–1915 (2008)

15. Monoyios, D., Vlachos, K.: Multiobjective genetic algorithms for solving the impairment-aware routing and wavelength assignment problem. IEEE J. Opt. Commun. Netw. **3**(1), 40–47 (2011)

16. Nelson, L.E., Jopson, R.M.: Introduction to polarized mode dispersion in optical networks. J. Opt. Fiber Commun. Rep. **1**(4), 312–344 (2004)

17. Kaur, K., Singh, H.: An algorithm of impairment aware routing for wavelength division multiplexed optical networks. Microwave Opt. Technol. Lett. **57**(7), 1632–1636 (2015)

Super-Router: A Collaborative Filtering Technique Against DDoS Attacks

Akshat Gaurav[✉] and Awadhesh Kumar Singh

Department of Computer Engineering, National Institute of Technology,
Kurushatra, Haryana, India
akshatgaurav470@gmail.com, aksingh@nitkkr.ac.in

Abstract. DDoS attack is one of the well known cyber attacks of Internet era, which affects on the availability of the network. In 1999, though Computer Incident Advisory Capability (CIAC) reports the first ever DDoS attack, but first major DDoS attack was recorded in year 2000 on some of the big websites e.g., Yahoo, Amazon, CNN, eBay etc. due to which their services went offline for few hours and huge amount of revenue losses were recorded. Since then DDoS attacks become favourite attacks of antagonists. There are so many different defense techniques available to detect and filter malicious traffic, but none of these methods could adequately filter out the malicious traffic. In this context, this paper proposed a new filtering scheme, Super-router, which uses collaborative filtering technique to filter malicious traffic. More specifically, Super-router uses unicast method of communication between filters which reduces the communication overheads and response time of individual filters. This makes Super-router an effective defense against DDoS attacks for high speed networks.

Keywords: DDoS attack · Super-router method · TCP-SYN attack · SQL slammer attack · NTP attack

1 Introduction

The main objective of DDoS attacks is to overwhelm the victim's system, server or network with large amount of fake traffic generated from many compromised computers named as Zombies [1,2]. These Zombies are selected either automatically or manually by handlers, which are directly chosen by the attacker. This combined network of handlers and zombies known as Botnet [1], Fig. 1 represents the basic architecture of DDoS attacks. Broadly DDoA attacks is classified as Bandwidth attack and Resource exploitation attack.

- **Bandwidths attack-** Attacker floods the victim's bandwidth by unwanted traffic, so it is unable to provide the services to legitimate users
- **Resource depletion attack-** Attacker tries to consume the available resources of the victim's machine so that victim may not be able to serve the legitimate user.

© Springer Nature Singapore Pte Ltd. 2017
D. Singh et al. (Eds.): ICAICR 2017, CCIS 712, pp. 294–305, 2017.
DOI: 10.1007/978-981-10-5780-9_27

Now days DDoS attacks are very popular as launching a single attack is easily feasible by using available tools such as Trinoo [4], Tribe Flood Attack [TFN] [5], TFN2K [6], Mstream [7], Shaft [8], Kinght [8], Low Orbit Ion Cannon (LOIC), High Orbit Ion Cannon (HOIC).

Easy availability of attack tools is one of the reasons why attacks are increasing every year. In [3] the present statistics of DDoS attacks are given. In Q1 of 2016, 4500 DDoS attacks were registered, in which 70% used the Echo chargen, UDP flooding, reflection based DNS, or TCP flooding method. Moreover, 55% of total attacks in Q1 of 2016 were on gaming industry and, 19 recorded attacks rated of more than 100 Gbps, highest of them has an attack rate of 298 Gbps. During Q1 of 2016 attackers mostly target layer 3 and layer 4 of network protocol for the attack which is 142.14% more than Q1 of 2015. Every present organization like Education, gaming, media & software industry, are affected by DDoS attacks. Thus, we can deduce that DDoS attack is one of the biggest cyber threats of every organization which uses internet for its operation.

In 1999, Computer Incident Advisory Capability reports the first DDoS attack, after then many methods and solutions were proposed on the defense techniques, to mitigate attack effects. There are mainly three defense methods:

- **Attack Prevention-** Pre-attack scenario or the methods taken before the attack to reduce attack effect on the victims system, Load balancing, setting up the Honeypots [9], use of proper scanning techniques are some of the examples of this method.
- **Attack Trace back-** This method is used to trace back the source of the attack, Probabilistic packet marking technique [10] is one of the examples of this technique.
- **Attack Filtering-** Filters are used to filter out the malicious traffic. These filters are generally installed on the routers and thus, they detect and stop the attack traffic before it could cause any significant damage.

Attack filtering is a domain of our research. There are many techniques which have been developed to differentiate the malicious traffic from the legitimate one. Kalkan et al. [11] classify the attack detection techniques according to the collaboration between the routers and the response time of routers thus, attack filtering process can be divided in to four groups.

- **Reactive and Individual-** In this type of filtering, filter remains active only for attack period and process the packets according to its own stored information and data, Hopcount filtering [12] is one of the examples of this type of filtering.
- **Reactive and Cooperative-** Filter remains active for attack duration and it also shares its data with different filters, Pushback technique [13], AITF [14], PFS [15] are some of the examples of this type of technique.
- **Proactive and Individual-** In this process filter remains active during all the time and does filtering according to its stored information, Ingress/Egress Filtering [16], RDPF [17], PackeScore [18] uses this technique to filter attack traffic.

- **Proactive and Cooperative-** Different filters collaborate with each other
  to filter out the malicious traffic. Moreover, these filters remain active before
  the attack. Thus it starts filtering the attack traffic at earlier stage of attack,
  ScoreForCore [11] is an example of this type of filtering technique.

An efficient DDoS defense system should be uncomplicated and extensible
enough to detect new and unknown attacks which are generated by different
sources. Moreover, it should detect the attack traffic quickly and efficiently i.e.,
it should have high detection rate and less response time. But none of the present
defence technique completely fulfils these requirements.

The proposed model, in this paper establish a defense mechanism which
provides security against verity of DDoS attacks. This mechanism is a hybrid
model consists of Collaborative filtering approach with Packet marking method.
It has an ability of deter the attack packets before they expand into the network
and damage the victim's system.

Rest of the paper is organized as follows. Section 2 presents related work
where as Sect. 3 presents the proposed model. Section 4 describes the performance evaluation and Sect. 5 has conclusion and future work.

2   Related Work

In the previous section different filtering mechanisms were discussed. Some of
the important proactive, cooperative filtering mechanisms which has proposed
in recent past are mentioned here.

Kim et al. [18] proposed an individual and proactive filtering mechanism,
PacketScore, in this scheme the packet scores of each incoming packet is calculated and if the value is less than the predefined threshold, the packet is
discarded. The main limitation of this approach is its inability to detect more
than one type of attacks at the same time also the memory requirements for
storing the packet scores is high.

Mahajan et al. [13] presented a collaborative technique to detect the DDoS
attack. This model is named as Pushback. According to this model if any router
faces congestion then it requests the corresponding upstream router to limit its
down- stream traffic rate. The advantage of this method is that the bandwidths
of downstream routers are saved as all the malicious packets are filtered by
upstream routers and they have to pass only the legitimate packets. But if the
attackers are uniformly distributed in the network then this model may not give
the desired results.

Franois et al. [19] proposed a collaborative and proactive technique, FireCol
to detect DDoS attack. This technique forms a virtual ring of IPS (Intrusion
Detection Systems) around the victim and then these IPS collaborate with each
other to detect the attack traffic according to the set of rules. To avail the services
of these IPS user has to register with their ISP (Internet Service Provider).
After registration each user gets a unique ID, TTL (time of subscription) and
supported capacity. Different users can set their detection rules and support

capacity according to their requirements but if users are large than this technique may overburden the IPS and reduce its response time.

Kalkan and Alagz [11] proposed ScoreForCore, a filtering mechanism which uses proactive and collaborative method to filter DDoS attack traffic. This approach can detect more than one type of attack at the same time, for this each router selects the attribute pairs randomly which defines the specific attack type and then during attack time these values of attribute pairs are compared with the attribute pairs deviated most during the attack. But if the router did not have the information about the most deviated attribute pairs then it gets this information from its neighboring routers by broadcasting its request into the network. The main limitation of this model is that it uses broadcasting technique which increases the message complexity of the system and also reduces the response time of the system.

3   Proposed Approach

In this proposed model two different routers collaborate with each other to filter out the malicious traffic thus, it is a reactive and collaborative type of filtering method as both of the routers act as single unit, a new name Super-router is used to address this combination. In Super-router combination each router has its own separate working and they are named as Packet Marker and Packet Analyser according to their working Fig. 1 represent the insight of the super router combination.

- **Packet Marker**- This is a router which marks the outgoing traffic if the incoming traffic is suspicious or not following defined standard rules.
- **Packet Analyser**- This router filters the packets if incoming traffic is suspicious and its most of the packets are marked.

3.1   Selection of Attributes

The main objective of Super-router combination is to detect and filter out different DDoS attacks by analyzing the score of the incoming packets. For this purpose different attributes are extracted from the incoming packets and then score of each packet is calculated according to the extracted attributes value. In order to reduce the memory storage, proposed model uses only six unique attributes, which uniquely define most of the present known attacks. These attributes are IP address, port number, protocol type, packet size, TTL value and TCPFlag.

In the proposed model Packet marker and Packet analyzer randomly selects the attributes which completely defines the different attack types, like for the detection of TCP SYN attack Packet marker and Packet analyzer calculates score by analyzing ProtocolType and TCPFlag attributes respectively. There is no need of calculating and storing all the attributes value, so the memory requirements of each router are reduced.

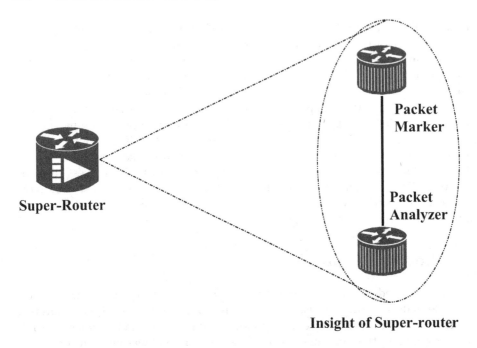

Insight of Super-router

Fig. 1. Concept of super-router

3.2   Packet Score Calculation

Each router of Super-router combination uses PacketScore [18] method to process the incoming packets. In PacketScore method score of each incoming packet is calculated and compared with certain threshold and if packet score is less than threshold then it is consider as malicious packet. Super-router model uses above concept and packet score of each incoming packet is calculated by using formula given below

$$Score(S_i) = \frac{iCAP/TCAP}{iCNP/TCNP} \tag{1}$$

In above formula iCAP and iCNP represent number of packets of specific attributes during attack time and no attack time respectively; and TCAP and TCNP represent total traffic during attack time and no attack time respectively.

3.3   Threshold Calculation

Packet score value for each selected time period is calculated and stored in the Score Book and then these scores are used to calculate the threshold value by using load shedding algorithm [20] for the next time period. According to the load shedding algorithm for the calculation of threshold value for $(i + 1)^{th}$ seconds, firstly current incoming traffic is calculated (ψ_i) and then acceptable traffic is calculated (ϕ_i) for i^{th} seconds. Thus threshold value for $(i+1)^{th}$ seconds is T_{i+1} and it is given as follows.

$$T_{i+1} = 1 - \frac{\psi_i}{\phi_i} \qquad (2)$$

3.4   Packet Discarding

The score of packets for $(i+1)^{th}$ time period is compare with the threshold (Th) value calculated in i^{th} time period. Thus, if score of the packets are less then the threshold(Th) than they are consider as malicious packets.

3.5   Description of Algorithm

The algorithm that is executed in each router of Super-router scheme is explain in this section and for better understanding, Table. 1 represents the abbreviations those are use in the algorithm.

Table 1. Attributes used in algorithm

Term	Explanation
P_k	k^{th} incoming packet
$A_i[k]$	i^{th} attribute of kth packet
$S_i[k]$	Score of ith attribute of kth packet
M[k]	Marker value of kth packet
Dr_N	Data rate during no attack time
Dr_A	Data rate during attack time
iCNP	Packet Count of ith attribute during no attack period
iCAP	Packet Count of ith attribute during attack period
TCNP	Total packets during no attack time
TCAP	Total packets during attack time
Th	Threshold

During attack period when the attack rate (Dr_A) is more than the normal rate (Dr_N) each filter in Super-router combination stores the attribute value and marker value of every incoming packet Pk in a register A[k] and in an array M[k] respectively. After that the score of the packet, S(k), is calculated according to attribute values and then this score is compare with the threshold value (Th). if the score is less than the threshold value and packet is not marked then filter simply mark the packet but, if the packet is marked then filter discard the respective packet. This algorithm is expressed in Algorithm 1.

```
Algorithm 1. Router side operation
Input : Incoming Packet P_k
Output : Weather Packet is Malicious or Legitimated
Begin
A_i[k] ⇐ Null ; /* set attribute value as null
M[k] ⇐ Null ; /* set marker value as null
S_i[k] ⇐ Null ; /* set packet score as null
if Dr_A > Dr_N then
   for Each incoming Packet P_k do
      A_i[k] ⇐ P_k ; /* Store the attribute value
      M[k] ⇐ P_k ;/* Store the marker value
      Calculate the packet score S_i(k) ;
      if S_i[k] > Th then
        return Packet is Legitimated ;
      else
        if M[k] is set then
          return Packet is Malicious ;
        else
          Set the marker value in P_k ;
          return Packet is Legitimate ;
        end if
      end if
   end for
end if
End
```

4   Performance Evaluation and Results

OMNeT++ [21] is a discrete event simulator used for modelling different communication networks. In OMNeT++ different models connected with each other hierarchically and communicate with each other by message passing at discrete time intervals.

In order to simulate the proposed model, simulation process is divided in to two configurations:

- **Idle Period-** In this configuration only legitimated users are present thus score book forming process take place in this configuration.
- **Attack Period-** In this configuration many attackers are introduced into the system which are generating attack traffic. During this configuration packet marking and packet discarding process takes place.

Each configuration contains one network file, which in turn consists of hosts, channel, routers and attacker (in attack period). Hosts are legitimate devices which generate normal request at random interval of time. Attackers are the malicious devices which flood the network with excessive traffic. Routers are the devices which are used for filtering and routing the packets from source to destination and channels are used to connect different modules.

4.1 Simulation Environment

In this section performance of proposed scheme is evaluated and compared with Packet Score and ScoreForCore schemes. For this a simulate environment is set up which consist of 200 hosts, 50 attackers and packets generated by host and attackers are in the range of 10 MB to 20 MB and 100 KB to 500 KB respectively and this simulation process runs for 500 s.

To compare the proposed scheme with other PacketScore and ScoreForCore schemes nine parameters are used as the performance criteria these are Precision (PL), Recall (RL), True Negative Rate (TNR), Negative Predictive Value (NPV), f-measure (FM), f-measure complement (FMC), Message complexity, Time complexity and Space complexity. The three schemes are evaluated according to performance criteria during below attack scenarios:

- **TCP SYN attack**- This is a flooding attack in which attacker generate large amount of TCP packets, so to detect this, Protocol type and TCP flag values are extracted from the incoming packet (*Protocol Type* = TCP, *TCP flag* = 40).
- **SQL slammer attack**- This attack exploits the buffer overflow vulnerability to attack the systems which are using unpatched Microsoft SQL server, so to detect this attack Protocol type, destination port and packet size values are extracted (*protocol type* = UDP, *destination port* = 1434, *packet size* in between 371 and 400 bytes)
- **NTP attack**- In this type of attack attacker exploits the NTP server to flood the victim system with large amount of UDP packets so for this attack Protocol type, destination port and packet size values are extracted from the attack packet(*Protocol type* = NTP, *destination port* = 123, *packet size* = 90 bytes)

4.2 Result Comparison

According to the parameters defined in the previous section, the results of the simulation are compared with existing filtering techniques i.e. PacketScore and ScoreForCore method.

- **Message Complexity**- ScoreForCore method uses broad- cast method to collect the information during attack time. So in worst case scenario number of query packets generated are X*Y*Z (where X, Y, Z are the number of routers which are one, two and three hop away). Because Super-router uses unicast method for communication, so the number of message generated is significantly less than ScoreForCore. Figure 2 clearly represents this scenario.
- **Time Complexity**- In worst case if router did not have the information then ScoreForCore sends a query message to its neighbors and a neighbor which has the information sends the reply message. This process takes approximate time of 6 hops. But Super-router does not wait for query and reply message so time complexity is less as compared to ScoreForCore. Figure 3 represent this situation.

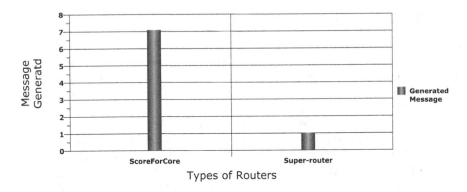

Fig. 2. Number of messages generated by super-router and ScoreForCore methods

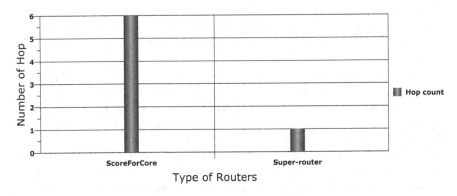

Fig. 3. Reaction time comparison between super-router and ScoreForCore schemes

- **Space Complexity-** ScoreForCore stores packet score for all the single attributes and one pair of attribute during no attack period. Packet score method also stores the score of all single attributes but Super-router stores only the score of its selected attribute, i.e. if all single attributes are 6 then ScoreForCore stores the score of 6+1(six single and one pair) attributes and Packet score method stores score of all 6 attributes but Super-router stores the score of 1 attribute. So we can say that Super-router is required less space for storing the attributes. Figure 4 represents this scenario.
- **Performance Matrix-** The output results of the proposed scheme from the simulation are compare with existing techniques i.e. ScoreForCore method and PacketScore method in Table 2.

In Table 2, PL, RL, TNR, NPV, FM and FMC stands for Precision, Recall, True negative rate, Negative predicate value, F-measure, F-measure complement respectively. From Table 2 it is also clear that the Super-router scheme detects the malicious traffic in all three attack scenarios more efficiently as compare to other two schemes.

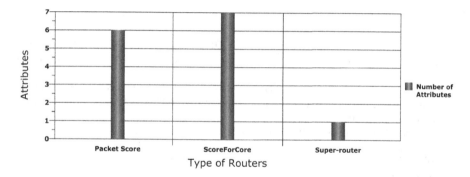

Fig. 4. Minimum attributes required by packet score, ScoreForCore and super-router schemes to filter malicious traffic

Table 2. Result comparison of super-router (SR) with packet score (PS) and Score-ForCore (SFC) schemes

Attack type	Model	PL	RL	TNR	NPV	FM	FMC
TCP-SYN attack	PS	0.73	0.49	0.59	0.89	0.73	0.80
	SFC	1	0.99	0.99	1	0.99	0.99
	SR	1	0.99	0.99	1	0.99	0.99
SQL slammer attack	PS	0.98	0.86	0.92	0.98	0.92	0.95
	SFC	1	1	1	1	1	1
	SR	1	0.99	0.99	1	0.99	0.99
NTP attack	PS	0.99	0.82	0.90	0.99	0.89	0.94
	SFC	1	0.99	0.99	1	0.99	0.99
	SR	1	0.99	0.99	1	0.99	0.99

5   Conclusion

In this paper a novel approach 'Super-router' was proposed, which was based on proactive and cooperative type of filtering method to detect DDoS attacks in High Speed Networks. Super-router was formed by the co-operation of two routers named, Packet Marker and Packet Analyzer and they communicate with each other to filter the outgoing packets so overall message overhead was considerably low, moreover both routers were one hop away so the response time is also less as compare to other filtering methods. The filtering performance of super-router was evaluated according to the performance matrix which includes precision, recall, true negative rate, negative predictive value, F-measure, F-measure complement in three different attack scenarios and the results showed that the proposed model accurately and efficiently detects the attack traffic as compare to current filtering techniques.

References

1. Mirkovic, J., Reiher, P.: A taxonomy of DDoS attack and DDoS defense mechanisms. ACM SIGCOMM Comput. Commun. Rev. **34**(2), 39–53 (2004). doi:10. 1145/997150.997156
2. Douligeris, C., Mitrokotsa, A.: DDoS attacks and defense mechanisms: classification and state-of-the-art. Comput. Netw. **44**(5), 643–666 (2004). doi:10.1016/j. comnet.2003.10.003
3. Q2 State of Internet Security Report. http://www.akamai.com
4. Dittrich, D.: The DoS project's "trinoo" distributed denial of service attack tool. University of Washington (1999). http://staff.washington.edu/dittrich/misc/ trinoo.analysis.txt
5. Dittrich, D.: The tribe flood network distributed denial of service attack tool. University of Washington (2002)
6. Barlow, J., Thrower, W.: TFN2K an analysis (2000). http://security.royans.net/ info/posts/bugtraq_ddos2.shtml
7. Dittrich, D., Weaver, G., Dietrich, S., Long, N.: The "mstream" distributed denial of service attack tool (2000). http://staff.washington.edu/dittrich/misc/mstream. analysis.txt3
8. Gupta, B.B., Joshi, R.C., Misra, M.: Distributed denial of service prevention techniques. Int. J. Comput. Electr. Eng. IJCEE **2**(2), 268–276 (2012). arXiv preprint arXiv:1208.3557 (2010)
9. Weiler, N.: Honeypots for distributed denial-of-service attacks. In: Proceedings of the 11th IEEE International Workshops on Enabling Technologies: Infrastructure for Collaborative Enterprises, WET ICE, pp. 109–114 (2002). doi:10.1109/ENABL. 2002.1029997
10. Bhavani, Y., Reddy, P.N.: An efficient IP traceback through packet marking algorithm. Int. J. Netw. Secur. Appl. IJNSA **2**, 132–142 (2010)
11. Kalkan, K., Alagz, F.: A distributed filtering mechanism against DDoS attacks: ScoreForCore. Comput. Netw. **108**, 199–209 (2016). doi:10.1016/j.comnet.2016. 08.023
12. Jin, C., Wang, H., Shin, K.G.: Hop-count filtering: an effective defense against spoofed DDoS attacks. In: Proceedings of the 10th ACM Conference on Computer and Communications Security, pp. 30–41 (2003). doi:10.1145/948109.948116.
13. Mahajan, R., Bellovin, S.M., Floyd, S., Ioannidis, J., Paxson, V., Shenker, S.: Controlling high bandwidth aggregates in the network. ACM SIGCOMM Comput. Commun. Rev. **32**(3), 62–73 (2002). doi:10.1145/571697.571724
14. Argyraki, K.J., Cheriton, D.R.: Active internet traffic filtering: real-time response to denial-of-service attacks. In: USENIX Annual Technical Conference, General track, pp. 135–148 (2005)
15. Seo, D., Lee, H., Perrig, A.: PFS: probabilistic filter scheduling against distributed denial-of-service attacks. In: 36th Conference on Local Computer Networks (LCN), pp. 9–17. IEEE (2011). doi:10.1109/LCN.2011.6114645
16. Ferguson, P.: Network ingress filtering: defeating denial of service attacks which employ IP source address spoofing (2000)
17. Park, K., Lee, H.: On the effectiveness of route-based packet filtering for distributed DoS attack prevention in power-law internets. ACM SIGCOMM Comput. Commun. Rev. **31**(4), 15–26 (2001). doi:10.1145/964723.383061
18. Kim, Y., Lau, Y.C., Chuah, M.C., Chao, H.J.: PacketScore: a statistics-based packet filtering scheme against distributed denial-of-service attacks. IEEE Trans. Dependable Secure Comput. **3**(2), 141–155 (2006). doi:10.1109/TDSC.2006.25

19. Franois, J., Aib, I., Boutaba, R.: FireCol: a collaborative protection network for the detection of flooding DDoS attacks. IEEE/ACM Trans. Netw. (TON) **20**(6), 1828–1841 (2012). doi:10.1109/TNET.2012.2194508
20. Kasera, S., Pinheiro, J., Loader, C., Karaul, M., Hari, A., LaPorta, T.: Fast and robust signaling overload control. In: 9th International Conference on Network Protocols, pp. 323–331 (2001). doi:10.1109/ICNP.2001.992913
21. OMNeT++. http://www.omnetpp.org
22. Kaur, R., Sangal, A.L., Kumar, K.: Modeling and simulation of DDoS attack using Omnet++. In: International Conference on Signal Processing and Integrated Networks (SPIN), pp. 220–225 (2014). doi:10.1109/SPIN.2014.6776951

A Systematic Survey on Congestion Mechanisms of CoAP Based Internet of Things

Ananya Pramanik[1], Ashish Kr. Luhach[2], Isha Batra[1(✉)],
and Upasana Singh[3]

[1] Lovely Professional University, Jalandhar, India
Isha.17451@lpu.co.in
[2] CTIEMT, Jalandhar, India
[3] University of Kwazulu-Natal, Durban, South Africa

Abstract. An IoT is a ubiquitous intelligent technology that enables interaction among intelligent devices via Internet. It consists of the lossy and low powered networks (LLN) connected sensors having limited power and bandwidth. For the messaging protocol, IFTF has standardized with a lightweight RESTful application layer protocol known as CoAP. It runs on the unreliable UDP layer for communication, reliability and congestion control. With the increase in no of transmissions, congestion in the network increases and it becomes difficult to overcome it using the conventional CoAP mechanism. Therefore, a new paradigm has been approached for the advancement known as CoAP congestion Control Mechanism (CoCoA). In this paper, there is a systematic survey of the traditional CoAP along with the new paradigm approaches and their algorithms is discussed. Also, a brief introduction of its working, limitations and evaluation parameters such as throughput, latency, and re-transmission are taken into consideration for survey.

Keywords: Internet of Things · CoAP · Congestion control · CoCoA · Backoff algorithm

1 Introduction

Internet of Things in a novel paradigm to connect people, things, data and application through internet to enable them for remote access, interactive integrated services and management. It is a unique way to identify the objects in the coming future by "Unique Address" in the networking field of computer science, such as by Radio Frequency Identification (RFID), barcode, sensors, actuators, LAN etc. [1]

For the standardization of the application layer protocol Internet Engineering Task Force (IETF) had proposed Constrained Application Protocol (CoAP) which function on the REST (Representational State Transfer) architecture. In CoAP has a basic congestion control protocol for the reliability that based on the retransmission timeout (RTO) together with exponential RTO backoff to deal with the congestion in the network.

The internet protocols that we use were not compatible for the constrained devices. So, taking this into account to interact with low power and resources limited deices

© Springer Nature Singapore Pte Ltd. 2017
D. Singh et al. (Eds.): ICAICR 2017, CCIS 712, pp. 306–317, 2017.
DOI: 10.1007/978-981-10-5780-9_28

CoAP and Message Queue Telemetry Transport (MQTT) are two messaging protocol were introducing in the IoT. Here we will mainly focus on the CoAP because of its popularity and deployment in the constrained devices having low overhead, resources capability and having HTTP like semantics.

CoAP is known as a Representational State Transfer style (RESTful) protocol which helps in the deployment of the connection between the clients and servers over the Internet. This mechanism is done by the help of sensor measurements or actuator states. This protocol is implied on UDP layer by default which is although did not provide end-to-end reliability which is needed for the applications. For this CoAP introduces end-to-end acknowledgements (ACKs). It is done by setting a confirmable (CON) flag in an outgoing CoAP message from the destination node for end-to-end ACK. In CON message, it is designed for the reliable communication. They reply with ACK and retransmits ACK without 2-3 s if the sender does not receive ACK before expiration of the timer the time is doubled for every consecutive failure. The second one is if it does not care about the message failure and sender do not wait for ACK the Non-Confirmable (NON) message is send. This scenario can be seen in implementation of real time and multicasting data transfer.

In this paper, we are presenting a review on the systematic survey on congestion mechanism of CoAP based Internet of things. Various Congestion control mechanism was discussed along with their algorithms. The working, limitations and evaluation of parameters like throughput, latency and retransmission gives the glimpse of overview of the congestion control mechanism in CoAP.

Rest of the paper is organized as follows: Sect. 2. Gives the idea how congestion control is different in IoT than WSN Sect. 3 gives the problem formulation in Congestion Control in CoAP Sect. 4 here various mechanism related to Congestion control in CoAP is discussed and their algorithms for detecting congestion. Furthered its working, limitation and parameters of evaluation is discussed.

2   How Congestion Control is Different in IoT than WSN?

When we talk about standalone WSNs (not connected to Internet), the traffic is less and mainly contributed by up-link (nodes to sink) traffic only. However, down-link (sink to nodes) traffic also occurs in query based applications but it does not contribute much to the traffic and congestion, since in standalone WSNs, sensor nodes' main task is to sense and route the data towards sink.

On the other hand, when WSN is connected to Internet (through Gateway), many real-time Internet applications open their way to the sensor network through Gateway node. In this scenario, both up-link and down-link traffic can be observed in equal quantity since many application users sitting on the other side of WSN may directly log in to any sensor node and execute the required task. This whole process increases the network traffic significantly which leads to congestion. That's why many in-network processing techniques are being used to reduce the packet transmissions inside WSN. Saving resources such as energy is the prime concern of the researches in industry as well as academics.

Further mostly transmission control protocol users transport layer for reliable communication. But due to short communication in IoT, TCP is not sufficient. As TCP needs more time for setting up connection control but the volume of data transfers is very low in IoT, thus TCP is impractical for IoT works on two principles.

Point 1 *The various large amount of data is transmitted at the same time.*
Point 2 *Due to heterogeneous network IoT nodes moves onto other networks,* thus increase in the network node (Table 1).

Table 1. Difference between congestion detection between IoT and WSN

Parameters	IoT	WSN
Property	WSN + Internet + Cloud Storage + Mob/Web application	Things connected to wireless network and gather data or monitor the environment by sensor nodes
Interaction layer	Application layer	Transport layer
Application layer protocol	UDP	TCP/UDP
Mechanism	Various back-off algorithm at CoAP	Routing schemes with centralized strategy, dedicated scheme with distributed strategy
Gateway	6lowpan	IEEE 802.15.4

3 Problem Formulation

CoAP based systems are designed for simple electronic devices that allow them to interact over internet. However, targeted low power device might not be capable enough to handle large no of requests and data loses. The main objective of network is to have reliable communication but in a congested network a reliable retransmission of ACK is necessary. So, there arise many congestion control problems like accidental collision or cross layer detection between sender and client or when the MAX_RE-TRANSMIT counter value reached and the message ACK is not reached. So, taking all this into account backoff algorithm like exponential backoff algorithm and Fibonacci backoff algorithm developed. But these algorithms work according to the traffic load there is not accuracy in them. Further there is a problem in implementation of CoAP over streaming services for the multicast and asynchronous message exchange. Thus, retrieved multiple data blocks by a single message that are loss due to accidental collision and channel error tis somehow reduce backoff delay the congestion.

All these approaches minimize congestion in a network but for more reliability in a congested network new CoAP Congested Mechanism Approach (CoCoA) was proposed. It uses a variable RTO estimator for the estimation of the ACK message to reduce congestion in the network. It was compared with default CoAP control mechanism. As a result, it performs better than Default CoAP. By changing parameters of CoCoA like variable backoff factors, backoff thresholds, and initial and maximum

RTOs, new scheme was proposed known as CoCoA-Fast (CoCoA-F). in this it gives throughput same but retransmission increases as compared to CoCoA but throughput of CoAP is still more. For more analysis to distinguish between wireless losses and congestion losses a 4-State Estimator scheme is introduced. Which reduces disproponate RTT value. Further we will be enhancing CoAP for reducing latency, data losses by adding request handling mechanism which will terminate and reestablish request connection in case if device is too busy and a re-transmission mechanism will be implemented to reduce lags and back-off delays in request processing. This may improve application performance in congested network (Fig. 1).

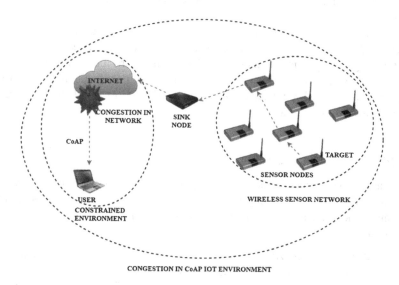

CONGESTION IN CoAP IOT ENVIRONMENT

Fig. 1. Detection of congestion in application layer of CoAP IoT environment.

4 Mechanism of Various Congestion Control in CoAP

Work has been done in WSN related to the congestion control mechanism. But existing congestion control protocols cannot be directly applied to the CoAP in IoT as they are lack in reliability, not able to flow control in UDP (User Datagram Protocol and devices are restricted due to its Low-Power and Lossy networks. So, in this section congestion control protocols are presented which are reliable to the application layer to the CoAP.

4.1 Traditional CoAP Congestion Control with Exponential Back-off

Traditional protocol is not applicable on the low data volume application protocols such as CoAP. Here RTT (Round Trip Time) is used for the calculation of RTO (Retransmission Time Out). In it upto conservative fixed value of 3 s when no RTT estimated can be obtained, controlling the transmission behavior by not sending more than one UDP datagram per RTT on average to a destination, detecting packet loss and exponential back-off [2] the transmission timer when a lost event is occurred.

In the back-off algorithm CoAP must track two endpoints first for each confirmable message it sends, the track should be maintained for its acknowledgement (or reset) known as timeout and a counter is maintained if there is any retransmission of message. Here an initial ACK_TIMEOUT is marked for a random duration between [ACK_-TIMEOUT] and [ACK_TIMEOUT * ACK_RANDOM_FACTOR]. In this case when time out is occurred and retransmission counter is less than MAX_RETRANSMIT the retransmission timeout is incremented and time out is doubled. If MAX_RE-TRANSMIT is reached before the acknowledgement, then the message is cancelled and gives the information of the failure otherwise the transmission was considered to be successful.

The main problems that can arise in the tradition congestion control may be case of the accidental collision or the cross-layer detection between the requestor when sender may be cancel the confirmable message ACK even before the MAX_RETRASMIT counter value has reached. In this case receiver, may elicit some different ACK for the message which has not been detected. Here the ACK was lost and there is no need for the retransmission of the request.

4.2   Adaptive Backoff Algorithm

Traditional internet protocol is not directly applicable to the IoT as due to its resource limitation of the devices. For this Binary Exponential Backoff or Truncated Binary Exponential Backoff algorithms are used for the retransmission of the missed congestion in the networks.

Exponential *Backoff Algorithm* [3]. In this algorithm whether the collision over between two nodes it takes sometimes to retransmit. Then a random value(k) is taken from $(0 \ldots 2n - 1)$ when waiting time calculate by k * Tslot. As in the algorithm whenever the retransmission attempts increase exponentially. But there is a drawback in this algorithm as after each collision window size increases which also increases the waiting time of nodes to access the channel and there is also loss of channel bandwidth (Fig. 2).

Fibonacci Backoff Algorithm. The Fibonacci equation $fib(n) = fib(n - 1) + fib(n - 2)$ and $fib(0) = 0$, $fib(1) = 1$ where $n \geq 0$. Here in it the waiting time increase slowly but as when there is more collision between the IoT nodes the increment factor is decreased. Here drawback of this algorithm is that as the timeout value is small which led to unnecessary retransmission within the nodes (Fig. 3).

The conclusion and outcome of these algorithm are in Exponential Backoff Algorithm rapidly increases for the packet delay if there is low traffic in the networks. But for Fibonacci Backoff Algorithm it slowly increases for packet delay if there is low traffic. Thus, according both the algorithms the change according to the traffic load and this phenomenon is termed as Adoptive Backoff Algorithm.

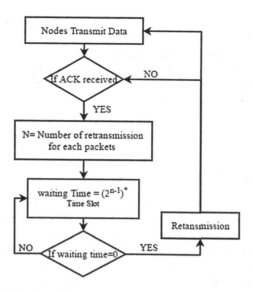

Fig. 2. Flow chart for exponential backoff algorithm [3]

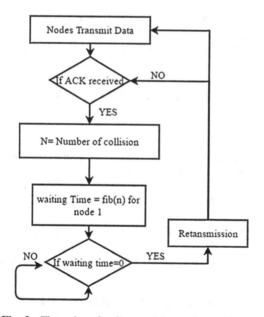

Fig. 3. Flow chart for fibonacci backoff algorithm [3]

4.3 Effective Steaming Over CoAP

The main purpose of this scheme is that it handles the packet losses due to accidental collision or channel error and reduces the effect unnecessary back-off delay. Here the efficiency of the packets sends in the form of block over the CoAP layer

(Web Based Layer). In the streaming scheme the data packets which are send over lossless and lossy networks [4].

The proposed Block Request and Recovery (BRR) mechanism works with the multiple blocks. The multiple block is request with the one block request (BREQ). If the network is not congested, then multiple blocks are retrieved by a single BREQ request. This will enhance the throughput of the network. But in case of congested network retrieving multiple block with a single BREQ request will make the channel busy for longer time without increasing throughput. So, BREQ should be determined carefully.

4.4   Alternate Congestion Control Algorithms

Default CoAP congestion control protocol reliability based upon retransmission timeout (RTO) mechanism and Exponential Backoff Algorithm is used but for more advance algorithm is used but for more advance congestion control a new alternative congestion control a new alternative congestion control algorithm is proposed known as CoAP simple Congestion Control/Advance (CoCoA) [5].

In this paper evaluates the performance of the default CoAP for congestion network with the proposed alternate CoCoA RTO was updated by measured RTTs value. The following are the RTT based algorithms.

TCP Based RTO Algorithm. In this algorithm RTO value is calculated using smoothed average of the RTT(SRTT) and RTT variation (RTTVAR). Initially the value of RTO is set to atleast 1. After the 1st RTT measurement SRTT value is set as R and value of RTOVAR is set as R/2. Thus, RTO is calculated as.

$$RTO = SRTT + max(G * k * RTTVAR) \tag{1}$$

Where G = clock granularity
k = 4

On subsequent updating of RTT we update value of RTO and get R', SRTT and RTTVAR value from the following equations

$$SRTT = (1 - \alpha) * SRTT + \alpha * R' \tag{2}$$

$$RTTVAR = (1 - \beta) * RTTVAR + \beta * |SRTT - R'| \tag{3}$$

When RTO timer expires the value of RTO is doubles on the subsequent retransmissions.

CoCoA Algorithm. CoCoA runs two RTO estimators for estimation which are: a strong estimators which uses ACKs of the original transmissions and a weak estimator that uses ACKs of transmissions. Following are the equations to find overall RTO estimators for strong and weak estimators.

$$RTO = 0.256 * E_{weak} + 0.75 * RTO \tag{4}$$

$$RTO = 0.5 * E_{strong} + 0.5 * RTO \qquad (5)$$

Where initially value of RTO is 2 s.

CoCoA uses variable backoff factor depending upon estimated RTO but for TCP it uses fixed backoff factor which is 2. If value of RTO is between 1 s and 3 s the backoff factor is 2 i.e. the whole equation of RTO is multiplied by 2. Below 1 s backoff factor is 3 but when backoff factor is above 3 s backoff factor is 1.5.

For the conclusion of the CoCoA and Two TCP-based Congestion algorithm known as alternative congestion control mechanism proposed by IETF. The result show that Default CoAP algorithm is better in higher time completion time that Alternative Congestion Algorithm but it is more scalable and efficient that Default CoAP in high congestion network.

4.5   CoCoA (Advance Congestion Control Protocol CoAP)

There is a restriction in the congestion control mechanism in UDP based application such as in CoAP due to its Low Power and Lossy Networks CoCoA for CoAP deals more efficiently to handle the congestion in the network. For the confirmable messages and ACKs it uses RTTs (Round Trip Times) for the packet exchange in CoAP between two motes i.e. sensors motes to calculate parameterized Retransmission Time-out (RTO) that is calculated over time which depends on the RTT value calculated by the motes. Some experiments in paper [6, 7] for the evaluation of parameters to distinguish between different congestion control algorithms in IoT. The dynamically used and approached congestion control mechanism is standardized by IETF is CoAP and CoCoA algorithms which is further discussed below.

Here in this paper [8] a comparative study of CoAP and CoCoA for congestion control Protocol is performed. For the experiment Contiki operating system was used a firmware for the sensor motes and implemented in the Cooja simulation framework. For the evaluation, a basic grid tropology of 18 motes or clients sending data to the data collector or server and a router which helps to connect the sensor network within the internet. RPL was setup before the experiment was performed and for the motes connectivity its waits for 180 s. Various traffic was generated from 0.5 s to 60 s to study the behavior of the algorithm in lossy scenarios. In this scenario of no wireless lose with different packet frequency there is a same throughput seen in CoAP and CoCoA. But with packet with frequency 2packets/sec CoCoA has higher throughput. Further in case of lossy environment throughput of CoAP is better that CoCoA it is due to losses are proportion to distance. But for retransmission CoCoA performs better than CoAP.

4.6   Congestion Avoidance Algorithm in SNS Environment

As the no of devices increases in the IoT network there is a burst of traffic which cause a congestion in the network. Here in this paper [9] a new flow congestion algorithm has been proposed which is controlled by the network in SDN (Software Defined Networking) environment. The main purpose of congestion control by this protocol is link utilization which is calculated by the SDN controller and then OpenFlow configuration protocol is applied to switches by recalculated rerouting algorithm.

OpenFlow has the logically centralized controller that holds the single control plane for the network. Many a devices containing only data planes will respond to the command given by centralized controller. All the network paths in the network and command are described by the OpenFlow controller. Thus this paradigm was implied to SDN environment to simplify and optimize the network (Figs. 4, 5 and Tables 2, 3).

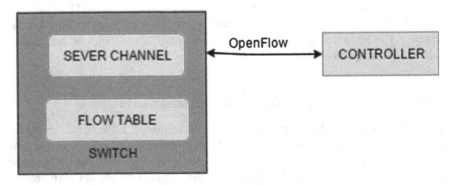

Fig. 4. Connection between the control plane and data plane

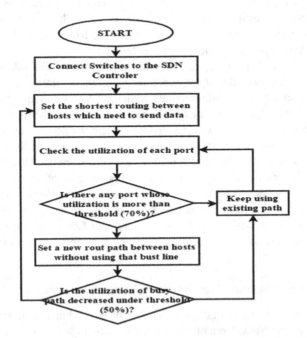

Fig. 5. Flow chart for description of SDN network working [9]

Table 2. Output evaluation of different congestion algorithms

Protocols	Output evaluation
Default CoAP	–
Effective streaming algorithm	Latency is under 1.2 s and throughput is 32% enhancement than default CoAP
Exponential backoff algorithm	Algorithm rapidly increases for the packet delay if there is low traffic in the networks
Fibonacci backoff algorithm	Algorithm slowly increases for packet delay if there is low traffic
CoCoA	Higher throughput than default CoAP
CoCoA- F	Throughput is same, retransmission increases than CoCoA, throughput less than default CoAP
4-state estimator scheme	CoCoA 4-state-strong achieves 35–60% higher throughput as compared to the default CoCoA scheme, with only 20% more retransmissions
Flow control algorithm	Minimize the high congestion by reset the flow

Table 3. Comparing different congestion control parameters

Protocol	Congestion notification	Congestion control	Evaluation type	Evaluation parameters	Compared with
Tradition CoAP	–	Back-Off algorithm	Simulation	–	Default
Adaptive backoff algorithm	Serial port and hyperterminal window	Exponential backoff algorithm	Arduino board	Throughput and mobility speed	Adaptive backoff algorithm
Adaptive backoff algorithm	Serial port and hyperterminal window	Fibonacci backoff algorithm	Arduino board	Throughput and mobility speed	Adaptive backoff algorithm
Effective streaming algorithm	Block Wise transfer	Multiple data blocks	Simulation Ns3	Latency, throughput	Default CoAP
Alternate congestion control algorithms	RTO Estimators	CoCoA and two TCP-based congestion algorithm	Netem Linux emulator and californium	Client completion time, scalability, efficiency	Default CoAP
Cocoa	RRT	Two RTO estimator algorithm (strong, weak)	Contiki Os Cooja simulation	Throughput in lossy and lossless environment	Default CoAP
CoCoA-F	RRT	Cocoa algorithm	Contiki Os Cooja simulation	Throughput in lossy environment	CoCoA and default CoAP

(continued)

Table 3. (*continued*)

Protocol	Congestion notification	Congestion control	Evaluation type	Evaluation parameters	Compared with
4-state estimator scheme	Variable backoff factor	Cocoa-strong algorithm	Contiki OS Cooja simulation	Distinguish between the wireless losses and congestion losses	–
SDN environment	Using VLC player Application size 10 k Byte avg bitrate 240 kbps	Flow control algorithm	Mininet and Onos with Wireshark	Throughput, RTT avg,	Legacy network

5   Conclusion

CoAP specifies various congestion control mechanism for the reliability of the network. In this paper, we carried out working and evaluation parameters for various CoAP mechanism such as Default CoAP, Effective Streaming Algorithm, Adaptive backoff algorithm, CoCoA and congestion is SDM environment. It has been observed that congestion in loss less environment is less than lossy environment. Thus, this leads to the retransmission of message which causes latency and less throughput in the network. To some extend CoCoA minimize the latency and throughput in the network as compared to default CoAP control mechanism. It uses 4-state estimator scheme to make network more reliable. Further we will be working on re-transmission mechanism which will be implemented to reduce lags and back-off delays in the request processing in congested network. This may improve the network performance in case of congestion.

References

1. Atzori, L., Iera, A., Morabito, G.: The Internet of Things: a survey. Comput. Netw. **54**(15), 2787–2805 (2010)
2. Tobergte, D.R., Curtis, S.: RFC 7252 - the constrained application protocol (CoAP). J. Chem. Inf. Model. **53**(9), 1689–1699 (2013)
3. Swarna, M., Ravi, S., Anand, M.: Adaptive backoff algorithm for congestion control in IoT. **9**(4), 205–214 (2016)
4. Choi, G., Kim, D.: Efficient streaming over CoAP, 476–478 (2016)
5. Järvinen, I., Daniel, L., Kojo, M.: Experimental evaluation of alternative congestion control algorithms for constrained application protocol (CoAP), p. 5 (2015)
6. Betzler, A., Gomez, C., Demirkol, I., Paradells, J.: CoAP congestion control for the Internet of Things, 154–160 (2016)

7. Chen, Y., Kunz, T.: Performance evaluation of IoT protocols under a constrained wireless access network. In: 2016 International Conference Selected Topics in Mobile Wireless Networking, MoWNeT 2016 (2016)

8. Bhalerao, R., Subramanian, S.S., Pasquale, J.: An analysis and improvement of congestion control in the CoAP Internet-of-Things protocol. In: 2016 13th IEEE Annual Consumer Communications Networking Conference CCNC 2016, pp. 889–894 (2016)

9. Song, S., Lee, J., Son, K., Jung, H., Lee, J.: A congestion avoidance algorithm in SDN environment. In: International Conference on Information Networking, March 2016, pp. 420–423 (2016)

Increasing Route Availability in Internet of Vehicles Using Ant Colony Optimization

Nitika Chowdhary[1(✉)] and Pankaj Deep Kaur[2]

[1] Department of Computer Science and Engineering,
Lyallpur Khalsa College of Engineering, Jalandhar, India
nitikachowdhary@ieee.org
[2] Department of Computer Science and Engineering,
GNDU RC Jalandhar, Jalandhar, India
pankajdeep.csejal@gndu.ac.in

Abstract. Smart City, where a large number of self-configurable and intelligent devices communicate with each other, provides a platform for collaborative decision making processes affecting virtually every other device present in the ecosystem. Internet of Vehicles (IoV) forms a major part of thus ecosystem that comprises of mobile vehicles capable of generating, storing and moreover processing the data flowing through the system. The vehicles continuously communicate with each other and with the external environment to collect and process real-time information. This collaboration provides a means to build up optimized routing decisions that may lead to the improvement in overall congestion suffered by the network. In this paper, we apply two optimization algorithms Any Colony and Firefly Optimization, on the real-time data collected from various vehicular sources to provide them optimized and congestion-free routes. Various road parameters have been considered that may affect the selection of a particular route toward the destination. The results of experimental setup, conducted using two open source simulators NS2 and SUMO, have shown a predominant enhancement by reducing the average travelling time of the vehicles in the complete system taken into consideration.

Keywords: Route optimization · Internet of vehicles · Ant colony optimization

1 Introduction

Internet of Things (IoT) is collectively comprised of astute self-configuring technologies with RFID tags, physical attributes and simulated personalities which work together in collaboration with each other. As the actuators or sensors deployed in IoT are capable of exchanging data among different platforms, so they become efficient enough to be used in numerous smart applications such as the renowned Smart City application. Upon integration of living and non-living world, a knowledgeable environment is created by IoT [1, 2].

Short range communication devices such as Radio Frequency Identifier (RFID), Zigbee, Millimeter Wave, Bluetooth etc. are used for forwarding this sensed data to vehicles. Smart infrastructures known as Road Side Units (RSUs) are deployed road

© Springer Nature Singapore Pte Ltd. 2017
D. Singh et al. (Eds.): ICAICR 2017, CCIS 712, pp. 318–331, 2017.
DOI: 10.1007/978-981-10-5780-9_29

side which integrate themselves, make connectivity to RSU clouds and thus help guiding road operations to vehicles. In Vehicle-to-Vehicle communication, a vehicle might join an RSU if vehicle is coming in its range or might leave the set of vehicles of a particular RSU if no longer coming under that range (as shown in Fig. 1).

In IoV, intelligent onboard units are deployed for gathering target information, vehicle's status details, driving location and profile information. Likewise, between vehicles and data capturing devices (onboard sensors which collect information through various geographical positions), V2S (Vehicle to Sensor) communication is built up. V2P provide interaction between people and vehicles whereas V2V provides interaction between different vehicles. Other communication is done through V2B that provides various business applications. Vehicles pass the received information to the targeted node and thus assist their neighboring vehicles in routing. Objects in IoV environment, thus provide entertainment along with safe and secure travelling to the onboard passengers.

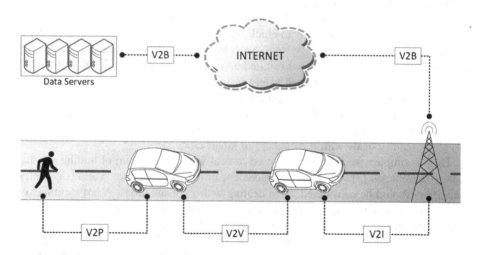

Fig. 1. Architecture of Internet of Vehicles

Vehicle Routing Problem (VRP) is a well-known optimization issue that has been prevalent in the area of traffic systems and navigations. From the literature, we observed that a large portion of navigation systems and route optimization have been undertaken by considering only two metrics, distance and time. Contrariwise, in a real-world environment, there are many complicated attributes that need to be undertaken (path quality, user's satisfaction, etc.) along with the traditional attributes like distance and time. This study aims at identifying a set of possible low cost routes that can somehow reduce overall cost in terms of multi-objective parameters. The studies have shown that traditional mechanisms targeting VRP, for instance, Dijkstra, A-star algorithms, are not quite efficient in solving multi-path and multi-objective attribute routing in IoV. As a result, it is imperative to build an efficient and advanced multi-optimal function technique that could enable identification of optimal routes in an IoV environment.

The paper organization is as follows. Section 2 discusses the related previous works. Section 3 discusses the parameters and approaches used in this paper for route optimization i.e., ant colony and firefly optimization algorithms. Section 4 presents the simulation parameters that were used to carry out the desired experiment. Section 5 provides a discussion on the results obtained from the experimental setup. Finally, Sect. 6 concludes this study.

2   Related Previous Works

Dynamic topology of a network is a deciding factor for performance of any routing protocol in IoV and application feasibility. A practical investigation of time and space features is being provided using various key metrics. Real-world topology of roads and real-time data is being analyzed to procreate actual traffic flows. Emergency is a major concern among vehicles. A comprehensive view of vehicle emergency warning system is being detailed including V2V (Vehicle to Vehicle) Communication and roadside infrastructure. In the proposed system, vehicles get alternative route information in detail. Increasing traffic density has resulted into large number of accidents. Eventually, government needs to improve road safety instead of road quality. Smart cities utilize the concept of intelligent road transportation system.

Below we discuss some of the related works that have dealt with the same problem. The context of their approach applicability is somewhat different from our approach as this study mainly deals with the concept of smart cities.

Earlier, simplex parameters were used to deal with the problem of finding optimal routes for vehicles [3]. With the advancement in the infrastructure, various complex parameters should be considered when dealing with such situations. A large number of applications also serve the purpose of providing such similar information. Driver oriented route optimization was first introduced by Choi et al. [4].

Different optimization algorithms including Dijkstra [5], A-star, genetic [6], etc. have been applied for the same. However, the context of applications has been limited to non-compound situations. Dethloff [7] as formulated equation for effective logistics between the source and multiple destinations that minimizes the total distance travelled. Meta-heuristics have been widely studies in a number of studies like, Ai and Kachitvichyanukul [8], Gajpal and Abad [9], and Montané and Galvão [10].

Sahoo et al. [11] used Ant Colony Optimization technique for optimizing the vehicle routes in VANETs. They combined ACO with zone based clustering to further enhance the routing results. AbdAllah et al. [12] solves dynamic routing problem by applying multiple modifications to the genetic algorithm. Their modified genetic algorithm outperformed a number of previously published literature works available on dynamic route management.

Oranj et al. [13] designed an algorithm for efficient routing based on ant colony optimization and DYMO (Dynamic MANET On-demand) protocol. Their algorithm can effectively monitor changes in the environment to perform re-routing of vehicles. Pan et al. [14] solved the problem issues pertaining to the privacy of a vehicle location and intensive computation resulting in increasing vehicles. They proposed a scheme named DIVERT, which can effectively avoid forming any type of congestion in the network by performing dynamic re-routing of the selected vehicles.

2.1 Problem Formulation

Any road network can be portrayed as a specific set of nodes and edges. Nodes act as intersections whereas edges act as the path or the road linking those intersections. Let G be a graph that defines a particular road network. Then $G = (N, E)$ represents the set of nodes and edges. For every edge E, there lies a set of two edges between which this road is defined. A particular edge has its own characteristics defined by multiple metrics. Based on these characteristics, an optimal route is selected. We have based our study on identifying sequential set of edges from a specific source toward a particular destination.

3   Optimization Algorithms

In this paper, we use two optimization techniques Ant Colony and Firefly, to find minimum cost routes for a particular source and destination pair. This section discusses these two optimization algorithms in detail.

3.1   Ant Colony Optimization

ACO is population based meta-heuristic optimization technique, which allows researchers to resolve problems related to NP-hard combinatorial optimization [15]. ACO has been quite popular when dealing with VRP and the existing literature has also considered solving other issues like parking recommendation, etc. using this technique. When using ACO for vehicle routing, usually a record is maintained that stores already visited nodes and the approximate travelling times required to reach them respectively.

The procedure followed by the Ant Colony Optimization algorithms is as follows. At first, the ants perform arbitrary chase for nourishment and after that re-enter their nest on discovering one. During their travel, they set down pheromone, a fragrant substance, on the land. The pheromone amount is in direct connection to the sustenance amount. It gets to be distinctly less demanding for next arrangement of ants for they would be pulled in by pheromone trails as opposed to strolling in an arbitrary manner.

The more would be the pheromone, the more ants would be pulled in towards that way which would additionally expand the pheromone amount on it, constituting it to be the best way. In the long run, all ants would get pulled in to that way. Different ants watch the trail and get pulled in towards it. The trail will accordingly develop rapidly. This essential can subsequently take care of the combinatorial enhancement issues. The flow chart depicting Ant Colony Optimization algorithm is shown in Fig. 2.

This trail finally defines the optimized route. The algorithm for ant colony optimization is shown in Algorithm 1.

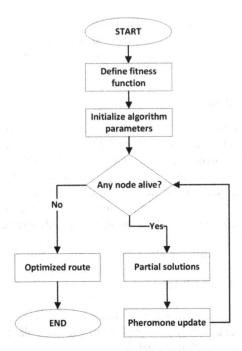

Fig. 2. Flow chart of ant colony optimization

Algorithm 1: Ant colony optimization pseudo code
01:   **Input:** Prob$_{Size}$, *Populationsize, n, α, γ, Θ, g0*
02:   **Output:** *O*
03:   *O* ← Solution (Prob$_{Size}$);
04:   *Ocost* ← CostCalculation (*Ph*);
05:   Init ← $\dfrac{1.0}{Prob_{size} \; X \; O_{cost}}$;
06:   Pheromone ← Initialize(init);
07:   **while** Stop() **do**
08:   **for** *x* = 1 **to** *n* **do**
09:   *Pi* ← Solution(Pheromone, Prob$_{Size}$, *γ*, *g0*);
10:   *Pxcost* ← CostCalculation (*Px*);
11:   **if** *Pxcost* ≤ *Ocost* **then**
12:   *Ocost* ← *Pxcost*;
13:   *O* ← *Px*;
14:   **end**
15:   LocalDecay (Pheromone, *Px, Pxcost, Θ*);
16:   **End**
17:   GlobalDecay (Pheromone, *Pbest,Ocost, α*);
18:   **end**
19:   **return** *O*;

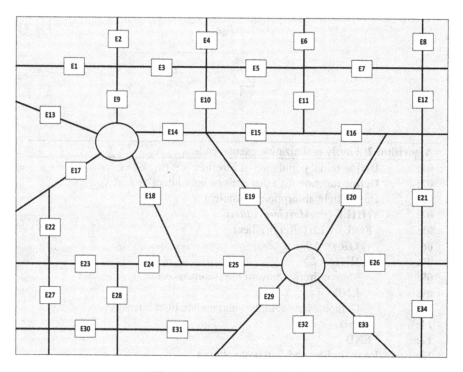

Fig. 3. Fabricated road network

At first, we have taken n ants, every one of which is appointed an irregular starting point on the domain. Ants develop a course by always strolling to another point by means of probabilistic control of their closest neighbor move. At the point when the trail has been developed totally, pheromone amount is changed to upgrade the best trail. There are fixed iteration to meet a halting criterion.

θ refers to the coefficient of local pheromone whose value is 0.1. γ refers to the heuristic coefficient and is set between 2 and 5. $g0$ defines greediness factor whose value is 0.9 and n is the total number of ants.

3.2   Firefly Optimization

Firefly optimization is a meta-heuristic algorithm proposed by Yang [16]. This algorithm is based on the flashing behavior of fireflies. In contrast to ACO, where other ants are attracted by pheromones, fireflies use a flash signal system to attract other flies. Some pre-requisite assumptions in this algorithm are that the fireflies are uni-sexual, attractiveness if directly proportional to their respective brightness, and a firefly will move randomly if there is no firefly having greater brightness with the current firefly. Equations (1) and (2) depicts the functions corresponding to attractiveness and distance between two fireflies respectively. Algorithm 2 represents the pseudocode of the firefly optimization algorithm.

$$\beta(r) = \beta_0 e^{-\gamma r^2} \tag{1}$$

$$r_{ij} = \sqrt{\sum_{k=1}^{d} \left(x_{i,k} - x_{j,k}\right)^2} \tag{2}$$

Algorithm 2: Firefly optimization pseudo code
01:      **Define** Initial population of Fireflies X = $(x_1, x_2, x_3, \ldots\ldots, x_n)^{\mathrm{T}}$
02:      **Define** function $f(X_i)$ that defines light intensity L_i at X_i
03:      **Define** light absorption coefficient μ
04:      **WHILE** ($t < MaxGeneration$)
05:       **FOR** $i = 1{:}n$ (all n fireflies)
06:        **FOR** $j = 1{:}i$
07:         **IF** ($L_j > L_i$)
08:          Move firefly i toward j in d-dimension
09:         **END**
10:         Compute new solutions and update light intensity
11:        **END**
12:       **END**
13:      Rank fireflies and find best solution
14:      **END**

4 Simulation Scenarios

In this section, various simulation parameters like input map, road defining parameters and simulation tools are outlined.

4.1 Input Road Network

To study the effect of optimization on a road network, we built a custom road network with different road elements with varying parameters so as to provide comprehensive variations between routes. Our road network consists of 34 edges providing different experience to the travelers. The optimized route defines spanning subset of the complete road network. Figure 3 shows the road network that has been used to perform different simulations. The subsequent subsection defines the road parameters that were considered in this study for assessing the quality of a road.

4.2   Input Road Metrics

The following road metrics are used to evaluate the characteristics of a road element defined by a particular edge.

- *Distance, M_1.* This metric defines the length of a particular road element. Routes may be selected based on their length as shorter router will be preferred more as compared to the other longer routes. Other metrics also decide the selection of the optimal route.
- *Cost, M_2.* This metric defines the cost of travelling through a particular road element. The cost usually comprises toll tax or any other monetary expenses required to travel on that road element.
- *Congestion, M_3.* Real-time data of congestion in the particular road element assists in deciding the final optimized route so as to avoid any further congestion in the network. This value rapidly changes with time depending on the number of vehicles using this road element.

This set of three parameters $<M_1, M_2, M_3>$ is assigned to each road element of the map. Table 1 shows the parameter values of all the road elements in the road network that were used to carry out the experiments. Figure 4 shows the flow chart of our complete experimental setup used to build and evaluate different scenarios.

Table 1. Normalized metric values of edges in the road network

Edge	M_1	M_2	M_3
E1	5	3.71	5.85
E2	8	9.04	7.15
E3	6	7.3	8.69
E4	6	9.25	3.65
E5	9	5.98	0.06
E6	8	8.82	5.09
E7	9	6.01	1.94
E8	8	3.04	0.69
E9	6	0.96	4.74
E10	7	0.69	2.48
E11	10	4.38	7.09
E12	7	5.77	2.9
E13	7	3.31	3.9
E14	5	2.2	8.77
E15	6	9.39	1.52
E16	6	3.52	7.75
E17	5	1.83	8.36
E18	5	7.25	3.26
E19	5	5.3	5.57
E20	7	8.7	4.81

(continued)

Table 1. (*continued*)

Edge	M_1	M_2	M_3
E21	8	1.52	5.61
E22	7	6.16	0.82
E23	5	3.43	4.68
E24	9	7.27	9.15
E25	8	9.9	8.88
E26	9	3.78	3.74
E27	9	9.2	5.48
E28	6	9.06	5.75
E29	6	7.46	7.97
E30	7	1.11	7.25
E31	7	7.74	2.78
E32	9	3.05	2.28
E33	10	5.1	7.64
E34	10	8.53	9.86

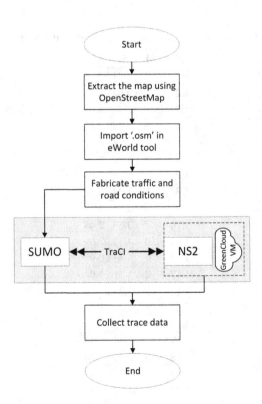

Fig. 4. Flow diagram of experimental setup

The simulations are performed on two open source software tools, NS2[1] and SUMO[2], which have gained high reputation among the researchers. Table 2 shows various parameters that control the simulation environment.

Table 2. Simulation parameters

Parameter	Value
Technology	ITS-G5/IEEE 80211.p
Frequency band	10 MHz @5.9 GHz
Fading	log-distance
TSD, TSM size	100 Bytes
Vehicle velocity	Uniform (20 m/s - 40 m/s)
Data collection window	5 s
Optimization window	30 s
Data rate	Variable
Interface type	Wireless Physical Interface
Mobility model	Random way point
Number of vehicles	100, 140, 180, ..., 380

The mobility traces of the road network taken into consideration are initially prepared using the tool SUMO. These mobility traces are then used in NS2 to perform the required operations of optimization and re-routing to achieve higher performance in terms of vehicle travelling time.

5 Experiment Results and Discussion

The data is collected after every 5 s and route optimization is performed after every 30 s. Without applying the optimization, vehicles follow randomly selected route toward their respective destinations.

This leads to congestion in some road elements and increase in the cumulative expenses incurred as a result. When the optimization technique is applied, the road elements with high real time traffic congestion is downgraded and is not preferred as a possible route by the vehicles.

Therefore, if in any case congestion occurs, further deterioration of the congestion can be avoided by optimizing the routes of other vehicles. Apart from this, other factors of the road elements like cost and distance also aid in re-routing process. Thus, an optimization that considers all such factors is bound to provide a driver friendly routes in such a way that there is significant gain in the overall performance of the network.

---

[1] www.isi.edu/nsnam/ns/.

[2] sumo.dlr.de/.

Figures 5 and 6 shows the increase in the cumulative travelling time of the network with increase in the number of vehicles for ant colony and firefly optimizations respectively. As the number of vehicles increases, congestion is likely to occur. This congestion during normal conditions could result in high loss to the network in terms of time. However, with optimization at hand, it is clearly visible that the time does not significantly increase.

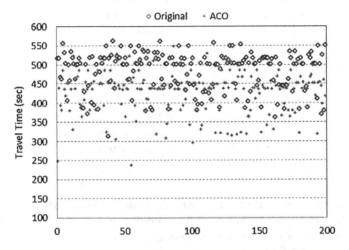

Fig. 5. Travelling time of different vehicles with ACO

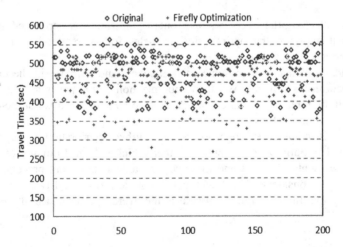

Fig. 6. Travelling time of different vehicles with firefly optimization

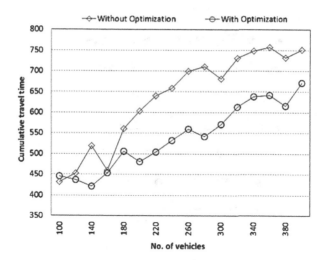

Fig. 7. Cumulative travelling time with increase in the number of vehicles in the network

Figure 7 depicts a significant enhancement of the traveling time of vehicles with and without application of the optimization technique. The average of the travelling time during normal conditions was quite high as compared to the travelling time when the optimization was applied. Not only is the travelling time improved, but the cost of migrating through a route is also diminished as the routes with less cost are selected provided they are not congested.

Table 3 represents the routes between three set of edges. It only represents the two least cost routes possible between the edge pair set. The cost of getting from one edge to another edge is also given in Table 3. Figure 8 highlights the time taken by both the optimization algorithms, ant colony and firefly, in order to compute the least cost routes between the edges. It is evident from the results that ant colony optimization algorithm was taking less time in contrast to the time taken by firefly optimization algorithm with the increase in number of vehicles.

Table 3. Set of possible routes between the selected points

R	Path	Cost
	E1 to E33	
R_1	E1 → E9 → E10 → E15 → E16 → E20 → E33	192
R_3	E1 → E3 → E5 → E7 → E12 → E21 → E26 → E33	240
	E22 to E12	
R_1	E22 → E17 → E14 → E15 → E16 → E12	164
R_3	E22 → E23 → E24 → E25 → E20 → E12	179
	E30 to E21	
R_1	E30 → E31 → E29 → E26 → E21	130
R_3	E30 → E28 → E24 → E25 → E26 → E21	171

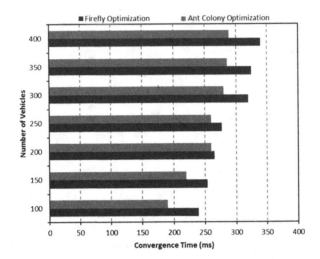

Fig. 8. Travelling time of different vehicles

6 Conclusion

Internet of Vehicles (IoV) is an integral part of overall Internet of Things (IoT) infrastructure. The conventional Vehicular Ad-hoc Networks have gone an inevitable evolution into a smart and self-sustaining transportation technology to server future generation needs. An important aspect of such technology is to provide emergency related services. IoV is also capable in providing the support for safety message dissemination in case of any emergency related issues.

Vehicles serve as standalone nodes of communication that can sense data, processes data, and even disseminate the required data to the surrounding environments. Hence, coordination of the vehicles in the system will boost the performance of the overall network. In this work, we use ant colony and firefly optimization methods on the locational data received from the network vehicles to provide real-time optimal routes based on the various network element factors. The experiments are performed using NS2 and SUMO, results from which confirms a high degree of improvement in the overall travelling time of a vehicle with application of such optimizations. It is also evident from the results that ant colony optimization algorithm is performing better than the firefly optimization algorithm in terms of both reducing the overall travelling time and time required for computation of least cost routes.

References

1. Medagliani, P., Leguay, J., Duda, A., Rousseau, F., Duquennoy, S., Raza, S., Ferrari, G., Gonizzi, P., Cirani, S., Veltri, L., Monton, M.: Internet of Things Applications-From Research and Innovation to Market Deployment, pp. 287–313. The River Publishers, Amsterdam (2014)

2. Gubbi, J., Buyya, R., Marusic, S., Palaniswami, M.: Internet of things (IoT): a vision, architectural elements, and future directions. Future Gener. Comput. Syst. **29**(7), 1645–1660 (2013)

3. Li, J.: Vehicle routing problem with time windows for reducing fuel consumption. J. Comput. **7**(12), 3020–3027 (2012)

4. Choi, W.-K., Kim, S.-J., Kang, T.-G., Jeon, H.-T.: Study on method of route choice problem based on user preference. In: Apolloni, B., Howlett, R.J., Jain, L. (eds.) KES 2007. LNCS, vol. 4694, pp. 645–652. Springer, Heidelberg (2007). doi:10.1007/978-3-540-74829-8_79

5. Pazooky, S., Rahmatollahi Namin, S., Soleymani, A., Samadzadegan, F.: An evaluation of potentials of genetic algorithm in shortest path problem. In: EGU General Assembly Conference Abstracts, vol. 11, pp. 80–98 (2009)

6. Kanoh, H.: Dynamic route planning for car navigation systems using virus genetic algorithms. Int. J. Knowl. Based Intell. Eng. Syst. **11**(1), 65–78 (2007)

7. Dethloff, J.: Relation between vehicle routing problems: an insertion heuristic for the vehicle routing problem with simultaneous delivery and pick-up applied to the vehicle routing problem with backhauls. J. Oper. Res. Soc. **53**(1), 115–118 (2002)

8. Ai, T.J., Kachitvichyanukul, V.: A particle swarm optimization for the vehicle routing problem with simultaneous pickup and delivery. Comput. Oper. Res. **36**(5), 1693–1702 (2009)

9. Gajpal, Y., Abad, P.: An ant colony system (ACS) for vehicle routing problem with simultaneous delivery and pickup. Comput. Oper. Res. **36**(12), 3215–3223 (2009)

10. Montané, F., Galvão, R.D.: A tabu search algorithm for the vehicle routing problem with simultaneous pick-up and delivery service. Comput. Oper. Res. **33**(3), 595–619 (2006)

11. Sahoo, A., Swain, S.K., Pattanayak, B.K., Mohanty, M.N.: An optimized cluster based routing technique in VANET for next generation network. In: Satapathy, S., Mandal, J., Udgata, S., Bhateja, V. (eds.) Information Systems Design and Intelligent Applications. Advances in Intelligent Systems and Computing, vol. 433, pp. 667–675. Springer, New Delhi (2016). doi:10.1007/978-81-322-2755-7_69

12. AbdAllah, A.M.F., Essam, D.L., Sarker, R.A.: On solving periodic re-optimization dynamic vehicle routing problems. Appl. Soft Comput. **55**, 1–12 (2017)

13. Oranj, A.M., Alguliev, R.M., Yusifov, F., Jamali, S.: Routing algorithm for vehicular ad hoc network based on dynamic ant colony optimization. Int. J. Electron. Electr. Eng. **4**(1), 79–83 (2016)

14. Pan, J.S., Popa, I.S., Borcea, C.: Divert: a distributed vehicular traffic re-routing system for congestion avoidance. IEEE Trans. Mob. Comput. **16**(1), 58–72 (2017)

15. Dorigo, M., Gambardella, L.M.: Ant colony system: a cooperative learning approach to the traveling salesman problem. IEEE Trans. Evol. Comput. **1**(1), 53–66 (1997)

16. Yang, X.-S.: Firefly algorithms for multimodal optimization. In: Watanabe, O., Zeugmann, T. (eds.) SAGA 2009. LNCS, vol. 5792, pp. 169–178. Springer, Heidelberg (2009). doi:10.1007/978-3-642-04944-6_14

Classification Based Network Layer Botnet Detection

Shivangi Garg$^{(\boxtimes)}$ and R.M. Sharma

Department of Computer Engineering, National Institute of Technology,
Kurukshetra, Haryana, India
shvgarg1992@gmail.com, rmsharma123@rediffmail.com

Abstract. Botnets has emerged as the capacious cyber security menace that is encountered by the institutions as well as population around the terrene. It has matured into becoming the primal carrier for launching the most serious menace such as DDOS attacks, spreading of spams, stealing of user's sensitive information (Banking info, credit card info etc.) and more. Generally, the community of common users are unaware of security standards that make them even more susceptible to bot attacks. A sententious amount of research for botnet detection and analysis has been done but significant amount of work has not been done in terms of contributing a community herded tool for bots. We propose an idea to perform filtration and classification on data received by Botflex that can help to reduce processing overhead and throughput of IDS will be improved. Botflex have limited set of detection parameters which are extended in our proposed approach.

Keywords: Botnet · Network layer · Filtration · Classification · Behaviour based IDS

1 Introduction

For any user or system connected to internet, BotNet is undoubtedly a potential security threat to their connectivity and service quality. Any common user including employees of big organizations, government officials or home users who are actively connected to internet, faces various security threats in daily life like scamming, spamming, spear phishing, cyber frauds, denial of service and botnet based DDOS attack [1, 2], as they are integral part of cyberspace. A large swarm of computers acts under the control of a single master mind called attacker via some control centre is called a Botnet. Botnets size varies from network of thousands of computers to more than millions of computers [2, 3]. Currently Botnets are posing a serious menace to the society as they are growing and spreading at an exponential rate.

Basically botnet has at least three-layer network consisting of botherder, bots and a target machine. Botherder sends instructions to bots and as per commands bots attacks the target [2]. Other layers such as control servers and proxies (called as stepping stones) are used to hide the identity of the real attacker and make the network robust and flexible. A basic Botnet network is shown in Fig. 1. Their tremendous size and their specialty of deception and elusion used to shield their identity and spawn them as

© Springer Nature Singapore Pte Ltd. 2017
D. Singh et al. (Eds.): ICAICR 2017, CCIS 712, pp. 332–342, 2017.
DOI: 10.1007/978-981-10-5780-9_30

popular and infamous [4]. It also makes them eligible to operate under radar for longer period of time. Current statistics:

- According to golden state report 2015–14, California bank faced the cyber theft of more than $900,000 and in last four years around 50 million records of Californian have been breached [3]
- kaspersky lab in Q2 of 2016, detected 83,048 mobile ransomware Trojans from a total of 250 millions unique malicious and potentially unwanted objects. [5]
- For mobile devices, Risk Tool malicious software topped the ranking of detected malware. 54 millions unique malign URLs were also determined. [5].
- The percentage of zero day vulnerabilities has been raised by 125% from 2014 to 2015 and every week a new zero day vulnerability is raised [6].

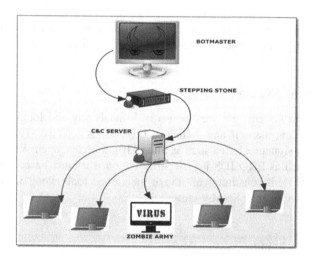

Fig. 1. Basic botnet structure

Due to lack of community driven tool it is very challenging for society to tackle this severe and growing threat. Many techniques have been introduced that make use of powerful IDS systems as an underlying architecture to detect the botnets. After BotHunter [7] which worked on snort IDS, Botflex [8] took few step forward in providing a community driven network based botnet detection tool. Rather than working on signature based IDS, this method uses behavior based IDS, named Bro [9] in order to make it possible to detect unknown botnets, although it also have few limitations, Problems with botflex [8] are following:

- Time taken to process 500 GB data traces is increased by half an hour for basic network intrusion detection system.
- Bro's throughput is reduced by ~ 4 K packets per seconds.

Our approach is to filter and classify the traffic at worker level machines configured with Bro IDS only. Botflex will be integrated with NIDS at controller node only. Ultimately processing time for IDS will decrease as it will directly feed botflex with traffic passed from worker nodes and hence throughput will also increase.

- Other problem is sensor module parameters that are needs to be extended so we have added some more parameters to perform better detection at each lifecycle phase.

The paper is further classified as follows: Sect. 2 gives a comparative literature analysis on earlier detection techniques on network layer. Section 3, discusses the proposed approach and detailed framework along with its working using different modules. Section 4 gives the evaluated results using various factors such as throughput, memory utilization, CPU utilization and finally, Sect. 5 concludes the findings of the paper and future directions.

2 Related Work

The work related to proposed approach is broadly categorized into available IDS systems and existing techniques for network based botnet detection.

2.1 IDS Systems Available

Intrusion detection systems are very powerful in analyzing and logging the network traffic and generating alerts if any malicious behavior is detected. The available IDS systems are either signature based such as Snort [10], Suricata, open WIPS, or behavior based systems such as BRO IDS [9]. Security Onion is a linux based distribution for IDS and NMS [11], it constitutes all above mentioned tools along with many other systems like ELSA, Squirt, Snorby etc.

2.2 Existing Techniques

BotHunter [7] is the first freely available network based detection tool and is based on Snort IDS system. BotHunter works on vertical correlation i.e. it exploits the behavior of an individual host. Specifically, the property of bots of sharing common set of actions during various phases of their lifecycle is exploited by BotHunter. BotHunter monitors a network and activities related to inbound and outbound scanning are captured. Then some malware activity detection and payload analysis is performed and alerts are generated based on Snort rules. But the model has some limitations as it fails to identify unknown botnets and do not capture encrypted c&c communication. Other technique proposed is BotMiner [12] based on horizontal correlation. It exploited the fact that botnet works in coordinated manner so any coordinated pattern points to presence of malicious patterns. Clustering method is used in this approach to make the detection more efficient and refined. This technique is very effective with the detection rate of approx 99%. The problem with this technique is its vulnerability to evasion technique as attacker can easily evade the BotMiner approach by manipulating the communication patterns.

Zhao et al. [13] proposed a novel approach to recognize botnet activity based on behavior analysis of network traffic. It classifies network traffic by using machine learning technique. This method successfully works for encrypted communication protocols as traffic analysis methods are independent of packet payload. Signature based techniques other then BotHunter are [14–16] which work on identifying the unknown botnet in the real time traffic.

Other anomaly based approaches are [12, 17, 18] that performs detection by analyzing the behavior of botnet traffic. The limitations of correlation based approaches is removed by Botflex [8] by employing both vertical and horizontal correlation methods together with a decision module where a CEP engine is used for the first time which is built within a network based IDS.

Botflex is a community-driven domain specific botnet detection solution which is flexible, extensible and having a simple user interface. Gu proposed another detection approach, BotSniffer [19]. The new and basic idea in BotSniffer is that it detects malicious activities based on spatial-temporal correlation and observe similarity patterns in network data that are derived from activities related to botnet. BotSniffer performs well for both IRC and HTTP based botnets. But it is ineffective for unknown bots. Comparison of all above mentioned techniques is shown in the Table 1.

Table 1. Comparison of existing literature survey

	Bothunter	Botsniffer	Botminer	Zhao	Botflex
Correlation	Vertical	Spatial-temporal	Horizontal	Machine learning	Horizontal-vertical
Encryption detection	No	No	Yes	Yes	Yes
Zero-day detection	No	No	Yes	Yes	Yes
Effectiveness (%)					
TPR	79.6	100	99	95	89
FPR	6.6	low	1	5	6.6

3 Proposed Framework

The proposed model basically consists of two modules.

3.1 IDS- Cluster Model

To introduce clustering, three virtual machines are taken running linux system simultaneously on each machine. Two machines are selected as filter machines and one is controller and collector. Set up is shown in Fig. 2. Controller machine is equipped with our NIDS system having Botflex configured on it.

Bro [9] consists of three layers namely network layer, event engine and policy interpreter. The network layer captures the packet from outside traffic using libpcap. This traffic is converted to packet stream and fed to event engine. The input taken

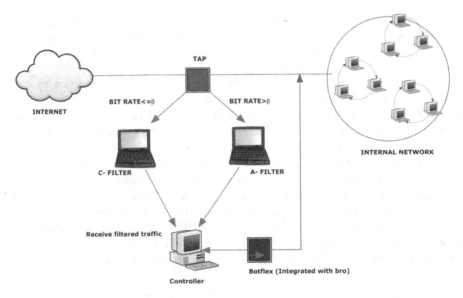

Fig. 2. Experimental set up

by engine is converted into events and data structures. Finally top layer manipulates this received event using pre-defined policies.

Botflex resides in top layer where botnet detection will be done. So our idea is to perform the filtration and data or traffic reduction at filter machines and finally that traffic will be passed to the controller machine. One filter machine is referred as C-filter and other is A-filter. The incoming traffic will be divided into these two, based on the bit rate (using a threshold value β). Generally high bit rate traffic is considered to be having traces of some flooding activity so high bit rate traffic will be passed through A-filter and rest through C-filter. Other model is classification model.

3.2   Classification Model

Here along with basic filtering, classification will be done at each filter machine. As shown in Figs. 3 and 4. In C- filter [12], filtering is done on the communication related parameters or behavioral parameters. First basic filtering will be done on the basis of parameters shown in the Fig. 3. The connections which are not fully established will be filtered out. These traffic traces are primarily generated by scanning activity for e.g. (sender sends SYN packets with pending TCP hand-shake). In white-list filtering, the network flows with well known destinations such as Google, yahoo etc. are filtered out. After basic filtering and white listing, classification will be performed.

Similar activities are performed at A-filter machine as shown in Fig. 4. with some scanning, spamming and other malicious traffic refinement parameters. Classification is the final step here, naïve Bayes classifier is used which worked for the parameters like duration, role, average bytes per packet, average bits per second. After all these filtration

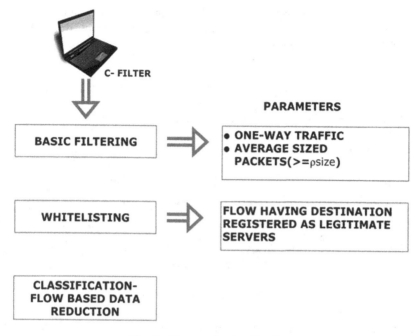

Fig. 3. Communication filtration

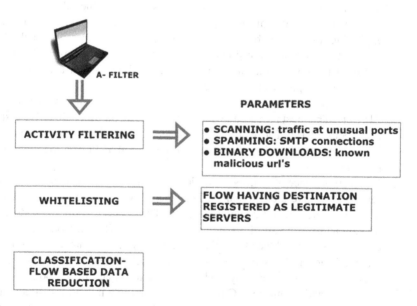

Fig. 4. Activity filtration

the final controller machine having Botflex will receive very fine grained data/packets to perform detection. Botflex need to process only small amount of data to perform botnet detection and its processing time will improve with compare to Bro IDS.

Botnet lifecycle is a key aspect of botnet [2]. Main aim of a researcher is to detect the botnets as early as possible in order to avoid its severe impact. Botnet lifecycle consist of five stages as shown in Fig. 5.

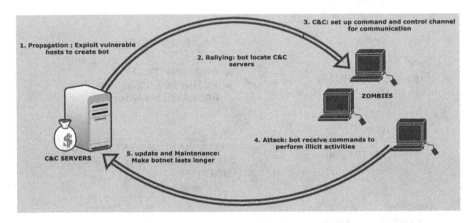

Fig. 5. Different phases in botnet lifecycle

Stage 1: Contagion: This phase includes the various active and passive methods through which botmaster will form its zombie army [1, 2]. Main motive of this phase is to recruit more and more bots for the botnet. Active methods include the scanning of entire internet to search for vulnerable hosts and exploiting the vulnerabilities to inject bot binaries. Passive method of propagation includes web downloads, where websites are specially crafted to install the bot binaries automatically to the host system using specially crafted javascripts or any active content.

Another one is by using infected media like hard drives, pen drives, CD's etc. The most remarkable attack was in 2009 on Iran's SCADA system using Stuxnet [3]. The worm was propagated using USB sticks. Koobface botnet uses social engineering techniques to install and infect the vulnerable host [1].

Stage 2: Connection: once the army is build, now bots need to locate the C&C servers to receive the commands. The C&C servers can be located either by using ip address or by domain name [2]. The bot receive the IP address or domain name as a part of bot binary or separately. The hardcoded addresses can be easily blacklisted by the security researcher that's why seeding method is generally used by p2p botnets. In this method, a list is maintained at each server as is regularly updated as per the state of each bot.

Stage 3: Command and Control: C&C plays a significant role in working of botnet as without C&C botnet is just a random collection of lame machines. C&C communication can be build upon existing protocols like IRC, the communication scheme used in early 2000 or by using http protocol which makes the malicious traffic easy to bypass the firewall rules [2]. But due to their centralized nature these architectures are vulnerable to detection. So botmaster switched to decentralized approach in which even detection of one or more bots does not affect the working of entire botnet which makes detection of entire botnet harder. As per current research social platforms like skype, facebook, VOIP etc. are considered to be the new emerging C&C communication channel [1]. But this architecture has problem of high message delays so a new hybrid communication architecture was evolved which overcome the disadvantages of above mentioned architectures. Other C&C communication can be build upon neoteric protocols [3]. These include the most recent botnet techniques such as social botnet, mobile botnets, cloud botnets. To establish communication channel between bots and C&C server, user accounts on popular social media sites such as facebook were used by whitewell as stepping-stones (social bots). Twitter social engine also being used to develop C&C communication by many popular botnet such as sninfs, torpig, Ramnit etc. [2].

Stage 4: Collation (Attack): After all recruitment process, locating the C&C and finally establishing connections botnet targets the victim in order to fulfill its purpose. The purpose can be anything like spreading spam mails, to perform DDos attack to take revenge, to have fun, popularity, to ruin someone's reputation in market. In 2007, the Estonian cyber attack made use of botnets to collapse the infrastructure of Estonia. In 2007, Georgia attack, Russia used botnets to perform large scale DDos attack. The purpose can also to breach national security by gathering information using botnets as APT's. [21]. In 2013, FBI arrested 10 international hackers who hacked the bank accounts of the users using botnets and made an amount of $850 millions using that information [1].

Stage 5: Update and Maintenance: This step is executed in order to make the botnet lasts longer. in order to increase their probability and duration of survival botnets operate stealthily to evade detection at each level. This can be achieved by using rootkits, obfuscation methods using polymorphisms at bot level. The C&C servers can hide using IP flux or domain flux techniques [21]. Proxies are also used by botmaster as a stepping stones to keep the activities more stealthy. Table 2. shows the summary of expected botnet traffic generated at each phase along with their distinct features from normal traffic.

Table 2. Extended detection parameters

Phase	Existing parameters [7]	Additional parameters
Inbound Scan	• IP sweep • Port scan	• Low bit rate • Increased number of scan at same port [2] • Increased no of probes at same port [2]
Exploit	• Match with blacklists	
Binary downloads	• Small size • Suspicious extensions • Match in MHR	
Attack	• Spam • Port scan	• Overlapped SMTP connections • High scan rate

4   Evaluation and Results

We evaluate our proposed model on dataset [20] provided by Botflex which consists of
381 IP addresses assigned to mid to small sized enterprises by Nayatel's local network.
Total 48,606 unique IP addresses are considered.

4.1   Extended Parameters Module

The parameters in sensor module of Botflex are extended as shown in Table 2. The
graph shown in Fig. 5 shows the contribution of each lifecycle phase on detection rate
(TPR). For early detection exploit phase must have some strong parameters which
provide the basis for system to trigger directly before any attack takes place. Generally
this can be done by examining bit rate, port scan and port probing as mentioned in the
Table 2.

Figure 6 shows the contribution of each phase in detection rate of extended module
with respect to Botflex as well as Bothunter. As shown in graph the major contribution
is given by the parameters described in C&C phase in detection rate. In Botflex, egg
download phase has the least contribution towards TPR followed by attack and exploit
phase.

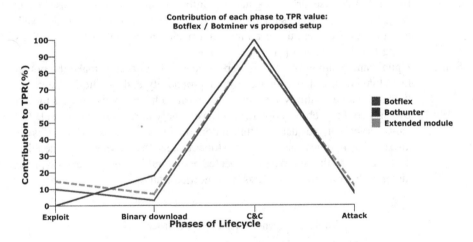

Fig. 6. Contribution of lifecycle phases to TPR [8]

4.2   Memory Utilization

We will evaluate the performance of our proposed method in terms of throughput given
by Bro IDS and comparing it with the setup with and without Botflex configuration.
Botflex reduces the throughput of Bro IDS by 4 k packets/sec and thus increases the
detection rate by 30 min [8]. Botflex also doubles the memory utilization of the system.
In our approach we are using separate filter machines so memory used by Bro IDS will

not be affected, therefore packets will be processed faster and also, machine equipped with Botflex will receive only filtered data that will speed up detection time for same amount of data.

4.3 CPU Utilization

The CPU usage ($\sim 50\%$) is consistent with Bro IDS with or without the presence of Botflex. In our approach CPU usage at filter level machines is same as used by Bro IDS and at detection level system CPU usage which is same as it mentioned in [8], so overall there is not much effect on CPU usage with average data rate of 28 k packets/sec.

5 Conclusion and Future Plan

Botnets is a powerful and amplifying threat against cyberspace as they provide an effective platform for most of cybercrimes primarily Distributed Denial of Service (DDoS) attacks against various popular targets, malware promulgations, phishing, and click frauds. They have ability to hide themselves from detection using various evasion techniques at different levels of botnet such as bot level, C&C level, etc. Their easy availability and reliability make them extremely popular for malicious usage. These challenging abilities enable various new trends in botnet anatomy such as social botnet, cloud botnet detection, etc. The primary requirement of botnet detection that is left unaddressed by most of the detection techniques includes detection at early phases, novel detection, and adaptability of detection model. Botminer had failed to address all these challenges. Botflex is a novel approach working in direction of providing tool to the community but it has some critical limitations like overhead, time delays and limited set of detection parameters. Through our approach it is possible to reduce the overhead on bro IDS and speed up the processing, detection rate and improve overall efficiency of Botflex. Our future work is to make Botflex fast and even more efficient in terms of its detection rate and processing time to tackle more sophisticated and complex bot attacks.

References

1. Karim, A., Salleh, R.B., Shiraz, M., Shah, S.A.A., Awan, I., Anuar, N.B.: Botnet detection techniques: review, future trends, and issues. J. Zhejiang Univ. SCI. C **15**, 943–983 (2014). doi:10.1631/jzus.C1300242
2. Khattak, S., Ramay, N.R., Khan, K.R., Syed, A.A., Khayam, S.A.: A taxonomy of botnet behavior, detection and defense. IEEE Commun. Surv. Tutorials **16**, 898–924 (2014). doi:10.1109/SURV.2013.091213.00134
3. Silva, S.S.C., Silna, R.M.P., Pinto, R.C.G., Salles, R.M.: Botnet: a survey. Comput. Netw. **57**, 378–403 (2013). Elsevier
4. Gross, G.: Detecting and destroying botnets. Netw. Secur. **2016**(3), 7–10 (2016)

5. https://securelist.com/files/2016/05/Q1_2016_MW_report_FINAL_eng.pdf. Accessed 28 Nov 2016
6. https://www.symantec.com/security-center/threat-report. Accessed 25 Feb 2017
7. Gu, G., Porras, P., Yegneswaran, V., Fong, M., Lee, W.: BotHunter: detecting malware infection through IDS-driven dialog correlation. In: Proceedings of the 16th USENIX Security Symposium, Boston, MA, USA 2007, vol. 7, pp. 1–16 (2007)
8. Khattak, S., Ahmed, Z., Syed, A.A., Khayam, S.A.: BotFlex: a community-driven tool for botnet detection. J. Netw. Comput. Appl. **58**(2015), 144–154 (2015)
9. Paxson, V.: Bro: A System for Detecting Network Intruders in Real-Time. In: Proceedings of the 7th USENIX Security Symposium San Antonio, Texas, vol. 31, pp. 2435–2463 (1998)
10. Gómez, J., Gil, C., Padilla, N., Baños, R., Jiménez, C.: Design of a snort-based hybrid intrusion detection system. In: Omatu, S., Rocha, M.P., Bravo, J., Fernández, F., Corchado, E., Bustillo, A., Corchado, J.M. (eds.) IWANN 2009. LNCS, vol. 5518, pp. 515–522. Springer, Heidelberg (2009). doi:10.1007/978-3-642-02481-8_75
11. http://blog.securityonion.net/p/securityonion.html. Accessed 25 Feb 2017
12. Gu, G., Perdisci, R., Zhang, J., Lee, W.: BotMiner: clustering analysis of network traffic for protocol- and structure-independent botnet detection. In: Proceedings of the 17th USENIX Security Symposium, San Jose, CA, USA 2008, vol. 5, pp. 139–154 (2008)
13. Zhao, D., Traore, I., Sayed, B., Lu, W., Saad, S., Ghorbani, A., et al.: Botnet detection based on traffic behavior analysis and flow intervals. Computer Security **39**(2013), 2–16 (2013)
14. Haq, O., Ahmed, W., Syed, A.A.: Titan: enabling low overhead and multi-faceted network fingerprinting of a bot. In: Proceedings of the 2014 44th Annual IEEE/IFIP International Conference on Dependable Systems and Networks. DSN 2014. Washington, DC, USA, pp. 37–44. IEEE Computer Society (2014). doi:10.1109/DSN.2014.20
15. Shin, S., Xu, Z., Gu, G.: EFFORT: a new host- network cooperated framework for efficient and effective bot malware detection. Comput. Netw. **57**, 2628–2642 (2013)
16. Zand, A., Vigna, G., Yan, X., Kruegel, C.: Extracting probable command and control signatures for detecting botnets. In: Proceedings of the 29th Annual ACM Symposium on Applied Computing (SAC 2014), New York, NY, USA, pp. 1657–1662. ACM (2014). doi:10.1145/2554850.2554896
17. Sakib, M.N., Huang, C.-T.: Using anomaly detection based techniques to detect HTTP-based botnet C&C traffic. In: 2016 IEEE International Conference on Communications (ICC). IEEE, pp. 1–6 (2016). doi:10.1109/ICC.2016.7510883
18. Chen, C.-M., Lin, H.-C.: Detecting botnet by anomalous traffic. J. Inf. Secur. Appl. **21**, 42–51 (2015)
19. Gu, G., Zhang, J., Lee, W.: BotSniffer: detecting botnet command and control channels in network traffic. In: Proceedings of the 15th Annual Network and Distributed System Security Symposium (2008)
20. https://github.com/sheharbano/BotFlex. Accessed 25 Feb 2017
21. Alieyan, K., ALmomani, A., Manasrah, A., Kadhum, M.M.: A survey of botnet detection based on DNS. Neural Comput. Appl. **28**, 1541–1558 (2015). Springer, Heidelebrg

An Efficient and Reliable Data Gathering Protocol Based on RSU Identification

Arun Malik[1]([⊠]) and Babita Pandey[2]

[1] Department of Computer Science and Engineering,
Lovely Professional University, Phagwara, India
arunmalikhisar@gmail.com
[2] Department of Computer Applications, Lovely Professional University,
Phagwara, India
shukla_babita@yahoo.co.in

Abstract. Vehicular Ad hoc Networks (VANETs) can act as an essential platform for providing various types of safety and non-safety applications by collecting the data sensed by the vehicles during their journey. To collect data in an efficient manner exclusive of network congestion is a very challenging task. In this paper, an efficient data gathering protocol based on Road side unit (RSU) identification approach is proposed for collecting the essential data sensed by the vehicle during their journey in an efficient manner without network congestion. The proposed protocol is able to reduce the communication overhead and average delay and capable of increasing the packet delivery ratio. Moreover, the proposed protocol is compared with the RSU activated data gathering protocol based on beacon broadcast. With the help of simulation results it has been identified that the proposed data gathering protocol considerably improves the efficiency of data collection as compared to RSU activated data gathering protocol based on beacon broadcast on the basis of communication overhead, average delay and packet delivery ratio.

Keywords: VANET · RSU · OBU · AU

1 Introduction

The intelligent vehicles possessing the facility of sensing, computation and wireless transmission along with road side units (RSUs) are the primary components of VANET. The transmission of messages is attained among vehicles or among a vehicle and RSU over a wireless standard called WAVE. This technique of communication transfers an ample range of data to the drivers and users, facilitates safety applications to increase security of roads and offers a relaxed driving. VANET consists of on board unit (OBU), RSU and application unit (AU). A resource command processor (RCP) in OBU consists of read/write memory inured to keep and recover data. An OBU provides a dedicated interface called as user interface to join with other OBUs and a network tool depends on IEEE 802.11p radio technology for dedicated short range wireless communications. In addition to this for non safety applications OBU may consist of another network device depends on additional radio technologies such as IEEE

© Springer Nature Singapore Pte Ltd. 2017
D. Singh et al. (Eds.): ICAICR 2017, CCIS 712, pp. 343–354, 2017.
DOI: 10.1007/978-981-10-5780-9_31

802.11a/b/g/n. An AU is mounted in the vehicles that carry out the applications by utilizing the communication capabilities of the OBU's. A trustworthy device for safety applications like accident warning, routing system with the ability of transmitting and receiving messages or an ordinary device like personal digital assistant to execute internet applications are the examples of AU. AU can be implanted into a vehicle or can be fixed with the OBU in a single substantial unit. To provide a devoted short range of communication depends on IEEE 802.11p radio technology, the RSU is outfitted with the particular network device. To provide communication within the infrastructural network, the RSUs can also be outfitted with other network devices. Characteristics of VANET are different from other ad hoc network. The unique characteristics of VANET that distinguish it from other ad hoc networks are as follow:

(a) Frequent changes in network topology: The topology of VANET is highly dynamic due to high speeds of moving vehicles. As driver needs to respond to the information got from the system because of which driver conduct is influenced due to which network topology change.

(b) Adequate power: As the vehicles in VANET are capable of providing constant power to the OBU through the long life battery due to which there are no power constraints in VANET.

(c) Dynamic network density: The network density in VANET is dynamic due to the traffic density on the road that can be far above the ground in case of traffic jam on the road or very low, as in sub urban areas.

(d) Different communication scenarios: Broadly, VANET works in two types of communication scenarios namely highway traffic scenarios and city traffic scenario. The environment is comparatively simple and straightforward in highway traffic as compared to city traffic scenario.

(e) Mobility prediction: As vehicles are controlled by road topology due to which vehicles in VANET travel in an arbitrary way. Moreover, vehicles have to follow traffic signals, road signs and react to moving vehicles on road leading to certainty in terms of their mobility.

(f) Broad range network: In crowded urban areas like highways, city centre and at the entry of the huge cities size of the network could be very large.

VANET offers various types of applications for the improvement of traffic safety and to facilitate the users with numerous commercial applications. VANET application can be divided into two major categories: *Safety and non-safety associated applications.*

Safety associated applications are also known as Intelligent Transport Applications (ITAs). ITAs are the primary application of VANET which are used as integral part of Intelligent Transport System (ITS). On board navigation, collated traffic control, study of traffic jams on the fly are the examples of ITAs. Traffic frequency and vehicular speeds monitored by the existing road side unit (RSU) are transferred to a centralized server that utilize this data to calculate traffic flow regulation and ideal traffic light schedules. This type of comprehensive "feedback" loop can be highly decreased by VANETs where vehicles communicate the road scenarios among themselves. The mobile nodes in VANET can even transmit information to the RSU in situation of accident due to which warning can be provided to the oncoming traffic about jam and immediate contact to the emergency rescue team can be possible. Such types of applications generally utilize broadcast or multicast routings schemes for transmitting and receiving messages [6]. [7] Safety associated application can be classified as:

(a) Dynamic traffic: The real time traffic information can be stored at the RSU and can be provided to the vehicular nodes whenever and wherever required.
(b) Collaborative exchange of messages: Vehicles will collaboratively exchange messages among themselves and with the RSU.
(c) Post accident warning: When a vehicle met with an accident it can broadcast message about its location to the neighboring vehicles as well as rescue team or highway patrol for help.
(d) Road Risk control warning: Vehicles can send messages to other vehicles information regarding rockslide or road characteristics warning like road curves, sudden downhill etc.
(e) Combined accident warning: Send the alert messages to both the vehicles potentially under crash route so that they can change their way.
(f) Monitoring the traffic: Traffic can be monitored by installing the camera at the RSU that provides help in the campaign of low or no tolerance against driving offenses.

Non safety associated applications are the applications that permit the user to establish communication with other vehicles and with Internet service providers (ISPs) to improve the drivers and passengers convenience. Non safety related services provided by the VANET include internet connectivity to the moving vehicles on road so that users can be able to download music, drop e-mails, watch online movies and video songs or play video games. Generally, some static or dynamic authorized networks to internet gateways are joined with the networks, due to which they can transmit the messages between VANET and the internet. Unicast routing is used as a fundamental communication methods in such types of applications [6]. [7] Non safety associated applications are classified can be classified as:

(a) Accessing of Internet: Vehicle can have access to internet by the virtue of RSU if RSU is acting as router.
(b) Online Video Transfer: The driver can request for online video transfer of his favorite movies.
(c) Path Deviation: In case of traffic jam path and tour planning can be easily done by the drivers.
(d) Browsing the Internet: One can utilize the time in a traffic jam very effectively by surfing the internet, by sending and downloading the e-mails and by browsing the social sites etc.
(e) Fuel Saving: Government can utilize the toll collection application to collect the toll tax from the vehicles without stopping them at the toll booths. Utilization of this application can save around 3% of fuel which is wasted by manually collection of tool tax, where vehicles on an average wait normally for 2–5 min.

Most of the safety related applications are dynamic, which would require high assurance of quality of service related to latency, communication overhead and security. To avoid a feasible mishap on the road a safety message has to reach to the desired vehicles within a part of a second. Due to this drivers of the vehicles can take immediate and proper measures to avoid the accident. Security in VANETs is the primary concern for its effective implementations. Probable security actions include a technique which can give assurance that information was produced by a trustworthy source (neighboring vehicles or RSUs), in addition to this a technique which can provide assurance that information was not replaced with or changed once it was produced. Non safety related applications that entail monetary transactions (like collecting toll at toll booths) needs the ability to perform a secure and safe transaction.

All the above mentioned safety and non safety related applications can be attained by offering vehicle to vehicle and vehicle to RSU communication at free of cost [1]. In VANETs, Onboard sensors are mounted on the vehicles to collect the various types of vehicular sensor data for providing the useful data such as speed and position of neighbouring vehicles, audio and video data, hurdles on the road, traffic jams and many more [2]. These onboard sensors mounted on vehicles in VANETs sense the data on a very large scale in dense traffic area to support the applications of traffic jams, accidents, hurdles on the road and monitoring the pollution generated by the vehicles in urban traffic scenario.

It is a big challenging task to collect the enormous amount of data on a large scale in dense traffic region in an efficient manner due to restriction of resources and communication conflicts in networks [3]. Moreover, high mobility and varying node density in VANET impose a big challenge in the task of data collection in an efficient manner with high scalability and reliability. Therefore data collection in VANET in an efficient manner with high reliability and scalability is still an open issue.

In this work, collection of data is performed in crowded traffic area where large number of vehicles sends the useful information like traffic jam, position and speed of vehicles, environment conditions, condition of road segments etc. in the form of data which is spatially associated to the RSU that act as a center of data for multi hop transmissions. To reduce the redundant information and to increase the efficiency in communication by maximum utilization of the spatially associated data send by the vehicle to RSU. In earlier days, large number of technologies was used that requires human interaction for data collection due to which traffic was disrupted. But now a day several technologies have been emerged that collect the data automatically without the disruption of traffic by not involving human interaction.

In this paper, an efficient data gathering protocol based on Road side unit (RSU) identification approach is proposed for collecting the essential data sensed by the vehicle during their journey in an efficient manner without network congestion. Moreover, the proposed protocol is compared with the RSU activated data gathering protocol based on beacon broadcast. The proposed protocol is able to achieve the goal of effective communication among vehicle and RSUs without increasing the communication and computational overhead increasing the packet delivery ratio. The primary contribution of this paper is as follow:

A novel data gathering protocol based on Road side unit (RSU) identification approach is proposed for collecting the essential data sensed by the vehicle during their journey. The proposed protocol is compared with the RSU activated data gathering protocol based on beacon broadcast. Simulations are performed to validate the efficiency and performance of proposed data gathering protocol.

Rest of the paper is described as follow. Section 2 describes the related works done in the field of data collection in VANET. Section 3 describes the existing RSU activated data gathering protocol based on beacon broadcast. Section 4 describes the proposed data gathering protocol based on Road side unit (RSU) identification approach Sect. 5 discuss the performance evaluation of the proposed protocol on the basis of simulation results. Section 6 concludes the paper.

2 Related Works

In [4] by utilizing cluster networking technique a protocol named as trafficGather is proposed. This protocol partition the road segments into a chain of road blocks where each road block is covered by a network cluster. This protocol allows the vehicle to send the useful information associated with the vehicles and road blocks in a particular time slots.

A protocol designated as MobEyes act as an effective middleware to collect and transmit the data sensed by the vehicles travelling in urban area to RSUs and among the neighboring vehicles is proposed in [5]. This protocol utilize the mobility of vehicles for diffusing the summaries of data sensed the vehicles among each other and to establish a low cost index for questioning the observed data.

In [6] a protocol termed as cluster gathering protocol that uses specific vehicular sensor network architecture where the telecommunication provider operates the ad hoc network. This protocol extracts the valuable information about the traffic condition in a specific geographical region by combining non valuable data sensed by the individual vehicle. Traffic load on the network is reduced by this protocol by means of unlicensed spectrum communication medium.

In [7] to collect the data which is spatially associated in an efficient manner a unique scheme named as compressive sensing based data collection is proposed. This scheme efficient collect the data on large scale, compress the collected data and extract the useful data in an accurate manner by applying compressive sensing theory. This scheme results in low communication overhead due to less computation and low communication control.

In [8] a novel multi hop data collection and dissemination scheme is described to handle the dynamic data collection and dynamic data exchange among vehicles and RSUs that are equipped with sensors. The primary motive of this scheme is to attain the accessibility of large scale data with reduced latency and communication overhead.

In [9] an original data collection scheme termed as PADAVAN is proposed in this paper with the help of which users can offers the data in an unsigned manner by averting the attackers from submitting huge amount of fake data. This scheme consists of n time's secret authentication scheme to provide protection to the privacy of collected data itself.

In [10] based on compressed sensing an essential data collection scheme is proposed. In this scheme both the in network data aggregation technique and the technique for compressed sensing are combined together to decrease the communication cost as low as possible for collection of data in VANET.

3   RSU Activated Data Gathering Protocol

In VANET RSUs are spotted at fixed location in the network. Each RSU covers a specific region containing the specific number of road segments over a given geographical area. After a particular time slot (t seconds) a beacon is broadcast by the RSU to all the vehicles within its range to collect the data of the road segments traversed by the vehicles during its trip. Every beacon message broadcast by the RSU consists of address of the RSU from which it is generated. As soon as vehicle receives the beacons from the RSU, it creates a data packet containing the useful information related to the road segments. Each vehicle has its unique identity and each vehicle will sends the data related to the road segments between the two consecutive beacon messages sends by the designated RSU. Data packet design for RSU activated data gathering protocol is shown in Fig. 1.

Message data packet Type	Message data packet creation time	Message data packet sequence number
Address of source which is sending the Data packet	Address of receiver which receiving the Dat packet	
Road section Size traversed by the vehicle	PLMT[]	

Fig. 1. Data packet design for RSU activated data gathering protocol

3.1   Algorithm

```
For each Vehicle Vk and RSU in the network
Vk traverse the road section RSk
If Vk get new RSk then
Add the new RSk to the partial lane map table PLMT[]
End if
Broadcast beacon by RSU to the vehicles in its range
// Where beacon consist of address of RSU and beacon timer
If Vk receives beacon then
Vk sends its identity and PLMT[] to the RSU from which it receives
the beacon
// by using RSU address in the beacon
End if
RSU receives vehicle identity and PLMT[] from vehicles
If new Vk then
Create new entry for Vk in road map table RMPT[][]
Add PMLT[] to RMPT[Vk][]
Else
Add PMLT[] to RMPT[Vk][]
End if
End for
```

4 Proposed Data Gathering Protocol Based on RSU Identification Approach

In this protocol vehicle first broadcast the message to identify the closest RSU within its range of sensors fixed in the form of onboard unit in it. Each Vehicle traversed so many road sections or path lanes in its trip from source to destination. Before sending the complete information related to the road sections or path lanes traversed by the vehicle after reaching to destination to the RSU, it first broadcast a RSU identification message to all the RSUs within its range for their address. As soon as address of closest RSU is identified, the information of the complete path traversed by the vehicle during its trip is sent to the closest RSU. Data packet design for the proposed data gathering protocol is shown in Fig. 2.

Message data packet Type	Message data packet creation time	Message data packet sequence number
Address of source which is sending the Data packet	Address of receiver which receiving the Dat packet	
RS_k		

Fig. 2. Data packet design for proposed data gathering protocol

4.1 Algorithm

```
For each vehicle Vₖ and RSU in the network
If Vₖ traverse the road section RSₖ then
Get the road section RSₖ
If Vₖ get new RSₖ
then;
Add the new RSₖ to the Complete path map table CPMT[]
End if
End if
If complete path is traverse by the Vₖ from source to destination
then
RSU identification beacon is transmit by the Vₖ with its identity
to all neighboring RSUs
If RSU received (Vₖ identity, RSU identification beacon)
then
RSU send its Address (RAddr) to Vₖ
If address of RSU is received by Vₖ
then
Vₖ send its identity and CPMT[] to the closest RSU.
If RSU received (vehicle identity and CPMT[]) from Vₖ
then
```

```
Create new record for Vk in Road Map table RMPT[][]
Add CPMT[] to RMPT[][]
End if
End if
End if
End for
```

5 Results and Discussion

5.1 Simulation Environment

Omnet ++ is used for simulation of networking scenario and mobility of vehicle is traced by sumo framework. Simulation scenario is shown in Figs. 3 and 4.

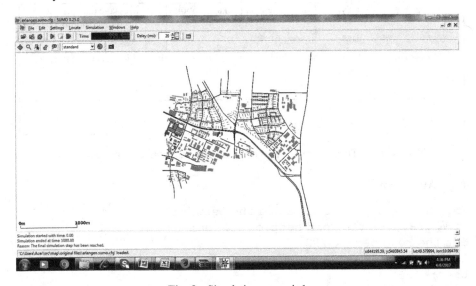

Fig. 3. Simulation scenario1

In simulation scenario, 800 m × 600 m dimensions of space is used where minimum and maximum speed of the vehicles are 0 m per second and 120 m per second. Moreover, density of traffic varies from 50 to 350 vehicles. Radio range is 200 m. Size of the data packet is 512 bytes per second. Bandwidth size is 2 Mbps and random mobility of the vehicles is used in the simulation scenario. Simulation parameters for sumo and omnet ++ are mentioned in Table 1.

5.2 Evaluation of Performance

To compute the performance of proposed data gathering protocol, simulations are performed using both the data gathering protocol i.e. RSU activated data gathering protocol and proposed data gathering protocol based on RSU identification approach. Performance of both the scheme is calculated and compared on the basis of

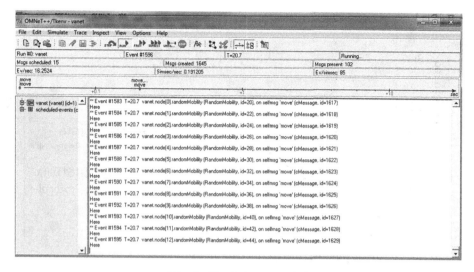

Fig. 4. Simulation scenario2

Table 1. Parameters for simulations

Parameters	Value
Space dimensions	800 m × 600 m
Minimum speed	0 m/s
Maximum speed	100 m/s
Radio range	200 m
Size of data packets	512 bytes per packet
Bandwidth	2 Mbps
Traffic type	Constant bit rate
Channel type	Wireless
Number of vehicles	50, 100, 150, 200, 250, 300
MAC	IEEE802.11 g

computational overhead (which is described as excess computation time that is required to send the data packets from vehicle to RSU), latency (time taken by the data packet to return to its sender) and packet delivery ratio (ratio of number of data packets reached to the receiver to the number of data packets sent by the sender).

Figure 5 represents the computational overhead with respect to number of vehicles for both the data gathering protocol in different traffic density. The computational overhead increases as the density of traffic increases. Results of simulation represents that increase in computational overhead of proposed data gathering protocol is less as compared to the RSU activated data gathering protocol.

Figure 6 represents the latency of both the data gathering protocol in different traffic density. Latency increases as the density of traffic increases. Results of simulation represents that increase in latency of proposed data gathering protocol is less as compared to the RSU activated data gathering protocol.

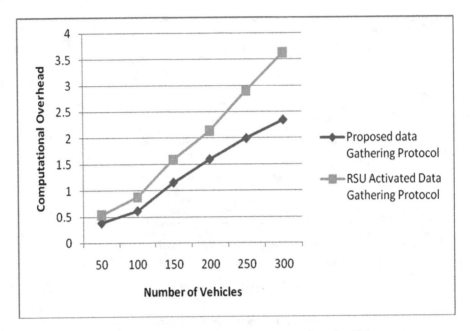

Fig. 5. Computational overhead versus number of vehicles

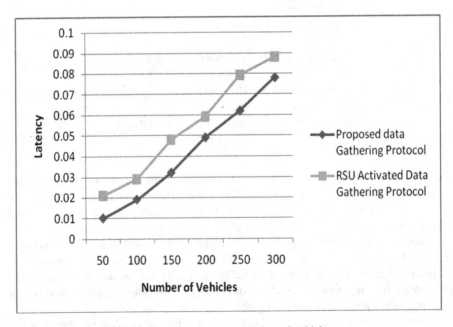

Fig. 6. Latency versus number of vehicles

Figure 7 represents the packet delivery ratio of both the data gathering protocol in different traffic density. Packet delivery ratio decreases as the density of traffic increases. Results of simulation represents that decrease in packet delivery ratio of proposed data gathering protocol is less as compared to the RSU activated data gathering protocol.

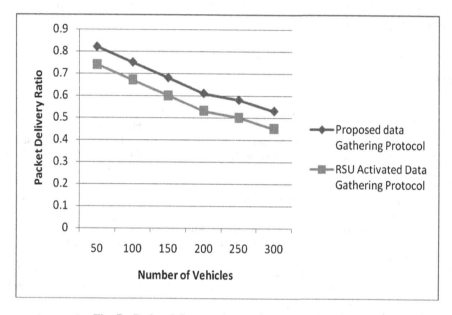

Fig. 7. Packet delivery ratio versus number of vehicles

Comparison of both the data collection protocol on the basis of computational overhead, latency and packet delivery ratio is summarized in Table 2.

Table 2. Comparison of data collection protocols

Protocols	Computational overhead	Latency	Packet delivery ratio
RSU activated data gathering protocol	High	High	Low
Proposed data gathering protocol	Low	Low	High

6   Conclusion

In this paper an efficient data gathering protocol based on RSU identification approach to collect the data in an efficient manner exclusive of network congestion for VANETs. In this proposed data gathering protocol vehicle first identify the closest RSU before sending its full path information traversed by vehicle from source to destination in VANET. Moreover, the performance evaluation of the proposed data gathering protocol can assure attractive performance in terms of efficiency and reliability as compared to RSU activated data gathering protocol. Simulation results reflects that the proposed protocol performs better in terms of communication overhead, latency and packet delivery ratio as compared to the RSU activated data gathering protocol. In future, security features can be embedded in the proposed data gathering protocol to improve the performance.

References

1. Li, Z., Liu, C., Chigan, C.: GPAS: a general purpose automatic survey system based on vehicular ad hoc networkS. IEEE Wirel. Commun. **18**(4), 61–66 (2011)
2. Uichin, L., Biao, Z., Gerla, M., Magistretti, E., Bellavista, P., Corradi, A.: Mobeyes: smart mobs for urban monitoring with a vehicular sensor network. IEEE Wirel. Commun. **13**(5) (2006)
3. Torrent-moreno, M., Santi, P., Cnr, T.: Fair sharing of bandwidth in VANETs. In: Proceedings of the 2nd ACM International Workshop on Vehicular Ad Hoc Networks, pp. 49–58 (2005)
4. Chang, W., Lin, H., Chen, B.: TrafficGather: An efficient and scalable data collection protocol for vehicular ad hoc networks. In: IEEE CCNC 2008 PROCEEDINGS, pp. 365–369 (2008)
5. Lee, U., Magistretti, E., Gerla, M., Bellavista, P., Member, S., Corradi, A.: Dissemination and harvesting of urban data using vehicular sensing platforms. IEEE Trans. Veh. Technol. **58**(2), 882–901 (2009)
6. Salhi, I., Cherif, M.O., Senouci, S.M.: A new architecture for data collection in vehicular networks. In: IEEE Conference on Communications, pp. 2–7 (2009)
7. Liu, C.: Compressive sensing based data collection in VANETs. In: IEEE Wireless Communications and Networking Conference, pp. 1756–1761 (2013)
8. Mansour, L., Moussaoui, S.: RDAP: requested data accessibility protocol for vehicular sensor networks. In: International Conference on Smart Communications in Network Technologies (2013)
9. Tomandl, A., Herrmann, D., Federrath, H.: PADAVAN : privacy-aware data accumulation for vehicular ad-hoc networks. In: 10th IEEE International Conference on Wireless and Mobile Computing, pp. 487–493 (2014)
10. Feng, C., Li, K., Li, Z., Jiang, S.: A compressed sensing approach to monitor urban traffic with data aggregation in VANETs. In: 43rd IEEE International Conference on Parallel Processing Workshops (2016)

A Neural Network Model for Intrusion Detection Using a Game Theoretic Approach

Pallavi Kaushik$^{(\boxtimes)}$ ⓘ and Kamlesh Dutta ⓘ

Computer Science and Engineering, NIT-Hamirpur, Himachal Pradesh, India
pallavikaushik27@gmail.com, kdnith@gmail.com

Abstract. The problem of intrusion detection in the computer networks is not new and various methodologies have been formulated to address the same. A game-theoretic representation was also formulated, using one of the oldest game playing techniques, the minimax algorithm to solve this problem. It exploited the adversary like situation between the intruder and the Intrusion Detection System (IDS) and the essence of this approach lies in the assumption that the intruder and the IDS have complete knowledge of the network and each other's strategy. The solution for the intrusion detection problem via game theory gives the detection probability by which the IDS can detect the malicious packets on a given network when the probabilities with which the intruder sends the malicious packets on the various paths leading him to the target are known to the IDS. However, in the real world scenario, the role of the intruder and the IDS is dynamic, if the attack is detected or goes undetected the intruder tries to breach the network again with a different approach or the IDS tries to defend the network with a different strategy respectively. The next strategy for either of the two can be learnt by experience and thus, this paper, models an artificial neural network to represent this game-theoretic representation. The modeled neural network gives the detection probability of an attack by the IDS when the probabilities of sending malicious packets on the various paths leading the intruder to the target are given as an input pattern to the neural network.

Keywords: Artificial intelligence · Game theory · Artificial neural network · Intrusion detection

1 Introduction

With the proliferation in the number of applications having its infrastructure based on the communication networks, ranging from something as gigantic and crucial as satellites to something as minuscule as the wireless sensors, the problem, and the threat of a breach in security has increased. The data runs unchecked and unrestricted on the networks, serving as a playground for the intruders, who have the expertise to extract it, understand it and manipulate it. Thus, the need for an efficient intrusion detection system has never been more pressing. Various intrusion detection techniques [1–6] have been proposed and used.

The intruder and the Intrusion Detection System (IDS) can be viewed from the perspective of the two rational decision making competitors. The success of one is

© Springer Nature Singapore Pte Ltd. 2017
D. Singh et al. (Eds.): ICAICR 2017, CCIS 712, pp. 355–367, 2017.
DOI: 10.1007/978-981-10-5780-9_32

deemed as the failure of the other and both the intruder and the IDS take decisions prioritizing their own objectives. Game theory is known to model such adversary situations with algorithms like minimax [7], negamax [8], SSS [9], Monte Carlo Tree Search (MCTS) [10], etc. The minimax algorithm can be applied in our situation because it works for two player zero-sum perfect information games. The intruder and the IDS can be taken to be the two players of the game and only one can be the winner, i.e. either the intrusion is detected (IDS wins) or it is not (intruder wins). This paper gets its motivation from [11], where a game-theoretic representation of the problem of intrusion detection has been given in the form of the minimax algorithm. However, [11] presents only one solution for a given network. It gives the probabilities with which the intruder must send the malicious packets on each path that leads him to the target and the sampling probabilities with which the IDS must sample each link in the network in order to detect the attack with maximum probability. However, in the real world scenario the role of the intruder and the IDS is dynamic, if the attack is detected or goes undetected the intruder tries to breach the network again with some different combination or the IDS tries to defend the network with a different strategy respectively. The next strategy for either of the two can be learnt by experience and the various machine learning techniques are known to do that [12]. One of such techniques, the Artificial Neural Networks (ANN) [13] that gets its motivation from the functioning of the human brain has been used in tasks pertaining to classification, recognition and prediction. ANNs are highly robust, adaptable, efficient and effective in the prediction tasks and have also been used in a wide range of applications where planning is required in the adverse environment such as game playing [14–16], power control [17, 18], stock market predictions [19], financial management [20], etc. Moreover, they require fewer assumptions, provide high prediction accuracy and are used for extracting knowledge from a large set of data. Thus, if the previous moves of the intruder and the IDS are present, the neural network can be made to learn from it and render the next best strategy for either of the intruder or the IDS.

In this paper, a neural network model of the intruder and the intrusion detection system using a game-theoretic approach is presented. The paper is organized into 5 Sections. Section 1 introduces the basic concepts and motivation of using a neural network with the game theoretic approach for developing an intrusion detection system. Section 2 presents the literature review of the some methodologies that use neural networks or game theory for intrusion detection. Section 3 describes the game-theoretic approach adopted for the intrusion detection problem as derived in [11], including its various assumptions. The artificial neural network that has been modeled keeping this representation as the base is explained in Sect. 4. Section 5 presents the conclusion and the future scope of the proposed model for IDS.

2   Related Works

Intrusion is an attempt to compromise the policies like confidentiality, integrity of a system and intrusion detection is the analysis and monitoring of the system or the communication network to see if any activity violates the standard security practices and user policies. The intrusion detection techniques can be classified into two major classes – anomaly based [21] and signature based [22].

Any activity that deviates from the usual or expected behavior of the user is treated as an anomaly. Such anomalies can be the result of an intrusion. Hence, the anomaly based intrusion detection systems detect intrusion in the communication network by monitoring the user activities and checking for any anomaly. This approach is known to create a large number of false alarms because the behavior of even the authorized user can change with time, but it has a potential to detect a new intrusion activity. Various techniques are used for anomaly detection like data mining [23, 24], machine learning [25–28] and statistical analysis [29, 30].

The signature based intrusion detection techniques make use of the stored signatures of the various attacks. It is based on the notion that the malicious packets or attacks bear a certain signature and any new packet can be deemed as malicious if it matches with any of the stored signatures. The basic advantage of this technique is that known attacks can be detected with fewer false positive rates, but the major drawback is that the signatures of the various attacks that an attacker can lodge need to be known and stored a priori for this technique to work efficiently. However, it fails to detect any new attack. Various techniques like supervised learning [31], expert systems [32] and data mining [33] have been used to achieve signature based detection.

As in this paper, we model a neural network for intrusion detection using a game theoretic approach, a few neural network models and game theoretic based applications for intrusion detection have been mentioned next.

2.1 Neural Networks for Intrusion Detection

Artificial neural networks are frequently used for the classification tasks and hence, have been used to model both the anomaly based and signature based intrusion detection system.

A competitive learning based neural network model which could detect the known, as well as the unknown attacks has been given in [34]. This neural network is as accurate as the Self Organizing Maps (SOM) and takes one fourth of the computation time as taken by SOM.

A multilayer neural network model has been used in [35] that not only classifies whether there is an attack or not but also determines the type of attack.

A hierarchical neural network has been presented in [36] that recognizes new attacks by monitoring those aspects of the network that are predictable in advance like the protocols. Hence, the neural network was able to predict the attacks that were not present in the training set.

A neural network model using the AdaBoost algorithm has been proposed in [37]. This model has the highest detection rates and lowest false alarm rates when compared to methods like Support Vector Machines (SVM), hierarchical SOM, genetic clustering, etc.

2.2   Game Theory and Intrusion Detection

Game theory categorizes the games mainly into three categories- cooperative games [38], non cooperative games [39] and repeated games [40]. Cooperative games are those where the players work together considering each other's resources in order to achieve a common goal. Non cooperative games are those where each player makes moves in order to achieve maximum benefit for themselves and at the same time minimizing the benefit of the other player. Repeated games is the class of games where the game is played for a few rounds and the players can observe the outcomes of previous rounds before playing the next round. All these three categorizations have been applied to the intrusion detection problems in one form or the other.

Cooperative Games. This technique has been used by Saad et al. [41] to propose a merger and split approach for the Wireless Sensor Networks (WSN). The approach results in reduced energy consumption by the nodes as the nodes come together to form a coalition and aim at maximizing the utility of their group. The reduced energy leads to an increase in the life span of the nodes belonging to the group.

The problem where many intruders come together and work in alliance to attack the same target has been represented in the form of a cooperative game in [11]. The solution to this problem has then been suggested based on the minimax algorithm.

Various other papers that have used cooperative games to solve various problems in the communication networks [42–44].

Non Cooperative Games. Various papers have used this approach to solve intrusion detection problem in the Mobile Ad hoc NETworks (MANET) [45], WSN [46], wired networks [47], distributed sensor networks [48], Ad Hoc wireless networks [49] etc. The model has been used for risk assessment in the network [50] and also to determine the security and dependability level in the network. It has also been used in [51] for analyzing intrusion detection in access control systems. [52] analyses the attacker and IDS behavior under dynamic information by modeling the scenario as a two player non cooperative game.

Repeated Games. Agah and Das [53] have used repeated games in their work to prevent the denial of service attacks in the routing layer of the wireless sensor networks. The concept of repeated games has been used in [54] for packet routing in WSNs. They have also been used in [55] to achieve optimal energy consumption by the nodes of WSN thus, prolonging their lifetime.

3   Game Formulation for Single Intruder Sending Multiple Packets

Otrok et al. [11] proposed a model for intrusion detection in wired networks which uses a game theoretic approach for finding an optimal sampling strategy within the given budget constraint set for the network. The neural network model for intrusion detection proposed by us, aims at employing this strategy for finding the probability by which intrusion is detected in a given network. In this section we elaborate the game theoretic approach as proposed in [11].

The game theoretic approach used for intrusion detection, is based on a non coop-erative perfect information zero-sum game. The approach assumed that the intruder and the target are known to the IDS and the infrastructure of the network is wired. The intruder is capable of sending n malicious packets to the target and the intrusion is said to be detected if the IDS can detect at least m malicious fragments out of n, where $m \leq n$. The IDS keeps a check on the network by sampling the traffic on each link in the paths that could lead the intruder to the target. Let Z be the set of paths, represented as P_1, P_2, ..., P_z leading the intruder to the target where $Z = \{P_1, P_2, ..., P_z\}$. The probability of sampling a malicious packet on link e on a path P ε Z is assumed as p_e. Let the traffic flow on each link e be given by t_e. Thus, the sampling rate s_e for link e will be given by

$$s_e = t_e * p_e \tag{1}$$

Since, sampling each and every packet in the network will be very expensive, a sampling budget constraint, represented as SB is present. The sampling probabilities are, hence, bound by the constraint as given in Eq. (2).

$$\sum_{e \, \varepsilon \, P} t_e * p_e \leq SB \tag{2}$$

Let p be the set of probabilities, p_e for all e ε P that satisfy Eq. (2) for given traffic flows on each link in a given network. The number of set p, will be more than one, hence, let the set of p be represented as p'.

Since, the intruder can send malicious packets via any path, so the probability of the intruder sending the malicious packet via a path P is represented as q(P). For each path P_1, P_2, ..., P_z ε Z, the intruder has a probability vector $Q = \{q(P_1), q(P_2), ..., q(P_z)\}$, such that Eq. (3) holds.

$$\sum_{P \, \varepsilon \, Z} q(p) = 1 \tag{3}$$

The set of such Q for which Eq. (3) holds is represented by Q'. The probability of sampling a malicious fragment travelling from the intruder to the target, given by β is as represented in Eq. (4)

$$\beta = \sum_{P \, \varepsilon \, Z} q(P) \, [1 - \prod_{e \, \varepsilon \, P} (1 - p_e)] \tag{4}$$

The intrusion will be detected, if at least m out of n packets (m $\leq$ n) are sampled. Thus, the IDS will detect the intrusion with probability,

$$\sum_{k=m}^{n} \beta^k * (1-\beta)^{n-k} \tag{5}$$

In order for the IDS to be efficient, it must maximize the detection probability given in Eq. (5) and at the same time, to make an effective attack the intruder must try to minimize this maximum detection probability. This scenario is apt for the application of the game theory method, the minimax algorithm which has two players namely, Max and Min. Max tries to maximize his returns and Min tries to minimize them and both the players make moves considering only their own benefits. In the given intrusion detection scenario the IDS corresponds to the player Max and the intruder corresponds to the player Min.

The game problem formulation for the above scenario, assuming the intruder and the IDS are the two players, will be as given in Eq. (6).

$$\text{function}(V) = \min_{n \in N, Q \in Q'} \max_{p \in p'} \sum_{k=m}^{n} \beta^k * (1-\beta)^{n-k} \tag{6}$$

where the intruder will try to minimize the function V and on the other hand, the main objective of the IDS will be to maximize it. To avoid the mathematical complexity, it is assumed that the intrusion detection requires detection of only m malicious packets out of n. For m malicious packets, Eq. (6) reduces to

$$V = \min_{n \in N, Q \in Q'} \max_{p \in p'} \beta^m * (1-\beta)^{n-m} \tag{7}$$

For a fixed number of total malicious packets n and the known probability set $Q \in Q'$ of sending the malicious packets on paths in the set Z, the part of the problem that needs to be solved from the perspective of the IDS is

$$\max_{p \in p'} \beta^m * (1-\beta)^{n-m} \tag{8}$$

To obtain the maximum value of the Eq. (8), values for m and β need to be maximized. As shown in [11] Eqs. (9) and (10) have been derived that would maximize m and β respectively.

$$m = n * \beta \tag{9}$$

$$\beta = \max_{p \in p'} \sum_{P \in Z} [q(P) \sum_{e \in P} p_e] \tag{10}$$

In order to maximize β, Eq. (10) needs to be evaluated. For an intrusion detection process to be successful, the present model considers that at least m malicious packets must be detected.

If it is assumed that the intruder sends only one malicious packet along the network [47] and a fixed strategy is followed by both the intruder and the IDS, then the expected number of times the malicious packet is detected by the IDS is given by Eq. (11).

$$\sum_{P \in Z} q(P) \left[\sum_{e \in P} p_e \right] \tag{11}$$

For this case the game theoretic model is

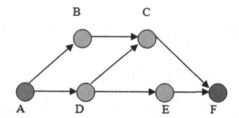

Fig. 1. The communication network

$$\min_{Q \in Q'} \max_{p \in p'} \sum_{P \in Z} q(P) \left[\sum_{e \in P} p_e \right] \tag{12}$$

It can be seen that for a fixed Q, Eq. (12) is similar to Eq. (10) and thus the proposed neural network can be used to solve it too. Solving Eq. (10) will not require an additional work to calculate the detection probability in the case of single malicious packet unlike the case of multiple malicious packets, where the value of m also needs to be calculated to get the final result.

4   Neural Network Model for Intrusion Detection

The game theoretic representation of the intruder and the IDS as described in Sect. 3 provides a theoretical background for developing our proposed neural network. Since, the topology of the computer network is graph based the neural network can be used to model the same. The proposed model is explained with the help of an example of communication network comprising of the intruder node, target node and other nodes participating in the communication (Fig. 1).

The nodes A and F denote the intruder and the target respectively. The other nodes (B, C, D, E) are participating in the communication between A and F. There are three

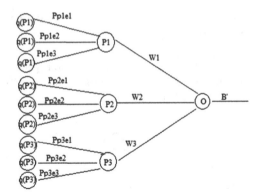

Fig. 2. Neural network model based on a game theoretic approach

paths that lead the intruder to the target. These paths, A-B-C-F, A-D-C-F and A-D-E-F are represented as P_1, P_2 and P_3 respectively. Thus, set $Z = \{P_1, P_2, P_3\}$.

As per our problem mentioned in Sect. 3, the probabilities with which the intruder will send the infected packets on each path P_1, P_2 and P_3 are known and represented as $q(P_1)$, $q(P_2)$ and $q(P_3)$. These will serve as our inputs. Thus, $Q = \{q(P_1), q(P_2), q(P_3)\}$. The Eq. (10) is our problem that needs to be solved and for it we need to find the best sampling probability for each link, e in each path, $P \varepsilon Z$ with which the IDS should sample the packets. The sampling probabilities for each link, s_e are the weights for neurons of the hidden layer, H_1.

The neural network model for the network in Fig. 1 is as represented in Fig. 2. An overview of the neural network is given in the following points.

1. The input layer consists of n neuron, where n is the sum of $l(P_1)$, $l(P_2)$, ..., $l(P_z)$, $l(P)$ representing the number of links in path $P \varepsilon Z$. The input to each input neuron is the probability $q(P)$ of the intruder sending the malicious nodes to path P.
2. It consists of a hidden layer, say H_1. The number of neurons in H_1 is equal to the distinct number of paths from the intruder to target i.e. number of elements in set Z.
3. There is one output neuron.

The neurons are represented by circles. The weights between the input layer and hidden layer are the sampling probabilities of each link and are represented as p_{P1e1} for link e_1 on path P_1 and so on. The weights between the neurons in the hidden layer and the output layer are represented as W1, W2 and W3. The activation function for all neurons in H_1 is linear and is a simple summer. The output from this function for neuron i, where i is a neuron in H_1 and l is the number of inputs to neuron i, is:

$$\sum_{j=1}^{1} q(P_i) * p_{Piej} \tag{13}$$

The weights p_{P1e1}, p_{P1e2} and p_{P1e3} are the sampling probabilities of links e_1, e_2 and e_3 in path P_1. Similarly, p_{P2e1}, p_{P2e2}, p_{P2e3} and p_{P3e1}, p_{P3e2}, p_{P2e3} are the sampling probabilities of links of path P_2 and P_3 respectively. Neurons P_1, P_2 and P_3 render their output O_1, O_2 and O_3 respectively as:

$$O_1 = q(P_1)\, p_{P1e1} + q(P_1)p_{P1e2} + q(P_1)p_{P1e3} \tag{14}$$

$$O_2 = q(P_2)p_{P2e1} + q(P_2)p_{P2e2} + q(P_2)p_{P2e3} \tag{15}$$

$$O_3 = q(P_3)p_{P3e1} + q(P_3)p_{P3e2} + q(P_3)p_{P3e3} \tag{16}$$

Thus, the final output ß', given by neuron O is:

$$\text{ß}' = \sum_{i=1}^{\text{Count}\{Z\}} O_i * w_i \tag{17}$$

Each of the outputs O_1, O_2 and O_3 represent the following part of the Eq. (10):

$q(P)\left[\sum_{e \in P} p_e\right]$ for paths P1, P2 and P3 respectively.

The weights W1, W2 and W3 are fixed as 1 and need not be changed throughout the training of the neural network. The output ß' from output neuron O, represents the value of Eq. (10), which represents the value of ß, the probability of detection of the malicious packets by the IDS. We need to find values of the sampling probabilities (p_e) for each link or the weights for neurons in H_1 that connect it to the input layer so that we get a maximum value of ß. Thus, we train the neural network on the value of maximum ß [Eq. (10)]. This value ß' is dependent on the weights that we want to adjust.

$$E(n) = \text{ß} - \text{ß}' \tag{18}$$

Equation (18) represents the error in the output for i^{th} iteration of training set, where E is the error, ß is the desired output and ß is the output obtained by the neural network. Weights W1, W2 and W3 will not be updated. The value of E must be compensated by the output of H_1 neurons. We use gradient descent algorithm to adjust the weights

$$W = p_{Ptei} + \alpha(\text{ß} - \text{ß}')q(P_t) \tag{19}$$

Where, W is the updated weight, p_{Ptei} is the old weight for neuron t for e_i input (for all edges e on path P_t), α is the learning rate, ß is the expected output, ß' is the obtained output and $q(P_t)$ is the input to the neuron t. In Eq. (19) all the parameters are known except the learning rate, α. Hence, its choice is crucial and challenging for the proper training of the neural network model. The value of the learning rate should not be too small or too large as if it is too large then the global minima of the squared error function will not be reached and the gradient descent algorithm will take a huge number of iterations to converge or it might not converge at all. If the learning rate it too small then the global minima of the squared error function will be reached ultimately but the gradient descent algorithm will take more than required time to converge. The neural network can be simulated for various values of α and the one giving least mean square error can be selected for the training. The number of iterations used for training the neural network also plays an important role and they can also be known via simulating the network for various values of iterations.

This will enable the neural network to render the most appropriate probability with which the IDS can detect an intrusion in the network. The neural network is to be trained for the value of maximum β i.e. the probability of sampling a malicious packet from the intruder to the target for a given the number of packets sent by the intruder and having the probability vector Q as input.

5   Conclusion and Future Scope

The artificial neural networks have been used to solve various problems effectively. Though for intrusion detection they are mainly used for classifying the different attacks or categorizing the activities as malicious or not. The intruder and IDS can be viewed from the perspective of non cooperating competitors. The present paper exploits this idea and models a neural network using a game theoretic representation of the intruder and the IDS. The present paper introduces a novel approach to find the probability with which the IDS can detect intrusion in a network by using the game theoretic representation of the intrusion detection problem (single intruder sending malicious packets). The proposed neural network finds the probability of intrusion detection when the number of malicious packets sent by the intruder is fixed and the probability of his sending the malicious packets on various paths leading him to the target are known. The proposed neural network can also be used in the case of a single intruder sending a single malicious packet to the target.

This paper opens various prospectives for future research. The modeling of the game theoretic representation for the intrusion detection problem can be tried to be solved with other soft computing techniques also apart from the neural networks like the support vector machines. The proposed neural network can also be improved by using identification and probabilistic point selection techniques for generating the training set. The game theoretic representations of the intrusion detection problem exist for the wireless networks too, hence they can also be implemented using some soft computing technique in the light of the present paper. In the present paper only a single intruder has been considered so the future research can be carried out to see how the model can be represented for cooperative intruders.

Acknowledgement. The first author would also like to thank the Ministry of Human Resource and Development (MHRD), Government of India for funding her M.Tech program.

References

1. Denning, D.E.: An intrusion-detection model. IEEE Trans. Softw. Eng. **2**, 222–232 (1987). doi:10.1109/TSE.1987.232894
2. Richard, A.K., Giovanni, V.: Intrusion detection: a brief history and overview. Computer **35**, supl27–supl30 (2002). doi:10.1109/MC.2002.1012428
3. Chih, F.T., Yu, F.H., Chia, Y.L., Wei, Y.L.: Intrusion detection by machine learning: a review. Expert Syst. Appl. **36**, 11994–12000 (2009). doi:10.1016/j.eswa.2009.05.029

4. Wun, H.C., Sheng, H.H., Hwang, P.S.: Application of SVM and ANN for intrusion detection. Comput. Oper. Res. **32**, 2617–2634 (2005). doi:10.1016/j.cor.2004.03.019
5. Gang, W., Jinxing, H., Jian, M., Lihua, H.: A new approach to intrusion detection using artificial neural networks and fuzzy clustering. Expert Syst. Appl. **37**, 6225–6232 (2010). doi:10.1016/j.eswa.2010.02.102
6. Mrutyunjaya, P., Manas, R.P.: Network intrusion detection using Naive Bayes. IJCSNS Int. J. Comput. Sci. Netw. Secur. **7**, 258–263 (2007). https://pdfs.semanticscholar.org/1a5c/191da4aa733c80311ef4057c16dc899819cd.pdf
7. Donald, E.K., Ronald, W.M.: An analysis of alpha beta pruning. Artif. Intell. **6**, 293–326 (1975). doi:10.1016/0004-3702(75)90019-3
8. George, T.H., Gary, P., Stanley, S.: Chapter 7: path finding in AI. In: Algorithms in a Nutshell, pp. 213–217. Oreilly Media (2008)
9. Stockman, G.C.: A minimax algorithm better than alpha-beta? Artif. Intell. **12**, 179–196 (1979). doi:10.1016/0004-3702(79)90016-X
10. Cameron, B.B., Edward, P., Daniel, W., Simon, M.L., Peter, I.C., Philipp, R., Stephen, T., Diego, P., Spyridon, S., Simon, C.: A survey of Monte Carlo tree search methods. IEEE Trans. Comput. Intell. AI Games **4**, 1–43 (2012). doi:10.1109/TCIAIG.2012.2186810
11. Hadi, O., Mona, M., Chadi, A., Mourad, D., Prabir, B.: Game theoretic models for detecting network intrusions. Comput. Commun. **31**, 1934–1944 (2008). doi:10.1016/j.comcom.2007.12.028
12. Michalski, R.S., Jaime, G.C., Tom, M.M.: Machine Learning: An Artificial Intelligence Approach. Springer Science & Business Media, Heidelberg (2013)
13. Yegnanarayana, B.: Chapter 1: basics of artificial neural networks. In: Artificial Neural Networks. PHI Learning Pvt. Ltd., pp. 15–39 (2009)
14. Chellapilla, K., David, B.F.: Evolving an expert checkers playing program without using human expertise. IEEE Trans. Evol. Comput. **5**, 422–428 (2001). doi:10.1109/4235.942536
15. David, S., Aja, H., Chris, J.M., Arthur, G., Laurent, S., George, V.D.D., Julian, S., et al.: Mastering the game of go with deep neural networks and tree search. Nature **529**, 484–489 (2016)
16. Andrew, N.L., Edward, G., Thomas, C.H.: Evolution of neural controllers for competitive game playing with teams of mobile robots. Robot. Auton. Syst. **46**, 135–150 (2004). doi:10.1016/j.robot.2004.01.001
17. Park, D.C., El-Sharkawi, M.A., Marks, R.J., Atlas, L.E., Damborg, M.J.: Electric load forecasting using an artificial neural network. IEEE Trans. Power Syst. **6**, 442–449 (1991). doi:10.1109/59.76685
18. Quan, H., Srinivasan, D., Khosravi, A.: Short-term load and wind power forecasting using neural network-based prediction intervals. IEEE Trans. Neural Netw. Learn. Syst. **25**, 303–315 (2014). doi:10.1109/TNNLS.2013.2276053
19. Ticknor, J.L.: A Bayesian regularized artificial neural network for stock market forecasting. Expert Syst. Appl. **40**, 5501–5506 (2013). doi:10.1016/j.eswa.2013.04.013
20. Kristjanpoller, W., Minutolo, M.C.: Gold price volatility: a forecasting approach using the artificial neural Network–GARCH model. Expert Syst. Appl. **42**, 7245–7251 (2015). doi:10.1016/j.eswa.2015.04.058
21. Pedro, G.T., Verdejo, J.D., Gabriel, M.F., Enrique, V.: Anomaly-based network intrusion detection: techniques, systems and challenges. Comput. Secur. **28**, 18–28 (2009). doi:10.1016/j.cose.2008.08.003
22. Tarek, S.S.: Wired and wireless intrusion detection system: classifications, good characteristics and state-of-the-art. Comput. Stand. Interfaces **28**, 670–694 (2006). doi:10.1016/j.csi.2005.07.002

23. Wenke, L., Salvatore, J.S., Kui, W.M.: Adaptive intrusion detection: a data mining approach. Artif. Intell. Rev. **14**, 533–567 (2000). doi:10.1023/A:1006624031083

24. Lee, W., Nimbalkar, R.A., Yee, K.K., Patil, S.B., Desai, P.H., Tran, T.T., Stolfo, S.J.: A data mining and CIDF based approach for detecting novel and distributed intrusions. In: Debar, H., Mé, L., Wu, S.F. (eds.) RAID 2000. LNCS, vol. 1907, pp. 49–65. Springer, Heidelberg (2000). doi:10.1007/3-540-39945-3_4

25. Valdes, A., Skinner, K.: Adaptive, model-based monitoring for cyber attack detection. In: Debar, H., Mé, L., Wu, S.Felix (eds.) RAID 2000. LNCS, vol. 1907, pp. 80–93. Springer, Heidelberg (2000). doi:10.1007/3-540-39945-3_6

26. Nong, Y., Mingming, X., Syed, M.E.: Probabilistic networks with undirected links for anomaly detection. In: Proceedings of the IEEE Systems, Man, and Cybernetics Information Assurance and Security Workshop, West Point, NY, pp. 175–179 (2000)

27. Gun, K., Nur, Z.H., Malcolm, I.H.: A hierarchical SOM-based intrusion detection system. Eng. Appl. Artif. Intell. **20**, 439–451 (2007). doi:10.1016/j.engappai.2006.09.005

28. Mei-Ling, S., Shu-Ching, C., Kanoksri, S., LiWu, C.: A novel anomaly detection scheme based on principal component classifier. In: Proceedings of the IEEE Foundations and New Directions of Data Mining Workshop, Melbourne, FL, USA, pp. 172–179 (2003)

29. Stuart, S., James, A.H., Joseph, M.M.: Practical automated detection of stealthy portscans. J. Comput. Secur. **10**, 105–136 (2002). doi:10.3233/JCS-2002-101-205

30. Nong, Y., Syed, M.E., Qiang, C., Sean, V.: Multivariate statistical analysis of audit trails for host-based intrusion detection. IEEE Trans. Comput. **51**, 810–820 (2002). doi:10.1109/TC. 2002.1017701

31. Alan, B., Chandrika, P., Rasheda, S., Boleslaw, S., Mark, E.: Network-based intrusion detection using neural networks. Intell. Eng. Syst. Through Artif. Neural Netw. **12**, 579–584 (2002)

32. Kathleen, A.J., David, H.D., Cathy, A.S.: An expert system application for network intrusion detection. In: National Computer Security Conference, Washington, DC (United States), 1–4 October (1991)

33. Wenke, L., Savatore, J.S., Kui, W.M.: Data mining in work flow environments- experiments in intrusion detection. In: Proceedings of the 1999 Conference on Knowledge Discovery and Data Mining (KDD 1999) (1999)

34. John, L.Z., Ali, G.: Network intrusion detection using an improved competitive learning neural network. In: Proceedings of Second Annual Conference on Communication Networks and Services Research, pp. 190–197. IEEE-Computer Society (2004). doi:10.1109/DNSR. 2004.1344728

35. Mehdi, M., Mohammad, Z.: A neural network based system for intrusion detection and classification of attacks. In: Proceedings of the 2004 IEEE International Conference on Advances in Intelligent Systems-Theory and Applications. Luxembourg-Kirchberg, Luxembourg. IEEE Press, 15–18 November 2004

36. Susan, C.L., David, V.H.: Training a neural network based intrusion detector to recognize novel attacks. IEEE Trans. Syst. Man Cybern.-Part A: Syst. Hum. **31**, 294–299 (2001). doi:10.1109/3468.935046

37. Weiming, H., Wei, H., Steve, M.: Adaboost-based algorithm for network intrusion detection. IEEE Trans. Syst. Man Cybern. Part B (Cybern.) **38**, 577–583 (2008). doi:10.1109/TSMCB. 2007.914695

38. Bezalel, P., Peter, S.: Introduction to the Theory of Cooperative Games, vol. 34. Springer Science and Business Media, Heidelberg (2007)

39. Eric, D.: Non-cooperative games. Ann. Math. **54**, 286–295 (2014). doi:10.2307/1969529

40. Robert, A.H., Erik, D.D.: Games, Puzzles and Computation. AK Peters, Limited, Natick (2009)

41. Walid, S., Zhu, H., Mérouane, D., Are, H., Tamer, B.: Coalitional game theory for communication networks. IEEE Sig. Process. Mag. **26**, 77–97 (2009). doi:10.1109/MSP. 2009.000000
42. Kai, M., Xinping, G., Bin, Z.: Symmetrical cooperative strategies in wireless networks: a cooperative game approach. In: 29th Chinese Control Conference (CCC), Beijing, China, pp. 4175–4179. IEEE, 29–31 July 2010
43. Tanya, R., Shridhar, M.M., Ali, G.: Robust estimation and detection in ad hoc and sensor networks. In: IEEE International Conference on Mobile Adhoc and Sensor Systems (MASS), Vancouver, BC, Canada, pp. 236–245. IEEE, 9–12 October 2006. doi:10.1109/ MOBHOC.2006.278562
44. Vanbien, L., Zhiyong, F., Ping, Z., Yi, H., Xiaomeng, W.: A dynamic spectrum allocation scheme with interference mitigation in cooperative networks. In: Wireless Communications and Networking Conference, WCNC 2008, pp. 3175–3180. IEEE (2008). doi:10.1109/ WCNC.2008.554
45. Hadi, O., Noman, M., Lingyu, W., Mourad, D., Prabir, B.: A game-theoretic intrusion detection model for mobile ad hoc networks. Comput. Commun. **31**, 708–721 (2008). doi:10.1016/j.comcom.2007.10.024
46. Haksub, K., Hyungkeuk, L., Sanghoon, L.: A cross-layer optimization for energy-efficient MAC protocol with delay and rate constraints. In: IEEE International Conference on Acoustics, Speech and Signal Processing (ICASSP), Prague, Czech Republic, pp. 2336–2339. IEEE, 22–27 May 2011. doi:10.1109/ICASSP.2011.5946951
47. Kodialam, M., Lakshman, T. V.: Detecting network intrusions via sampling: a game theoretic approach. In: INFOCOM 2003 Twenty-Second Annual Joint Conference of the IEEE Computer and Communications, San Francisco, California, USA, vol. 3, pp. 1880–1889, March 2003. doi:10.1109/INFCOM.2003.1209210
48. Shamik, S., Mainak, C., Kevin, K.: A game theoretic framework for power control in wireless sensor networks. IEEE Trans. Comput. **59**, 231–242 (2010). doi:10.1109/TC.2009. 82
49. Animesh, P., Park, J-M.: A game theoretic approach to modeling intrusion detection in mobile ad hoc networks. In: Proceedings from the Fifth Annual IEEE SMC Information Assurance Workshop, pp. 280–284. IEEE (2004).doi:10.1109/IAW.2004.1437828
50. He, W., Xia, C., Wang, H., Zhang, C., Ji, Y.: A game theoretical attack-defense model oriented to network security risk assessment. In: International Conference on Computer Science and Software Engineering, vol. 3, pp. 1097–1103. IEEE (2008). doi:10.1109/CSSE. 2008.1062
51. Tansu, A., Tamer, B.: A game theoretic analysis of intrusion detection in access control systems. In: 43rd IEEE Conference on Decision and Control, vol. 2, pp. 1568–1573. IEEE (2004). doi:10.1109/CDC.2004.1430267
52. Sintayehu, D., Kyle, G., Ladan, G., Reza, G., Srikanta, K.: Reliable data fusion in wireless sensor networks: a dynamic bayesian game approach. In: Proceedings of 2009 IEEE Military Communications Conference, Boston, MA, USA, 18–21 October. IEEE Press (2009). doi:10.1109/MILCOM.2009.5379987
53. Afrand, A., Sajal, K.D.: Preventing DoS attacks in wireless sensor networks: a repeated game theory approach. Int. J. Netw. Secur. **5**, 145–153 (2007)
54. Charles, P., Zhu, H., Liu, K.J.R.: Cooperation enforcement and learning for optimizing packet forwarding in autonomous wireless networks. IEEE Trans. Wirel. Commun. **7**, 3150–3163 (2008). doi:10.1109/TWC.2008.070213
55. Zhang, X., Cai, Y., Zhang, H.: A game-theoretic dynamic power management policy on wireless sensor network. In: International Conference on Communication Technology, ICCT 2006, Guilin, China, pp. 1–4. IEEE (2006).doi:10.1109/ICCT.2006.341932

Author Index

Printed in the United States
By Bookmasters